Lecture Notes in Comp

Edited by G. Goos, J. Hartmanis and

Springer

Berlin
Heidelberg
New York
Barcelona
Hong Kong
London
Milan
Paris
Singapore
Tokyo

Richard Connor   Alberto Mendelzon (Eds.)

Research Issues in Structured and Semistructured Database Programming

7th International Workshop
on Database Programming Languages, DBPL'99
Kinloch Rannoch, UK, September 1-3, 1999
Revised Papers

Springer

Series Editors

Gerhard Goos, Karlsruhe University, Germany
Juris Hartmanis, Cornell University, NY, USA
Jan van Leeuwen, Utrecht University, The Netherlands

Volume Editors

Richard Connor
University of Strathclyde
Department of Computer Science
Glasgow G1 1XH, Scotland, UK
E-mail: richard@cs.strath.ac.uk

Alberto Mendelzon
University of Toronto
Department of Computer Science
6 King's College Road, Toronto, Ontario, Canada M5S 3H5
E-mail: mendel@db.toronto.edu

Cataloging-in-Publication Data applied for

Die deutsche Bibliothek - CIP-Einheitsaufnahme

Research issues in structured and semistructured database programming ;
revised papers / 7th International Workshop on Database Programming
Languages, DBPL '99, Kinloch Rannoch, UK, September 1 - 3, 1999.
Richard Connor ; Alberto Mendelzon (ed.). - Berlin ; Heidelberg ; New
York ; Barcelona ; Hong Kong ; London ; Milan ; Paris ; Singapore ;
Tokyo : Springer, 2000
  (Lecture notes in computer science ; 1949)
  ISBN 3-540-41481-9

CR Subject Classification (1998): H.2, H.3

ISSN 0302-9743
ISBN 3-540-41481-9 Springer-Verlag Berlin Heidelberg New York

Springer-Verlag Berlin Heidelberg New York
a member of BertelsmannSpringer Science+Business Media GmbH
© Springer-Verlag Berlin Heidelberg 2000
Printed in Germany

Typesetting: Camera-ready by author, data conversion by DA-TeX Gerd Blumenstein
Printed on acid-free paper   SPIN 10781315   06/3142   5 4 3 2 1 0

Editors' Foreword

The Seventh International Workshop on Database Programming Languages (DBPL99) took place in Kinloch Rannoch, Perthshire, UK from the 1st to the 3rd of September 1999. This series of workshops focuses on the interaction of theory and practice in the design and development of database programming languages. The workshop has occurred biennially since 1987, and was previously held in:

Roscoff, Finistère, France (1987)
Salishan, Oregon, USA (1989)
Nafplion, Argolida, Greece (1991)
Manhattan, New York, USA (1993)
Gubbio, Umbria, Italy (1995)
Estes Park, Colorado, USA (1997)

The workshop, as always, was organised as a mixture of invited speakers, informal paper presentations and discussion. Attendance at the workshop was limited to those who submitted papers and members of the Programme Committee, to ensure a sufficiently small forum for useful discussion. Before finding their way into this volume, papers were refereed by at least three members of the Programme Committee. Sixteen of the 31 submitted papers were accepted for presentation at the workshop. In the tradition of the series, authors were encouraged to improve their papers based on both referees' comments and ensuing discussion at the workshop, and resubmit them for publication in this volume, after which a further stage of refereeing took place. The result, we believe, is a volume of high-quality and well-polished papers.

Two invited presentations were given, by Luca Cardelli (Microsoft Research Labs, Cambridge, UK) and Alon Levy (University of Washington). We are particularly grateful to Luca Cardelli for working his presentation into a full paper for inclusion in the volume, a task well beyond the call of duty!

The sessions of the workshop were arranged under the following headings:

Querying and query optimisation
Languages for document models
Persistence, components and workflow
Typing and querying semi-structured data
Active and spatial databases
Unifying semi-structured and traditional data models

It is interesting to note that the subject area of the workshop represents a significant departure from previous workshops. All of the papers are concerned with data-intensive computational systems. However, the number of papers roughly arranged by category of interest are as follows:

This is a fairly typical spread of interest for a DPBL workshop, except for the sudden emergence of semistructured data as a major theme. Databases, as defined in any text book, deal with significantly large collections of highly structured data. However, it seems that the DBPL community has implicitly decided that semi-structured data, traditionally viewed as unstructured from a database perspective, is now a major theme within the database research domain.

The workshop sessions contained the following papers:

Invited talk: semi-structured computation

In this paper Cardelli shows how his work on mobile ambient systems can be transferred to the domain of semi-structured data. The key observation is that both contexts are based upon imperfect knowledge of labeled graphs, and the paper gives an insight into a radically new model for computation over semi-structured data.

Querying and query optimisation

Libkin and Wong discuss conditions under which it is possible to evaluate certain database queries in the context of query languages that do not allow their explicit definition. This may be achieved by the incremental maintenance of the query result over changes to the data, rather than by a defined computation over the current given state.

Aggelis and Cosmodakis show an optimisation method for nested SQL query blocks with aggregation operators, derived from the theory of dependency implication. In some cases this allows the merging of MAX, MIN blocks to allow the same optimisation strategy as tableau equivalence to be used.

Grahne and Waller consider string databases, which they define as a collection of tables, the columns of which contain strings. They address the issue of designing a simple query language for string databases, based on a simple first-order logic extended by a concatenation operator.

Languages for document models

Maneth and Neven introduce a document transformation language, with similar expressive power to XSL, using regular expressions. A further language is introduced which replaces simple pattern matching by monadic second-order logic formulae. Various properties of this language are investigated.

Neven contrasts document models defined using extended context-free grammars (in which the right-hand side of expansions may contain regular expressions) with standard context-free grammars. An important difference is the ability to order child nodes. The investigation is into extensions of attribute grammars that may be usefully applied within the extended context.

Persistence, components and workflow

McIver et al. address the inherent problems of the application of the componentware paradigm in the context of databases. They introduce Souk, a language-independent paradigm for performing data integration, designed to allow the rapid construction of integrated solutions from off-the-shelf components.

Printezis, Atkinson and Jordan investigate the pragmatic issue of the misuse of the *transient* keyword within the Java[1] language. Originally intended to allow explicit closure severance within persistent versions of the language, it is now multiply interpreted by different implementations, allowed because of the loose definition of the language. The paper shows why most current interpretations are inappropriate and describes a more useful one for the context of a persistent Java system.

Dong et al. show a method for translating distributed workflow schemata into a family of communicating flowcharts, which are essentially atomic and execute in parallel. Semantics-preserving transformations over these sets of flowcharts can be used to optimise the overall workflow according to the physical infrastructure available for its execution.

Typing and querying semi-structured data

Bergholz and Freytag discuss the querying of semi-structured data. They propose that queries may be divided into two parts, the first part deriving a match between the data and a partial schema, the second part manipulating that part of the data that matches the schema. The first part of the query can be re-used for a number of different queries requiring the same structure.

Buneman and Pierce investigate a new use of the unlabelled union type for typing semi-structured data. This overcomes the problems of the normal strategy of combining typed data sources in a semi-structured collection, which is to throw away all the existing type information. The union treatment shown allows type information, albeit in a weakened form, to be maintained without losing the inherent flexibility of the semi-structured format.

Buneman, Fan and Weinstein concentrate on a restricted semi-structured data model, where outgoing edges are constrained to have unique labels. In this model, which is representative of a large body of semi-structured collections, many path constraint problems, undecidable in the general model, are decidable. The limits of these results are studied for some different classes of path constraint language.

---

[1] Java is a trademark of Sun Microsystems.

Active and spatial databases

Geerts and Kuijpers are interested in 2-dimensional spatial databases defined by polynomial inequalities, and in particular in the issue of topological connectivity. This is known not to be first-order expressible in general. They show a spatial Datalog program which tests topological connectivity for arbitrary closed and bounded spatial databases, and is guaranteed to terminate.

Kuper and Su show extensions to linear constraint languages which can express Euclidean distance. The operators under study work directly on the data, unlike previous work which depends upon the data representation.

Bailey and Poulovassilis consider the termination of rules, which is a critical requirement for active databases. This paper shows an abstract interpretation framework which allows the modeling of specific approximations for termination analysis methods. The framework allows the comparison and verification of different methods for termination analysis.

Unifying semi-structured and traditional data models

Granhe and Lakshmanan start from the observation that the state-of-the-art in semi-structured querying is based on navigational techniques, which are inherently detached from standard database theory. First, the semantics of querying is not entirely defined through the normal input/output typing of queries. Second, the notion of genericity is largely unaddressed within the domain, and indeed the emerging trend is for query expressions to be dependent on a particular instance of a database.

Lahiri et al. investigate an integration of structured and semi-structured databases. They describe Ozone, a system within which structured data may contain references to semi-structured, and vice versa. The main contribution is towards the unification of representing and querying such hybrid data collections.

Acknowledgements

DBPL99 was co-chaired by Richard Connor and Alberto Mendelzon. The Programme Committee members were:

Luca Cardelli	(Microsoft Cambridge)
Richard Connor	(University of Strathclyde)
Alan Dearle	(University of St Andrews)
Stephane Grumbach	(INRIA, Versailles)
Laks Lakshmanan	(Concordia University)
Leonid Libkin	(Bell Labs)
Gianni Mecca	(Università di Basilicata)
Alberto Mendelzon	(University of Toronto)
Fausto Rabitti	(CNUCE-CNR, Pisa)
Peter Schwarz	(IBM Almaden)
Dan Suciu	(AT&T)
David Toman	(University of Waterloo)

We would also like to thank: David Lievens and Steve Neely for practical help during the workshop and with the preparation of the preprint proceedings; Elizabeth MacFarlane for organising the finances, and the staff of the Kinloch Rannoch Hotel for providing a traditional warm Scottish welcome. Advice from Tony Printezis on single malt whisky was well received by the workshop participants, as was the whisky itself.

The next DPBL workshop will be co-chaired by Giorgio Ghelli and Gösta Grahne, and will take place in Italy in September 2001.

August 2000   Richard Connor
                                                        Alberto Mendelzon

Table of Contents

Typing and Querying Semistructured data

Active and Spatial Databases

Unifying Semistructured and Traditional Data Models

Semistructured Computation

Luca Cardelli

Microsoft Research

1 Introduction

This paper is based on the observation that the areas of *semistructured databases* [1] and *mobile computation* [3] have some surprising similarities at the technical level. Both areas are inspired by the need to make better use of the Internet. Despite this common motivation, the technical similarities that arise seem largely accidental, but they should still permit the transfer of some techniques between the two areas. Moreover, if we can take advantage of the similarities and generalize them, we may obtain a broader model of data and computation on the Internet.

The ultimate source of similarities is the fact that both areas have to deal with extreme dynamicity of data and behavior. In semistructured databases, one cannot rely on uniformity of structure because data may come from heterogeneous and uncoordinated sources. Still, it is necessary to perform searches based on whatever uniformity one can find in the data. In mobile computation, one cannot rely on uniformity of structure because agents, devices, and networks can dynamically connect, move around, become inaccessible, or crash. Still, it is necessary to perform computations based on whatever resources and connections one can find on the network.

We will develop these similarities throughout the paper. As a sample, consider the following arguments. First, one can regard data structures stored inside network nodes as a natural extension of network structures, since on a large time/space scale both networks and data are semistructured and dynamic. Therefore, one can think of applying the same navigational and code mobility techniques uniformly to networks and data. Second, since networks and their resources are semistructured, one can think of applying semistructured database searches to network structure. This is a well-known major problem in mobile computation, going under the name of resource discovery.

2 Information

2.1 Representing Dynamic Information

In our work on mobility [3, 5] we have been describing mobile structures in a variety of related ways. In all of these, the spatial part of the structure can be represented abstractly as an edge-labeled tree.

For example, the following figure shows at the top left a nested-blob representation of geographical information. At the bottom left we have an equivalent representation in the nested-brackets syntax of the Ambient Calculus [5]. When hierarchical information is used to represent document structures, a more appropriate graphical representation is in terms of nested folders, as shown at the bottom right. Finally, at the top right we have a more schematic representation of hierarchies in terms of edge-labeled trees.

R. Connor and A. Mendelzon (Eds.): DBPL'99, LNCS 1949, pp. 1–16, 2000.

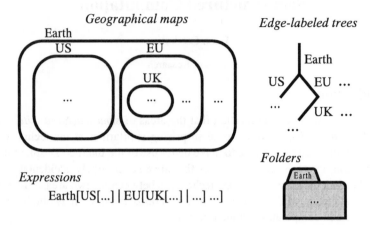

Geographical maps

Edge-labeled trees

Folders

Expressions

Earth[US[...] | EU[UK[...] | ...] ...]

We have studied the Ambient Calculus as a general model of mobile computation. The Ambient Calculus has so far been restricted to edge-labeled trees, but it is not hard to imagine an extension (obtained by adding recursion) that can represent edge-labeled directed graphs. As it happens, edge-labeled directed graphs are also the favorite representation for semistructured data [1]. So, basic data structures used to represent semistructured data and mobile computation, essentially agree. Coincidence?

It should be stressed that edge-labeled trees and graphs are a very rudimentary way of representing information. For example, there is no exact representation of record or variant data structures, which are at the foundations of almost all modern programming languages. Instead, we are thrown back to a crude representation similar to LISP's S-expressions.

The reason for this step backward, as we hinted earlier, is that in semistructured databases one cannot rely on a fixed number of subtrees for a given node (hence no records) and one cannot even rely of a fixed set of possible shapes under a node (hence no variants). Similarly, on a network, one cannot rely on a fixed number of machines being alive at a given node, or resources being available at a given site, nor can one rule out arbitrary network reconfiguration. So, the similarities in data representation arise from similarities of constraints on the data.

In the rest of this section we discuss the representation of mobile and semistructured information. We emphasize the Ambient Calculus view of data representation, mostly because it is less well known. This model arose independently from semistructured data; it can be instructive to see a slightly different solution to what is essentially the same problem of dynamic data representation.

2.2 Information Expressions and Information Trees

We now describe in more detail the syntax of *information expressions*; this is a subset of the Ambient Calculus that concerns data structures. The syntax is interpreted as representing *finite-depth edge-labeled unordered trees*; for short: *information trees*.

The tree that consists just of a root node is written as the expression **0**:

0   represents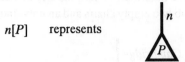

A tree with a single edge labeled n from the root, leading to a subtree represented by P, is written as the expression $n[P]$:

$n[P]$ represents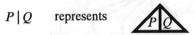

A tree obtained by joining two trees, represented by P and Q, at the root, is written as the expression $P \mid Q$.

$P \mid Q$ represents

A tree obtained by joining an infinite number of equal trees, represented by P, at the root, is written as the expression $!P$. (This can be used to represent abstractly unbounded resources.)

$!P$ represents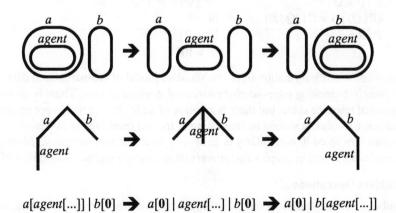

The description of trees in this syntax is not unique. For example the expressions $P \mid Q$ and $Q \mid P$ represent the same (unordered) tree; similarly, the expressions $0 \mid P$ and P represent the same tree. More subtle equivalences govern $!$. We will consider two expression equivalent when they represent the same tree.

The Ambient Calculus uses these tree structures to describe mobile computation, which is seen as the evolution of tree structures over time. The following figure gives, first, a blob representation of an *agent* moving from inside node a to inside node b, with an intermediate state where the agent is traveling over the network.

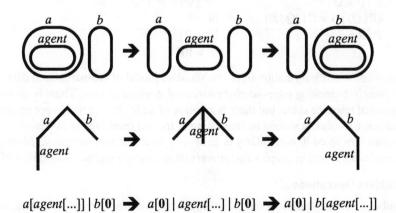

$a[agent[...]] \mid b[0]$ ➜ $a[0] \mid agent[...] \mid b[0]$ ➜ $a[0] \mid b[agent[...]]$

Then, the same situation is represented as transformation of information trees, where hierarchy represents containment and the root is the whole network. Finally, the same situation is represented again as transformation of information expressions. The Ambient Calculus has additional syntax to represent the actions of the agent as it travels from *a* to *b* (indicated here by "..."); we will discuss these actions later.

Note that information trees are not restricted to be finite-branching. For example, the following information tree describes, in part, the city of Cambridge, the Cambridge Eagle pub, and within the pub two empty chairs and an unbounded number of full glasses of beer.

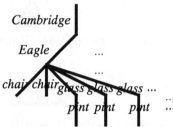

This tree can be represented by the following expression:

Cambridge[*Eagle*[*chair*[0] | *chair*[0] | !*glass*[*pint*[0]]] | ...]

Here is another example: an expression representing the (invalid!) fact that in Cambridge there is an unlimited number of empty parking spaces:

Cambridge[!*ParkingSpace*[0] | ...]

Equivalence of information trees can be characterized fairly easily, even in presence of infinite branching. Up to the equivalence relation induced by the following set of equations, two information expressions are equivalent if and only if they represent the same information tree [9]. Because of this, we will often confuse expressions with the trees they represent.

$$P \mid Q = Q \mid P \qquad\qquad !(P \mid Q) = !P \mid !Q$$
$$(P \mid Q) \mid R = P \mid (Q \mid R) \qquad !0 = 0$$
$$P \mid 0 = P \qquad\qquad !P = P \mid !P$$
$$!P = !!P$$

In contrast to our information trees, the standard model of semistructured data consists of *finitely-branching edge-labeled unordered directed graphs*. There is no notion of unbounded resource there, but there is a notion of node sharing that is not present in the Ambient Calculus. It should be interesting to try and combine the two models; it is not obvious how to do it, particularly in terms of syntactical representation. Moreover, the rules of equivalence of graph structures are more challenging; see Section 6.4 of [1].

2.3 Ambient Operations

The Ambient Calculus provides operations to describe the transformation of data. In the present context, the operations of the Ambient Calculus may look rather peculiar, because they are intended to represent agent mobility rather than data manipulation. We present them here as an example of a set of operations on information trees; other sets of operations are conceivable. In any case, their generalization to directed graphs does not seem entirely obvious.

Information expressions and information trees are a special case of *ambient expressions* and *ambient trees*; in the latter we can represent also the dynamic aspects of mobile computation and mutable information. An ambient tree is an information tree where each node in the tree may have an associated collection of concurrent threads that can execute certain operations. The fact that threads are associated to nodes means that the operations are "local": they affect only a small number of nodes near the thread node (typically three nodes). In our example of an *agent* moving from *a* to *b*, there would usually be a thread in the agent node (the node below the *agent* edge) that is the cause of the movement.

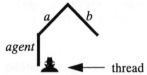

Therefore, the full Ambient Calculus has both a spatial and a temporal component. The spatial component consists of information trees, that is, semistructured data. The temporal component includes operations that locally modify the spatial component. Rather than giving the syntax of these operations, we describe them schematically below. The location of the thread performing the operations is indicated by the thread icon.

The operation *in n*, causes an ambient to enter another ambient named *n* (i.e., it causes a subtree to slide down along an *n* edge). The converse operation, *out n*, causes an ambient to exit another ambient named *n* (i.e., it causes a subtree to slide up along an *n* edge). The operation *open n* opens up an ambient named *n* and merges its contents (i.e., it collapses an edge labeled *n*); these contents may include threads and subtrees. Finally, the spawning operation creates a new configuration within the current ambient (i.e., it creates a new tree and merges its root with the current node).

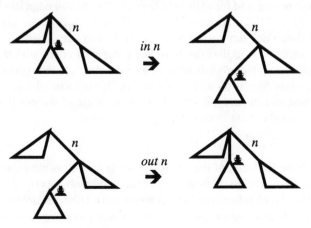

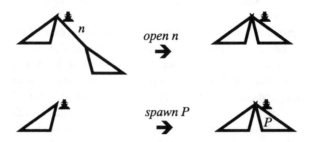

It should be clear that, by strategically placing agents on a tree, we can rearrange, collapse, and expand sections of the tree at will.

2.4 Summary

We have seen that there are some fundamental similarities of data representation in the areas of semistructured data and mobile computation. Moreover, in the case of mobile computation, we have ways of describing the manipulation of data. (In semistructured database, data manipulation is part of the query language, which we discuss later.)

3 Data Structures

We discuss briefly how traditional data structures (records and variants) fit into the semistructured data and ambients data models.

3.1 Records

A *record r* is a structure of the form $\{l_1=v_1, ..., l_n=v_n\}$, where l_i are distinct labels and v_i are the associated values; the pairs l_i,v_i are called record *fields*. Field values can be extracted by a *record selection* operation, $r.l_i$, by indexing on the field labels.

Semistructured data can naturally represent record-like structures: a root node represents the whole record, and for each field $l_i=v_i$, the root has an edge labeled l_i leading to a subtree v_i. Record fields are unordered, just like the edges of our trees. However, semistructured data does not correspond exactly to records: labels in a record are unique, while semistructured data can have any number of edges with the same label under a node. Moreover, records usually have uniform structure throughout a given collection of data, while there is no such uniformity on semistructured data.

It is interesting to compare this with the representation of records in the Ambient Calculus. There, we represent records $\{l_1=v_1, ..., l_n=v_n\}$ as:

$$r[l_1[... v_1 ...] | ... | l_n[... v_n ...]]$$

where r is the name (address) of the record, which is used to name an ambient $r[...]$ representing the whole record. This ambient contains subambients $l_1[...] ... l_n[...]$ representing labeled fields (unordered because | is unordered). The field ambients contain the field values $v_1, ..., v_n$ and some machinery (omitted here) to allow them to be read and rewritten.

However, ambients represent mobile computation. This means that, potentially, field subambients $l_i[...]$ can take off and leave, and new fields can arrive. Moreover, a new field can arrive that has the some label as an existing field. In both cases, the stable structure of ordinary records is destroyed.

3.2 Variants

A *variant* v is a structure of the form $[l=v]$, where l is a label and v is the associated value, and where l is restricted to be a member of a finite set of labels $l_1 ... l_n$. A *case analysis* operation can be used to determine which of these labels is present in the variant, and to extract the associated value.

A variant can be easily represented in semistructured data, as an edge labeled l leading to a subtree v, with the understanding that l is a unique edge of its parent node, and that l is a member of a finite collection $l_1 ... l_n$. But the latter restrictions are not enforced in semistructured data. A node meant to represent a variant could have zero outgoing edges, or two or more edges with different labels, or even two or more edges with the same label, or an edge whose label does not belong to the intended set. In all these situations, the standard case analysis operation becomes meaningless.

A similar situation happens, again, in the case of mobile computation. Even if the constraints of variant structures are respected at a given time, a variant may decide to leave its parent node at some point, or other variants may come to join the parent node.

3.3 Summary

We have seen that fundamental data structures used in programming languages becomes essentially meaningless both in semistructured data and in mobile computation. We have discussed the untyped situation here, but this means in particular that fundamental notions of types in programming languages become inapplicable. We discuss type systems next.

4 Type Systems

4.1 Type Systems for Dynamic Data

Because of the problems discussed in the previous section, it is quite challenging to devise type systems for semistructured data or mobile computation. Type systems track invariants in the data, but most familiar invariants are now violated. Therefore, we need to find weaker invariants and weaker type systems that can track them.

In the area of semistructured data, ordinary database schemas are too rigid, for the same reasons that ordinary type systems are too rigid. New approaches are needed; for example, *union types* have been proposed [2]. Here we give the outline of a different solution devised for mobile computation. Our task is to find a type system for the information trees of Section 2, subject to the constraint that information trees can change dynamically, and that the operations that change them must be typeable too.

4.2 A Type System for Information Trees

The type system we present here may appear to be very weak, in the sense of imposing very few constraints on information trees. However, this appearance is deceptive: within this type system, when applied to the full Ambient Calculus, we can represent standard type systems for the λ-calculus and the π-calculus [6]. Moreover, more refined type systems for mobility studied in [4] enforce more constraints by forcing certain substructures to remain "immobile". Here we give only an intuitive sketch of the type system; details can be found in [6].

The task of finding a type systems for information trees is essentially the same as the task of finding a type system for ordinary hierarchical file systems. Imagine a file system with the following constraints. First, each folder has a name. Second, each name has an associated data type (globally). Third, each folder of a given name can contain only data of the type associated with its name. Fourth, if there is a thread operating at a node, it can only read and write data of the correct type at that node. Fifth, any folder can contain any other kind of folder (no restrictions).

In terms of information trees, these rules can be depicted as follows. Here we add the possibility that the nodes of information tree may contain atomic data (although in principle this data can also be represented by trees):

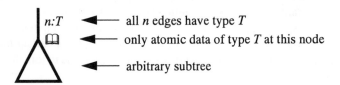

Next, we need to examine the operations described in section 2.3 (or any similar set of operations) to make sure they can be typed. The type system can easily keep track of the global associations of types to names. Moreover, we need to type each thread according to the type of data it can read, write, or merge (by performing *open*) at the current node.

The *in* and *out* operations change the structure of the tree (which is not restricted by the type system) but do not change the relationship between an edge and the contents of the node below it; so no type invariant is violated. The *open* operation, though, merges the contents of two nodes. Here the type system must guarantee that the labels above those two nodes have the same type; this can be done relatively easily, by keeping track of the type of each thread, as sketched above. Finally, the *spawn* operation creates a new subtree, so it must simply enforce the relationship between the edges it creates and the attached data.

This is a sensible type system in the sense that it guarantees well-typed interactions: any process that reads or writes data at a particular node (i.e., inside a particular folder) can rely on the kind of data it will find there. On the other hand, this type system does not constrain the structure of the tree, therefore allowing both heterogeneity (for semistructured data) and mutability (for mobile computation).

Note also that this type system does not give us anything similar to ordinary record types. Folder types are both weaker than record types, because they do not enforce uniformity of substructures, and stronger, because they enforce global constraints on the typing of edges.

4.3 Summary

Because of the extreme dynamicity present both in semistructured data and in mobile computation, new type systems are needed. We have presented a particular type system as an example of possible technology transfers: we have several ready-made type systems for mobile computation that could be applicable to semistructured data.

5 Queries

Semistructured databases have developed flexible ways of querying data, even though the data is not rigidly structured according to schemas [1]. In relational database theory, query languages are nicely related to query algebras and to query logics. However, query algebras and query logics for semistructured database are not yet well understood.

For reasons unrelated to queries, we have developed a specification logic for the Ambient Calculus [7]. Could this logic, by an accident of fate, lead to a query language for semistructured data?

5.1 Ambient Logic

In classical logic, assertions are simply either *true* or *false*. In *modal logic*, instead, assertions are true or false relative to a *state* (or *world*). For example, in epistemic logic assertions are relative to the knowledge state of an entity. In temporal logic, assertions are relative to the execution state of a program. In our Ambient Logic, which is a modal logic, assertions are relative to the current place and the current time.

As an example, here is a formula in our logic that makes an assertion about the shape of the current location at the current time. It is asserting that right now, right here, there is a location called *Cambridge* that contains at least a location called *Eagle* that contains at least one empty *chair* (the formula **0** matches an empty location; the formula **T** matches anything):

$$Cambridge[Eagle[chair[\mathbf{0}] \mid \mathbf{T}] \mid \mathbf{T}]$$

This assertion happens to be true of the tree shown in Section 2.2. However, the truth of the assertion will in general depend on the current time (is it happy hour, when all chairs are taken?) and the current location (Cambridge England or Cambridge Mass.?).

Formulas of the Ambient Logic

η	a name n or a variable x
$\mathcal{A}, \mathcal{B} : \Phi ::=$	
T	true
$\neg \mathcal{A}$	negation
$\mathcal{A} \vee \mathcal{B}$	disjunction
0	void
$\eta[\mathcal{A}]$	location
$\mathcal{A} \mid \mathcal{B}$	composition
$\diamondsuit \mathcal{A}$	somewhere modality
$\Diamond \mathcal{A}$	sometime modality

$\mathcal{A}@\eta$	location adjunct
$\mathcal{A}\triangleright\mathcal{B}$	composition adjunct
$\forall x.\mathcal{A}$	universal quantification over names

More generally, our logic includes both assertions about trees, such as the one above, and standard logical connectives for composing assertions. The following table summarizes the formulas of the Ambient Logic. The first three lines give classical propositional logic. The next three lines describe trees. Then we have two modal connective for assertions that are true somewhere or sometime. After the two adjunctions (discussed later) we have quantification over names, giving us a form of predicate logic; the quantified names can appear in the location and location adjunct constructs.

5.2 Satisfaction

The exact meaning of logical formulas is given by a *satisfaction relation* connecting a tree with an formula. The term *satisfaction* comes from logic; for reasons that will become apparent shortly, we will also call this concept *matching*. The basic question we consider: is this formula satisfied by this tree? Or: does this tree match this formula?

The satisfaction relation between a tree P (actually, an expression P representing a tree) and a formula $\mathcal{A}$ is written:

$$P \vDash \mathcal{A}$$

For the basic assertions on trees, the satisfaction/matching relation can be described as follows; for graphical effect we relate tree shapes to formulas:

- **0**: *here now* there is absolutely nothing:

    •   matches   **0**

- $n[\mathcal{A}]$: *here now* there is one edge called *n*, whose descendant satisfies the formula $\mathcal{A}$:

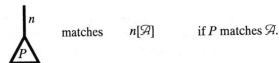

    matches $n[\mathcal{A}]$ if P matches $\mathcal{A}$.

- $\mathcal{A} \mid \mathcal{B}$: *here now* there are exactly two things next to each other, one satisfying $\mathcal{A}$ and one satisfying $\mathcal{B}$:

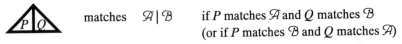

    matches $\mathcal{A} \mid \mathcal{B}$ if P matches $\mathcal{A}$ and Q matches $\mathcal{B}$
                                (or if P matches $\mathcal{B}$ and Q matches $\mathcal{A}$)

- $\diamondsuit\mathcal{A}$: *somewhere now*, there is a place satisfying $\mathcal{A}$:

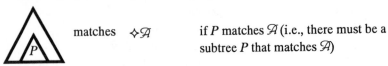

    matches $\diamondsuit\mathcal{A}$ if P matches $\mathcal{A}$ (i.e., there must be a
                                subtree P that matches $\mathcal{A}$)

- $\Diamond \mathcal{A}$: *here sometime*, there is a thing satisfying $\mathcal{A}$, after some reductions:

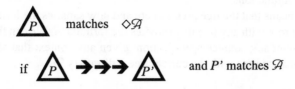

The propositional connectives and the universal quantifier have fairly standard interpretations. A formula $\neg \mathcal{A}$ is satisfied by anything that does not satisfy $\mathcal{A}$. A formula $\mathcal{A} \vee \mathcal{B}$ is satisfied by anything that satisfies either $\mathcal{A}$ or $\mathcal{B}$. Anything satisfies the formula **T**, while nothing satisfies its negation, **F**, defined as $\neg$**T**. A formula $\forall x.\mathcal{A}$ is satisfied by a tree P if for all names n, the tree P satisfies $\mathcal{A}$ where x is replaced by n.

Many useful derived connectives can be defined from the primitive ones. Here is a brief list:

- *Normal Implication:* $\mathcal{A} \Rightarrow \mathcal{B} \triangleq \neg \mathcal{A} \vee \mathcal{B}$. This is the standard definition, but note that in our modal logic this means that P matches $\mathcal{A} \Rightarrow \mathcal{B}$ if whenever P matches $\mathcal{A}$ then *the same* P matches $\mathcal{B}$ at the same time and in the same place. As examples, consider $Borders[\textbf{T}] \Rightarrow Borders[Starbucks[\textbf{T}] \mid \textbf{T}]$, stating that a $Borders$ bookstore contains a $Starbucks$ shop, and $(NonSmoker[\textbf{T}] \mid \textbf{T}) \Rightarrow (NonSmoker[\textbf{T}] \mid Smoker[\textbf{T}] \mid \textbf{T})$, stating that next to a non-smoker there is a smoker.

- *Everywhere:* $\sqcap \mathcal{A} \triangleq \neg \Diamond \neg \mathcal{A}$. What is true everywhere? Not much, unless we qualify it. We can write $\sqcap (\mathcal{A} \Rightarrow \mathcal{B})$ to mean that everywhere $\mathcal{A}$ is true, $\mathcal{B}$ is true as well. For example, $US[\sqcap (Borders[\textbf{T}] \Rightarrow Borders[Starbucks[\textbf{T}] \mid \textbf{T}])]$.

- *Always:* $\square \mathcal{A} \triangleq \neg \Diamond \neg \mathcal{A}$. This can be used to express temporal invariants, such as: $\square Pisa[LeaningTower[\textbf{T}] \mid \textbf{T}]$.

- *Parallel Implication:* $\mathcal{A} \mid \Rightarrow \mathcal{B} \triangleq \neg(\mathcal{A} \mid \neg \mathcal{B})$. This means that it is not possible to split the root of the current tree in such a way that one part satisfies $\mathcal{A}$ and the other does not satisfy $\mathcal{B}$. In other words, every way we split the root of the current tree, if one part satisfies $\mathcal{A}$, then the other part must satisfy $\mathcal{B}$. For example, $Bath[\sqcap (NonSmoker[\textbf{T}] \mid \Rightarrow Smoker[\textbf{T}] \mid \textbf{T})]$ means that at the $Bath$ pub, anywhere there is a non-smoker there is, nearby, a smoker. Note that parallel implication makes the definition of this property a bit more compact than in the earlier example about smokers.

- Nested Implication: $n[\Rightarrow \mathcal{A}] \triangleq \neg n[\neg \mathcal{A}]$. This means that it is not possible that the contents of an n location do not satisfy $\mathcal{A}$. In other words, if there is an n location, its contents satisfy $\mathcal{A}$. For example: $US[\sqcap Borders[\Rightarrow Starbucks[\textbf{T}] \mid \textbf{T}]]$; again, this is a bit more compact than the previous formulation of this example.

5.3 Adjunctions

The adjunction connectives, $\mathcal{A} \triangleright \mathcal{B}$ and $\mathcal{A}@n$, are of special interest; they are the logical inverses, in a certain sense, of $\mathcal{A} \mid \mathcal{B}$ and $n[\mathcal{A}]$ respectively. In ordinary logic, we have a fundamental adjunction between conjunction and implication given by the property: $\mathcal{A} \wedge \mathcal{B}$ entails C iff $\mathcal{A}$ entails $\mathcal{B} \Rightarrow C$. Similarly, in our logic we have that $\mathcal{A} \mid \mathcal{B}$ entails C

iff $\mathcal{A}$ entails $\mathcal{B} \triangleright C$, and that $n[\mathcal{A}]$ entails C iff $\mathcal{A}$ entails $C@n$. We now explore the explicit meaning of these adjunctions.

The formula $\mathcal{A} \triangleright \mathcal{B}$ means that the tree present here and now satisfies the formula $\mathcal{B}$ when it is merged at the root with any tree that satisfies the formula $\mathcal{A}$. We can think of this formula as a requirement/guarantee specification: given any context that satisfies $\mathcal{A}$, the combination of that context with the current tree will satisfy $\mathcal{B}$.

    matches $\mathcal{A} \triangleright \mathcal{B}$

if for all that match $\mathcal{A}$ we have that 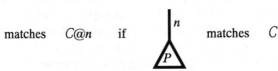 matches $\mathcal{B}$

For example, consider a representation of a fish consisting of a certain structure (beginning with *fish*[...]), and a certain behavior. A prudent fish would satisfy the following specification, stating that even in presence of *bait*, the *bait* and the *fish* remain separate:

$$fish[...] \quad \vDash \quad bait[\mathbf{T}] \triangleright \Box(fish[\mathbf{T}] \mid bait[\mathbf{T}])$$

On the other hand, a good *bait* would satisfy the following specification, stating that in presence of a *fish*, it is possible that the *fish* will eventually ingest the bait:

$$bait[...] \quad \vDash \quad fish[\mathbf{T}] \triangleright \Diamond fish[bait[\mathbf{T}] \mid \mathbf{T}]$$

These two specifications are, of course, incompatible. In fact, it is possible to show within our logic that, independently of any implementation of *fish* and *bait*, the composition of the *fish* spec with the *bait* spec leads to a logical contradiction.

The formula $C@n$ means that the tree present here and now satisfies the formula C when it is placed under an edge named n. This is another kind of requirement/guarantee specification, regarding nested contexts instead of parallel contexts: even when "thrown" inside an n context, the current tree will manage to satisfy the property C.

    matches $C@n$ if matches C

For example, an aquarium fish should satisfy the following property, stating that the fish will survive when placed in a (persistent) tank:

$$(\Box tank[fish[\mathbf{T}] \mid \mathbf{T}]) @ tank$$

5.4 From Satisfaction to Queries

A satisfaction relation, such as the one defined in the previous section, is not always decidable. However, in our case, if we rule out the $!P$ operator on trees, which describes infinite configurations, and also the $\mathcal{A} \triangleright \mathcal{B}$ formulas, which involve a quantification over an infinite set of trees, then the problem of whether $P \vDash \mathcal{A}$ becomes decidable [7]. A decision procedure for such a problem is also called a *modelchecking* algorithm. Such an algorithm implements essentially a matching procedure between a tree and a formula, where the result of the match is just success of failure.

For example, the following match succeeds. The formula can be read as stating that there is an empty chair at the *Eagle* pub; the matching process verifies that this fact holds in the current situation:

$$Eagle[chair[John[\mathbf{0}]] \mid chair[Mary[\mathbf{0}]] \mid chair[\mathbf{0}]]$$
$$\vDash Eagle[chair[\mathbf{0}] \mid \mathbf{T}]$$

More generally, we can conceive of collecting information during the matching process about which parts of the tree match which parts of the formula. Further, we can enrich formulas with markers that are meant to be bound to parts of the tree during matching; the result of the matching algorithm is then either failure or an association of formula markers to the trees that matched them.

We thus extend formulas with *matching variables*, $\mathcal{X}$, which are often placed where previously we would have placed a $\mathbf{T}$. For example by matching:

$$Eagle[chair[John[\mathbf{0}]] \mid chair[Mary[\mathbf{0}]] \mid chair[\mathbf{0}]]$$
$$\vDash Eagle[chair[\mathcal{X}] \mid \mathbf{T}]$$

we obtain, bound to $\mathcal{X}$, either somebody sitting at the *Eagle*, or the indication that there is an empty chair. Moreover, by matching:

$$Eagle[chair[John[\mathbf{0}]] \mid chair[Mary[\mathbf{0}]] \mid chair[\mathbf{0}]]$$
$$\vDash Eagle[chair[(\neg\mathbf{0})\wedge\mathcal{X}] \mid \mathbf{T}]$$

we obtain, bound to $\mathcal{X}$, somebody (not $\mathbf{0}$) sitting at the *Eagle*. Here the answer could be either *John*[$\mathbf{0}$] or *Mary*[$\mathbf{0}$], since both lead to a successful global match. Moreover, by using the same variable more than once we can express constraints: the formula *Eagle*[*chair*[$(\neg\mathbf{0})\wedge\mathcal{X}$] | *chair*[$\mathcal{X}$] | $\mathbf{T}$] is successfully matched if there are two people with the same name sitting at the *Eagle*.

These generalized formulas that include matching variables can thus be seen as *queries*. The result of a successful matching can be seen as a possible answer to a query, and the collection of all possible successful matches as the collection of all answers.

For serious semistructured database applications, we need also sophisticated ways of matching names (e.g. with wildcards and lexicographic orders) and of matching paths of names. For the latter, though, we already have considerable flexibility within the existing logic; consider the following examples:

- *Exact path*. The formula $n[m[p[\mathcal{X}]] \mid \mathbf{T}]$ means: match a path consisting of the names n, m, p, and bind $\mathcal{X}$ to what the path leads to. Note that, in this example, other paths may lead out of n, but there must be a unique path out of m and p.

- *Dislocated path*. The formula $n[\diamondsuit(m[\mathcal{X}] \mid \mathbf{T})]$ means: match a path consisting of a name n, followed by an arbitrary path, followed by a name m; bind $\mathcal{X}$ to what the path leads to.

- *Disjunctive path*. The formula $n[p[\mathcal{X}]] \vee m[p[\mathcal{X}]]$ means: bind $\mathcal{X}$ to the result of following either a path n,p, or a path m,p.

- *Negative path.* The formula $\diamond m[\neg(p[\mathbf{T}] \mid \mathbf{T}) \mid q[\mathcal{X}]]$ means: bind $\mathcal{X}$ to anything found somewhere under m, inside a q but not next to a p.
- *Wildcard and restricted wildcard.* $m[\exists y.y \neq n \wedge y[\mathcal{X}]]$ means: match a path consisting of m and any name different from n, and bind $\mathcal{X}$ to what the path leads to. (Inequality of names can be expressed within the logic [7]).

5.5 Adjunctive Queries

Using adjunctions, we can express queries that not only produce matches, but also reconstruct a results.

Consider the query:

$$m[\mathcal{X}@n]$$

This is matched by a tree $m[P]$ if P matches $\mathcal{X}@n$. By definition of P matching $\mathcal{X}@n$, we must verify that $n[P]$ matches $\mathcal{X}$. The latter simply causes the binding of $\mathcal{X}$ to $n[P]$, and we have this association as the result of the query. Note that $n[P]$ is not a subtree of the original tree: it was constructed by the query process. A similar query, $\diamond m[\mathcal{X}@q@n]$, means: if somewhere there is an edge m, wrap its contents P into $q[n[P]]$, and return that as the binding for $\mathcal{X}$.

Consider now the query

$$n[0] \triangleright \mathcal{X}$$

We have that P matches $n[0] \triangleright \mathcal{X}$ if for all Q that match $n[0]$, $P \mid Q$ matches $\mathcal{X}$. This immediately gives a result binding of $P \mid Q$ for $\mathcal{X}$. But what is Q? Fortunately there is only one Q that matches the formula $n[0]$, and that is the tree $n[0]$. So, this query has the following meaning: compose the current tree with $n[0]$, and give that as the binding of $\mathcal{X}$. Note, again, that this composition is not present in the original tree: it is constructed by the query. In this particular case, the infinite quantification over all Q does not hurt. However, as we mentioned above, we do not have a general matching algorithm for $\triangleright$, so we can at best handle some special cases.

It is not clear yet how much expressive power is induced by adjunctive queries, but the idea of using adjunctions to express query-and-recombination seems interesting, and it comes naturally out of an existing logic. It should be noted that basic questions of expressive power for semistructured database query languages are still open.

In other work [8], we are using a more traditional SQL-style *select* construct for constructing answers to queries. The resulting query language seems to be very similar to XML-QL [1], perhaps indicating a natural convergence of query mechanisms. However, it is also clear that new and potentially useful concepts, such as adjunctive queries, are emerging from the logical point of view.

5.6 Summary

We have seen that what was originally intended as a specification logic for mobile systems can be interpreted (with some extension) as a powerful query language for semistructured data. Conversely, although we have not discussed this, well-known efficient techniques for computing queries in databases can be used for modelchecking certain classes of mobile specifications.

6 Update

Sometimes we wish to change the data. These changes can be expressed by computational processes outside of the domain of databases and query languages. For example, we can use the Ambient Calculus operations described in Section 2.3 to transform trees. In general, if we have a fully worked-out notion of semistructured computation, instead of just semistructured data, then we already have a notion of semistructured update.

In database domains, however, we may want to be able express data transformations more declaratively. For example, transformations systems based on tree grammar transducers have been proposed for XML. It turns out that in our Ambient Logic we also have ways of specifying update operations declaratively, as we now discuss.

6.1 From Satisfiability to Update

In the examples of queries given so far we have considered only a static notion of matching. Remember, though, that we also have a temporal operator in the logic, $\Diamond\mathcal{A}$, that requires matching $\mathcal{A}$ after some evolution of the underlying tree. If we want to talk about update, we need to say that *right now*, we have a certain configuration, and *later*, we achieve another configuration.

To this end, we consider a slightly different view of the satisfaction problem. So far we have considered questions of the form $P \vDash \mathcal{A}$ when both P and $\mathcal{A}$ are given. Consider now the case where only $\mathcal{A}$ is given, and where we are looking for a tree that satisfies it; we can write this problem as $X \vDash \mathcal{A}$. In some cases this is easy: any formula constructed only by composing $\mathbf{0}$, $n[\mathcal{A}]$, and $\mathcal{A} \mid \mathcal{B}$ operations is satisfied by a unique tree. If other logical operators are used, the problem becomes harder (possibly undecidable).

Consider, then, the problem $X \vDash \mathcal{A} \triangleright \Diamond \mathcal{B}$. By definition, we have that X matches $\mathcal{A} \triangleright \Diamond \mathcal{B}$ if when composed with any tree P that matches $\mathcal{A}$, the composition $P \mid X$ can evolve into a tree that satisfies $\mathcal{B}$. Therefore, whatever X is, it must be something that transforms a tree satisfying $\mathcal{A}$ into a tree satisfying $\mathcal{B}$. In other words, X is a *mutator* of arbitrary $\mathcal{A}$ trees into $\mathcal{B}$ trees, and $X \vDash \mathcal{A} \triangleright \Diamond \mathcal{B}$ is a specification of such a mutator.

So, we can see $X \vDash \mathcal{A} \triangleright \Diamond \mathcal{B}$ as an inference problem where we are trying to synthesize an appropriate mutator. We believe that this is very much in the database style, where transformations are often specified declaratively, and synthesized by sophisticated optimizers. Of course, this problem can be hard. Alternatively, if we have a proposed mutator P to transform $\mathcal{A}$ trees into $\mathcal{B}$ trees, we can try to verify the property $P \vDash \mathcal{A} \triangleright \Diamond \mathcal{B}$, to check the correctness of the mutator.

6.2 Summary

We have seen that query languages for semistructured data and specification logics for mobility can be related. In one direction, this can gives us new query languages for semistructured data, or at least a new way of looking at existing query languages. In the other direction, this can gives us modelchecking techniques for mobility specifications.

Conclusions

In conclusion, we have argued that semistructured data and mobile computation are naturally related, because of a hidden similarity in the problems they are trying to solve.

From our point of view, we have discovered that the Ambient Calculus can be seen as a computational model over semistructured data. As a consequence, type systems already developed for the Ambient Calculus can be seen as weak schemas for semistructured data. Moreover, the Ambient Logic, with some modifications, can be seen as a query language for semistructured data.

We have also discovered that it should be interesting to integrate ideas and techniques arising from semistructured databases into the Ambient Calculus, and in mobile computation in general. For example, the generalization of the Ambient Calculus to graph structures, the use of database techniques for modelchecking, and the use of semistructured query languages for network resource discovery.

We hope that, conversely, people in the semistructured database community will find this connection interesting, and will be able to use it for their own purposes. Much, of course, remains to be done.

Acknowledgments

This paper arose from discussions with Giorgio Ghelli about semistructured databases.

References

[1] Abiteboul, S., Buneman, P., Suciu, D.: **Data on the Web**. Morgan Kaufmann Publishers, San Francisco, 2000.

[2] Buneman, P., Pierce, B.: **Union Types for Semistructured Data.** Proceedings of the International Database Programming Languages Workshop, 1999. Also available as University of Pennsylvania Dept. of CIS technical report MS-CIS-99-09.

[3] Cardelli, L.: **Abstractions for Mobile Computation.** Jan Vitek and Christian Jensen, Editors. *Secure Internet Programming: Security Issues for Mobile and Distributed Objects.* LNCS. 1603, 51-94, Springer, 1999.

[4] Cardelli, L., Ghelli, G., Gordon, A.D.: **Mobility Types for Mobile Ambients.** ICALP'99. LNCS 1644, 230-239, Springer, 1999.

[5] Cardelli, L., Gordon, A.D.: **Mobile Ambients.** FoSSaCS'98, LNCS 1378, 140-155, Springer, 1998.

[6] Cardelli, L., Gordon, A.D.: **Types for Mobile Ambients.** POPL'99, 79-92, 1999.

[7] Cardelli, L., Gordon, A.D.: **Anytime, Anywhere. Modal Logics for Mobile Ambients.** Proceedings POPL'00, 365-377, 2000.

[8] Cardelli, L., Ghelli, G.: **A Query Language for Semistructured Data Based on the Ambient Logic.** To appear.

[9] Engelfriet, J.: **A Multiset Semantics for the π-calculus with Replication**. TCS **153**, 65-94, 1996.

On the Power of Incremental Evaluation in SQL-like Languages

Leonid Libkin[1][*] and Limsoon Wong[2][**]

[1] Bell Laboratories, 600 Mountain Avenue, Murray Hill, NJ 07974, USA.
`libkin@bell-labs.com`
[2] Kent Ridge Digital Labs, 21 Heng Mui Keng Terrace, Singapore 119613.
`limsoon@krdl.org.sg`

Abstract. We consider IES($\mathcal{SQL}$), the incremental evaluation system over an SQL-like language with grouping, arithmetics, and aggregation. We show that every second order query is in IES($\mathcal{SQL}$) and that there are PSPACE-complete queries in IES($\mathcal{SQL}$). We further show that every PSPACE query is in IES($\mathcal{SQL}$) augmented with a deterministic transitive closure operator. Lastly, we consider ordered databases and provide a complete analysis of a hierarchy on IES($\mathcal{SQL}$) defined with respect to arity-bounded auxiliary relations.

1 Introduction

In the context of querying in a database system, for varied reasons such as efficiency and reliability, the user is often restricted to a special ambient language of that database system. For example, in commercial relational database systems, the user is restricted to use SQL to express queries. These special query languages are usually not Turing-complete. Consequently, there are queries that they cannot express. For example, relational algebra cannot test if a given table has an even number of rows and SQL cannot produce the transitive closure of a table containing the edge relationships of an unordered graph. The preceeding discussion on query expressibility is based on the classical "static" setting, which assumes that the query must compute its answer from "scratch." That is, the input to a query is given all at once and the output must be produced all at once.

However, a database normally builds its tables over a period of time by a sequence of insertions and deletions of individual records. Therefore, it is reasonable to consider query expressibility in the following non-classical "dynamic" or "incremental" setting. The writer of the query knows in advance, before the database is built, which query he has to write. In such an environment, he can take into consideration and has access to the history of updates to the intended input tables of the query. What he has available to him at any moment is considerably more than the classical query writer. For example, in addition

---

[*] Part of this work was done while visiting INRIA and Kent Ridge Digital Labs.
[**] Part of this work was done while visiting Bell Labs.

R. Connor and A. Mendelzon (Eds.): DBPL'99, LNCS 1949, pp. 17-30, 2000.

to the current state of the input table, he would have access to the next incoming update (the tuple being inserted or deleted), the current answer to the query (assuming that it is his plan to keep a copy of the answer), and possibly some auxiliary information (assuming that it is his plan to keep the auxiliary information). Following [8, 12, etc], we call this non-classical setting of querying databases "incremental query evaluation."

There are two kinds of incremental query evaluation in general. The first kind is where a query is definable in the ambient language. In this case, incremental evaluation is possible simply by re-executing the query from scratch every time an answer to the query is needed. The main challenge here is how to write the query in a smarter way to avoid re-executing the query from scratch all the time[12, 13, etc.] The second kind is where a query is *not* definable in the ambient language in the classical sense. Then the question arises as to whether this same query can be expressed in the non-classical sense, where we allow the query writer access to the extra incremental information mentioned earlier. This second kind of incremental query evaluation is the main interest of this paper. The main questions addressed in this setting deal with conditions under which it is possible to evaluate queries incrementally.

Let us motivate this second kind of incremental query evaluation by a very simple example using the relational calculus (first-order logic) as the ambient language. Let PARITY be the query that returns true iff the cardinality of a set X is even. This query cannot be expressed in relational calculus, but it can be incrementally evaluated. Indeed, on the insertion of an x into X, one replaces the current answer to PARITY by its negation if $x \notin X$, and keeps it intact if $x \in X$. On the deletion of an x from X, one negates the current answer if $x \in X$, and keeps the answer unchanged if $x \notin X$. Clearly, this algorithm is first-order definable.

We denote the class of queries that can be incrementally evaluated in a language $\mathcal{L}$, using auxiliary relations of arity up to k, $k > 0$, by $\mathsf{IES}(\mathcal{L})_k$. We let $\mathsf{IES}(\mathcal{L})_\epsilon$ be the class of queries incrementally evaluated in $\mathcal{L}$ without using any auxiliary data (like the PARITY example above). Finally, $\mathsf{IES}(\mathcal{L})$ is the union of all $\mathsf{IES}(\mathcal{L})_k$.

The most frequently considered class is $\mathsf{IES}(\mathcal{FO})$, which uses the relational calculus as its ambient language. There are several examples of queries belonging to $\mathsf{IES}(\mathcal{FO})$ that are not definable in $\mathcal{FO}$ [21, 7]. The most complex example is probably that of [9], which is a query that is in $\mathsf{IES}(\mathcal{FO})$ but cannot be expressed even in first-order logic enhanced with counting and transitive closure operators. It is known [7] that the arity hierarchy is strict: $\mathsf{IES}(\mathcal{FO})_k \subset \mathsf{IES}(\mathcal{FO})_{k+1}$, and that $\mathsf{IES}(\mathcal{FO}) \subseteq \mathrm{PTIME}$. Still, for most queries of interest, such as the transitive closure of a relation, it remains open whether they belong to $\mathsf{IES}(\mathcal{FO})$. It also appears [9] that proving lower bounds for $\mathsf{IES}(\mathcal{FO})$ is as difficult as proving some circuit lower bounds.

Most commercial database systems speak SQL and most practical implementations of SQL are more expressive than the relational algebra because they have aggregate functions (e.g., `AVG`, `TOTAL`) and grouping constructs (`GROUPBY`,

HAVING). This motivated us [19] to look at incremental evaluation systems based on the "core" of SQL, which comprises relational calculus plus grouping and aggregation. Somewhat surprisingly, we discovered the following. First, queries such as the transitive closure and even some PTIME-complete queries, can be incrementally evaluated by core SQL queries (although the algorithms presented in [19] were quite ad hoc). Second, the arity hierarchy for core SQL collapses at the second level.

Our goal here is to investigate deeper into the incremental evaluation capabilities of SQL-like languages. In particular, we want to find nice descriptions of classes of queries that can be incrementally evaluated. The first set of results shows that the classes are indeed much larger than we suspected before. We define a language $\mathcal{SQL}$ that extends relational algebra with grouping and aggregation, and show that:

1. Every query whose data complexity is in the polynomial hierarchy (equivalently: every second-order definable query) is in IES($\mathcal{SQL}$).
2. There exists PSPACE-complete queries in IES($\mathcal{SQL}$).
3. Adding deterministic transitive closure to $\mathcal{SQL}$ (a DLOGSPACE operator) results in a language that can incrementally evaluate every query of PSPACE data complexity.

In the second part of the paper, we compare the IES hierarchy in the cases of ordered and unordered types. We show that the IES($\mathcal{SQL}$)$_k$ hierarchy collapses at level 1 in the case of ordered types. We further paint the complete picture of the relationship between the classes of the ordered and the unordered hierarchies; see Figure 2.

As one might expect, the reason for the enormous power of SQL-like languages in terms of incremental evaluation is that one can create and maintain rather large structures on *numbers* and use them for coding queries. In some cases, this can be quite inefficient. However, we have demonstrated elsewhere [6] that coding an algorithm for incremental evaluation of transitive closure in SQL is reasonably simple. Moreover, it has also been shown [22] that the performance is adequate for a large class of graphs. Thus, while the proofs here in general do not lend themselves to efficient algorithms (nor can they, as we show how to evaluate presumably intractable queries), the incremental techniques can well be used in practice. However, proving that certain queries cannot be incrementally evaluated in SQL within some complexity bounds appears beyond reach, as doing so would separate some complexity classes, cf. [15].

Organization In the next section, we give preliminary material, such as a theoretical language $\mathcal{SQL}$ capturing the grouping and aggregation features of SQL, the definition of incremental evaluation system IES, a nested relational language, and the relationship between the incremental evaluation systems based on the nested language and aggregation.

In Section 3, we prove that IES($\mathcal{SQL}$), the incremental evaluation system based on core SQL, includes every query whose data complexity is in the polynomial hierarchy. We also give an example of a PSPACE-complete query which belongs to $\mathsf{IES}(\mathcal{SQL})$, and show that $\mathcal{SQL}$ augmented with the deterministic transitive closure operator can incrementally evaluate every query of PSPACE data complexity.

In Section 4, we consider a slightly different version of $\mathcal{SQL}$, denoted by $\mathcal{SQL}^<$. In this language, base types come equipped with an order relation. We show that the $\mathsf{IES}(\mathcal{SQL}^<)_k$ hierarchy collapses at the first level, and explain the relationship between the classes in both $\mathsf{IES}(\mathcal{SQL})_k$ and $\mathsf{IES}(\mathcal{SQL}^<)_k$ hierarchies.

2   Preliminaries

Languages $\mathcal{SQL}$ and $\mathcal{NRC}$ A functional-style language that captures the essential features of SQL (grouping and aggregation) has been studied in a number of papers [18,5,15]. While the syntax slightly varies, choosing any particular one will not affect our results, as the expressive power is the same. Here we work with the version presented in [15].

The language is defined as a suitable restriction of a *nested* language. The type system is given by

$$\begin{aligned}
\textsc{Base} &:= b \mid \mathbb{Q} \\
rt &:= \textsc{Base} \times \ldots \times \textsc{Base} \\
t &:= \mathbb{B} \mid rt \mid \{rt\} \mid t \times \ldots \times t
\end{aligned}$$

The base types are b and $\mathbb{Q}$, with the domain of b being an infinite set $\mathcal{U}$, disjoint from $\mathbb{Q}$. We use $\times$ for product types; the semantics of $t_1 \times \ldots \times t_n$ is the cartesian product of domains of types $t_1, \ldots, t_n$. The semantics of $\{t\}$ is the finite powerset of elements of type t. We use the notation rt for record types, and let $\mathbb{B}$ be the Boolean type.

A database schema σ is a collection of relation names and their types of the form $\{rt\}$. For a relation $R \in \sigma$, we denote its type by $\mathrm{tp}_\sigma(R)$. Expressions of the language over a fixed relational schema σ are shown in Figure 1. We adopt the convention of omitting the explicit type superscripts in these expressions whenever they can be inferred from the context. We briefly explain the semantics here. The set of free variables of an expression e is defined in a standard way by induction on the structure of e and we often write $e(x_1, \ldots, x_n)$ to explicitly indicate that $x_1, \ldots, x_n$ are free variables of e. Expressions $\bigcup\{e_1 \mid x \in e_2\}$ and $\sum\{e_1 \mid x \in e_2\}$ bind the variable x (furthermore, x is not allowed to be free in e_2 for this expression to be well-formed).

For each fixed schema σ and an expression $e(x_1, \ldots, x_n)$, the value of $e(x_1, \ldots, x_n)$ is defined by induction on the structure of e and with respect to a σ-database D and a substitution $[x_1 := a_1, \ldots, x_n := a_n]$ that assigns to each variable x_i a value a_i of the appropriate type. We write $e[x_1 := a_1, \ldots, x_n := a_n](D)$ to denote this value; if the context is understood, we shorten this to $e[x_1 := a_1, \ldots, x_n := a_n]$ or just e. We have equality test on both base types. On the rationals, we have the order and the usual arithmetic operations. There is the tupling operation $(e_1, \ldots, e_n)$ and projections $\pi_{i,n}$ on tuples. The value of $\{e\}$ is the singleton set containing the value of e; $e_1 \cup e_2$ computes the union of two sets, and $\emptyset$ is the empty set.

To define the semantics of $\bigcup$ and $\sum$, assume that the value of e_2 is the set $\{b_1, \ldots, b_m\}$. Then the value of $\bigcup\{e_1 \mid x \in e_2\}$ is defined to be

$$\bigcup_{i=1}^{m} e_1[x_1 := a_1, \ldots, x_n := a_n, x := b_i](D).$$

The value of $\sum\{e_1 \mid x \in e_2\}$ is $c_1 + \ldots + c_m$, each c_i is the value of $e_1[x_1 := a_1, \ldots, x_n := a_n, x := b_i]$, $i = 1, \ldots, m$.

$$\frac{}{x^t : t} \quad \frac{R \in \sigma}{R : \mathrm{tp}_\sigma(R)} \quad \frac{}{0, 1 : \mathbb{Q}} \quad \frac{e_1, e_2 : \mathbb{Q}}{e_1 + e_2, \ e_1 - e_2, \ e_1 * e_2, \ e_1 \div e_2 : \mathbb{Q}}$$

$$\frac{e_1, e_2 : b}{= (e_1, e_2) : \mathbb{B}} \quad \frac{e_1, e_2 : \mathbb{Q}}{= (e_1, e_2) : \mathbb{B}} \quad \frac{e_1, e_2 : \mathbb{Q}}{< (e_1, e_2) : \mathbb{B}} \quad \frac{e : \mathbb{B} \quad e_1 : t \quad e_2 : t}{\textit{if } e \textit{ then } e_1 \textit{ else } e_2 : t}$$

$$\frac{e_1 : t_1 \quad \ldots \quad e_n : t_n}{(e_1, \ldots, e_n) : t_1 \times \ldots \times t_n} \quad \frac{i \leq n \quad e : t_1 \times \ldots \times t_n}{\pi_{i,n} \, e : t_i}$$

$$\frac{e : rt}{\{e\} : \{rt\}} \quad \frac{e_1 : \{rt\} \quad e_2 : \{rt\}}{e_1 \cup e_2 : \{rt\}} \quad \frac{}{\emptyset^{rt} : \{rt\}}$$

$$\frac{e_1 : \{rt_1\} \quad e_2 : \{rt_2\}}{\bigcup\{e_1 \mid x^{rt_2} \in e_2\} : \{rt_1\}} \quad \frac{e_1 : \mathbb{Q} \quad e_2 : \{rt\}}{\sum\{e_1 \mid x^{rt} \in e_2\} : \mathbb{Q}}$$

Fig. 1. Expressions of $\mathcal{SQL}$ over schema σ

Properties of $\mathcal{SQL}$ The relational part of the language (without arithmetic and aggregation) is known [18, 3] to have essentially the power of the *relational algebra*. When the standard arithmetic and the $\sum$ aggregate are added, the language becomes [18] powerful enough to code standard SQL aggregation features such as the GROUPBY and HAVING clauses, and aggregate functions such as TOTAL, COUNT, AVG, MIN, MAX, which are present in all commercial versions of SQL [1].

Another language that we frequently use is the nested relational calculus $\mathcal{NRC}$. Its type system is given by

$$t ::= b \mid \mathbb{B} \mid t \times \ldots \times t \mid \{t\}$$

That is, sets nested arbitrarily deep are allowed. The expressions of $\mathcal{NRC}$ are exactly the expressions of $\mathcal{SQL}$ that do not involve arithmetic, except that there is no restriction to flat types in the set operations.

Incremental evaluation systems The idea of an incremental evaluation system, or IES, is as follows. Suppose we have a query Q and a language $\mathcal{L}$. An IES($\mathcal{L}$) for incrementally evaluating Q is a system consisting of an input database, an answer database, an optional auxiliary database, and a finite set of "update" functions that correspond to different kinds of permissible updates to the input database. These update functions take as input the corresponding update, the input database, the answer database, and the auxiliary database; and collectively produce as output the updated input database, the updated answer database, and the updated auxiliary database. There are two main requirements: the condition $O = Q(I)$ must be maintained, where I is the input database, and O is the output database; and that the update functions must be expressible in the language $\mathcal{L}$. For example, in the previous section we gave an incremental evaluation system for the PARITY query in relational calculus. That system did not use any auxiliary relations.

Following [21, 7, 8, 19], we consider here only queries that operate on relational databases storing elements of the base type b. These queries are those whose inputs are of types of the form $\{b \times \ldots \times b\}$. Queries whose incremental evaluation we study have to be generic, that is, invariant under permutations of the domain $\mathcal{U}$ of type b. Examples include all queries definable in a variety of classical query languages, such as relational calculus, datalog, and the while-loop language. The criteria for permissible update are restricted to the insertion and deletion of a single tuple into an input relation.

While the informal definition given above is sufficient for understanding the results of the paper, we give a formal definition of IES($\mathcal{L}$), as in [19], which is very similar to the definitions of FOIES [7] and Dyn-$\mathcal{C}$ [21]. Suppose the types of relations of the input database are $\{rt_1\}, \ldots, \{rt_m\}$, where $rt_1, \ldots, rt_m$ are record types of the form $b \times \ldots \times b$. We consider elementary updates of the form $ins_i(x)$ and $del_i(x)$, where x is of type rt_i. Given an object X of type $S = \{rt_1\} \times \ldots \times \{rt_m\}$, applying such an update results in inserting x into or deleting x from the ith set in X, that is, the set of type $\{rt_i\}$. Given a sequence $\mathcal{U}$ of updates, $\mathcal{U}(X)$ denotes the result of applying the sequence $\mathcal{U}$ to an object X of type S.

Given a query Q of type $S \to T$ (that is, an expression of type T with free variables of types $\{rt_1\}, \ldots, \{rt_m\}$), and a type T_{aux} (of auxiliary data), consider a collection of functions $\mathcal{F}_Q$:

$$
\begin{aligned}
&f_{\text{init}} : S \to T & &f_{\text{init}}^{\text{aux}} : S \to T_{\text{aux}} \\
&f_{\text{del}}^i : rt_i \times S \times T \times T_{\text{aux}} \to T & &f_{\text{del}}^{\text{aux},i} : rt_i \times S \times T \times T_{\text{aux}} \to T_{\text{aux}} \\
&f_{\text{ins}}^i : rt_i \times S \times T \times T_{\text{aux}} \to T & &f_{\text{ins}}^{\text{aux},i} : rt_i \times S \times T \times T_{\text{aux}} \to T_{\text{aux}}
\end{aligned}
$$

Given an elementary update u, we associate two functions with it. The function $f_u : S \times T \times T_{\text{aux}} \to T$ is defined as $\lambda(X, Y, Z).f_{\text{del}}^i(a, X, Y, Z)$ if u is $del_i(a)$, and as $\lambda(X, Y, Z).f_{\text{ins}}^i(a, X, Y, Z)$ if u is $ins_i(a)$. We similarly define $f_u^{\text{aux}} : S \times T \times T_{\text{aux}} \to T_{\text{aux}}$.

Given a sequence of updates $\mathcal{U} = \{u_1, \ldots, u_l\}$, define inductively the collection of objects: $X_0 = \emptyset : S$, $RES_0 = f_{\text{init}}(X_0)$, $AUX_0 = f_{\text{init}}^{\text{aux}}(X_0)$ (where $\emptyset$ of type S is a product of m empty sets), and

$$X_{i+1} = u_{i+1}(X_i)$$
$$RES_{i+1} = f_{u_{i+1}}(X_i, RES_i, AUX_i)$$
$$AUX_{i+1} = f_{u_{i+1}}^{\mathrm{aux}}(X_i, RES_i, AUX_i)$$

Finally, we define $\mathcal{F}_Q(\mathcal{U})$ as RES_l.

We now say that there exists an *incremental evaluation system* for Q in $\mathcal{L}$ if there is a type T_{aux} and a collection $\mathcal{F}_Q$ of functions, typed as above, such that, for any sequence $\mathcal{U}$ of updates, $\mathcal{F}_Q(\mathcal{U}) = Q(\mathcal{U}(\emptyset))$. We also say then that Q is *expressible in* IES($\mathcal{L}$) or *maintainable in* $\mathcal{L}$. If T_{aux} is a product of flat types $\{rt\}$, with rts having at most k components, then we say that Q is in IES($\mathcal{L}$)$_k$.

Since every expression in $\mathcal{NRC}$ or $\mathcal{SQL}$ has a well-typed function associated with it, the definition above applies to these languages.

Properties of IES Clearly, every query expressible in $\mathcal{L}$ belongs to IES($\mathcal{L}$)$_\epsilon$. What makes IES interesting is that many queries that are not expressible in $\mathcal{L}$ can still be incrementally evaluated in $\mathcal{L}$. For example, the transitive closure of undirected graphs belongs to IES($\mathcal{FO}$)$_2$ [21, 7]. One of the more remarkable facts about IES($\mathcal{FO}$), mentioned already in the introduction, is that the arity hierarchy is strict: IES($\mathcal{FO}$)$_k \subsetneq$ IES($\mathcal{FO}$)$_{k+1}$ [7]. Also, every query in IES($\mathcal{FO}$) has PTIME data complexity.

A number of results about IES($\mathcal{SQL}$) exist in the literature. We know [4] that $\mathcal{SQL}$ is unable to maintain transitive closure of arbitrary graphs without using auxiliary relations. We also know that transitive closure of arbitrary graphs remains unmaintainable in $\mathcal{SQL}$ even in the presence of auxiliary data whose degrees are bounded by a constant [5]. On the positive side, we know that if the bounded degree constraint on auxiliary data is removed, transitive closure of arbitrary graphs becomes maintainable in $\mathcal{SQL}$. In fact, this query and even the alternating path query belong to IES($\mathcal{SQL}$)$_2$. Finally, we also know [19] that the IES($\mathcal{SQL}$)$_k$ hierarchy collapses to IES($\mathcal{SQL}$)$_2$. We shall use the following result [19] several times in this paper.

Fact 1 IES($\mathcal{NRC}$) $\subseteq$ IES($\mathcal{SQL}$).   □

3 Maintainability of Second Order Queries

We prove in this section that we can incrementally evaluate all queries whose data complexity is in the polynomial hierarchy PHIER (equivalently, all queries expressible in second order logic). The proof, sketched at the end of the section, is based on the ability to maintain very large sets using arithmetic, which suffices to model second-order expressible queries.

Theorem 1. *$\mathcal{SQL}$ can incrementally evaluate all queries whose data complexity is in the polynomial hierarchy. That is, PHIER $\subseteq$ IES($\mathcal{SQL}$).*   □

The best previously known [19] positive result on the limit of incremental evaluation in $\mathcal{SQL}$ was for a PTIME-complete query. Theorem 1 shows that the class of queries that can be incrementally evaluated in $\mathcal{SQL}$ is presumably much larger than the class of tractable queries. In particular, every NP-complete problem is in IES($\mathcal{SQL}$).

The next question is whether the containment can be replaced by equality. This appears unlikely in view of the following.

Proposition 1. *There exists a problem complete for PSPACE which belongs to* IES($\mathcal{SQL}$). □

Note that this is *not* sufficient to conclude the containment of PSPACE in IES($\mathcal{SQL}$), as the notion of reduction for dynamic complexity classes is more restrictive than the usual reduction notions in complexity theory, see [21]. In fact, we do not know if PSPACE is contained in IES($\mathcal{SQL}$). We can show, however, that a mild extension of $\mathcal{SQL}$ gives us a language powerful enough to incrementally evaluate all PSPACE queries. Namely, consider the following addition to the language:

$$\frac{e : \{rt \times rt\}}{dtc(e) : \{rt \times rt\}}$$

Here *dtc* is the deterministic transitive closure operator [16]. Given a graph with the set of edges E, there is an edge (a, b) in its deterministic transitive closure iff there is a deterministic path $(a, a_1), (a_1, a_2), ..., (a_{n-1}, a_n), (a_n, b)$ in E; that is, a path in which every node a_i, $i < n$, and a have outdegree 1. It is known [16] that *dtc* is complete for DLOGSPACE. We prove the following new result.

Proposition 2. $\mathcal{SQL}$ + *dtc can incrementally evaluate all queries of* PSPACE *data complexity. That is,* PSPACE $\subseteq$ IES($\mathcal{SQL}$ + dtc). □

We now sketch the proofs of these results. We use the notation $\wp(B^k)$ to mean the powerset of the k-fold cartesian product of the set $B : \{b\}$ of atomic objects. The proof of Theorem 1 involves two steps. In the first step, we show that $\wp(B^k)$ can be maintained in $\mathcal{NRC}$ for every k, when B is updated. In the second step, we show that if the domain of each second order quantifier is made available to $\mathcal{NRC}$, then any second order logic formula can be translated to $\mathcal{NRC}$. The first of these two steps is also needed for the proof of Propositions 2 and 1, so we abstract it out in the following lemma.

Lemma 1. $\mathcal{NRC}$ *can incrementally evaluate* $\wp(B^k)$ *for every* k *when* $B : \{b\}$ *is updated.*

Proof sketch. Let PB_k^o and PB_k^n be the symbols naming the nested relation $\wp(B^k)$ immediately before and after the update. We proceed by induction on k. The simple base case of $k = 1$ (maintaining the powerset of a unary relation) is omitted. For the induction case of $k > 1$, we consider two cases.

Suppose the update is the insertion of a new element x into the set B. By the induction hypothesis, $\mathcal{NRC}$ can maintain $\wp(B^{k-1})$. So we can create the following nested sets: $Y_0 = \{\{(x, ..., x)\}\}$ and $Y_i =$

$\{\{(z_1, \ldots, z_i, x, z_{i+1}, \ldots, z_{k-1}) \mid (z_1, \ldots, z_{k-1}) \in X\} \mid X \in PB^n_{k-1}\}$, for $i = 1$, ..., $k - 1$. Let *cartprod* be the function that forms the cartesian product of two sets; this function is easily definable in $\mathcal{NRC}$. Let *allunion* be the function that takes a tuple $(S_1, \ldots, S_k)$ of sets and returns a set of sets containing all possible unions of $S_1, \ldots, S_k$; this function is also definable in $\mathcal{NRC}$ because the number of combinations is fixed once k is given. Then it is not difficult to see that $PB^n_k = \{X \mid Y \in (PB^o_k \ cartprod \ Y_0 \ cartprod \ Y_1 \ cartprod \cdots cartprod Y_{k-1}), X \in allunion(Y)\}$.

Suppose the update is the deletion of an existing element x from the set B. Then all we need is to delete from each of $PB_1, \ldots, PB_k$ all the sets that have x as a component of one of their elements, which is definable in $\mathcal{NRC}$.   □

Proof sketch of Theorem 1. Let $Q : \{rt\}$ be a query in PHIER, with input relations $R_1, \ldots, R_m$ of types $\{rt_i\}$. Then Q is definable by a second-order formula with n free first-order variables, where n is the arity of rt. Suppose this formula is $\phi(x) = \mathbf{Q}_1 S_1 \ldots \mathbf{Q}_p S_p \alpha(x, S_1, \ldots, S_p)$; where α is a first-order formula in the language of R_is, S_is, and equality; $\mathbf{Q}$s are the quantifiers $\forall$ and $\exists$; and each S_i has arity k_i. Then, to maintain Q in $\mathcal{NRC}$, we have to maintain: (a) the active domain B of the database $R_1, \ldots, R_m$, and (b) all $\wp(B^{k_i})$. Note that the definition of IES($\mathcal{NRC}$) puts no restriction on types of auxiliary relations. Since a single insertion into or deletion from a relation R_i results in a fixed number of insertions and deletions in B that is bounded by the maximal arity of a relation, we conclude from Lemma 1 that all $\wp(B^{k_i})$ can be incrementally evaluated. Since $\mathcal{NRC}$ has all the power of first-order logic [3], we conclude that it can incrementally evaluate Q by maintaining all the powersets and then evaluating a first-order query on them.   □

Proof sketch of Proposition 1. It is not hard to show that with $\wp(B^k)$, one can incrementally evaluate the REACHABLE DEADLOCK problem, which is known to be PSPACE-complete [20].

Proof sketch of Proposition 2. Let Q be a PSPACE query. It is known then that Q is expressible in partial-fixpoint logic, if the underlying structure is ordered. We know [19] that an order relation on the active domain can be maintained in $\mathcal{SQL}$. We also know [2] that Q is of the form $\mathrm{PFP}_{y,S}\phi(x, y, S)$, where ϕ is a first-order formula. To show that Q is in IES($\mathcal{SQL} + dtc$) we do the following. We maintain the active domain B, an order relation on it, and $\wp(B^k)$ where $k = |y|$. We maintain it, however, as a *flat* relation of type $\{\mathbb{Q} \times b \times \ldots \times b\}$ where subsets are coded; that is, a tuple (c, a) indicates that a belongs to a subset of B^k coded by c. That this can be done, follows from the proof of IES($\mathcal{NRC}$) $\subseteq$ IES($\mathcal{SQL}$) in [19]. We next define a binary relation R_0 of type $\{\mathbb{Q} \times \mathbb{Q}\}$ such that a pair (c_1, c_2) is in it if applying the operator defined by ϕ to the subset of B^k coded by c_1 yields c_2. It is routine to verify that this is definable. Next, we note that the outdegree of every node of R_0 is at most 1; hence, $dtc(R_0)$ is its transitive closure. Using this, we can determine the value of the partial fixpoint operator.   □

Limitations of Incremental Evaluation in $\mathcal{SQL}$ Having captured the whole
of the polynomial hierarchy inside IES($\mathcal{SQL}$), can we do more? Proving lower
bounds in the area of dynamic complexity is very hard [21,9] and $\mathcal{SQL}$ is
apparently no exception. Still, we can establish some easy limitations. More
precisely, we address the following question. We saw that the powerset of B^k
can be incrementally evaluated in $\mathcal{NRC}$. Does this continue to hold for *iterated* powerset constructions? For example, can we maintain sets like $\wp(\wp(B^k))$,
$\wp(\wp(B) \text{ cartprod } \wp(B))$, etc.? If we could maintain $\wp(\wp(B^k))$ in $\mathcal{NRC}$, it would
have shown that PSPACE is contained in IES($\mathcal{SQL}$). However, it turns out the
Lemma 1 is close to the limit. First, we note the 2-DEXPSPACE data complexity
of IES($\mathcal{SQL}$).

Proposition 3. *For every query in* IES($\mathcal{SQL}$) *(even without restriction to flat
types) there exist numbers $c, d > 0$ such that the total size of the input database,
answer database, and auxiliary database after n updates is at most c^{d^n}.*

Proof. It is known that $\mathcal{SQL}$ queries have PTIME data complexity [18]. Thus, if
$f(n)$ is the size of the input, output and auxiliary databases after n updates, we
obtain $f(n+1) \leq Cf(n)^m$ for appropriately chosen $C, m > 0$. The claim now
follows by induction on n. □

We use $\wp^j(B^k)$ to mean taking the powerset j times on the k-fold cartesian
product of the set B of atomic objects. We know that $\wp(B^k)$ can be maintained
by $\mathcal{NRC}$. For the iterated case, not much can be done.

Corollary 1. *Let $j > 1$. $\wp^j(B^k)$ can be maintained by $\mathcal{NRC}$ when B is updated
iff $j = 2$ and $k = 1$.*

Proof sketch. First, we show that $\wp^2(B)$ can be maintained. Let $B : \{b\}$ denote
the input database. Let $PPB = \wp(\wp(B)) : \{\{\{b\}\}\}$ denote the answer database.
B is initially empty. PPB is initially $\{\{\}, \{\{\}\}\}$. Suppose the update is the
insertion of a new atomic object x into B. Let $\Delta = \{U \cup \{\{x\} \cup v \mid v \in V\} \mid U \in
PPB^o, V \in PPB^o\}$. Then $PPB^n = PPB^o \cup \Delta$ is the desired double powerset.
Suppose the update is the deletion of an old object x from B. Then we simply
delete from PPB all those sets that mention x. Both operations are definable in
$\mathcal{NRC}$.

That $\wp^j(B^k)$ cannot be maintained for $(j, k) \neq (2, 1)$, easily follows from the
bounds above, as $2^{2^{n^2}}$ is not majorized by c^{d^n} for any constants c, d. □

4   Low Levels of the IES hierarchy

We know that the class of queries that can be evaluated incrementally in $\mathcal{SQL}$ is
very large. We also know from earlier work [4,19] that with restrictions on the
class of auxiliary relations, even many PTIME queries cannot be maintained.
Thus, we would like to investigate the low levels of the IES($\mathcal{SQL}$) hierarchy. This
was partly done in [19], under a severe restriction that only elements of base
types be used in auxiliary relations. Now, using recent results on the expressive

power of SQL-like languages and locality tools from finite-model theory [14, 15], we paint the complete picture of the relationship between the levels of the hierarchy.

In many incremental algorithms, the presence of an order is essential. While having an order on the base type b makes no difference if binary auxiliary relations are allowed (since one can maintain an order as an auxiliary relation), there is a difference for the case when restrictions on the arity of auxiliary relations are imposed. We thus consider an extension of SQL denoted by $SQL^<$ which is obtained by a adding a new rule

$$\frac{e_1, e_2 : b}{<_b (e_1, e_2) : \mathbb{B}}$$

where $<_b$ is interpreted as an order on the domain of the base type b. The main result now relates the levels of the $\mathsf{IES}(SQL)_k$ and $\mathsf{IES}(SQL^<)_k$ hierarchies.

Theorem 2. *The relationships shown in the diagram in Figure 2 hold. Here* $A \longrightarrow B$ *means that* A *is a proper subset of* B, *and* $A \dashleftarrow \cdots \cdots \dashrightarrow B$ *means that* $A \nsubseteq B$ *and* $B \nsubseteq A$.

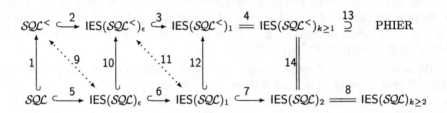

Fig. 2. $\mathsf{IES}(SQL)_k$ and $\mathsf{IES}(SQL^<)_k$ hierarchies

Proof sketch. The containment 13 was shown in this paper (Theorem 1). The hierarchy collapse 8, as well as the inclusion 6 and the maintenance of order 14 are from [19]. We also note that in SQL, one can incrementally evaluate a query q_0 such that $q_0(D) = 2^n$, where n is the size of the active domain of D. However, it is known that the maximal number SQL or $SQL^<$ can produce is at most polynomial in the size of the active domain and the maximal number stored in the database. This shows inclusions 2, 5 and half of 9: $\mathsf{IES}(SQL)_\epsilon \nsubseteq SQL^<$.

Next, consider an input of type $\{b\}$, and a query

$$q_1(X) = \begin{cases} 2^{|X|} & \text{if } |X| \text{ is a power of 2} \\ 0 & \text{otherwise} \end{cases}$$

This query belongs to $\mathsf{IES}(SQL)_1$, as we can maintain the set $\{0, 1, 2, \ldots, 2^{|X|}\}$ and then use standard techniques to test for the powers of 2. However, $q_1 \notin$

$\mathsf{IES}(\mathcal{SQL}^<)_\epsilon$. Indeed, if $|X| = 2^m - 1$, then $q_1(X) = 0$ and thus on an insert into X, the maintenance query would have to produce an integer exponential in the size of the input. This shows 3, 6, and half of 11: $\mathsf{IES}(\mathcal{SQL})_1 \not\subseteq \mathsf{IES}(\mathcal{SQL}^<)_\epsilon$.

The proof of collapse 4 proceeds similarly to the proof of 8 in [19]. To reduce arity 2 to arity 1, we maintain a large enough initial segment of natural numbers (but still polynomial) which we use to code tuples by numbers, where an element of base type b is coded by its relative position in the ordering of the active domain, and tuples are coded using the standard pairing function. Then 4 and 7 imply 12.

For the remaining relationship, we use locality techniques from finite-model theory [10, 11, 14]. We shall now consider queries on tuples of flat relations of types $\{b \times \ldots \times b\}$ into a relation of type of the same form. Given an input database D, which is a tuple of relations $R_1, \ldots, R_k$, we define the Gaifman graph $\mathcal{G}(D)$ on its active domain as an undirected graph with (a, b) being an edge in it if one of R_is has a tuple that contains both a and b. By a distance in D, we mean the distance in its Gaifman graph. Given a tuple t, by $S_r^D(t)$ we mean the set of all elements of the active domain of D at a distance at most r of some element of t. These are *neighborhoods* of tuples, which can be considered as databases of the same schema as D, by restricting the relations of D onto them. Two tuples are said to have the same r-type if their r-neighborhoods are isomorphic. That is, there is a bijection $f : S_r^D(t_1) \to S_r^D(t_2)$ such that $f(t_1) = t_2$ and for every tuple u of elements of $S_r^D(t_1)$, $u \in R_i$ implies $f(u) \in R_i$, and for every v in $S_r^D(t_2)$, $v \in R_i$ implies $f^{-1}(v) \in R_i$.

We now say (see [14], where connection with Gaifman's theorem [11] is explained) that a query Q is *local* if there exists an integer r such that, if t_1 and t_2 have the same r-type in D, then $t_1 \in Q(D)$ iff $t_2 \in Q(D)$. We shall use the fact [15] that every query of pure relational type (no rationals) in $\mathcal{SQL}$ is local.

Now 1 follows from locality of $\mathcal{SQL}$, and the fact that $\mathcal{SQL}^<$ expresses all queries definable in first-order logic with counting over ordered structures (see [15]), which is known to violate locality [14]. For other relationships, consider the following query. Its input type is $\{b \times b\} \times \{b\}$; its output is of type $\{b\}$. We shall refer to the graph part of the input as G and to the set part as P; that is, the input is a pair (G, P). A pair is *good* if G is the graph of a successor relation, and P is its initial segment. A query q is *good* if it has the following properties whenever its input is good: (1) If $n = 2^{|P|}$, where n is the number of nodes in G, then $q(G, P)$ is the transitive closure of the initial segment defined by P; (2) If $n \neq 2^{|P|}$, then $q(G, P) = \emptyset$. It can be shown that there is a good query q in $\mathcal{SQL}^<$—this is because with counting power we can encode fragments of monadic second-order on small portions of the input [14].

As the next step, we show that no such good q can belong to $\mathsf{IES}(\mathcal{SQL})_1$. This shows the second half of 11 (that $\mathsf{IES}(\mathcal{SQL}^<)_\epsilon \not\subseteq \mathsf{IES}(\mathcal{SQL})_1$), 10, 12, and second half of 9. It also shows 7, because we know $\mathcal{SQL}^< \subseteq \mathsf{IES}(\mathcal{SQL})_2$. To prove this, we first reduce the problem to inexpressibility of a good query in $\mathcal{SQL}$ in the presence of additional unary relations. This is because we can consider an input in which $2^{|P|-1} = n$. For such an input, the answer to q is $\emptyset$, but on an insert into P it becomes the transitive closure of the segment defined by P. As the next step, we show that locality of $\mathcal{SQL}$ withstands adding *numerical* relations, those of type $\{\mathbb{Q} \times \ldots \times \mathbb{Q}\}$, as long as there is no ordering on b. To prove this, we first code $\mathcal{SQL}$ into an infinitary logic with counting, as was done in [15], and then modify the induction argument from [17] to prove locality in the presence of extra numerical relations. Finally, a finite number, say m, of unary relations of type $\{b\}$, amounts to coloring nodes of a graph with 2^m colors. If we assume that q is definable with auxiliary unary relations, we fix a number r witnessing its locality, and choose n big enough so that there would be two identically colored disjoint neighborhoods of points a and b in P. This would mean that the r-types of (a, b) and (b, a) are the same, but these tuples can clearly be distinguished by q. This completes the proof. $\square$

5 Open Problems

We have shown that PHIER $\subseteq$ IES($\mathcal{SQL}$), but it remains open whether a larger complexity class can be subsumed. One possibility is that all PSPACE queries are maintainable in $\mathcal{SQL}$. While we showed that there is a PSPACE-complete problem in IES($\mathcal{SQL}$), this does not mean that all PSPACE queries are maintainable, as IES in general is not closed under the usual reductions (polynomial or first-order), and we do not yet know of any problem complete for PSPACE under stronger reductions, defined in [21], that would belong to IES($\mathcal{SQL}$).

The proof of PHIER $\subseteq$ IES($\mathcal{SQL}$) does not lend itself to an efficient algorithm for queries of lower complexity. In fact, it is not clear if such algorithms exist in general, and proving, or disproving their existence, is closely tied to deep unresolved problems in complexity. However, coding the maintenance algorithms for some useful queries (e.g., the transitive closure) in SQL is quite easy [6] and in fact the maintenance is quite efficient for graphs of special form [22]. Thus, while general results in this area are probably beyond reach, one could consider restrictions on classes of inputs that would lead to efficient maintenance algorithms.

References

1. S. Abiteboul, R. Hull, and V. Vianu. *Foundations of Databases.* Addison-Wesley, 1995.
2. S. Abiteboul, V. Vianu. Computing with first-order logic. *JCSS* 50 (1995), 309–335.
3. P. Buneman, S. Naqvi, V. Tannen, and L. Wong. Principles of programming with complex objects and collection types. *Theoretical Computer Science,* 149(1):3–48, September 1995.
4. G. Dong, L. Libkin, and L. Wong. On impossibility of decremental recomputation of recursive queries in relational calculus and SQL. In *DBPL'95,* page 8.
5. G. Dong, L. Libkin, and L. Wong. Local properties of query languages. In *Theoretical Computer Science,* to appear. Extended abstract in *ICDT'97.*
6. G. Dong, L. Libkin, J. Su and L. Wong. Maintaining the transitive closure of graphs in SQL. In *Int. J. Information Technology,* 5 (1999), 46–78.

7. G. Dong and J. Su. Arity bounds in first-order incremental evaluation and definition of polynomial time database queries. *Journal of Computer and System Sciences* 57 (1998), 289–308.

8. G. Dong, J. Su, and R. Topor. Nonrecursive incremental evaluation of Datalog queries. *Annals of Mathematics and Artificial Intelligence*, 14:187–223, 1995.

9. K. Etessami. Dynamic tree isomorphism via first-order updates to a relational database. In *PODS'98*, pages 235–243.

10. R. Fagin, L. Stockmeyer, M. Vardi, On monadic NP vs monadic co-NP, *Information and Computation*, 120 (1994), 78–92.

11. H. Gaifman, On local and non-local properties, *in* "Proceedings of the Herbrand Symposium, Logic Colloquium '81," North Holland, 1982.

12. A. Gupta, I. S. Mumick and V. S. Subrahmanian. Maintaining views incrementally. In *SIGMOD'93*, pages 157–166.

13. A. Gupta and I.S. Mumick. Maintenance of materialized views: problems, techniques, and applications. *Data Engineering Bulletin* 18 (1995), 3–18.

14. L. Hella, L. Libkin and J. Nurmonen. Notions of locality and their logical characterizations over finite models. *J. Symb. Logic*, 64 (1999), 1751–1773.

15. L. Hella, L. Libkin, J. Nurmonen and L. Wong. Logics with aggregate operators. In *LICS'99*, pages 35–44.

16. N. Immerman. Languages that capture complexity classes. *SIAM Journal of Computing*, 16:760–778, 1987.

17. L. Libkin. On counting logics and local properties. In *LICS'98*, pages 501-512.

18. L. Libkin and L. Wong. Query languages for bags and aggregate functions. *Journal of Computer and System Sciences* 55 (1997), 241–272.

19. L. Libkin and L. Wong. Incremental recomputation of recursive queries with nested sets and aggregate functions. In *DBPL'97*, pages 222–238.

20. C. Papadimitriou. *Computational Complexity*. Addison Wesley, 1994.

21. S. Patnaik and N. Immerman. Dyn-FO: A parallel dynamic complexity class. *Journal of Computer and System Sciences* 55 (1997), 199–209.

22. T.A. Schultz. ADEPT – The advanced database environment for planning and tracking. *Bell Labs Technical Journal*, 3(3):3–9, 1998.

Optimization of Nested SQL Queries
by Tableau Equivalence

Vasilis Aggelis and Stavros Cosmadakis

University of Patras, Patras, Greece

Abstract. We present a new optimization method for nested SQL query blocks with aggregation operators. The method is derived from the theory of dependency implication and tableau minimization. It unifies and generalizes previously proposed (seemingly unrelated) algorithms, and can incorporate general database dependencies given in the database schema.

We apply our method to query blocks with MAX, MIN aggregation operators. We obtain an algorithm which does not infer arithmetical or aggregation constraints, and reduces optimization of such query blocks to the well-studied problem of tableau minimization. We prove a *completeness* result for this algorithm: if two MAX, MIN blocks can be merged, the algorithm will detect this fact.

1 Introduction

The practical importance of optimizing queries in relational database systems has been recognized. Traditional systems optimize a given query by choosing among a set of execution plans, which include the possible orders of joins, the available join algorithms, and the data access methods that are used [SAC+79, JK84]. Such optimizers work well for the basic SELECT-FROM-WHERE queries of SQL [MS93]. However, they can perform poorly on *nested* SQL queries, which may include subqueries and views.

Since nesting of queries is a salient feature of the SQL language as used in practice, optimization of such queries was considered early on. One line of research has concentrated on extending the traditional "selection propagation" techniques to nested queries. In these approaches, traditional optimizers are enhanced with additional execution plans, where selection and join predicates are applied as early as possible [MFPR90a, MFPR90b, MPR90, LMS94]. Another line of work has proceeded in an orthogonal direction, introducing execution plans which correspond to alternative structures of nesting. In particular, these approaches consider the possibilities of merging query blocks, denesting queries, commuting aggregation blocks with joins, and commuting GROUP BY with join [Day87, GW87, Kim82, Mur92, PHH92, YL94, HG94].

In this paper we propose an approach which unifies and generalizes the approaches mentioned above. We apply the "selection propagation" idea to certain data dependencies that are implicit in aggregation blocks. Propagation of SQL predicates [MFPR90a, MFPR90b, MPR90, LMS94] is a special case of propagation of these dependencies. At the same time, propagating these dependencies

R. Connor and A. Mendelzon (Eds.): DBPL'99, LNCS 1949, pp. 31-42, 2000.

can produce execution plans with alternative nesting structure, as in [Day87, GW87, Kim82, Mur92, PHH92, YL94, HG94].

In addition to expressing in a common framework previously proposed query transformations which seemed unrelated, our approach incorporates naturally general data dependencies that may be given in the database schema. It extends transformations which commute joins with aggregation operators (or GROUP BY) and merge query blocks [Day87, PHH92, YL94, HG94], in that it does not require adding tuple ids to the grouping addributes; and it can handle joins on aggregation attributes as well as on grouping attributes. Also, transformations which denest subqueries [GW87, Kim82, Mur92] only consider query blocks nested within each other, whereas our method does not depend on the order of nesting.

We illustrate our method by means of a small example. We consider the following database schema (of a hypothetical university database)[1]:

ids(Name, Idnum)
enrolled(Name, Idnum, Course)
timetable(Course, Hours)

The relation **ids** records the id numbers of students. The relation **enrolled** records the courses a student is enrolled in (and his/her id number); **timetable** records the number of hours a course is taught per week. These base relations do not contain duplicates.

The following dependencies are given in the database schema:

1. **enrolled**. Name,Idnum $\subseteq$ **ids**. Name,Idnum
2. **ids**: Name $\rightarrow$ Idnum

The first is an inclusion dependency (IND) stating that: every pair consisting of a student name and id number that appears in the **enrolled** relation, also appears in the **ids** relation. The second is a functional dependency (FD) stating that: student name is a key of the **ids** relation.

In Figure 1 we show a SQL definition for a view **maxhours** and a nested query Q.

The view **maxhours** gives, for each student, his id number; and the maximum number of hours of teaching (per week) of any of the courses he is enrolled in. The view **maxhours** is used to define the nested query Q, which gives, for each student, his id number and the maximum number of hours of teaching (per week) of any of the courses he is enrolled in; provided that there exist at least two courses which are taught for at least that many hours per week.

In Figure 2 we show the result of applying our optimization method to the nested query Q.

The query Q' results by transforming Q in the following ways.

First, the join with the **ids** relation in the main block of Q is eliminated. This simplification is arrived at using the aggregation block of the view **maxhours**,

---

[1] We use a non-normalized schema for brevity; the optimization method works for normalized and for non-normalized schemas.

and the dependencies of the schema. To justify the simplification we reason informally as follows. The join with the `enrolled` relation in `maxhours` is more restrictive than the join with the `ids` relation in the main block of Q, because of the IND 1. Also, the FD Name→Idnum can be seen to hold for the `enrolled` relation, because of the FD 2 and the IND 1; consequently, the value of the Idnum attribute of Q can be taken from the Idnum attribute of the `enrolled` relation, and thus from the Idnum attribute of `maxhours` (instead of the Idnum attribute of the `ids` relation).

The second optimization of Q is that the subquery in the WHERE clause has been replaced by a view `countcourses`, which gives, for each number of hours some course is taught for, the number of courses that are taught for at least that many hours per week. Note that the common *nested iteration* method of evaluating the subquery in Q requires retrieving the `timetable` relation once for each tuple of the view `maxhours` referenced in the main block of Q. On the other hand, Q' can be evaluated by single-level joins containing the join relations explicitly; this enables the optimizer to use a method such as *merge join* [SAC+79] to implement the joins, often at a great reduction cost over the nested iteration method [Kim82][2].

Observe also that the view `countcourses` contains the joins with the `enrolled` and `timetable` relations, appearing in the view `maxhours`. Including these joins makes the view `countcourses` safe, and produces a potentially cheaper execution plan, as it reduces the number of groups to be aggregated.

Optimization algorithms for nested SQL queries are often described as algebraic transformations, operating on a query graph which captures the relevant information in the query [MFPR90a, MFPR90b, MPR90, LMS94, Day87, GW87, Kim82, Mur92, PHH92, YL94, HG94]. In our method, we use the alternative *tableau* formalism that has been introduced in the context of conjunctive queries [AHV95, Ull89]. In Section 2 we sketch how this formalism is used to describe nested SQL queries.

In Section 3 we describe our optimization method; we use the chase procedure and the concept of tableau equivalence, which have been introduced for optimizing conjunctive queries in the presence of general data dependencies. One importance difference of SQL queries from conjunctive queries is the presence of duplicates in the result of a typical SQL query [IR95, CV93]. Our method optimizes correctly SQL queries where the number of duplicates is part of the semantics, and should not be altered by optimization[3].

We also describe in Section 3 how to fine-tune our method for the case of SQL queries with MAX, MIN operators. We obtain in this case an optimization algorithm which does not infer any arithmetical or aggregation constraints.

In Section 4 we focus on the special case of *merging* of SQL query blocks with MAX, MIN operators. We show that, if such merging is possible, it will be discovered by our optimization method. Such completeness results can not

---

[2] Detailed cost models illustrating the gain in complexity can be found in [Kim82, GW87].

[3] The number of duplicates is irrelevant to the semantics of our example query Q.

hold for algebraic transformations of SQL queries: designing complete systems of algebraic transformations requires rather technical devices, having to do with the equality predicate [YP82, IL84, C87].

In Section 5 we summarize our contributions, and point out some directions for further research.

ids(Name, Idnum)
enrolled(Name, Idnum, Course)
timetable(Course, Hours)

1. enrolled. Name,Idnum $\subseteq$ ids. Name,Idnum
2. ids: Name $\rightarrow$ Idnum

V: CREATE VIEW maxhours(Name, Idnum, Hours) AS
         SELECT e.Name, e.Idnum, MAX(t.Hours)
         FROM enrolled e, timetable t
         WHERE e.Course $=$ t.Course
         GROUPBY e.Name, e.Idnum

Q: SELECT i.Name, i.Idnum, m.Hours
    FROM ids i, maxhours m
    WHERE m.Name $=$ i.Name AND
          $2 \leq$ (SELECT COUNT (u.Course)
                  FROM timetable u
                  WHERE u.Hours $\geq$ m.Hours)

Fig. 1. Example database schema and query

Q': SELECT m.Name, m.Idnum, m.Hours
     FROM maxhours m, countcourses k
     WHERE m.Hours $=$ k.Hours AND
           $2 \leq$ k.Count

W: CREATE VIEW countcourses(Hours, Count) AS
         SELECT t.Hours, COUNT(u.Course)
         FROM enrolled e, timetable t, timetable u
         WHERE e.Course $=$ t.Course AND
               u.Hours $\geq$ t.Hours
         GROUPBY t.Hours

Fig. 2. Optimized example query

2   SQL Queries as Tableaux

Tableaux are a declarative formalism which captures the SELECT-PROJECT-JOIN queries of the relational calculus [AHV95, Ull89]. It is well-known that tableaux can express the basic SELECT-FROM-WHERE queries of SQL. In this Section we describe (by example) a natural extension of tableaux which expresses SQL queries with nested blocks and aggregation operators. The tableaux we describe in this Extended Abstract express *existential* SQL queries, i.e., conditions which have to hold for *some* tuples in the database. Queries with *universal* conditions – OUTER JOIN, null values, ALL quantifiers – are not expressible.

For each query block we construct one tableau; subqueries or views within a query become separate tableaux. Figure 3 shows the tableaux for our example query in Figure 1.

A typical row of a tableau has the form R(x, y, ...), where R is the name of a base relation, a SQL predicate or a query block; and x, y, ... are variables local to the tableau, or constants.

The first row of a tableau gives the general form of a tuple in the result of the corresponding query block; it is called the *summary* row, and the variables it contains are called *distinguished*.

The subsequent rows of the tableau give the general form of the tuples that have to be present in the base relations, and in the results of other query blocks; they typically contain additional variables, called *nondistinguished*.

Thus, for the tableau corresponding to the view **maxhours** the summary row is **maxhours**(n, p, hmax). The tuple (n, p, hmax) will be in the result of **maxhours** just in case the relation **enrolled** contains some tuple (n, p, c); and the relation **timetable** contains some tuple (c, h). Notice that c, h are nondistinguished variables. The last line of the tableau expresses aggregation and grouping: it states that, for each fixed n and p, hmax is the maximum possible value of h. A similar formulation of aggregation is described in [Klug82].

A tableau corresponding to a subquery contains special *non-local* variables – they are local to the tableau obtained from the enclosing query block. Thus, the tableau corresponding to the subquery in Q, *Qsubquery*, contains a non-local variable **H**, which is local to the tableau corresponding to Q.

It is straightforward (but lenghty) to give an algorithm which will convert a SQL query to a tableau representation; and vice versa.

3   The Optimization Method

Optimization of tableaux (corresponding to conjunctive queries) has been studied extensively. The central notion is *equivalence*, i.e., finding a tableau which expresses the same query and can be evaluated more efficiently. The *chase* procedure is a general method to test equivalence of tableaux, in the presence of data dependencies [AHV95, Ull89].

Our method introduces, for each query tableau, an *embedded implicational dependency* (EID) [AHV95, F82] stating that certain tuples exist and certain

	Name	Idnum	Course	Hours
maxhours	n	p		hmax
enrolled	n	p	c	
timetable			c	h
		hmax = MAX h (n, p)		

	Name	Idnum	Hours
Q	n	p	**H**
ids	n	p	
maxhours	n	p'	**H**

	1st	2nd
$\leq$	2	C

	Count
$Qsubquery$	C

	Count
$Qsubquery$	c-count

	Course	Hours
timetable	c	g

	1st	2nd
$\geq$	g	**H**
	c-count = COUNT c	

Fig. 3. Tableaux for example query

predicates hold in the database. In general, we can obtain such an EID by simply replicating the tableau.

Each query tableau is subsequently optimized using the dependencies of the schema and the EIDs introduced. The algorithm executes two passes (as in [LMS94]):

The first pass proceeds in a *bottom-up* way. Each tableau is optimized using the EIDs of the tableaux it contains. We start from the tableau which contain no subqueries or views, and finish with the top-level tableau.

In the second pass, each tableau is optimized using the EIDs of the tableaux it is contained in, in a *top-down* way.

In each pass, the optimization of each tableau consists of two distinct operations:

The first operation is to introduce new predicates; and to simplify the joins, by eliminating rows of the tableau.

The second operation is to replace subqueries by views (cf. the Introduction); it is done only during the second pass.

We illustrate the two operations by means of our running example.

Figure 4 shows the EID obtained from the view **maxhours**. It states that, for each tuple (n, p, hmax) in the result of **maxhours**, the relation **enrolled** contains a tuple (n, p, c); and the relation **timetable** contains a tuple (c, hmax), for some c. Notice that the EID is simpler than the tableau of **maxhours**. Such simplified EIDs can be used for query blocks with the MAX, MIN aggregation operators.

Introduction of new predicates and simplification of joins are done as follows.

The tableau is chased with the appropriate EIDs, and the dependencies of the schema. Figure 5 shows (in part) the result of applying this procedure to the tableau for Q. New rows are added to the tableau; they appear after the triple line. Chasing the second row of the original tableau with the EID obtained from **maxhours**, adds the first two of the new rows. Chasing the first of the new rows with the IND 1 of the schema adds the third new row.

The chase also adds to the tableau the SQL predicates appearing in the EIDs. In the case of the equality predicate, variables in the tableau are equated. In Figure 5, such equating happens by applying the FD 2 of the schema to the first and last rows; this equates p' with p.

To simplify the joins, the tableau resulting from the chase is minimized. This is done by examining the rows of the original tableau *not used in the chase*, and eliminating those which are covered by the tuples introduced by the chase.

Remark. It is not necessary for the chase itself to terminate; the tableau can still be minimized, as soon as a row as above is discovered.

Thus, the first row of the tableau in Figure 5 can be eliminated, because it is duplicated in the last row (recall that p' has been equated with p).

The final optimized tableau is obtained by dropping the rows that were introduced by the chase. In our example, this gives the tableau for Q' in Figure 6.

Remark. If the number of duplicates is part of the semantics of a query block, minimization of the corresponding tableau is omitted.

Replacement of subqueries by views is done as follows.

The non-local variables of the tableau corresponding to a subquery are traced to the tableaux they are local to. The tuples containing those variables as local, are added to the subquery tableau. The resulting tableau is optimized using chase, as in the first operation.

Applying this operation to the tableau *Qsubquery* in Figure 3 (where **H** is a non-local variable) results in the tableau `countcourses` in Figure 6.

The correctness of our method is expressed in the following result.

Theorem 1. *Suppose a query* Q' *is obtained by optimizing a query* Q.

(i) On every database, the result of Q' *contains exactly the same tuples as the result of* Q.

(ii) If minimization is not used, each tuple is duplicated in the result of Q' *the same number of times as in the result of* Q.

(iii) If minimization is used, each tuple is duplicated in the result of Q' *at most as many times as in the result of* Q.

The argument is a straightforward application of the properties of tableau chase and minimization, and of the results of [IR95, CV93].

	Name	Idnum	Course	Hours
maxhours	n	p		hmax
enrolled	n	p	c	
timetable			c	hmax

Fig. 4. EID from the view `maxhours`

	Name	Idnum	Course	Hours
Q	n	p		**H**
ids	n	p		
maxhours	n	p'		**H**
		⋮		
enrolled	n	p'	c	
timetable			c	**H**
ids	n	p'		

Fig. 5. Chase on the tableau of Q

Q'	Name	Idnum	Hours
maxhours	n	p	**H**
	n	p	**H**

	Hours	Count
countcourses	**H**	C

	1st	2nd
$\leq$	2	C

	Hours	Count
countcourses	**H**	c-count

	Name	Idnum	Course	Hours
enrolled	n	p'	c'	
timetable			c'	**H**
timetable			c	g

	1st	2nd
$\geq$	g	**H**

c-count = COUNT c

Fig. 6. Tableaux for optimized example query

4   Completeness for Merging MAX, MIN Aggregation Blocks

It is not hard to see that nested SQL query blocks without aggregation can be merged. This is the Type-N and Type-J nesting considered in [Kim82]. In addition, Our optimization method can merge query blocks where MAX, MIN operators are used in the inner block.

An example of such merging is shown in Figure 7; our running example is varied by omitting the last conjunct of the WHERE clause of Q, to obtain Q_0. The optimized block is Q_0': essentially, Q_0 has been merged with the view **maxhours**.

There are cases where merging of MAX (MIN) query blocks can be shown to be impossible. Consider again the query Q in our example. It is not hard to see that, by adding appropriately chosen tuples to the base relations, we can change the result of Q to *empty*: consider the semantics of the last conjunct of the WHERE clause of Q. In contrast, this cannot happen for Q_0', or its equivalent Q_0.

Definition 2. A query is *simple* if its result cannot be changed to *empty* by adding tuples to the database relations.

Proposition 3. *A SQL query defined by a single* MAX *block is simple.*

An analogous Proposition holds for SQL queries defined by a single MIN block.

By the above remarks, SQL query blocks cannot be merged into a single MAX block, unless the query defined is simple.

We can now state our completeness result.

Theorem 4. *If a SQL query is simple, the optimization method transforms it into a single* MAX *block.*

The proof uses the properties of the chase to construct a database which demonstrates that the query is not simple (if the optimization method cannot transform the query into a single MAX block).

An analogous result holds for transforming SQL queries into a single MIN block.

Q_0: SELECT i.Name, i.Idnum, m.Hours
    FROM ids i, maxhours m
    WHERE m.Name = i.Name

Q_0': SELECT m.Name, m.Idnum, m.Hours
    FROM maxhours m

Fig. 7. Example of merging aggregation blocks

5   Conclusions

We have presented a general optimization method for nested SQL queries, which unifies several known approaches and at the same time extends them in several nontrivial ways. We have applied our method to the case of query blocks with MAX, MIN aggregation operators. For such queries, we have obtained an algorithm which avoids the complications of inferring arithmetical or aggregations constraints [SRSS94, NSS98]; thus, it becomes possible to use algorithms for optimizing queries without constraints [DBS90, CR97, ASU79a, ASU79b, JKlug84, CM77] to optimize nested SQL query blocks with MAX, MIN.

We believe our approach will be fruitfully applicable in other cases. A natural proposal is to apply it to aggregation operators which are known to be delicate to analyze, such as COUNT [Kim82, GW87, Mur92].

Finally, it should be possible to extend our approach to incorporate other optimization algorithms [RR98, S.et.al.96, SPL96] within our general framework.

References

[AHV95]	S. Abiteboul, R. Hull, V. Vianu. Foundations of databases. Addison-Wesley, 1995.
[ASU79a]	A. Aho, Y. Sagiv, J. Ullman. Efficient optimization of a class of relational expressions. *ACM TODS* 4(4), 1979.
[ASU79b]	A. Aho, Y. Sagiv, J. Ullman. Equivalence of relational expressions. *SIAM J. on Computing* 8(2), 1979.
[CM77]	A. Chandra, P. Merlin. Optimal implementation of conjunctive queries in relational databases. In *STOC 1977*.
[CV93]	S. Chaudhuri, M. Vardi. Optimization of real conjunctive queries. In *PODS 1993*.
[CR97]	C. Chekuri, A. Rajaraman. Conjunctive query containment revisited. In *ICDT 1997*.
[C87]	S. S. Cosmadakis. Database theory and cylindric lattices. In *IEEE Conf. on Foundations of Computer Science 1987*.
[Day87]	U. Dayal. Of nests and trees: a unified approach to processing queries that contain nested subqueries, aggregates, and quantifiers. In *VLDB 1987*.
[DBS90]	P. Dublish, J. Biskup, Y. Sagiv. Optimization of a subclass of conjunctive queries. In *ICDT 1990*.
[F82]	R. Fagin. Horn clauses and database dependencies. *JACM* 29(4), 1982.
[GW87]	R. Ganski, H. Wong. Optimization of nested SQL queries revisited. In *SIGMOD 1987*.
[HG94]	V. Harinarayan, A. Gupta. Generalized projections: a powerful query-optimization technique. Stanford University CS-TN-94-14, 1994.
[IL84]	T. Imielinski, W. Lipski. The relational model of data and cylindrical algebras. *JCSS* 28(1), 1984.
[IR95]	E. Ioannidis, R. Ramakrishnan. Containment of conjunctive queries: beyond relations as sets. *ACM TODS* 20(3), 1995.
[JKlug84]	D. Johnson, A. Klug. Testing containment of conjunctive queries under functional and inclusion dependencies. *JCSS* 28, 1984.
[JK84]	M. Jarke, J. Koch. Query optimization in database systems. *ACM Computing Surveys* 16(2), 1984.
[Kim82]	W. Kim. On optimizing an SQL-like nested query. *ACM TODS* 7(3), 1982.
[Klug82]	A. Klug. Equivalence of relational algebra and relational calculus query languages having aggregate functions. *JACM* 29(3), 1982.
[LMS94]	A. Levy, I. Mumick, Y. Sagiv. Query optimization by predicate move-around. In *VLDB 1994*.
[MFPR90a]	I. Mumick, S. Finkelstein, H. Pirahesh, R. Ramakrishnan. Magic is relevant. In *SIGMOD 1990*.
[MFPR90b]	I. Mumick, S. Finkelstein, H. Pirahesh, R. Ramakrishnan. Magic conditions. In *PODS 1990*.
[MPR90]	I. Mumick, H. Pirahesh, R. Ramakrishnan. The magic of duplicates and aggregates. In *VLDB 1990*.
[MS93]	J. Melton, A. Simon. Understanding the new SQL: a complete guide. Morgan Kaufmann, 1993.

[Mur92]   M. Muralikrishna. Improved unnesting algorithms for join aggregate SQL queries. In *VLDB 1992*.

[NSS98]   W. Nutt, Y. Sagiv, S. Shurin. Deciding equivalences among aggregate queries. In *PODS 1998*.

[PHH92]   H. Pirahesh, J. Hellerstein, W. Hasan. Extensible/rule based query rewrite optimization in Starburst. In *SIGMOD 1992*.

[RR98]   J. Rao, K. A. Ross. Reusing invariants: a new strategy for correlated queries. In *SIGMOD 1998*.

[SAC+79]   P. Selinger, M. Astrahan, D. Chamberlin, R. Lorie, T. Price. Access path selection in a relational database management system. In *SIGMOD 1979*.

[S.et.al.96] P. Seshadri et al. Cost based optimization for magic: algebra and implementation. In *SIGMOD 1996*.

[SPL96]   P. Seshadri, H. Pirahesh, T. Y. C. Leung. Complex Query Decorrelation. In *ICDE 1996*.

[SRSS94]   D. Srivastava, K. Ross, P. Stuckey, S. Sudarshan. Foundations of Aggregation Constraints. In *PPCP 1994*.

[Ull89]   J. D. Ullman. Database and Knowledge-Base Systems, Vols I and II. Computer Science Press, 1989.

[YL94]   W. Yan, P. Larson. Performing Group-By before Join. In *ICDE 1994*.

[YP82]   M. Yannakakis, C. Papadimitriou. Algebraic dependencies. *JCSS* 25(2), 1982.

User-Defined Aggregates in Database Languages

Haixun Wang and Carlo Zaniolo

Computer Science Department
University of California at Los Angeles
{hxwang,zaniolo}@cs.ucla.edu

Abstract. User-defined aggregates (UDAs) can be the linchpin of so-phisticated data mining functions and other advanced database applications, but they find little support in current database systems. In this paper, we describe the SQL-AG prototype that overcomes these limitations by supporting UDAs as originally proposed in Postgres and SQL3. Then we extend the power and flexibility of UDAs by adding (i) early returns, (to express online aggregation) and (ii) syntactically recognizable monotonic UDAs that can be used in recursive queries to support applications, such as Bill of Materials (BoM) and greedy algorithms for graph optimization, that cannot be expressed under stratified aggregation. This paper proposes a unified solution to both the theoretical and practical problems of UDAs, and demonstrates the power of UDAs in dealing with advanced database applications.

1 Introduction

The importance of new specialized aggregates in advanced applications is ex-emplified by rollups and data cubes that, owing to their use in decision support applications, have been included in all new releases of commercial DBMSs. Yet, we claim that database vendors, and to a certain extent even researchers, have overlooked User-Defined Aggregates (UDAs), which can play an even more critical and pervasive role in advanced database applications, particularly data mining. In this paper, we show that:

⋄ Many data mining algorithms rely on specialized aggregates.
⋄ The number and diversity of these aggregates imply that (rather than vendors adding ad hoc built-ins, which are never enough) a general mechanism should be provided to introduce new UDAs, in analogy to user-defined scalar functions of object-relational (O-R) DBMSs.
⋄ UDAs can be easily and efficiently incorporated in O-R DBMSs, in accordance with the UDA specs originally proposed in SQL3 [8]. This is also true for the UDA extensions discussed in this paper that greatly improve their flexibility and functionality.

R. Connor and A. Mendelzon (Eds.): DBPL'99, LNCS 1949, pp. 43–60, 2000.

2   Aggregates in Data Mining

As a first example, consider the data mining methods used for classification. Say, for instance, that we want to classify the value of PlayTennis as a 'Yes' or a 'No' given a training set such as that shown in Table 1.

Table 1. Tennis

Outlook	Temp	Humidity	Wind	PlayTennis
Sunny	Hot	High	Weak	No
Sunny	Hot	High	Strong	No
Overcast	Hot	High	Weak	Yes
Rain	Mild	High	Weak	Yes
Rain	Cool	Normal	Weak	Yes
Rain	Cool	Normal	Strong	Yes
Overcast	Cool	Normal	Strong	No
Sunny	Mild	High	Weak	No
Sunny	Cool	Normal	Weak	Yes
Rain	Mild	Normal	Weak	Yes
Sunny	Mild	Normal	Strong	Yes
Overcast	Mild	High	Strong	Yes
Overcast	Hot	Normal	Weak	Yes
Rain	Mild	High	Strong	No

The algorithm known as Boosted Bayesian Classifier [5] has proven to be the most effective at this task (in fact, it was the winner of the KDD'97 data mining competition). A *Naive Bayesian* [5] classifier makes probability-based predictions as follows. Let $A_1, A_2, \ldots, A_k$ be attributes, with discrete values, used to predict a discrete class C. (For the example at hand, we have four prediction attributes, $k = 4$, and $C = $ 'PlayTennis'). For attribute values a_1 through a_k, the optimal prediction is the value c for which $Pr(C = c | A_1 = a_1 \wedge \ldots \wedge A_k = a_k)$ is maximal. By Bayes' rule, and assuming independence of the attributes, this means to classify a new tuple to the value of c that maximizes the product of $Pr(C = c)$ with:

$$\prod_{j=1,\ldots,K} Pr(A_j = a_j | C = c)$$

But these probabilities can be estimated from the training set as follows:

$$Pr(A_j = a_j | C = c) = \frac{count(A_j = a_j \wedge C = c)}{count(C = c)}$$

The numerators and the denominators above can be easily computed using SQL aggregate queries. For instance, all the numerators values for the third column (the Wind column) can be computed as follows:

Example 1. Using SQL's count Aggregate

SELECT **Wind, PlayTennis, count(*)**
FROM **Tennis**
GROUP BY **Wind, PlayTennis**

Furthermore, the Super Groups construct contained in the recent OLAP extensions of commercial SQL systems[3] allows us to express this computation in a single query:

Example 2. Using DB2's grouping sets

SELECT **Outlook, Temp, Humidity, Wind,**
                  PlayTennis, count(*)
FROM **Tennis**
GROUP BY GROUPING SETS **(PlayTennis),**
        ((Outlook, PlayTennis), (Temp, PlayTennis),
        (Humidity, PlayTennis), (Wind,PlayTennis))

In conclusion, this award-winning classification algorithm can be implemented well using the SQL **count** aggregate, thanks to the multiple grouping extensions recently introduced to support OLAPs. A database-centric approach to data mining is often preferable to main-memory oriented implementations, because it ensures better scalability and performance on large training sets. Unfortunately, unlike the Bayesian classifier just discussed, most data mining functions are prohibitively complex and inefficient to express and execute using the (SQL-compliant) data manipulation primitives of current database systems [23]. In this paper, we claim that the simplest and most cost-effective solution to this problem consists in adding powerful UDA capabilities to DBMSs. Toward this goal, we implemented the UDA specifications originally proposed for SQL3 [8], (but not supported yet in commercial systems) and extended them with the mechanism of early returns discussed in the next section. While we use mostly data mining examples, UDAs are needed in many applications to overcome the limited expressive power of SQL; for instance, we found them essential in implementing temporal database queries [4].

3   UDAs and Early Returns

While the aggregate computations needed in a Bayesian classifier can be expressed using SQL built-ins, this is not the case for most data mining algorithms. For instance the SPRINT classifier [24] chooses on which attribute and value to split next using a gini index:

$$gini(S) = 1 - \sum_{j=1}^{c} p_j^2 \tag{1}$$

Here p_j denotes the relative frequency of class j in the training set S. For discrete domains (i.e., categorical attributes) this operation can be implemented using the standard count aggregate of SQL. However, the attribute values from continuous domains must be first sorted on the attribute value, and then the count must be evaluated incrementally for each new value in the sorted set. Now, incremental evaluation of aggregates is not fully supported in current DBMSs (even those providing support for rollups). Moreover, the objective of the *gini* computation is to select a point (and a column from the table) where the gini index is minimum. Thus, for each new value in the sorted set, (i) the running count for each class must be updated, and (ii) the value of the gini function at this point must be calculated and compared with the minimum so far, to see if the old value must be replaced with the new one; in fact, after every value has been examined, (iii) the minimum point for the gini must be returned, since this point will be used for the next split. Therefore, the gini computations involves the following aggregate-like operations: (i) computing a running count, (ii) composing two aggregates (via the intermediate gini function), and (iii) returning the *point* where the minimum is found (rather than the *value* of that minimum). None of these three operations can be easily expressed and efficiently supported in SQL2; but with UDAs originally proposed for SQL3 [8], they can be merged into a single and efficient computation that determines the splitting point in a single pass through the dataset.

While UDAs such as those proposed for SQL3 [8] are the right tool for computing a gini index, they cannot express many other aggregate computations, and, in particular, they cannot express online aggregation [6]. On-line aggregation is very useful in many situations, e.g., to stop as soon as the computation of an average converges within the desired accuracy, or when aggregates, such as count or sum, have crossed the minimum support level (e.g., in the A Priori algorithm). On-line aggregates find many applications in data mining [26], and greatly extend the power of UDAs.

We can solve these problems by allowing UDAs to produce "early returns", i.e., to return values during the computation, rather than only at the end of the computation as in traditional aggregates. The computation of rollups, running aggregates, moving window aggregates, and many others becomes simple and efficient using the mechanism of *early returns*, which allows the generation of partial results while the computation of the aggregate is still in progress [4].

For instance, while final returns can be used to find a point of global minimum for a function, such as the gini function, early returns will be used to compute the points where local extrema occur (i.e., the valleys and the peaks).

4   Extended UDA and SQL3

In this section, we discuss the SQL-AG language, whereas the the SQL-AG system is described in the next section. To introduce a UDA named myavg, according to the specifications proposed for SQL3 [8], we must proceed as shown in Example 3. Basically, the user must define three user-defined functions (UDFs) for the three cases INITIALIZE, ITERATE, and TERMINATE. The INITIALIZE (ITER-ATE) function defines how the first (successive) values in the set are processed. The TERMINATE function describes the final computation for the aggregate value. Thus, to compute the traditional average, the state will hold the variables sum and count; these are, respectively, initialized to the the first value of the set and to 1 by myavg_single. Then, for each successive value in the set, myavg_multi adds this value to sum and also increases count by 1. Finally, myavg_terminate returns sum/count.

Example 3. A UDA Definition

    AGGREGATE FUNCTION myavg(IN NUMBER)
    RETURNS NUMBER
    STATE state
    INITIALIZE myavg_single
    ITERATE myavg_multi
    TERMINATE myavg_terminate

The search for global minima for the gini index can be easily programmed using two UDFs gini-single and gini-multi. But, in the presence of ties, the gini-terminate function will return any of the points where the global minimum occurs, e.g., the first point. Therefore, the order in which the elements of a set are considered becomes important, and can influence the final result, and to the extent that this order is unknown, UDAs display a *nondeterministic* behavior. Traditional SQL built-ins are instead deterministic, i.e., they always return the same result on a given set. This nondeterministic behavior is not an impediment in formalizing the logic-based semantics of UDAs, and in writing effective queries; in fact, nondetermism is a critical feature in many real life applications.

An important extension introduced by SQL-AG is *early returns* that are specified using a PRODUCE myavg_produce function. For instance, with an online aggregation, the average of values computed so far can be returned every N records, where N is specified by a user or computed by a function that evaluates the rate of convergence. Early returns are useful in many other roles, besides online aggregation. For instance, in a time series we need to find local extrema, i.e., valleys and peaks, which are easily handled with early returns. In this case, the aggregate might not produce any final return, and this can be specified by TERMINATE NOP.

An important issue brought to a resolution by early returns is that of mono-tonicity: in the next section we prove that aggregates with only early returns (i.e., those declared with TERMINATE NOP) are monotonic and can be freely used in recursion. This provides a surprisingly simple solution to the problem of detecting monotone aggregation [15] that had remained open since Ross and Sagiv demonstrated the many useful applications of these aggregates [19]. Mono-tonic aggregates can be used to express graph traversal algorithms, greedy algo-rithms, Bill of Materials (BoM) applications and other computations that were previously viewed to be beyond the capabilities of SQL and Datalog [19,9,17,10].

For example, say that we have defined a mcount aggregate, where PRODUCE returns a new partial count for each new element in the set, and thus there is no final return. Therefore, mcount is a monotonic aggregate: for a set with cardinality 4, mcount will simply produce $1, 2, 3, 4$; when a new element is added to the set mcount returns $1, 2, 3, 4, 5$. Thus mcount is monotonic with respect to set containment, whereas the traditional count returns first $\{4\}$ and then $\{5\}$, where the latter set is not a superset of the former. (Observe, that mcount is monotonic and deterministic; the msum aggregate returning the sum so far is still monotonic, but nonderministic.)

Consider now the use of monotonic aggregates in solving recursive problems. The **Join-the-Party** problem states that some people will come to the party no matter what, and their names are stored in a sure(Person) relation. But others will join if at least three of their friends will be there. Here, friend(P, F) denotes that P regards F as a friend. A monotonic user-defined aggregate mcount is used inside a recursive query to solve this problem. The PRODUCE routine of mcount returns the intermediary count and its TERMINATE routine is defined as NOP.

Example 4. Join the Party in SQL-AG

```
WITH RECURSIVE willcome(Name) AS
(   SELECT Person FROM sure
UNION ALL
    SELECT f.P
    FROM willcome, friend f
    WHERE willcome.Name = f.F
    GROUP BY f.P
    HAVING mcount(f.F)=3
) SELECT Name FROM willcome
```

As we shall see later, this program has a formal logic-based semantics, inasmuch as it can be translated into an equivalent Datalog program that has stable model semantics [11]. On a more practical note, a host of advanced database applications, particularly data mining applications, benefit from our UDAs. For instance, it is possible to express complex algorithms such as the 'A Priori' algorithm using the monotonic version of count, resulting in more flexibility and opportunities for optimization. Since the result of a fixpoint computation on monotonic operators is not dependent on the particular order of execution, several variations of A Priori are possible; for instance, a technique where the computation of item-sets of cardinality $n+1$ starts before that of cardinality n is completed was proposed in [2]. We were also able to implement other data mining algorithms, such as SPRINT/PUBLIC(1) and iceberg queries [7] in SQL-AG, with very little effort. The UDAs were used here to build histograms, calculate the gini index, and to perform in one pass the complex comparisons of tree costs needed to implement PUBLIC(1) [18].

5   SQL-AG

Two versions of SQL-AG were implemented, the first on Oracle, using PL/SQL, and the second for IBM DB2. Here we describe this second version, which is significantly more powerful and efficient than the other. DB2 supports user-defined functions (UDFs) but not user-defined aggregates. The SQL-AG system supports SQL queries with UDAs by transforming them into DB2 queries that use scratchpad UDFs to emulate the functionality of the corresponding UDAs [3]. For instance, say that we want to find the average salary of employees by department, using the UDA myavg, instead of the SQL built-in; then we can write:

```
SELECT dept, myavg(salary)
FROM emp
GROUP BY dept
```

This query is translated by SQL-AG into the following query, which can be executed by DB2:

```
SELECT dept, myavg(dept)
FROM emp
WHERE myavg_groupby(dept, salary)=0
GROUP BY dept
```

Here, the funtion myavg_groupby performs the actual computation of the aggregate by applying to each record the INITIALIZE and ITERATE functions written by the user (i.e., the functions **myavg_single** and **myavg_multi** for Example 3), and then returning 0. Finally, for each dept the function myavg(dept) applies the TERMINATE function written by the user (i.e., **myavg_terminate** for Example 3) to the last values computed by myavg_groupby, returning the final result. Similar transformations are used to handle the case where the UDA only has early returns, and the more complex case where both early returns and final returns are used. More details about SQL-AG and its implementation can be found in [25].

We compared the performance of native DB2 builtins against SQL-AG UDAs on a Ultra SPARC 2 with 128 megabytes memory. We used a new UDA, myavg, which has the same functionality as the builtin aggregate avg. Figure 1 shows that, when aggregation contains no group-by columns, our UDAs incur in a modest performance penalty with respect to DB2 builtins. However, when group-by columns are used, then the UDAs of SQL-AG normally outperform DB2's builtin aggregates, as shown in Figure 2. This is due to the fact that DB2 implements grouping by pre-sorting all the records, while SQL-AG uses hashing. This advantage is lost if the group-by columns coincide with the primary key for the relation at hand, and thus the data is already in the proper order. In this case, our UDAs are somewhat slower than DB2 builtins—bottom curve in Figure 2.

Our performance comparison shows that, in general, user-defined aggregates can be expected to have performance comparable to that of builtins [1]. In fact,

---

[1] These results were obtained using DB2 UDFs in an unfenced mode [3]. Execution in the fenced mode was considerably slower.

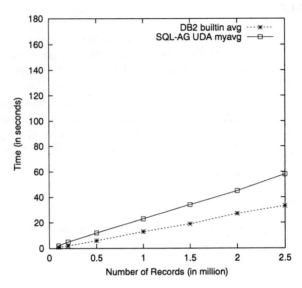

Fig. 1. Aggregates without Group-by

there are several situations where specialized UDAs will be preferred to builtin aggregates simply for performance reasons. For instance, all counts needed in Example 2 can be computed in one pass through the data using a hash-based approach (and SQL-AG allows the user to specify whether the implementation of each aggregate is hash-based or sort-based). In DB2, and other commercial systems, an implementation of GROUPING SETS normally results in a cascade of sorting operations. As illustrated by Figure 3, this resulted in a substantial speed-up, and improved scalability (DB2 on our workstation refused to handle more than 800000 records).

6   Aggregates in Logic

The procedural attachments used to define new aggregates in SQL-AG could leave the reader with the impression that these are merely procedural extensions, without the benefits of the formal logic-based semantics that provides the bedrock for relational query languages and the recent SQL extensions for recursive queries. Fortunately, this is not the case, and we next provide a logic based formalization for UDAs. This also yields a simple syntactic characterization of aggregates that are monotonic in the standard lattice of set-containment, and can therefore *be used without restrictions in recursive queries.* This breakthrough offers a simple solution to the monotonic aggregation problem, and allows us to express applications such as BoM and graph traversals that had long been problematic for SQL and Datalog [19,10,15].

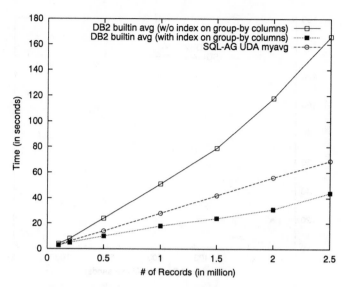

Fig. 2. Aggregates with Group-by Columns

Inductive Definition of Aggregates. Aggregate functions on (non-empty) sets can be defined by induction. The base case for induction is that of singleton sets; thus, for count, sum and max, we have $count(\{y\}) = 1$, $sum(\{y\}) = y$, and $max(\{y\}) = y$. Then, by induction, we consider sets with two or more elements; these sets have the following form: $S \sqcup \{y\}$, where $\sqcup$ denotes disjoint union (thus S is the "old" set while y is the "new" element). Then, our *specific inductive functions* are as follows: $sum(S \sqcup \{x\}) = sum(S) + x$, $count(S \sqcup \{x\}) = count(S) + 1$, $max(S \sqcup \{x\}) =$ **if** $x > max(S)$ **then** x **else** $max(S)$. Thus, expressing aggregates in Datalog can be broken down in two parts: (i) writing the rules for the specific inductive functions used for this particular aggregate, and (ii) writing the recursive rules that enumerate the elements of a set one-by-one as needed to apply the specific inductive functions. Part (i) is described next, and part (ii) is discussed in the next section. For concreteness, we use here the syntax of $\mathcal{LDL}{++}$ [20,28].

In $\mathcal{LDL}{++}$, the base base step in the computation of an aggregate is expressed by single rules that apply to singleton sets, while the induction step is expressed by multi rules that apply to sets with two or more elements. Thus, we obtain the following definitions for sum

$$single(sum, Y, Y).$$
$$multi(sum, Y, Old, New) \leftarrow New = Old + Y.$$

and for max

$$single(max, Y, Y).$$
$$multi(max, Y, Old, Y) \leftarrow \quad Y > Old.$$
$$multi(max, Y, Old, Old) \leftarrow Y <= Old.$$

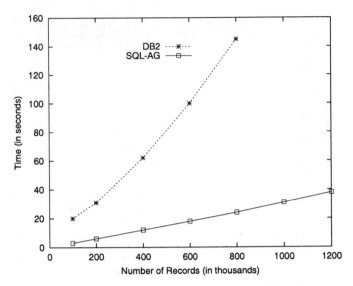

Fig. 3. DB2's grouping set vs. SQL-AG's UDA

Therefore, we use the first argument in the heads of the rules to hold the unique name of each aggregate.

Then, the *freturn* rules are used to specify the value to be returned at the end of the computation. For sum and max the return rules are as follows:

$$\text{freturn}(\text{sum}, Y, \text{Old}, \text{Old}). \quad \text{freturn}(\text{max}, Y, \text{Old}, \text{Old}).$$

The complete definition of the aggregate avg is as follows:

$$\text{single}(\text{avg}, Y, (Y, 1)).$$
$$\text{multi}(\text{avg}, Y, (\text{Sum}, \text{Count}), (\text{Nsum}, \text{NCount})) \leftarrow \text{Nsum} = \text{Sum} + Y,$$
$$\text{Ncount} = \text{Count} + 1.$$
$$\text{freturn}(\text{avg}, Y, (\text{Sum}, \text{Count}), \text{Avg}) \leftarrow \qquad \text{Avg} = \text{Sum}/\text{Count}.$$

The $\mathcal{LDL}$++ extension recently developed at UCLA also supports *early returns*, which must be specified using ereturn rules. Thus, if the user wants to see partial results from the computation of averages every 100 elements, the following rule must be added:

$$\text{ereturn}(\text{avg}, X, (\text{Sum}, \text{Count}), \text{Avg}) \leftarrow$$
$$\text{Count mod } 100 = 0, \text{Avg} = \text{Sum}/\text{Count}.$$

In order to find the average salary of employees grouped by department, the user can thus write:

$$\text{p}(\text{DeptNo}, \text{avg}\langle \text{Sal}\rangle) \leftarrow \text{empl}(\text{Ename}, \text{Sal}, \text{DeptNo}).$$

Thus, in this syntax, that is shared by both $\mathcal{LDL}++$ [28] and CORAL [17], aggregates, such as $\text{avg}\langle\ldots\rangle$, are used as arguments in the head of the rule, and the remaining non-aggregate arguments are interpreted as group-by attributes.

The head aggregate construct can be viewed as a meta-level construct with first order semantics; as shown in the next section, it can be expanded into the internal rules that, along with the single, multi, freturn and ereturn rules written by the user, express the formal meaning of aggregates in logic.

Let us now define a logic-based equivalent of the SQL-AG program of Example 4. We begin by defining mcount that returns the incremental count at each step:

$$\text{single}(\text{mcount}, Y, 1).$$
$$\text{multi}(\text{mcount}, Y, \text{Old}, \text{New}) \leftarrow \quad \text{New} = \text{Old} + 1.$$
$$\text{ereturn}(\text{mcount}, Y, \text{Old}, \text{New}) \leftarrow \text{Old} = \text{nil}, \text{New} = 1.$$
$$\text{ereturn}(\text{mcount}, Y, \text{Old}, \text{New}) \leftarrow \text{Old} \neq \text{nil}, \text{New} = \text{Old} + 1.$$

The first ereturn rule applies when $\text{Old} = \text{nil}$ (where nil is just a special value—not the empty list). Now, the condition $\text{Old} = \text{nil}$ is only satisfied when the first Y value in the set is found; thus, this rule is enabled together with single rule, and produces the integer 1. After that, the second ereturn rule applies repeatedly, in parallel with the multi rule, producing $2, \ldots, n$, where n the number of items counted so far.

The query, *"Find all departments with less than 7 employees"* can be expressed as follows:

$$\text{count\_emp}(D\#, \text{mcount}\langle E\#\rangle) \leftarrow \text{emp}(E\#, \text{Sal}, D\#).$$
$$\text{large\_dept}(D\#) \leftarrow \qquad \text{count\_emp}(D\#, \text{Count}), \text{Count} = 7.$$
$$\text{small\_dept}(D\#, \text{Dname}) \leftarrow \qquad \text{dept}(D\#, \text{Dname}), \neg\text{large\_dept}(D\#).$$

This example illustrates some of the benefits of online aggregation. Negated queries are subject to existential variable optimization; thus, in $\mathcal{LDL}++$ the search for new employees of a department stops as soon as the threshold of 7 is reached. But the traditional count must retrieve all employees in the department, no matter how high their count is.

Several authors have advocated extensions to predicate calculus with generalized existential quantifiers [13,14], to express a concept such as *"There exist at least seven employees"*. This idea is naturally supported by new aggregate $\text{atleast}\langle(K, X)\rangle$ that returns the value yes as soon as K instances of X are counted. This aggregate of Boolean behavior can be defined as follows:

$$\text{single}(\text{atleast}, (K, Y), 1).$$
$$\text{multi}(\text{atleast}, (K, Y), \text{Old}, \text{New}) \leftarrow \quad \text{Old} < K, \text{New} = \text{Old} + 1.$$
$$\text{ereturn}(\text{atleast}, (K, Y), K1, \text{yes}) \leftarrow K1 = \text{nil}, K = 1.$$
$$\text{ereturn}(\text{atleast}, (K, Y), K1, \text{yes}) \leftarrow K1 \neq \text{nil}, K1 + 1 = K.$$

Then, a predicate equivalent to the large_dept$(D\#)$ can be formulated as follows:

$$\text{lrg\_dpt}(D\#, \text{atleast}\langle(7, \text{Ename})\rangle) \leftarrow \text{empl}(\text{Ename}, \text{Sal}, D\#).$$

Here, because of the condition Old < K in the multi rule defining atleast, the search stops after seven employees, even for a positive goal ?lrg_dpt(D#, yes), for which no existential optimization is performed.

Observe that mcount and atleast aggregates define monotonic mappings with respect to set containment: in the next section, we prove that all UDAs defined with only early returns (e.g., online aggregates) are monotonic, and can be freely used in recursive queries and rules.

7 Formal Semantics and Monotonicity

The logic-based semantics of a program with aggregates can be defined by viewing it as a short-hand of another Datalog program without aggregates. For that, we need the ability of enumerating the elements of the set one-by-one. For instance, if we assumed that the set elements belong to a totally ordered domain, then we could visit them one-at-a-time in, say, ascending order. But such an assumption would violate the genericity principle [1]; moreover, it still requires nonmonotonic constructs to visit the elements one-by-one, thus preventing the use of aggregates in recursive rules. A better solution consists in using choice [21,22], or more precisely the dynamic version of choice [12], which can used freely in recursive rules. By enforcing functional dependencies on the result produced by the rules, this powerful construct allows us to derive the Ordering rules, below, which arrange the elements of the set in a simple chain.

Positive choice programs are equivalent to programs with negated goals; these programs are guaranteed to have one or more total stable models [11]. As shown in [12], choice is strictly more powerful than other nondeterministic construct previously defined, including the *witness* operator of Abiteboul&Vianu [1], and the static version of choice [12]. This added power allows us to express computations that would not have been possible using witness or static choice. In particular a positive choice program can be used to order the elements of a sets into a chain [12]. This operation is critical in our inductive definition of aggregates discussed next.

For instance, say that we have the following rule where we apply myagr on the Y-values grouped by X:

$$r : p(X, myagr\langle Y\rangle) \leftarrow q(X, Y).$$

The mapping from the body to head of this rule can expressed by (i) the $next_r$ rules that arrange the Y-values of q(Y) into a chain, (ii) the cagr rules that implement the inductive definition of the aggregate by calling the single and multi rules, and (iii) the yield-rules that produce the actual pairs in p by using the ereturn and freturn rules.

The $next_{r1}$ rules use the choice construct of $\mathcal{LDL}++$:
Ordering Rules:

```
next_r(X, nil, nil) ← q(X, Y).
next_r(X, Y1, Y2) ←   next_r(X, _, Y1), q(X, Y2),
                      choice((X, Y1), (Y2)), choice((X, Y2), (Y1)).
```

Aggregates can be defined by the following internal recursive predicate `cagr`:
cagr Rules

$$\text{cagr}(\text{myagr}, X, Y, \text{New}) \leftarrow \text{next\_r}(X, \text{nil}, Y), Y \neq \text{nil},$$
$$\text{single}(\text{myagr}, Y, \text{New}).$$
$$\text{cagr}(\text{myagr}, X, Y2, \text{New}) \leftarrow \text{next\_r}(X, Y1, Y2),$$
$$\text{cagr}(\text{myagr}, X, Y1, \text{Old}),$$
$$\text{multi}(\text{myagr}, Y2, \text{Old}, \text{New}).$$

The `cagr` rules implement the inductive definition of the UDA by calling on the `single` and `multi` predicates written by the user. Therefore, `single` is used once to initialize `cagr(myagr, X, Y, New)`, where Y denotes the first input value and New is value of the aggregate on a singleton set. Then, for each new input value, Y2, and Old (denoting the last partial value of the aggregate) are fed to the `multi` predicate, to be processed by the `multi` rules defined by the user and returned to head of the recursive `cagr` rule.

Here, we have left the bodies of these rules unspecified, since no "special" restriction applies to them (except that they cannot use the predicate p being defined via the aggregate, nor any predicate mutually recursive with p).

The predicates `ereturn` and `freturn` are called by the yield rules that control what is to be returned:
Early-Yield Rule:

$$p(X, \text{AgrVal}) \leftarrow \text{next\_r}(X, \text{nil}, Y), Y \neq \text{nil},$$
$$\text{ereturn}(\text{myagr}, Y, \text{nil}, \text{AgrVal}).$$
$$p(X, \text{AgrVal}) \leftarrow \text{next\_r}(X, Y1, Y2),$$
$$\text{cagr}(\text{myagr}, X, Y1, \text{Old}),$$
$$\text{ereturn}(\text{myagr}, Y2, \text{Old}, \text{AgrVal}).$$

The first early-yield rule applies to the first value in the set, and the second one to all successive values. The result(s) returned when all elements in the set have been visited is controlled by a final-yield rule:
Final-Yield Rule:

$$p(X, \text{AgrVal}) \leftarrow \text{next\_r}(X, \_, Y), \neg \text{next\_r}(X, Y, \_),$$
$$\text{cagr}(\text{myagr}, X, Y, \text{Old}),$$
$$\text{freturn}(\text{myagr}, Y, \text{Old}, \text{AgrVal}).$$

This general template defining the meaning of all aggregates is then customized by the user-supplied rules for `single`, `multi`, `ereturn`, and `freturn`, which all have mvavg as their first head argument (thus the aggregate name is used to avoid interference with other UDAs).

Monotonicity Observe that *negation is only used in the final yield rule*. When the aggregate definition contains no final-return rule (i.e., only early return

rules) then the final-yield rule can be eliminated and the remaining rules constitute a *positive choice program*. Now, positive choice programs *define monotonic
transformations*—an important result obtained in [12] that will be summarized
next.

As customary in deductive databases, a program P can be viewed as consisting of two separate components: an extensional component, denoted $edb(P)$,
and an intensional one, denoted $idb(P)$. Then, a positive choice program defines
a monotonic multi-valued mapping from $edb(P)$ to $idb(P)$, as per the following
theorem proven in [12]:

Theorem 1. *Let P and P' be two positive choice programs where $idb(P') =
idb(P)$ and $edb(P') \supseteq edb(P)$. Then, if M is a choice model for P, then, there
exists a choice model M' for P' such that $M' \supseteq M$.*

Thus, for a multi-valued function we only require that, as the value of the
argument increases, some of the values of the function also increase (we do not
require all values to increase). Furthermore, we say that we have a fixpoint
when one of the function values is equal to its argument. Each multi-valued
mapping also induces a nondeterministic (single-valued) mapping, defined as an
arbitrary choice among the values of the function. As shown in [12], for choice
programs, a fixpoint is reached by the inflationary repeated application of such
a nondeterministic mapping.

Furthermore the set of these fixpoints coincide with the stable models [11]
of the program obtained by rewriting the choice program into an equivalent
program with negation [21]. Thus, our next_r rules are formally defined by their
equivalent rules with negated goals:

$$\begin{aligned}
\text{next\_r}(X, Y1, Y2) &\leftarrow & \text{next\_r}(X, \_, Y1), q(X, Y2), \\
& & \text{chosen}(X, Y1, Y2). \\
\text{chosen}(X, Y1, Y2) &\leftarrow & \text{next\_r}(X, Y1, Y2), \neg\text{diffchoice}(X, Y1, Y2). \\
\text{diffchoice}(X, Y1, Y2) &\leftarrow & \text{chosen}(X, Y1, Y2'), Y2' \neq Y2. \\
\text{diffchoice}(X, Y1, Y2) &\leftarrow & \text{chosen}(X, Y1', Y2), Y1' \neq Y1.
\end{aligned}$$

This program, as every choice program reexpressed via negation, has one or
more (total) stable models [11], where each stable model satisfies all the FDs
defined by the choice goals [22,12].

Therefore, keeping with previous authors [16], we have defined the semantics
of aggregates in terms of stable models [11]; however, through the use of the
choice construct, we have avoided the computational intractability problems of
stable models. Furthermore in our semantics, choice rules are only used to de-
liver the **next** value Y2 generated by our rule r (for the given group-by value
X and the previous such value Y1): thus, an operational realization is very simple and efficient since it reduces to a get-next operation on data. Furthermore,
since aggregates define monotonic transformations in the usual lattice of set
containment, bottom-up execution techniques of deductive databases, such as
the semi-naive fixpoint, and magic sets, remain valid for these programs. Thus,
monotone aggregates can be added to deductive database systems with no change

in execution strategy—a conclusion that also applies to recursive queries with monotone aggregates in SQL DBMSs.

8   Programs with Monotone Aggregation

We now express several examples derived from [19] using our new monotonic aggregates [28].

Join the Party . The SQL-AG query of Example 4, can be expressed in $\mathcal{LDL}$ using the monotonic aggregate mcount and an additional predicate $c_f$riends.

$$\begin{aligned}
&\text{willcome}(P) \leftarrow &&\text{sure}(P). \\
&\text{willcome}(P) \leftarrow &&\text{c\_friends}(P, K), K >= 3. \\
&\text{c\_friends}(P, \text{mcount}\langle F\rangle) \leftarrow \text{willcome}(F), \text{friend}(P, F).
\end{aligned}$$

Here, we have set $K = 3$ as the number of friends required for a person to come to the party. Consider now a computation of these rules on the following database.

sure(mark).	friend(jerry, mark).
sure(tom).	friend(penny, mark).
sure(jane).	friend(jerry, jane).
	friend(penny, jane).
	friend(jerry, penny).
	friend(penny, tom).

Then, the basic semi-naive computation yields:

willcome(mark), willcome(tom), willcome(jane),

c_friends(jerry, 1), c_friends(penny, 1), c_friends(jerry, 2),

c_friends(penny, 2), c_friends(penny, 3), willcome(penny),

c_friends(jerry, 3), willcome(jerry).

This example illustrates how the standard semi-naive computation can be applied to queries containing monotone user-defined aggregates.

The Join-the-Party query of Example 4 eliminates the need for a c_friends predicate by using the 'having' construct . In $\mathcal{LDL}$++, we can obtain the same effect by using the aggregate atleast defined in Section 6, which is also monotone:

$$\begin{aligned}
&\text{wllcm}(F, \text{yes}) \leftarrow &&\text{sure}(F). \\
&\text{wllcm}(X, \text{atleast}\langle (3, F)\rangle) \leftarrow \text{wllcm}(F, \text{yes}), \text{friend}(X, F).
\end{aligned}$$

Unlike in the previous formulation, where a new tuple c_friends is produced every time a new friend is found, a new wllcm tuple is here produced only when the threshold of 3 is crossed.

Company Control Another interesting example is transitive ownership and control of corporations. Say that owns(C1, C2, Per) denotes the percentage of shares that corporation C1 owns of corporation C2. Then, C1 controls C2 if it owns more than, say, 50% of its shares. In general, to decide whether C1 controls C3 we must also add the shares owned by corporations such as C2 that are controlled by C1. This yields the transitive control predicate defined as follows:

$$\text{control}(C, C) \leftarrow \quad \text{owns}(C, \_, \_).$$
$$\text{control}(Onr, C) \leftarrow \quad \text{towns}(Onr, C, Per), Per > 50.$$
$$\text{towns}(Onr, C2, \text{msum}\langle Per \rangle) \leftarrow \text{control}(Onr, C1), \text{owns}(C1, C2, Per).$$

Thus, every company controls itself, and a company C1 that has transitive ownership of more than 50% of C2's shares controls C2 . In the last rule, towns computes transitive ownership with the help of msum that adds up the shares of controlling companies. Observe that any pair (Onr, C2) is added at most once to control, thus the contribution of C1 to Onr's transitive ownership of C2 is only accounted once.

9   Conclusion

The practical importance of database aggregates has long been recognized, but indepth treatments of this critical subject were lacking. In this paper, we have addressed both the theoretical and practical aspects of aggregates, including user-defined aggregates and online aggregation. Our logic-based formalization of aggregates provided a simple and practical solution to problem of monotone aggregation, a problem on which many previous approaches had achieved only limited success [17,15,10,19].

Various examples were also given illustrating power and flexibility of UDAs in advanced applications; several more examples, omitted because of space limitations, can be found in [25]. For instance, by adding greedy aggregates built upon priority queues, we expressed graph algorithms such as Dijkstra's single source least-cost path, or Prim's least-cost spanning tree. Also data mining functions, including tree classifiers and A Priori, can be formulated efficiently using our UDAs.

At UCLA, we developed the the SQL-AG prototype that supports the UDAs here described on top of DB2 [25], and we also developed a new version of $\mathcal{LDL}++$ [28] supporting the Datalog extensions described in this paper. The SQL-AG implementation is of particular significance, since it shows that UDAs are fully compatible with O-R systems, and can actually outperform builtin aggregates in particular applications.

We are currently investigating the issue of ease of use in UDAs. In fact, while UDAs in $\mathcal{LDL}++$ can be expressed using rules, several procedural language functions must be written to add a new UDA in SQL-AG or SQL3. However, our experience suggests that in most UDAs the computations to be performed by the INITIALIZE, ITERATE, TERMINATE, and PRODUCE functions are very simple, and can effectively be expressed using an (SQL-like) high-level language. We expect that this approach will enhance users' convenience, and portability. A simple SQL-like language for UDAs is described in [27].

References

1. Abiteboul S., Hull R. and Vianu V., Foundations of Databases, Addison Wesley, 1995.
2. S. Brin, R. Motwani, J. D. Ullman, S. L. Tsur, "Dynamic Itemset Counting and Implication Rules for Market Basket Data". In *SIGMOD'97*.
3. D. Chamberlin, "Using the new DB2, IBM's Object-Relational Database System," Morgan Kaufmann, 1996.
4. Cindy Xinmin Chen, Carlo Zaniolo: Universal Temporal Extensions for Database Languages. ICDE 1999: 428-437.
5. Charles Elkan. "Boosting and Naive Bayesian Learning". Technical report no cs97-557, Dept. of Computer Science and Engineering, UCSD, September 1997.
6. J. M. Hellerstein, P. J. Haas, H. J. Wang. "Online Aggregation". *SIGMOD, 1997*.
7. M. Fang, N. Shivakumar, H. Garcia-Molina, R. Motwani, J. D. Ullman, "Computing Iceberg Queries Efficiently". In *VLDB 1998*.
8. ISO/IEC JTC1/SC21 N10489, ISO//IEC 9075, "Committee Draft (CD), Database Language SQL", July 1996.
9. Finkelstein, S. J., N. Mattos, I. S. Mumick, and H. Pirahesh, Expressing Recursive Queries in SQL, ISO WG3 report X3H2-96-075, March 1966.
10. S. Ganguly, S. Greco, and C. Zaniolo, "Extrema Predicates in Deductive Databases," JCSS 51(2): 244-259 (1995).
11. M. Gelfond and V. Lifschitz. The Stable Model Semantics for Logic Programming. *Procs. Joint International Conference and Symposium on Logic Programming*, pp. 1070–1080, 1988.
12. F. Giannotti, D. Pedreschi, and C. Zaniolo, "Semantics and Expressive Power of Non-Deterministic Constructs in Deductive Databases," JCSS, to appear.
13. Gyssen, M., Van Gucht, D. and Badia, A., Query Languages with Generalized Quantifiers, in Applications of Logic Databases, R. Ramakrishan, Kluwer, 1995.
14. Hsu, P. Y. and Parker, D. S., "Improving SQL with Generalized Quantifiers," Proc. ICDE 1995.
15. A. Van Gelder. "Foundations of Aggregations in Deductive Databases." *Proc. of the Int. Conf. On Deductive and Object-Oriented databases*, 1993.
16. David B. Kemp and Peter J. Stuckey, "Semantics of logic programs with aggregates" *Proc. 1991 International Symposium on Logic Programming*, pages 387–401, October 1991.
17. D. Srivastava, R. Ramakrishnan, P. Seshadri, S. Sudarshan. Coral++: Adding Object-Orientation to a Logic Database Language. In *VLDB 1993: 158-170*.
18. R. Rastogi, K. Shim. "PUBLIC: A Decision Tree Classifier that Integrates Building and Pruning". VLDB 1998: 404-415.
19. K. A. Ross and Yehoshua Sagiv, "Monotonic Aggregation in Deductive Database", JCSS 54(1), 79-97 (1997).
20. S. A. Naqvi, S. Tsur *"A Logical Language for Data and Knowledge Bases"*, W. H. Freeman, 1989.
21. D. Saccà and C. Zaniolo. Stable models and non-determinism in logic programs with negation, *Proceedings of the Ninth ACM Symposium on Principles of Database Systems*, pages 205–217, 1990.

22. D. Saccà and C. Zaniolo, Deterministic and non-deterministic Stable Models, *Journal of Logic and Computation*, 7(5):555-579, October 1997.
23. S. Sarawagi, S. Thomas, R. Agrawal, "Integrating Association Rule Mining with Relational Database Systems: Alternatives and Implications". In *SIGMOD, 1998*.
24. J. C. Shafer, R. Agrawal, M. Mehta, "SPRINT: A Scalable Parallel Classifier for Data Mining". In *VLDB 1996*.
25. Haixun Wang, The SQL-AG System,
    http://magna.cs.ucla.edu/~hxwang/sqlag/sqlag.html
26. H. Wang and C. Zaniolo "User-Defined Aggregates in Datamining," ACM SIG-MOD Workshop on Research Issues in Data Mining and Knowledge Discovery, DMKD'99, May 30, 1999.
27. H. Wang, and C. Zaniolo "User Defined Aggregates in Object-Relational Systems" ICDE 2000 Conference, San Diego, CA, February 29-March 3, 2000.
28. C. Zaniolo et al. *LDL++* Documentation and Web Demo,
    http://www.cs.ucla.edu/ldl

How to Make SQL Stand for
String Query Language

Gösta Grahne[1] and Emmanuel Waller[2]

[1] Department of Computer Science, Concordia University
Montreal, Quebec, Canada H3G 1M8
grahne@cs.concordia.ca
[2] LRI, Université Paris-Sud
91405 Orsay Cedex, France
waller@lri.fr

Abstract. A *string database* is simply a collection of tables, the columns of which contain *strings* over some given alphabet. We address in this paper the issue of designing a simple, user friendly query language for string databases. We focus on the language $FO(\bullet)$, which is classical first order logic extended with a concatenation operator, and where quantifiers range over the set of all strings. We wish to capture all *string queries*, i.e., well-typed and computable mappings involving a notion of string genericity. Unfortunately, unrestricted quantification may allow some queries to have infinite output. This leads us to study the "safety" problem for $FO(\bullet)$, that is, how to build syntactic and/or semantic restrictions so as to obtain a language expressing only queries with finite output, hopefully all string queries. We introduce a family of such restrictions and study their expressivness and complexity. We prove that none of these languages express *all* string queries. We prove that a family of these languages is equivalent to a simple, tractable language that we call SriQueL, standing for *String Query Language*, which thus emerges a robust and natural language suitable for string querying.

1 Introduction

Current database management systems, especially those based on the relational model, have little support for string querying and manipulation. This can be a problem in several string-oriented application areas such as molecular biology (see e.g. [6,31]) and text processing, the latter becoming crucial with the burst of the Web, XML and digital libraries, among others. In such a system, a string is one of the basic data types of Codd's relational model [5], which means that the strings are treated as atomic entities; thus a string can be accessed only as a whole and not on the level of the individual characters occuring within it. Modern object-oriented systems are usually alike in this sense. Although they offer support for complex objects, strings are usually treated as atomic. In SQL, the only non-atomic operator is the LIKE-operator which can be used in simple pattern matching tasks such as finding a substring in a field; however,

R. Connor and A. Mendelzon (Eds.): DBPL'99, LNCS 1949, pp. 61–79, 2000.
© Springer-Verlag Berlin Heidelberg 2000

the expressive power of the operator is limited. In this paper, we address the issue of designing a general purpose query language for string databases, based on first order logic.

Lately we have witnessed in the database community an increased research activity into databases having strings, tuples and sets as the principal datatypes. The area deserves to be regarded as a subfield of database theory. It is called "string databases" or "sequence databases," depending on the authors. Here we shall use the former name.

We extend the relational model to include finite strings over some given finite alphabet Σ as primary objects of information. A relation of arity k in our model is then a finite subset of the k-fold Cartesian product of Σ^*, the set of all finite strings over Σ, with itself. In other words, each position in a tuple of a relation contains a string of arbitrary length instead of just a single atomic value. This definition was essentially introduced in [14] an later used in e.g. [17] and [24]. However, a brief excursion into the history books reveals for instance that Stockmeyer [34] was familiar with string relations. Earlier still Quine, [26] showed that first order logic over strings is undecidable.

¿From the point of view of design, in addition to *data extraction* features, such as "retrieve all palindromes," the string language needs also *data restructuring* constructs [14,17,24,35]. For example, given two unary relations, one might want to concatenate each string from one relation with a string from the other relation, as opposed to merely taking the Cartesian product of the two relations. The former returns a set of "new" strings, whereas the latter returns a set of pairs of strings previously existing in the input instance.

Adequate query languages for string databases have been the aim of several attempts, mainly [14,17,24] (see Section 6 for works less close to ours). These three provide full power languages, based on sophisticated primitives, namely transducers, datalog with or without negation, and an original logic equivalent to multi-tape automata. However, in addition to finding complete languages, there is a need to define, and understand in depth, languages à la SQL, user-friendly, and of low time complexity, without recursion and within LOGSPACE. The "user-friendly" aspect was part of the motivation of the theory of range restriction, inspiring numerous works (see e.g. [1], Chap. 5.3 and 5.4).

In this paper we return to the spirit of "the founding fathers" ([34,26]). In other words, we will use as string-language relational calculus with an interpreted concatenation function. Our syntax will be called $FO(\bullet)$, where the symbol $\bullet$ stands for concatenation. We will define various semantics, one of them yielding our main language. Since according to a central authority in the field [37], SQL (i.e. FO) is "intergalactic dataspeak," we take a parsimonious stand to stick to FO as close as possible. In spite of its rather "formal" look, we believe the simplicity and low complexity of our main language to be well-suited for "everyday" database querying and programming. As a consequence we called it StriQueL, standing for *String Query Language*.

The contributions of this paper are the following. String queries are formally defined, with emphasis on string genericity. Given the syntax $FO(\bullet)$, we then consider first evaluating query formulas by making quantifiers range over the whole domain Σ^*. This yields the query language $[\![FO(\bullet)]\!]_{nat}$. The question is then: What are the relationships between $[\![FO(\bullet)]\!]_{nat}$ and string queries? Does the former capture all, or only some of the latter?

One can pursue a "top-down" or a "bottom-up" approach. The "top-down" approach would consist in taking the whole language $[\![FO(\bullet)]\!]_{nat}$, and restricting it syntactically without sacrificing expressive power. In this direction, we prove that the problem whether a formula expresses a string query is (not surprisingly) undecidable. We then undertake a "bottom-up" approach: designing a very simple language, obviously capturing only string queries, then empovering it little by little.

We first study three versions of a restricted semantics, where the quantifiers are not allowed to range over the full domain Σ^*, and we compare them to each other. In a parallel approach, we define syntactic restrictions yielding a language that, we believe, corresponds naturally in the string context to the intuitive relational "SQL level." That is, its comfort and expressivity are the ones we wish for "everyday" querying of the database by end-users. We call it $FO_{rr}(\bullet)$ (for *range-restricted*).

It turns out that $FO_{rr}(\bullet)$ is equivalent to one of our semantic restrictions. This result emphasises the robustness of the language. All these properties made us call it StriQueL—String Query Language.

Now, it is not surprising that we show that our StriQueL language does not express all string queries. More precisely, its complexity is shown to be of the same order of magnitude as its homologue the pure relational SQL, namely logarithmic space.

Although considered a quality for "everyday" use of string databases, these limitations in expressive power are not desirable for more advanced applications. We consider then how to overcome the limitations. We define a safe, non range-restricted, fragment of $FO(\bullet)$, through an operator schema Γ. It is based on an interesting extension, namely introducing an additional symbol in Σ along with particular constraints.

All languages introduced (except $[\![FO(\bullet)]\!]_{nat}$) are shown to compute only string queries, and to be actually evaluable (their semantics is constructive).

Although in molecular biology attempts of string manipulation have been proposed based on grammatical constructs, we believe first order logic over strings should provide an original and very flexible manipulation tool for this area. Moreover, it includes naturally some forms of pattern-matching capabilities. This issue is briefly discussed. Finally, the expressive power of the pure relational fragment of our languages is compared with pure relational FO.

The remainder of the paper is organised as follows. String queries and genericity, $[\![FO(\bullet)]\!]_{nat}$ and the discussion on the decidability of being a string query form Section 2. Section 3 introduces restrictions yielding our String Query Language, and contains a study of it. The Γ operator and the study of the corresponding language are presented in Section 4. In Section 5, we sketch the expressive power of our languages in terms of other formalisms, namely the pure relational and formal languages. Related works are detailed in Section 6, before concluding and presenting perspectives.

2   Definitions and Problems

In this section, we set up the basic definitions for our work. First, string queries are defined, emphasising string genericity. The syntax $FO(\bullet)$ and the semantics $[\![FO(\bullet)]\!]_{nat}$ are given. We then briefly discuss the difficulty of deciding whether a formula represents a string query. This difficulty is a strong motivation for our "bottom-up" approach to restricting the syntax or semantics for $FO(\bullet)$ (i.e., we shall begin with very simple syntax/semantics that we enrich little by little).

Throughout this paper we assume that a fixed finite alphabet Σ is given.

2.1   Queries and String Genericity

In our study of query languages for string databases, we first need to fix a definition of query. Although several definitions are possible, we choose in this paper one inspired from the traditional one in the relational model (see e.g. [1] for a definition and discussion of relational genericity). We adapt the traditional definition to string databases. Well-typedness and computability are essentially the same as in the relational case. String genericity is new. The idea of string genericity is to identify mappings that differ in only renaming of string symbols, i.e., letters of the fixed alphabet Σ.

A *relation* r of arity k in our model is a finite subset of the k-fold Cartesian product of Σ^*, the set of all finite strings over Σ, with itself. The arity of r, denoted $\alpha(r)$, is defined to be k. A *string database instance* I is a finite sequence of relations $(r_1, \ldots, r_n)$. The *schema* of I is $(\alpha(r_1), \ldots, \alpha(r_n))$.

We consider mappings from string databases to string relations. We'll sometimes call them also *string mappings* to emphasise the context. *Well-typedness* of a mapping simply says that the input and output schemas are fixed. Let us recall also computability [1], which immediately applies string mappings. A mapping h is *computable* if there exists a Turing machine M, such that for each instance I, given I encoded on the tape, M does the following. If $h(I)$ is defined, M computes the encoding of $h(I)$, writes it on the tape and stops. Otherwise M doesn't stop.

We now turn to the specificity of string mappings. First, recall that a mapping is *relational generic* if it is invariant under permutations of the domain (the domain being Σ^*). We will require in addition that permutations preserve the structure of strings. To this end we say that a permutation ρ of Σ^* is a *string morphism*, if for all u and v in Σ^*, $\rho(u.v) = \rho(u).\rho(v)$. In other words, symbols of Σ are "repainted" without changing the way they combine within strings. Now, a mapping h from string databases to string relations is *string generic* if for each permutation ρ of Σ^* which also is a string morphism, we have that for all instances I,

$$\rho(h(I)) = h(\rho(I)).$$

The concept of C-genericity for any finite subset C of Σ^* is defined as usual. C-genericity will be used to allow constants in query expressions.[1]

As stated in below, a relational generic mapping is also string generic, but some string generic mappings are not relational generic. This phenomenon is due to the fact that string isomorphisms of Σ^* are simply particular permutations of Σ^*. For instance, the mapping $R(u) \mapsto R(u.u)$ is string generic but not relational generic.

Fact 1 *Every relational generic mapping is string generic, but the converse does not hold.*

We now formally define string queries.

Definition 1 Let $(a_1, \ldots, a_k)$ be a database schema and b an arity. A *string query* of type $(a_1, \ldots, a_k) \to b$ is a partial string generic and computable mapping from the set of all database instances over $(a_1, \ldots, a_k)$ to the set of all relations of arity b.

2.2   A Family of Query Languages for the $FO(\bullet)$ Syntax

In this section, we assume classical notions and vocabulary (see e.g. the definition of FO in [1]) and focus on our new string primitive. The syntax $FO(\bullet)$ and a parameterised semantics $[\![FO(\bullet)]\!]_{\mathbf{d}}$ are presented. A difference with classical first order logic is that valuations and quantifiers only range over the domain $\mathbf{d}$ considered, where $\mathbf{d} \subseteq \Sigma^*$.

Syntax. We introduce here the syntax $FO(\bullet)$. It is an extension of first order predicate logic (FO) with a natural concatenation operator for strings, the *dot* operator, denoted $\bullet$. Terms are variables or constants from Σ^*, or of the form $t_1 \bullet t_2$, where t_1, t_2 are themselves terms. Formulas are built as usual from relation symbols and equality between terms, to give atoms; and inductively with the operators $\wedge, \vee, \neg, \exists, \forall$.

Semantics. Let be given terms t_1, t_2, an instance I and a valuation v for the variables appearing in t_1, t_2, i.e., a mapping from these variables to Σ^*. The *interpretation* of $t_1 \bullet t_2$ under I and v, denoted $I(t_1 \bullet t_2)$, is $I(t_1).I(t_2)$, where, in this expression, "." denotes the usual semantic concatenation of strings (associative, with neutral ϵ); and as usual $I(x) = v(x)$ for a variable x, and $I(u) = u$ for $u \in \Sigma^*$. Satisfaction of a formula φ of $FO(\bullet)$ is then inductively defined. Atoms and connectives $\wedge, \vee, \neg$ are as usual. The semantics of quantifiers $\exists, \forall$ is obtained by making variables range over some given domain $\mathbf{d} \subseteq \Sigma^*$ (see e.g. the definition of relativized interpretations in [1]).

---

[1] A way to define string genericity that might be considered more natural could be to define permutations ρ over Σ (instead of Σ^*), and then to extend ρ to strings in Σ^* and database instances in the straightforward way; this would avoid defining string morphisms.

Definition 2 Let $\varphi(\bar{x})$ be an $FO(\bullet)$ formula with $\bar{x}$ being a vector of its free variables. Given $\mathbf{d} \subseteq \Sigma^*$, the *mapping expressed by* φ *under the semantics* $\mathbf{d}$ is defined as

$$[\![\varphi]\!]_{\mathbf{d}}(I) = \{v(\bar{x}) : v \text{ is a valuation of } \bar{x} \text{ making } \varphi(\bar{x}) \text{ true in } I\},$$

where both v and the quantifiers of φ range over $\mathbf{d}$.

The *set of all mappings* expressed by query expressions in $FO(\bullet)$ under the semantics $\mathbf{d}$ is denoted $[\![FO(\bullet)]\!]_{\mathbf{d}}$.

At this point, we have in hand a rich and simple definition of a family of languages $[\![FO(\bullet)]\!]_{\mathbf{d}}$ based on the syntax $FO(\bullet)$ and parameterised by the domain $\mathbf{d}$. Our search for admissible semantic restrictions will go along the line of carefully defining more and more powerful domains $\mathbf{d}$.

2.3   Where and How to Look for the Right Language–Issues and Directions

In this section, we present our approach to a search for an admissible query languages for string databases.

Choosing a query language among ours now amounts to fixing the ranging domain $\mathbf{d}$. The natural choice for $\mathbf{d}$ would be to take the whole Σ^*. This is called the *natural semantics*, and defines a a query language $[\![FO(\bullet)]\!]_{nat}$ that we will consider now.

We want to write formulas φ in $FO(\bullet)$ such that the corresponding mapping $[\![\varphi]\!]_{nat}$ is a string query. The following fact is straightforward.

Fact 2 *There is an $FO(\bullet)$ formula φ such that $[\![\varphi]\!]_{nat}$ is not a string query.*

We are thus faced with the task of determining those formulas that express string queries (under the natural semantics). However, as stated below, a direct approach is doomed to fail.

Fact 3 *Given a formula φ in $FO(\bullet)$, it is undecidable whether $[\![\varphi]\!]_{nat}$ is a string query.*

Our purpose then becomes finding a syntactic fragment of $FO(\bullet)$ that captures *all and only* string queries under natural semantics. Our language StriQueL is a first step in this direction (see Section 3.3), but, due to its pragmatic low-complexity nature, it obviously does not express all string queries. The next step, beyond the scope of this paper, would be to design such a sound and complete language, or show that the class of string queries does not have an effective syntax.

As a starting point, one might look to the results of Makanin [8,23], from which it follows that the satisfiability problem for *conjunctive* $FO(\bullet)$ queries under natural semantics is decidable. However it is not clear if Makanin's techniques can be extended to show that a conjunctive $FO(\bullet)$ formula expresses a string query.

3   Restricting the Language

3.1   Semantic Restrictions

In this section, several progressively richer semantics, that is, semantics that allow expressing more and more string queries, are introduced. The expressivity of the query languages they generate are compared.

In the traditional relational setting, there are known ways to restrict the *FO*-language to only generate relational queries. The queries can then be evaluated using the so called active domain semantics (see e.g. [1]). This is due to the genericity property which enforces the output of queries to be within the active domain. In our setting string genericity allows to construct strings that are outside the active domain and an $FO(\bullet)$ formula can generate a string query even if the output is not included in the active domain. For instance take $\varphi(x) \equiv \exists y, z\,[(x = y \bullet z) \wedge R(y) \wedge R(z)]$, where the output will consist of concatenations of strings from the input instance. We therefore have to develop new techniques adapted to the string setting.

Before giving the formal definitions below, let us first give a flavour of the issue. The "bottom possibility," i.e., sticking to the relational concepts, consists in making the quantifiers range over the active domain, *adom*, (the strings in the input instances, but not their substrings). This use of the classical database notion of the active domain in the context of string queries appears in [15]. Unfortunately, extracting the square root of some strings in the input instance, as in e.g. $\varphi(x) \equiv R(x \bullet x)$, is possible only if the string x is itself in the input instance. Taking the extended active domain, *eadom*, (i.e., considering also substrings of string in the input instance) does the trick. The domain *eadom* was introduced in [24]. However, this domain does not allow to build up new strings using for instance the query $\varphi(x) \equiv \exists y\,[R(y) \wedge x = y \bullet y]$. If we in addition to substrings allow k concatenations of strings in the input instance we can handle the previous query. The corresponding domain is called $eadom^k$. This domain was not considered in previous works; however it can be seen as a combination of *eadom* and of the $adom^k$ used in [15].

The next step would be not bound the construction of new strings by some constant k. This would make the domain, and thus potentially the output, infinite. Consider for example the query $\varphi(x) \equiv \exists y, z\,[R(y) \wedge x = y \bullet z]$. Hence there is a need of a bound of some kind. But this bound could depend on the instance, as opposed to the query. Such a language is considered in Section 4.

In spite of its restrictions, used in an adequate manner, $eadom^k$ yields an appealing and useful language, as we shall see below.

We now proceed to the formal definitions. Given an instance I and a formula φ in $FO(\bullet)$, the *active domain of φ and I*, denoted $adom(\varphi,I)$, is the set of all strings occurring in φ or in the columns of the relations in I. The *extended active domain* of φ and I, denoted $eadom(\varphi,I)$, is $adom(\varphi,I)$ closed under substrings. For each strictly positive integer k, the set of strings obtained by concatenating at most k strings from $eadom(\varphi, I)$ gives us $eadom(\varphi, I)^k$.

We now consider the three above possibilities for the ranging domain **d**. We thus get three different string query languages, namely $[\![FO(\bullet)]\!]_{adom}$, $[\![FO(\bullet)]\!]_{eadom}$, and $[\![FO(\bullet)]\!]_{eadom^k}$. This gives us the following pleasant state of affairs.

Proposition 1 *For any $FO(\bullet)$ formula φ, and any $k \geq 2$, $[\![\varphi]\!]_{adom}$, $[\![\varphi]\!]_{eadom}$, and $[\![\varphi]\!]_{eadom^k}$ are string queries.*[2]

The issue in the next result (and again in Section 5), is whether enriching the semantics, and then restricting to mappings whose input/output is in the active domain, yields new string queries. In the following case it indeed does give more power.

Proposition 2 *Let $[\![FO(\bullet)]\!]_{eadom} \cap adom$ be the subset of those mappings in $[\![FO(\bullet)]\!]_{eadom}$ where the output contains only strings in adom. Then $[\![FO(\bullet)]\!]_{adom}$ is a proper subset of $[\![FO(\bullet)]\!]_{eadom} \cap adom$.*

Crux. The proof uses the following lemma which is false for string queries in $[\![FO(\bullet)]\!]_{eadom}$. The lemma is proved using techniques from [3].

Lemma 1. On instances with only one element, Boolean $[\![FO(\bullet)]\!]_{adom}$ queries are constant.

The next results says that allowing concatenations in the domain strictly increases the expressive power of the corresponding query language.

Proposition 3 $[\![FO(\bullet)]\!]_{eadom^k}$ *is a proper subset of* $[\![FO(\bullet)]\!]_{eadom^{k+1}}$, *for each $k \geq 1$.*

Now comparing $[\![FO(\bullet)]\!]_{eadom}$ to $[\![FO(\bullet)]\!]_{eadom^k} \cap eadom$, the latter equaling $[\![FO(\bullet)]\!]_{eadom^k}$ restricted to mappings that have output only containing strings from $[\![FO(\bullet)]\!]_{eadom}$, it turns out that $[\![FO(\bullet)]\!]_{eadom^k} \cap eadom$ is a succinct version of $[\![FO(\bullet)]\!]_{eadom}$.

Proposition 4 *For each $FO(\bullet)$ formula φ with m free variables $\{x_1, \ldots, x_m\}$ there exists a an $FO(\bullet)$ formula ψ with $k \times m$ free variables such that for all instances I, we have $[\![\varphi]\!]_{eadom^k}(I) = [\![\psi]\!]_{eadom}(I)$.*

As a consequence $[\![FO(\bullet)]\!]_{eadom}$ and $[\![FO(\bullet)]\!]_{eadom^k} \cap eadom$ has the same expressive power.

Proposition 5 $[\![FO(\bullet)]\!]_{eadom} = [\![FO(\bullet)]\!]_{eadom^k} \cap eadom$.

---

[2] Note that $[\![FO(\bullet)]\!]_{eadom^1} = [\![FO(\bullet)]\!]_{eadom}$

3.2   Syntactic Restrictions

We now define *range-restricted formulas* by restricting the syntax of the language, and evaluating queries under the natural semantics. Intuitively, the idea of range-restriction here, is to carefully track, throughout a formula, whether each variable will take its values among substrings of the instance (*eadom*), or a finite number of concatenations of them.

We use as a basis the method given in [1], Algorithm 5.4.3. The relational algorithm is extended by adding the following possibilities for φ.

Definition 3 *Let φ be a $FO(\bullet)$ formula. Then $rr(\varphi)$, the set of range-restricted variables of φ, is defined as follows:*

If φ is of the form $R(t_1, \ldots, t_n)$ then $rr(\varphi) =$ the set of all variables appearing in $t_1, \ldots, t_n$.
If φ is of the form $x = u$ or $u = x$, where $u \in \Sigma^*$ then $rr(\varphi) = \{x\}$.
If φ is of the form $u = v_1 \bullet x_1 \bullet \cdots \bullet v_n \bullet x_n \bullet v_{n+1}$, where u and the v_i's are in Σ^* (possibly ϵ) then $rr(\varphi) = \{x_1, \ldots, x_n\}$.
If φ is of the form $\varphi_1 \wedge x = v_1 \bullet x_1 \bullet \cdots \bullet v_n \bullet x_n \bullet v_{n+1}$ then $rr(\varphi) =$
    if $x \in rr(\varphi_1)$ then $rr(\varphi_1) \cup \{x_1, \ldots, x_n\}$;
    if all x_i's are in $rr(\varphi_1)$, then $rr(\varphi_1) \cup \{x\}$;
    otherwise $rr(\varphi_1)$.
Negation and existential quantification are as in [1].

A formula φ is said to be *range-restricted* if $rr(\varphi)$ equals the set of free variables in φ. The set of all range-restricted $FO(\bullet)$ formulas is denoted $FO_{rr}(\bullet)$.

Proposition 6 *For any $FO_{rr}(\bullet)$ formula φ, the mapping $[\![\varphi]\!]_{nat}$ is a string query.*

Crux. The idea is given in the proof of Theorem 7 below.

3.3   StriQueL, The String Query Language–Expressivity and Complexity

Theorem 7 $FO_{rr}(\bullet) = \bigcup_{k \geq 1} [\![FO(\bullet)]\!]_{eadom^k}$

Crux. Given a formula φ in $FO_{rr}(.)$ we compute k with the same algorithm as $rr(\varphi)$ in the following manner.

If φ is of the form $R(x)$ then $k_x = 1$.
If φ is of the form $x = u$ $(u \in \Sigma^*)$ then $k_x = 1$.
If φ is of the form $x = y \bullet u$ then $k_x = k_y + 1$.
If φ is of the form $x = y_1 \bullet y_2$ then $k_x = 2 \times max(k_{y_1}, k_{y_2})$.

On the basis of the robustness emphasised by this equivalence, and on its comfort, we take $FO_{rr}(\bullet)$ as being our string query language: StriQueL.

Evidently the StriQueL language does not express all string queries, just as SQL does not express all relational queries.

Theorem 8 *There is a string query outside* $[\![FO_{rr}(\bullet)]\!]_{nat}$.

Crux. The idea is to find a $[\![FO(\bullet)]\!]_{nat}$ formula φ that computes the concatenation of all the strings in some input instance I. If this is the case, φ cannot be range-restricted, because from Proposition 4 and Theorem 7 we know that the output of range restricted formulas are at most k concatenations of strings in I, for a given k independent of I.

We slightly adapt now the usual relational definition of data complexity for strings. Given a instance I, its size $|I|$ corresponds to the sum of the lengths of all the strings that occur in I. Complexity measures are now given in terms of $|I|$.

Theorem 9 *Let* φ *be an* $FO(\bullet)$ *formula and* I *an instance. Then* $[\![\varphi]\!]_{adom}(I)$, $[\![\varphi]\!]_{eadom}(I)$, *and* $[\![\varphi]\!]_{eadom^k}(I)$ *are computable in logarithmic space.*

Crux. The idea of the proof is more intricate than in the relational case, although it is based on the same principle. For $[\![\varphi]\!]_{adom}(I)$ the proof goes as in the usual setting. For $[\![\varphi]\!]_{eadom}(I)$ the crux is that a string in *eadom* can be described using two pointers (one for the beginning, one for the end) on the input instance, it is therefore easy to adapt the proof of $[\![\varphi]\!]_{adom}(I)$ to this case. The same holds for $[\![\varphi]\!]_{eadom^k}(I)$, with $2k$ pointers.

4   Beyond Constant Bounds

StriQueL, our language that was presented in previous section is, we believe, well-suited to "everyday" database programming and querying by end-users. However, some more advanced applications and/or programmers may want more powerful languages. For all semantics in the previous section, the number of concatenations in the creation of new strings is bounded by a constant independent of the input. (Nevertheless, in our StriQueL this constant depends on the query, and is not only arbitrarily fixed for the whole language as in, e.g., $[\![FO(\bullet)]\!]_{eadom^k}$.) It is clear that this constraint should be relaxed for certain situations.

Several possibilities arise thus for the domain, for instance the following: The domain could be *eadom*^{n} (or more generally $(\Sigma|_I)^n \subseteq \Sigma^n$), for some n depending on I, e.g. $n = |I|$, or $n = max\{|u| : u \in I\}$, or any arbitrary total function, or family of functions (for instance, $n = |I|$ being fixed, $\bigcup_{p\ \text{polynomial}} \Sigma^{p(n)}$). One of the more naive solutions yielding this might be for instance the following. Given I and $n = |I|$, take for domain *eadom*^{n}.

In this section, we provide a more powerful language, again a variant of $[\![FO(\bullet)]\!]_{nat}$. This language comes with a constructive semantics, i.e., an algorithm to compute the output of a query.

As we discussed above, such languages may range from ones capturing all string queries, down to *while/fixpoint*-like ones, or even simpler ones. We follow here again our "bottom-up" exploration and provide a rather simple one, though much more powerful than our previous StriQueL. Moreover, to explore a different direction than in previous sections, we introduce a slight variant in our semantics. We believe this variant also to be very promising for future work.

The language $[FO^{\#}(\bullet)]_{nat}$. Until now, we proceeded as follows. Given the alphabet Σ, the language $[FO(\bullet)]_{nat}$ over Σ was formally defined, allowing constants from Σ in the formulas (and in their inputs), and with quantifiers ranging over Σ^*. According to its definition, this language was given as input instances over Σ^*. Let now some new symbol not in Σ, say $\#$, be given. Consider $FO(\bullet)$ over $\Sigma \cup \{\#\}$, but now, the input of a formula is an instance over Σ^* only, that is, an instance in which $\#$ does *not* appear. We denote this language $[FO^{\#}(\bullet)]_{nat}$.

The language $FO_\Gamma(\bullet)$. What we shall do now, is to define a simple syntactic extension of $FO_{rr}(\bullet)$ (expressing a subset of $[FO^{\#}(\bullet)]_{nat}$), in which we allow particular subformulas having the property that a few designated quantified variables are allowed to range *arbitrarily* over $(\Sigma \cup \{\#\})^*$. We show however (in the same spirit as for $FO_{rr}(\bullet)$), based on the particular structure of these subformulas, that, given I, only a finite number of valuations can satisfy the formula φ defining the query, thus yielding a finite evaluation and a finite output.

To simplify the presentation of the syntax, we use a "macro" that we call Γ. More precisely, a formula in the language may now contain as a subformula an expression $\Gamma(\cdots)$. These subformulas are added to $FO_{rr}(\bullet)$ to yield the language $FO_\Gamma(\bullet)$. Note that, again, as for $FO_{rr}(\bullet)$, the formal semantics is simply that of $[FO^{\#}(\bullet)]_{nat}$ (i.e., with the full domain $(\Sigma \cup \{\#\})^*$). Formally, the $\Gamma(\cdots)$ expressions are replaced ("expanded") by their corresponding $FO^{\#}(\bullet)$ subformula, so that strictly speaking the syntax of $FO_\Gamma(\bullet)$ is a fragment of $FO^{\#}(\bullet)$.

Before introducing the formal details of the Γ operator, let us present its principles intuitively. In an expression $\Gamma(x, y, one\_step)$, x and y are strings, and *one_step* is an ordinary first order formula. This formula *one_step* defines a relationship between x and y that will have to be satisfied. With these three arguments, Γ will be doing the following.

First, a string $x\#s_1\#s_2\#\ldots\#s_n\#y$ is built (call it z in the following). Then, it is verified whether $one\_step(x, s_1)$ holds, then $one\_step(s_1, s_2)$, ..., until $one\_step(s_n, y)$. If all are true, then the formula $\Gamma(x, y, one\_step)$ is true.

Now, how is it that the number of such "big" strings z, and the evaluation of the $one\_step(s_i, s_{i+1})$'s, are both bounded? Intuitively, to achieve this, Γ generates only s_i's of strictly increasing size (thus bounded by $|y|$), and forces also *one_step* to be finitely evaluable (in fact, it has even to be quantifier-free).

Strictly speaking, this mechanism is encoded in a big "parameterized" first order formula, that we call Γ. By "parameterized", we simply mean that some subformula in $\Gamma(\cdots)$ will be the "parameter" $one\_step(\cdots)$. (This kind of construction is analogous to axiom schemata in axiomatic logic.) For the sake of the presentation, we choose a very simple variant of Γ. Richer variants can easily be defined.

We define a formula schema $\Gamma(x, y, one\_step)$, where one_step has two free variables, and has to be built using only conjunctions and disjunctions of equality atoms (no negations, and no quantifiers),[3] and the free variables of Γ are x, y. The variable x represents the "initial step" and y the "final step" in Γ. Examples of how to use Γ to build a $FO_\Gamma(\bullet)$ formula are given below.

$\Gamma(x, y, one\_step) \equiv$

$no\_\#(x) \wedge no\_\#(y) \wedge$

$\exists z, u : (z = \# \bullet x \bullet \# \bullet u \bullet \# \bullet y \bullet \#) \wedge$

$\forall z_1, v, w : (substring(z_1, z) \wedge z_1 = \# \bullet v \bullet \# \bullet w \bullet \# \wedge no\_\#(v) \wedge no\_\#(w)) \rightarrow$

$(\exists u_1, u_2 \ (w = u_1 \bullet v \bullet u_2 \wedge (u_1 \neq \epsilon \vee u_2 \neq \epsilon)) \wedge one\_step(v, w))$

Let denote this $FO^\#(\bullet)$ formula φ_Γ, and call it the "expansion" of our $\Gamma(\cdots)$ subformula shorthand. In the expansion the predicate $no\_\#$ checks easily that its argument does not feature the $\#$ symbol, and $substring$ is the obvious abbreviation. The beginning of the last line says that at each step, each v is a strict substring of w.

We extend the definition of range restriction to Γ, by adding one case to Definition 3 in Section 3.2. Notice that, with respect to range restriction, Γ is a "propagator" of range restriction, not a "generator". That is, it does not bound variables by itself, but it transmits bounds from y to x.

If $\varphi = \varphi_1 \wedge \Gamma(x, y, one\_step)$ then
if $y \notin rr(\varphi_1)$, then $rr(\varphi) = rr(\varphi_1)$;
if $y \in rr(\varphi_1)$, then $rr(\varphi) = rr(\varphi_1) \cup \{x\}$.

The language obtained is called $FO_\Gamma(\bullet)$. Its syntax is the syntax of $FO(\bullet)$ extended with the Γ operator, and its semantics is that of $[\![FO^\#(\bullet)]\!]_{nat}$, when Γ is expanded.[4]

We give below the queries $same\_length$ and $parity$ in $FO_\Gamma(\bullet)$. Note that strictly speaking, the symbol $\cent$ has to be simulated using only $\#$, making the real formula heavier.[5]

$same\_length(s_1, s_2) \equiv x = car(s_1) \bullet \cent \bullet car(s_2) \wedge y = s_1 \bullet \cent \bullet s_2 \wedge \Gamma(x, y, \psi),$

$\quad$ where $\psi(v, w) \equiv v = u_1 \bullet \cent \bullet u_2 \wedge w = u_3 \bullet \cent \bullet u_4 \wedge$

$$\left(\bigvee_{a \in \Sigma} u_3 = u_1 \bullet a \right) \wedge \left(\bigvee_{a \in \Sigma} u_4 = u_2 \bullet a \right),$$

---

[3] We could also for instance define it such that all new variables introduced by one_step be forced to be substrings of x or y. Also, one_step could be allowed to be any safe formula, e.g. range-restricted.

[4] To be more precise, a formula of $FO_\Gamma(\bullet)$ is one of $FO^\#(\bullet)$: all $\Gamma(\ldots)$ subformulas used above as shorthands are replaced by the actual $\varphi_{\Gamma(\ldots)}$ subformula. For instance our notation $\exists x, y : R(x, y) \wedge \Gamma(x, y, \psi)$ denotes the $FO^\#(\bullet)$ formula $\exists x, y : R(x, y) \wedge \varphi_{\Gamma(x,y,\psi)}$.

[5] This is done essentially by using two $\#$ symbols concatenated.

and the function *car* returns the first letter of its argument.

$$parity(x) \ \equiv \ \Gamma(\epsilon, x, \psi), \ \text{where} \ \psi(v, w) \ \equiv \bigvee_{\{a,b\} \subseteq \Sigma} w = v \bullet a \bullet b.$$

The following theorem characterises $FO_\Gamma(\bullet)$.

Theorem 10 *Let φ be a formula in $FO_\Gamma(\bullet)$. Then*

1. $\llbracket \varphi \rrbracket_{nat}$ *is a string query.*
2. *For any instance I, $\llbracket \varphi \rrbracket_{nat}(I)$ can be evaluated in space polynomial in the size of the longest string in the extended active domain $eadom(I, \varphi)$.*

Crux. We briefly consider point 1. Let s be the longest string in $eadom(I, \varphi)$. Let φ be of the form $\psi(\ldots, y, \ldots) \wedge \Gamma(x, y, one\_step)$, where $\psi(\ldots, y, \ldots)$ is an $FO_{rr}(\bullet)$ formula[6]. As in the proof of Theorem 8 we will get a bound, say k, on the variable y. Then, we have that $\llbracket \varphi \rrbracket_{nat}(I) \subseteq eadom^n$, where $n \leq 1 + 2 + \ldots + |s|^k$. This is because of the following: The only "dangerous" variables are the quantified ones in the expansion of Γ. Now y is the "output" of Γ, i.e., the last word concatenated in the existentially quantified long derivation $\exists z : z = x \bullet \# \bullet s_1 \bullet \# \bullet s_2 \bullet \# \bullet \ldots \bullet \# \bullet y$. As $|s_1| < |s_2| < \ldots < |y|$ (because of the constraint imposed by Γ on one_step), we get the maximal size of n for any string in the range of $\llbracket \varphi \rrbracket_{nat}(I)$. This shows that if y is bound to $eadom^k$ for some constant k depending only on φ, then Γ is safe because quantifiers need only to range over $eadom^n$.

Note that, once replaced by its expansion, Γ may not be range restricted. However, we just showed above its actual safety (provided y is itself range restricted). In other words, we mix here a syntactic means (range restriction), and a semantically safe operator (Γ).

5   Expressive Power—StriQueL *vs* Others

In this section, we compare our languages with formalisms outside string query languages. We first compare the pure relational fragment of our languages with pure relational *FO*. We end this section by a note on the difficulty of the comparison of $FO(\bullet)$ languages with formal languages. We however believe that such comparisons are a promising direction of research.

String genericity *vs* relational genericity. The issue here is to determine (1) whether our string languages express more queries than relational *FO*, and (2) whether we can compute purely relational generic queries that are not in relational *FO* (recall Definition 1 and definitions of both genericity concepts in Section 2.1). The answer to question (1) is yes: we already saw in Section 2.1 that there are string generic mappings that are not relational generic. In addition

---

[6] Note that y might be quantified in $\psi(\ldots, y, \ldots)$

we now have that such mappings can be expressed in our simplest semantics, namely the active domain semantics. The answer to question (2) is no. This last result has to be put in contrast with the case of $FO(<)$, for which the order *did* bring new generic relational queries [16,1]. We denote by $\Downarrow M$ the subset of mappings in M that are relational generic.

Proposition 11   1. There is a formula φ in $FO(\bullet)$, such that $[\![FO(\bullet)]\!]_{adom}$ is not a relational generic query.
   2. $[\![FO]\!]_{adom} = \Downarrow [\![FO(\bullet)]\!]_{adom} = \Downarrow [\![FO(\bullet)]\!]_{eadom^k}$

Crux. Given $FO(\bullet)$ formula φ such that $[\![\varphi]\!]_{adom}$ is a relational generic query we construct a FO formula ψ, such that $[\![\psi]\!]_{adom}(I) = [\![\varphi]\!]_{adom}(I)$, for any instance I. A case analysis shows that ψ and φ agree on instances where the active domain is composed of words of size 1. ¿From this and the fact that φ is relational generic, it follows that they must also agree on all models. This proof is inspired by techniques from [3].

On the relationship with formal languages. A string query is called *context-free* if there exists a context-free language $L \subseteq \Sigma^*$ such that the following holds: When given as input a unary relation r, the query returns $r \cap L$. The same definition extends to other classes of languages. Here we only give a conjecture grouping several representative situations.

Conjecture 1   1. The query $parity(x)$ is rational but not in $[\![FO(\bullet)]\!]_{nat}$.
   2. The query $\varphi(x) \equiv x = a^i \bullet b^j \bullet c^k$, where a and b are in Σ and $i \neq j$ or $j \neq k$, is context-free but not in $[\![FO(\bullet)]\!]_{nat}$.

Note that if we are allowed to use additional "marker-symbols," as in the query language $[\![FO^{\#}(\bullet)]\!]_{nat}$, then computing the parity query is easy. These examples suggest that putting in correspondence fragments of $[\![FO(\bullet)]\!]_{nat}$ and classes of formal languages may not be easy.

6   Related Works

Strings have been studied in databases, logic, formal language theory and computational complexity. In this section, we survey the main works in relationship with ours. We begin with databases, then turn to the others. Some definitions we used were introduced by other authors, as was pointed out in the text above. All the theorems that were explicitly stated above are novel.

Databases. Present-day database query languages offer little support for string relations. For example, the *Sequence Retrieving System (SRS)* [10], which has gained popularity in molecular biology, does not allow the database administrator to draw links from one preformatted data file to another [11], but only on its atomic non-sequence fields. Because the majority of current relational database management systems do not support application-specific data types such as sequences, some molecular biology database designers have begun to move towards object-oriented database technology [12]. Another solution, strongly advocated in for instance [7], is to introduce such types as relational domains, as we have done. In any case, the string handling concepts introduced in this work are in no way specific to the relational model; indeed, they are being applied for querying sequences of complex objects from object-oriented databases as well [2].

Our language differs from such languages as SEQ [32,33], where sequence elements and their underlying order type are distinct domains, in that queries in our application areas are more oriented towards parsing-type tasks than for example computing moving averages on temporally sequenced data [32].

One of the early declarative database languages for string databases was Richardsons [27]. This language used the modalities of temporal logic for expressing properties of strings. Each successive position in a string is seen to be the time wise "next" instance of that string. The temporal modalities lend themselves naturally to reasoning about strings. There are however well-known restrictions [38] to basic temporal logic. In particular, no recursion or iteration is achieved.

The works closer to ours begin with Wang [15], and Ginsburg and Wang [14]. They extended the relational calculus with interpreted *regular transducer functions*. Such a function has n input strings, and the result is a regular finite state transduction on the inputs. The resulting language captures all r. e. sets (and sets in the arithmetical hierarchy) [15]. The drastic expressive power of the language results from the use of powerful interpreted functions. Of course, the transducer mappings of Wang and Ginsburg are intended to serve as semantic programming primitives, but using them may turn rather heavy from the point of view of programming comfort.

Later, Grahne, Nykänen, and Ukkonen [17] proposed a string-extension of relational calculus based on modal logic. Their language has basically the same expressive power as that of Ginsburg and Wang. It has however the advantage that the string primitives do not have to be "plugged in," they have a declarative semantics that can be coupled with relational structures. The string programming primitive is a declarative specification of a multitape finite state automaton. The multitape automaton have proven to be useful in pattern matching problems [13,17]. The language has also been implemented [19]. A detailed study of safety and evaluability is done in [18].

Still later, Mecca and Bonner [24] used the interpreted functions of Ginsburg and Wang in a datalog-like language. Since Prolog with one function symbol already yields all r. e. sets [21], the Mecca-Bonner language has full Turing expressivity. In a series of sophisticated constructions [24] Mecca and Bonner restrict the language to capture sets in for instance PTIME, and hyper-exponential time. In the Mecca-Bonner language the programming primitive for recursion is datalog rules. String operations are expressed through the transducer functions, and if the programmer wants to iterate or recurse over strings, she has to mix the datalog rules and transducer functions, and stay within the syntactic restrictions given by Bonner and Mecca. W.r.t. expressivity, Bonner and Mecca consider computing string functions, i.e., mappings from a single relation containing a single string, and returning a single string.

In brief, compared to [14,17,24], we go back to the spirit of the "founding fathers". For the string programming primitive, we return to using only $\bullet$, simpler than all previous string programming primitives. And for the "host language", we return to FO, simpler than [17,24]. We study in depth a low-complexity language, whereas the abovementioned authors explore very powerful ones (except some PTIME fragment with transducers in [24]).

Logic, formal languages and computational complexity. The main direction in logic seems to have been in showing undecidability of various fragments of the theories of concatenation. In the case of first order, this amounts to variants of our $[\![FO(\bullet)]\!]_{nat}$. It initiated with Quine [26] (see also [36]). Makanin [23] shows the decidability of the existential fragment of the theory of concatenation, with consequences on word equations. We used the recent presentation in [8], which contain other references; however, nothing seems to have been done w.r.t. computing the set of all solutions [30] (not only a yes/no answer), which is the output of our queries.

From a pure formal languages point of view, Salomaa [29], Chap. III, presents an apparently isolated result around characterising type-0 (i.e., recursively enumerable) and type-1 languages.

In the classical marriage between strings and formal language theory [28,9], a model of a formula is a single string, not a whole collection of relations as in our study. As a consequence, issues, techniques and results are quite different.

In computational complexity, Stockmeyer [34] shows that the polynomial time hierarchy can be characterised in terms of (polynomially bounded) quantification over string relations.

In brief, in logic and related areas, to our knowledge, no study of a low power fragment as ours was undertaken.

7   Conclusion

Querying string databases has essentially focused until now on very powerful languages, i.e., variants of $[\![FO(\bullet)]\!]_{nat}$. Our main point in this paper was the proposal and in-depth study of a low complexity fragment of $[\![FO(\bullet)]\!]_{nat}$. Its simplicity being, we believe, well-suited for "everyday" database querying and programming, we called it StriQueL, standing for *String Query Language*.

More precisely, after having defined string queries, given the $FO(\bullet)$ syntax, we considered the general language $[\![FO(\bullet)]\!]_{nat}$ and defined our goal: all string queries. Discouraged by an undecidability result we obtained, we proceeded "bottom-up". Were successively introduced: semantics restrictions of $[\![FO(\bullet)]\!]_{nat}$ (i.e., $[\![FO(\bullet)]\!]_{adom}$, $[\![FO(\bullet)]\!]_{eadom}$, and $[\![FO(\bullet)]\!]_{eadom^k}$); then a syntactic restriction, $FO_{rr}(\bullet)$. We argued that this last one might deserve the name

StriQueL—String Query Language. Its was shown that its complexity is in logarithmic space, and that it does not express all string queries. To get more expressive power, $FO_\Gamma(\bullet)$ a fragment of $[\![FO^\#(\bullet)]\!]_{nat}$, was introduced. Some comparisons with formal languages and pure relational languages were also proven.

All languages considered (except $[\![FO(\bullet)]\!]_{nat}$ and $[\![FO^\#(\bullet)]\!]_{nat}$) were shown to express only string queries. It remains open whether there is a string query not in $[\![FO(\bullet)]\!]_{nat}$.

Perspectives. First, an efficient operational semantics for StriQueL was not considered in this paper: the design of an adequate algebra is definitely relevant.

Another direction will be the design and study of a more powerful variant of the Γ operator. A different direction, more in the "systematic" spirit of our StriQueL (or $FO_{rr}(\bullet)$), will be around the following notion of domain independence ($\Sigma^{\leq l}$ represents all string of size at most l):

A string mapping (defined by φ in the semantics $[\![FO(\bullet)]\!]_{nat}$) is said to be *domain independent* if, for each instance I, there exists a constant l, such that $[\![\varphi]\!]_{nat}(I) = [\![\varphi]\!]_{\Sigma^{\leq l}}(I)$.

Of course, one issue is to compute the constant l. In addition, some aspects of domain independence are rather involved in the relational case [20] so here, because of the nature of string genericity and the infinite domain Σ^*, new techniques have to be developed.

A parallel step will be to define analogous to *fixpoint* and *while* dealing with strings. One of our purposes in doing the present work was to gain a deeper understanding of the notion of string query; we believe these recursive languages can now be addressed.

Another interesting further question is how our results correlate with query languages for lists. Is it possible to apply some of them to lists with arbitrary element type (typically having an infinite domain)? How can query languages for lists be adopted for strings?

To close this perspective section, we believe the most interesting issue at this point is this: Is there an effective syntactic restriction of $[\![FO(\bullet)]\!]_{nat}$ yielding exactly the class of all string queries?

Acknowledgements

The authors whish to thanks Luc Segoufin for fruitful discussions on the subject, and Leonid Libkin and Victor Vianu for comments on an earlier version of this paper.

References

1. S. Abiteboul, R. Hull and V. Vianu. *Foundations of Databases.* Addison-Wesley, 1995.

2. N. Balkir, E. Sukan, G. Ozsoyoglu and Z. Oszoyoglu. VISUAL : A graphical icon-based query language. In *IEEE International Conferecne on Data Engineering*, 1996.
3. M. Benedikt, L. Libkin. Languages for Relational Databases over Interpreted Structures. In *Proc. ACM Symp. on Principles of Database Systems*, 1997.
4. M. Benedikt, L. Libkin. Safe Constraint Queries. In *Proc. ACM Symp. on Principles of Database Systems*, 1998.
5. E. F. Codd. A Relational Model of Data for Large Shared Data Banks. *Communications of ACM*, 13:6, 1970
6. J. Collado-Vides. The search for a grammatical theory of gene regulation is formally justified by showing the inadequacy of context-free grammars. *Computer applications in the Biosciences*, 7(3):321-326, 1991.
7. C. Date. *An introduction to database systems*. Addison-Wesley, 1994.
8. V. Diekert, Makanin's algorithm. Available at http://www.lri.fr/˜rtaloop/92.html
9. T. Eiter, G. Gottlob, Y. Gurevich. Existential Second-Order Logic over Strings. In *Proc. Symp. on Logic in Computer Science*, 1998.
10. T. Etzold and P. Argos. SRS - an indexing and retrieval tool for flat file data libraries. *Computer applications in the Biosciences*, 9(1):49-57, 1993.
11. T. Etzold and P. Argos. Transforming a set of biological flat file libraries to a fast access network. *Computer applications in the Biosciences*, 9(1):59-64, 1993
12. European Molecular Biologiy Network (EMBNET). *Strategies in Bioinformatics: a european perspective*, 1994.
13. Z. Galil, J. I. Seiferas. Time-Space-Optimal String Matching. *Journal of Computer and System Sciences* 26(3): 280-294, 1983.
14. S. Ginsburg, X. S. Wang. Pattern Matching by Rs-Operations: Toward a Unified Approach to Querying Sequenced Data. In *Proc. ACM Symp. on Principles of Database Systems*, 1992.
15. S. Ginsburg and W. Wang. Regular Sequence Operations and Their Use in Database Queries. *Journal of Computer and System Science* 56(1): 1-26 (1998)
16. Y. Gurevich. in [1], exercice 17.27.
17. G. Grahne, M. Nykänen, E. Ukkonen. Reasoning about Strings in Databases. In *Proc. ACM Symp. on Principles of Database Systems*, 1994.
18. G. Grahne, M. Nykänen. Safety, translation and evaluation of Alignment calculus. *First East-European Symposium on Advances in Database Information Systems (ABDIS'97)*, St-Petersburg, Russia, 1997.
19. G. Grahne, R. Hakli, M. Nykanen and E. Ukkonen. AQL: An alignment based language for querying string databases. *Proc. of the 9TH International Conference on Management of Data (Comad '98)*, Hyderabad, India, December 1998.
20. R. Hull, J. Su. Domain independence and the relational calculus. *Acta informatica*, 31:6, 1994.
21. J. W. Lloyd *Foundations of logic programming*. Springer, 1984.
22. J. Barwise (Ed). *Handbool of mathematical logic*. North-Holland, 1991.
23. G. S. Makanin. The problem of solvability of equations in a free semi-group. english translation in *Math. USSR Sbornik*, 32, 129-198, 1977.
24. G. Mecca, A. J. Bonner. Sequences, Datalog and Transducers. In *Proc. ACM Symp. on Principles of Database Systems*, 1995.
25. C. H. Papadimitriou. *Computational complexity*. Addison-Wesley, Chap. 17, 1994.
26. W. V. Quine. Concatenation as a basis for arithmetic. *Journal of Symbolic Logic*, 11(4):105-114, 1946
27. J. Richardson. Supporting lists in a data model (a timely approach). *Proc. of Intl. Conf. on Very Large Data Bases*, 1992.

28. G. Rozenberg, A. Salomaa (Eds). *Handbook of formal languages*. Springer, 1997.
29. A. Salomaa. *Formal languages*, Chap. 3, Academic Press, 1973.
30. K. Schulz. Personnal communication.
31. D. Searls. String variable grammar: a logic grammar formalism for the biological language of DNA. *Journal of Logic Programming*, pp. 73–102, 1995.
32. P. Seshadri, M. Livny and R. Ramakrishnan. SEQ: a model for sequence databases. *IEEE International Conference on Data Engineering*, pp. 232–239, 1995.
33. P. Seshadri, M. Livny and R. Ramakrishnan. The design and implementation of a sequence database system. *Proc. of Intl. Conf. on Very Large Data Bases*, 1996.
34. L. J. Stockmeyer. The polynomial-time hierarchy. *Theoretical Computer Science*, 3:1-22, 1977
35. B. Subramanian, T. Leung, S. Vandenberg and S. Zdonik. The AQUA appraoch to querying lists and trees in objsct-oriented databases. *IEEE International Conference on Data Engineering*, pp. 80–89, 1995.
36. R. Treinen. A new method for undecidability proofs of first order theories. *J. Symbolic Computation*, 14:437-457, 1992.
37. J. Ullman. *Principles of database and knowledge-base systems, Volume 1.* Computer Science Press, 1988.
38. P. Wolper. Temporal logic can be more expressive. *Information and Control*, 56:72-99, 1983.

Structured Document Transformations Based on XSL

Sebastian Maneth[1]* and Frank Neven[2]**

[1] Leiden University, LIACS
PO Box 9512, 2300 RA Leiden, The Netherlands
maneth@liacs.nl
[2] Limburgs Universitair Centrum, Universitaire Campus, Dept. WNI, Infolab,
B-3590 Diepenbeek, Belgium
frank.neven@luc.ac.be

Abstract. Based on the recursion mechanism of the XML transformation language XSL, the document transformation language $\mathcal{DTL}$ is defined. First the instantiation $\mathcal{DTL}^{\text{reg}}$ is considered that uses regular expressions as pattern language. This instantiation closely resembles the navigation mechanism of XSL. For $\mathcal{DTL}^{\text{reg}}$ the complexity of relevant decision problems such as termination of programs, usefulness of rules and equivalence of selection patterns, is addressed. Next, a much more powerful abstraction of XSL is considered that uses monadic second-order logic formulas as pattern language ($\mathcal{DTL}^{\text{mso}}$). If $\mathcal{DTL}^{\text{mso}}$ is restricted to top-down transformations ($\mathcal{DTL}_d^{\text{mso}}$), then a computational model can be defined which is a natural generalization to *unranked* trees of top-down tree transducers with look-ahead. The look-ahead can be realized by a straightforward bottom-up pre-processing pass through the document. The size of the output of an XSL program is at most exponential in the size of the input. By restricting copying in XSL a decidable fragment of $\mathcal{DTL}_d^{\text{mso}}$ programs is obtained which induces transformations of linear size increase (safe $\mathcal{DTL}_d^{\text{mso}}$). It is shown that the emptiness and finiteness problems are decidable for ranges of $\mathcal{DTL}_d^{\text{mso}}$ programs and that the ranges are closed under intersection with generalized Document Type Definitions (DTDs).

1 Introduction

XSL [4,2] is a recursive XML [5,1,23] transformation language and an XSL program can be thought of as an ordered collection of templates. Each template has an associated pattern (selection pattern) and contains a nested set of construction rules. A template processes nodes that match the selection pattern and constructs output according to the construction rules. The transformation starts at the 'root' of the input document and the construction rules specify, by

---

* The work of this author was supported by the EC TMR Network GETGRATS.
** Research Assistant of the Fund for Scientific Research, Flanders.

R. Connor and A. Mendelzon (Eds.): DBPL'99, LNCS 1949, pp. 80–98, 2000.

means of construction patterns, where in the XML document the transformation process should continue. In this paper we define a document transformation language $(\mathcal{DTL})$ based on the recursion and navigation mechanism embodied in XSL.

As is customary [21,16], we use an abstraction of XML documents that focuses on the document *structure* and consider a document as a *tree*. Such a tree is ordered and unranked (consider, e.g., a list-tag: the number of list entries is unbounded, which means that the number of children in the corresponding tree is unbounded). Figure 1 shows an XML document and the corresponding tree. In our notation the tree shown there is the string `product(sales(dom(a)dom(b)` `dom(c))sales(dom(d)for(e)for(f)))`. To enhance the expressiveness of Document Type Definitions (DTDs), which are modeled by extended context-free grammars, we also use a tree notion. Indeed, we define *generalized* DTDs as the tree regular grammars defined by Murata [18].

```
<product>
    <sales>
        <domestic> a </domestic>
        <domestic> b </domestic>
        <foreign> c </foreign>
    </sales>
    <sales>
        <domestic> d </domestic>
        <foreign> e </foreign>
        <foreign> f </foreign>
    </sales>
</product>
```

Fig. 1. Example of an XML document and the corresponding tree representation

First, we study the instantiation $\mathcal{DTL}^{\mathrm{reg}}$ of $\mathcal{DTL}$ that uses regular path expressions as selection and construction patterns. This instantiation closely resembles the navigation mechanism of XSL. We consider various decision problems for $\mathcal{DTL}^{\mathrm{reg}}$ programs. An important drawback of XSL is that programs do not always terminate. This is due to the `ancestor` function which allows XSL programs to move up in XML documents. We show that it is EXPTIME-complete to decide whether or not an $\mathcal{DTL}^{\mathrm{reg}}$ program terminates on all trees satisfying a generalized DTD. Further, we consider optimization problems, like usefulness of template rules and equivalence of selection patterns.

Next, we study $\mathcal{DTL}$ with monadic second-order logic (MSO) formulas as pattern language $(\mathcal{DTL}^{\mathrm{mso}})$ and focus on the natural fragment of $\mathcal{DTL}^{\mathrm{mso}}$ that induces top-down transformations. This means that the construction rules can only select *descendants* of the current node for further processing. Consequently, programs can no longer move up in the document and will always terminate. We denote this fragment by $\mathcal{DTL}_d^{\mathrm{mso}}$. We define a computational model for $\mathcal{DTL}_d^{\mathrm{mso}}$: the top-down tree transducer with look-ahead. This is a finite state device obtained as the natural generalization of the usual top-down tree transducer [24,8] over ranked trees. The basic idea of going from ranked to unranked trees is the one of Brüggemann-Klein, Murata and Wood [3]: replace recursive calls by regular (string) languages of recursive calls. We show that these transducers correspond exactly to $\mathcal{DTL}_d^{mso}$ programs. As in the ranked case the look-ahead used by the transducer can be eliminated by first running a bottom-up relabeling on the input tree. This means that the input tree has to be processed only twice in order to perform a transformation: first a bottom-up relabeling phase and then the top-down transformation (without look-ahead).

Unfortunately, the ranges of $\mathcal{DTL}_d^{mso}$ programs can in general not be described by (generalized) DTDs. For a given $\mathcal{DTL}_d^{mso}$ (or $\mathcal{DTL}^{reg}$) program this is even undecidable. We show that two relevant optimization problems for $\mathcal{DTL}_d^{mso}$ programs are decidable: (1) whether or not the range of a $\mathcal{DTL}_d^{mso}$ program is empty, and (2) whether or not the range of an $\mathcal{DTL}_d^{mso}$ program is finite. Further, we show that the class of output languages of $\mathcal{DTL}_d^{mso}$ programs is closed under intersection with generalized DTD's: given a $\mathcal{DTL}_d^{mso}$ program P and a generalized DTD $\mathcal{D}$, there always exists a $\mathcal{DTL}_d^{mso}$ program P' that only transforms an input tree when the result belongs to $\mathcal{D}$.

Since XSL programs can select nodes of an input tree several times ("copy"), the size of the output trees can be exponential in the size of the input trees. However, the original purpose of XSL was to add style specifications to XML documents.[1] Most XSL programs, therefore, do not change the input document very drastically. Hence, it makes sense to focus on transformations where the size increase is only linear. An obvious, but rather drastic way to obtain this, is to simply disallow copying of subtrees. ¿From a practical viewpoint, however, it is desirable to allow (some restricted type of) copying (see the example in Section 7.2). We define a dynamic notion that essentially requires that each subtree can only be processed (and hence copied) a bounded number of times. We call $\mathcal{DTL}_d^{mso}$ programs that are bounded copying *safe*. Consequently, a safe program runs in time linear in the size of the input tree. Although safeness is a dynamic notion we show that it is nevertheless decidable.

2 Preliminaries

2.1 Trees and Forests

For $k \in \mathbb{N}$, $[k]$ denotes the set $\{1, \ldots, k\}$; thus $[0] = \emptyset$. We denote the empty string by ε. In what follows let Σ be an alphabet. The set of all (resp. nonempty) strings over Σ is denoted by Σ^* (Σ^+, respectively). Note that $*$ and $+$ are also used in regular expression (see the examples in Section 2.2). For a set S we denote the set of all regular languages over S by $\text{Reg}(S)$. For a string $w = a_1 \cdots a_n$ and $i \in [n]$ with $a_1, \ldots, a_n \in \Sigma$ we denote by $w(i)$ the i-th letter a_i.

The *set of unranked trees over* Σ, denoted by $\mathcal{T}_\Sigma$, is the smallest set of strings $\mathcal{T}$ over Σ and the parenthesis symbols '(' and ')' such that for $\sigma \in \Sigma$ and $w \in \mathcal{T}_\Sigma^*$,

---

[1] There are now new proposals to make XSL into a fully fledged XML query language, see, e.g., the proposal by Bosworth [2].

$\sigma(w)$ is in $\mathcal{T}$. For $\sigma()$ we simply write σ. In the following, when we say tree, we always mean unranked tree. Let S be a set. Then $\mathcal{T}_\Sigma(S)$ denotes the set of trees t over $\Sigma \cup S$ such that symbols of S may only appear at the leafs of t. The *set* $\mathcal{T}_\Sigma^*$ *of unranked forests over* Σ is denoted by $\mathcal{F}_\Sigma$; furthermore, $\mathcal{F}_\Sigma(S) = \mathcal{T}_\Sigma^*(S)$.

For every tree $t \in \mathcal{T}_\Sigma$, the *set of occurrences* (or, *nodes*) *of* t, denoted by $\mathrm{Occ}(t)$, is the subset of $\mathbb{N}^*$ inductively defined as: if $t = \sigma(t_1 \cdots t_n)$ with $\sigma \in \Sigma$, $n \geq 0$, and $t_1, \ldots, t_n \in \mathcal{T}_\Sigma$, then $\mathrm{Occ}(t) = \{\varepsilon\} \cup \bigcup_{i \in [n]} \{iu \mid u \in \mathrm{Occ}(t_i)\}$. Thus, the occurrence ε represents the root of a tree and ui represents the i-th child of u. For every tree $t \in \mathcal{T}_\Sigma$ and every occurrence u of t, the *label of* t *at occurrence* u is denoted by $t[u]$; we also say that $t[u]$ occurs in t at node u. Define $\mathrm{rank}(t, u) = n$, where n is the number of children of u. The *subtree of* t *at occurrence* u is denoted by t/u. The *substitution* of a forest $w \in \mathcal{T}_\Sigma^*$ at occurrence u in t is denoted by $t[u \leftarrow w]$. Formally, these notions can be defined as follows: $t[\varepsilon]$ is the first symbol of t (in Σ), $t/\varepsilon = t$, $t[\varepsilon \leftarrow w] = w$, and if $t = \sigma(t_1 \cdots t_k)$, $i \in [k]$, and $u \in \mathrm{Occ}(t_i)$, then $t[iu] = t_i[u]$, $t/iu = t_i/u$, and $t[iu \leftarrow w] = \sigma(t_1 \cdots t_i[u \leftarrow w] \cdots t_k)$. Note that $t[u \leftarrow w]$ is in general a forest (for $u \neq \varepsilon$ it is a tree).

2.2   DTDs and Generalized DTDs

We model a DTD [5] as an extended context-free grammar. This is a context-free grammar that allows regular expressions on the right-hand side of productions. To illustrate the shortcomings of DTDs we recall the example from Ludäscher et al. [16,21]. Consider the following DTD G

$$
\begin{array}{ll}
\texttt{dealers} & \longrightarrow \texttt{dealer}^* \\
\texttt{dealer} & \longrightarrow \texttt{ad}^* \\
\texttt{ad} & \longrightarrow \texttt{usedcar\_ad} + \texttt{newcar\_ad}
\end{array}
$$

that models a list of dealers with advertisements for new and used cars. Note that the right-hand sides are regular expressions, i.e., $*$ and $+$ mean Kleene-star and set union, respectively. We now want to specify those derivation trees of the above grammar where each dealer has at least one used car ad. This cannot be specified with DTDs without changing the structure of the derivation trees. Therefore, we will define *generalized* DTDs as tree regular grammars introduced by Murata [18].

Definition 1. A *generalized DTD* is a tree regular grammar $\mathcal{D} = (N, \Delta, S, P)$, where N and Δ are alphabets of *nonterminals* and *terminals*, respectively, $S \in N$ is the *start nonterminal*, and P is a finite set of *productions* of the form $A \to t$, where $t \in \mathcal{F}_\Delta(\mathrm{Reg}(N))$, and if $A = S$, then t should be a tree with $t[\varepsilon] \notin \mathrm{Reg}(N)$.[2]

The language generated by $\mathcal{D}$, denoted by $L(\mathcal{D})$, is defined in the obvious way: $L(\mathcal{D}) = \{t \in \mathcal{T}_\Delta \mid S \Rightarrow_\mathcal{D}^* t\}$, where the derivation relation $\Rightarrow_\mathcal{D}$ induced by $\mathcal{D}$ is

---

[2] This is just a technicality to ensure the definition of trees only.

defined as $\xi_1 \Rightarrow_{\mathcal{D}} \xi_2$ if there is a node u in ξ_1 labeled by a regular language K and ξ_2 is obtained from ξ_1 by substituting u by the right-hand sides of X_1-,..., X_n-productions, where $X_1 \cdots X_n$ is a string in K. Here, an X-production is a production of the form $X \to t$.

Example 2. The following generalized DTD defines those derivation trees of G where all dealers have at least one used car ad. All strings that start with capital letters are nonterminals; all others are terminals; `Dealers` is the start symbol. For convenience, we denote the regular languages at leaves by regular expressions.

$$
\begin{aligned}
\texttt{Dealers} &\longrightarrow \texttt{dealers}(D) \\
\texttt{Dealer} &\longrightarrow \texttt{dealer}(U) \\
\texttt{UsedAd} &\longrightarrow \texttt{ad}(\texttt{usedcar\_ad}) \\
\texttt{NewAd} &\longrightarrow \texttt{ad}(\texttt{newcar\_ad}),
\end{aligned}
$$

where D and U are the regular languages given by the expressions `Dealer*` and `(UsedAd + NewAd)*UsedAd(UsedAd + NewAd)*`, respectively.

Generalized DTDs have the same expressive power as tree automata on unranked trees [3], which are essentially the specialized ltd's of Papakonstantinou and Vianu [21,3].

3   XSL

In this section we give some examples of XSL programs, which will motivate the definition of $\mathcal{DTL}$. XSL programs contain more features than we describe here.[3] We will focus on the navigational and restructuring ability of XSL.

Example 3. In Figure 2 an example of an XSL program P is shown. Figure 3 contains the output produced by processing the XML document in Figure 1. The program P contains three templates. A template consists of a selection pattern, which equals the `match` attribute, and of construction rules, which equal anything between `<xsl:template...>` and `</xsl:template>`. The translation process starts at the root of the document. The selection patterns determine which template should be applied at the current node. The construction rules describe the output and contain construction patterns. Construction patterns are the patterns that equal the `select` attribute in `xsl:apply-templates`; they select the nodes with which the transformation process should continue. If no construction pattern appears in a template, then all children of the current node are processed.

In P the templates are applied at `product`, `foreign` and `domestic` nodes respectively. In patterns, the construct / denotes *child of* and // denotes *descendant of*. The pattern `sales/domestic` then selects all `domestic` grandchildren of the current node whose parent is labeled with `sales`, and the pattern

---

[3] Although the XSL working draft [4] is still unstable and sometimes remains quite vague.

```
<xsl:stylesheet>

<xsl:template match="product">
  <OUT>
     <TABLE>
            <xsl:apply-templates select="sales//foreign"/>
     </TABLE>
     <TABLE>
            <xsl:apply-templates select="sales/domestic"/>
     </TABLE>
  </OUT>
</xsl:template>

<xsl:template match="foreign">
  '<xsl:apply-templates/>'
</xsl:template>

<xsl:template match="domestic">
  <xsl:apply-templates/>
</xsl:template>

</xsl:stylesheet>
```

Fig. 2. Example of an XSL program

sales//foreign selects all descendants of **sales**-labeled children of the current node which are labeled **foreign**. If several nodes are selected by a pattern, then they are processed in *document order* [5], which is the pre-order of the document (tree). The construction rules of the first template create two 'tables' and put them between **OUT** 'nodes'; in the first table all nodes that match the pattern **sales//foreign** are selected for further processing; in the second table all nodes that match the pattern **sales/domestic** are selected for further processing. Built-in template rules make sure that text nodes (like a, b,... in Figure 1) are copied through. The second template rule puts them between quotes, the third one doesn't.

XSL contains built-in template rules to allow recursive processing to continue in the absence of a successful pattern match by an explicit rule in the style sheet. In our language $\mathcal{DTL}$ we will not consider built-in rules as they can easily be simulated. Consequently, $\mathcal{DTL}$ programs will not transform every input tree. We will show (in the proof of Theorem 18) that the domain of a $\mathcal{DTL}$ program can be defined by a generalized DTD (more precisely, we show this for the 'descendant' case with MSO patterns, $\mathcal{DTL}_d^{\mathrm{mso}}$).

XSL essentially allows arbitrary regular expressions as selection and construction patterns. As is illustrated by the next example, construction patterns can also select ancestors as opposed to descendants.

Example 4. The function $\mathrm{ancestor}(p)$ selects the first ancestor of the current node that matches pattern p. For example, $\mathrm{ancestor}(\mathtt{chapter})/\mathtt{title}$ will se-

```
<OUT>
     <TABLE> 'c' 'e' 'f' </TABLE>
     <TABLE> a b d </TABLE>
</OUT>
```

Fig. 3. The output of the program in Figure 2 on the data in Figure 1

lect the `title` children of the first ancestor of the current node that is a `chapter`. This feature can cause undesirable behavior. Indeed, in Figure 4 an XSL program is shown that does not terminate on the XML document in Figure 1.

```
<xsl:stylesheet>

<xsl:template match="product">
  <TABLE>
          <xsl:apply-templates select="ancestor(product)"/>
  </TABLE>
</xsl:template>

</xsl:stylesheet>
```

Fig. 4. Example of an XSL program that does not terminate

If a node matches several template rules, then the rule with the highest priority is taken. The priority of a template rule is specified by the `priority` attribute of the rule.

The XSL working draft informally mentions *mode* attributes to allow to treat same parts of the document in different ways. A simple example which needs modes is the transformation of a list of items into two lists of corresponding serial numbers and prices (see Section 7.2). In $\mathcal{DTL}$ we model this by *states*.

4   The Document Transformation Language $\mathcal{DTL}$

We now define $\mathcal{DTL}$ without specifying the actual pattern language. Intuitively, a unary pattern selects nodes of trees, while a binary pattern selects pairs of nodes of trees. Formally, a *unary pattern* p over Σ is a subset of $\mathcal{T}_\Sigma \times \mathbb{N}^*$; a *binary pattern* p' over Σ is a subset of $\mathcal{T}_\Sigma \times \mathbb{N}^* \times \mathbb{N}^*$. Let $s \in \mathcal{T}_\Sigma$ and let $u, v \in \mathrm{Occ}(s)$ be nodes of s. If $(s, u) \in p$ (respectively, $(s, u, v) \in p'$), then we say that u *matches* p (respectively, (u, v) *matches* p'). Let Q be a finite set of states. A *construction function* f over Q and Σ is a function from Q to the set of binary patterns, such that $\forall q, q' \in Q : q \neq q' \rightarrow f(q) \cap f(q') = \varnothing$; this condition expresses that in a construction function all binary patterns should be disjoint. The set of all construction functions over Q and Σ is denoted by $\mathrm{CF}(Q, \Sigma)$.

Definition 5. A $\mathcal{DTL}$ *program* is a tuple $P = (\Sigma, \Delta, Q, q_0, R, \prec)$, where

- Σ is an alphabet of *input symbols*;
- Δ is an alphabet of *output symbols*;

- Q is a finite set of *states* (modes);
- $q_0 \in Q$ is the *initial* state;
- R is a finite *set of template rules* of the form (q, p, t) where $q \in Q$, p is a unary pattern over Σ (called *selection pattern*) and t is a forest in $\mathcal{F}_\Delta(\mathrm{CF}(Q, \Sigma))$; if $q = q_0$, then t is required to be a tree such that $t[\varepsilon] \notin \mathrm{CF}(Q, \Sigma)$.[4]
- $\prec$ is a total order on R, called the *priority order*.

We are now ready to define the transformation relation induced by P. Intuitively, P starts processing in its initial state q_0 at the root node ε of the input tree s. This is denoted by $q_0(\varepsilon)$. Now the highest priority template rule (q_0, p, t) for which ε matches p is applied. This means to replace $q_0(\varepsilon)$ by t, in which each construction function f is replaced by a sequence $q_1(v_1) \ldots q_m(v_m)$, where each v_i is a node of s selected by the pattern $f(q_i)$, i.e., $f(q_i)(s, \varepsilon, v_i)$ holds, and $v_1, \ldots, v_m$ are in pre-order. The transformation process then continues in the same manner at these nodes.

Formally, the *transformation relation induced by P on s*, denoted by $\Rightarrow_{P,s}$, is the binary relation on $\mathcal{T}_{\Delta \cup Q}(\mathrm{Occ}(s))$ defined as follows. For $\xi, \xi' \in \mathcal{T}_{\Delta \cup Q}(\mathrm{Occ}(s))$, $\xi \Rightarrow_{P,s} \xi'$, if there is a node $u \in \mathrm{Occ}(\xi)$ and a template rule $r = (q, p, t)$ in R such that

1. $\xi/u = q(v)$ with $q \in Q$ and $v \in \mathrm{Occ}(s)$,
2. $r = \max_{\prec}\{(q, p', t') \in R \mid (s, v) \in p'\}$,
3. $\xi' = \xi[u \leftarrow t\Theta]$, where Θ denotes the substitution of replacing every construction function $f \in \mathrm{CF}(Q, \Sigma)$ by the forest $q_1(v_1) \ldots q_m(v_m)$, where
   - $\{v_1, \ldots, v_m\} = \{u \mid (s, v, u) \in \bigcup_{q \in Q} f(q)\}$;
   - for $i \in [m]$, $(s, v, v_i) \in f(q_i)$; and
   - $v_1 <_{\mathrm{pre}} \cdots <_{\mathrm{pre}} v_m$. Here, $<_{\mathrm{pre}}$ denotes the pre-order of the tree.

The *transformation realized by P*, denoted by τ_P, is the function $\{(s, t) \in \mathcal{T}_\Sigma \times \mathcal{T}_\Delta \mid q_0(\varepsilon) \Rightarrow^*_{P,s} t\}$. Here, $\Rightarrow^*_{P,s}$ denotes the transitive closure of $\Rightarrow_{P,s}$. We give an example of a $\mathcal{DTL}$-transformation in the next section.

5   Regular Expressions as a Pattern Language for $\mathcal{DTL}$

We now define unary and binary patterns that closely resemble the patterns issued by XSL. Denote by $L(r)$ the language defined by the regular expression r. For a tree t and $v, v' \in \mathrm{Occ}(t)$, $\mathrm{path}(t, v, v')$ denotes the string formed by the node labels on the unique path from v to v' (the labels of v and v' included).

Unary patterns are defined as $p(x) \equiv u \cdot x \cdot d$, where u and d are regular expressions and x is a variable (u stands for up and d stands for down). For a tree s and a node v: $(s, v) \in p$ iff $\mathrm{path}(s, \varepsilon, v) \in L(u)$ and there is a leaf v' in s/v such that $\mathrm{path}(s, v, v') \in L(d)$.

Binary patterns are also defined by regular expressions. We have *up/down* patterns and *down* patterns:

---

[4] This is just a technicality to ensure tree to tree translations.

- An up/down pattern is of the form $p(x, y) \equiv x \cdot u \cdot d \cdot y$, where u and d are regular expressions, and x and y are variables. For a tree s and nodes v and v': $(s, v, v') \in p$ iff there exists an ancestor v'' of v and v' such that $path(s, v, v'') \in L(u)$ and $path(s, v'', v') \in L(d)$.
- A down pattern is of the form $p(x, y) \equiv x \cdot d \cdot y$, where d is a regular expression, and x and y are variables. For a tree s and nodes v and v': $(s, v, v') \in p$ iff v' is a descendant of v and $path(s, v, v') \in L(d)$.

Denote the instantiation of $\mathcal{DTL}$ with the above patterns by $\mathcal{DTL}^{\mathrm{reg}}$.

Example 6. The XSL program in Figure 2 can be described in $\mathcal{DTL}^{\mathrm{reg}}$ as follows. Let $Q = \{q_0\}$, Σ and Δ consist of all ASCII symbols, and let R consist of the following template rules. (In all the rules the construction function f is represented directly by the binary pattern $f(q_0)$.)

$(q_0, \Sigma^*\texttt{product} \cdot x \cdot \texttt{product} \Sigma^*, \texttt{<OUT>}(\texttt{<TABLE>}(x \cdot \texttt{product sales} \Sigma^* \texttt{foreign} \cdot y)$
$\qquad\qquad\qquad\qquad\qquad \texttt{<TABLE>}(x \cdot \texttt{product sales domestic} \cdot y)))$
$(q_0, \Sigma^*\texttt{foreign} \cdot x \cdot \texttt{foreign} \Sigma^*, \texttt{'}(x \cdot \texttt{foreign} \Sigma \cdot y)\texttt{'})$
$(q_0, \Sigma^*\texttt{domestic} \cdot x \cdot \texttt{domestic} \Sigma^*, (x \cdot \texttt{domestic} \Sigma \cdot y))$

The priority of the rules does not matter in this case and is therefore omitted. We also refrained from specifying the built-in XSL rules that just copy through the string content.

Let us now take a look at an example of the computation of a $\mathcal{DTL}^{\mathrm{reg}}$ program.

Example 7. Consider the simple program P with the single template rule $(q_0, \Sigma^* \cdot x \cdot \Sigma^*, \sigma(f))$ with $f(q_0) = x \cdot \Sigma\Sigma^* \cdot y$, where $\Sigma = \{\sigma\}$. Intuitively, P selects *all proper descendants* of the current node. Recall that the nodes that match a pattern are selected in *pre-order* of the input tree; this is true for *all* $\mathcal{DTL}$ programs. Let us now consider the monadic input tree $s = \sigma(\sigma(\sigma(\sigma)))$. We start with $q_0(\varepsilon)$ (recall that ε denotes the root of s). Now we apply the (only) q_0-rule that matches at the root of s. In its right-hand side the pattern $f(q_0) = x \cdot \Sigma\Sigma^* \cdot y$ has to be replaced by the sequence of (pre-order) nodes that match $x \cdot \Sigma\Sigma^* \cdot y$, where $x = \varepsilon$ (here, this will be *all* proper descendants). The computation proceeds as shown in Figure 5. Similarly the reader may imagine how the derivation of P for non-monadic input trees looks like.

We now establish the complexity of some relevant decision problems for $\mathcal{DTL}^{\mathrm{reg}}$ programs. In the following let $\mathcal{D}$ be a generalized DTD. We show that deciding whether or not a $\mathcal{DTL}^{\mathrm{reg}}$ program terminates cannot be decided efficiently and provide an EXPTIME algorithm.

Theorem 8. *Deciding whether or not a $\mathcal{DTL}^{\mathrm{reg}}$ program terminates on every tree in $L(\mathcal{D})$ is EXPTIME-complete.*

Sketch of Proof: EXPTIME-hardness is shown by a reduction from the circularity problem of attribute grammars which is EXPTIME-complete [15]. An attribute grammar consists essentially of an underlying context-free grammar G_0,

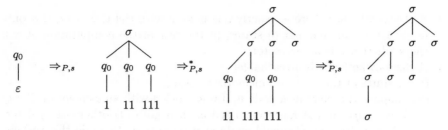

Fig. 5. A computation of P for input tree $s = \sigma(\sigma(\sigma(\sigma)))$

a set of attributes and a set of semantic rules that define the attribute values. We define the generalized DTD $\mathcal{D}$ such that it defines all abstract derivation trees of G_0 (cf., e.g., Lemma 5.5 in [17]); every node in such a tree is labeled by a production of G_0 (plus a 'sibling' number). The values of the attributes of a node (as defined by the semantic rules) depend on attributes of the parent and on attributes of its siblings. Attributes are, hence, defined locally. We take the attributes as the set of states of P. The program P now simulates all runs through the dependency graph of G on an input tree s as follows. (W.l.o.g. we can assume that all grammar symbols have the same set of attributes.) At the root of s, P selects every node in every state. At a node u the state a selects all nodes that the attribute occurrence a at u depends on. If a is a synthesized attribute, then this is determined by the semantic rules of p (the label of u) and otherwise (a inherited) it is determined by the semantic rules of the father of u. Clearly, P arrives at the same node twice in the same state (and hence does not terminate) iff an attribute occurrence depends on itself, i.e., iff G is circular.

We will reduce the termination problem to the emptiness problem of two-way non-deterministic tree automata with string regular look-around with negation ($2NTA^{sr}$). Intuitively, such an automaton can walk non-deterministically in two direction through the input tree and can check at any node whether a unary $\mathcal{DTL}^{reg}$ pattern holds or not (here is where the negation comes in). We omit the formal definition of the automaton and the rather involved proof of the next lemma which uses techniques developed by Neven and Schwentick [19]:

Lemma 9. *Emptiness of $2NTA^{sr}$s is EXPTIME-complete.*

Let $P = (\Sigma, \Delta, Q, q_0, R, \prec)$ be a $\mathcal{DTL}^{reg}$ program and $\mathcal{D}$ a generalized DTD. We say that a node v of a tree t is q-reachable for a state q if there exists a tree $s \in \mathcal{T}_{\Delta \cup Q}(\mathrm{Occ}(t))$, such that $q_0(\varepsilon) \Rightarrow^*_{P,t} s$ and $s/u = q(v)$ for some $u \in \mathrm{Occ}(t)$. If P does not terminate on all trees in $L(\mathcal{D})$, then there exists a tree t and $v \in \mathrm{Occ}(t)$ such that v is q-reachable and P returns at node v in state q. We call such nodes *attractors* (as the program always returns to them). We will now construct a $2NTA^{sr}$ A over the alphabet $\Sigma \cup (\Sigma \times Q)$ that accepts a tree t iff t has only one node labeled with an element of $\Sigma \times Q$ (say $t[u] = (\sigma, q)$) and P does not terminate on t', where t' is obtained from t by changing the label of u into σ. The automaton works as follows:

1. A first checks whether the input tree belongs to $L(\mathcal{D})$ (this requires a polynomial number of states in the size of A);

2. A checks whether there is exactly one node v with $t[v] \in \Sigma \times Q$; this only needs a constant number of states; in the rest of the computation A will check whether v is an attractor;

3. A checks whether v is q-reachable:

    (a) A starts at the root and memorizes state q_0;

    (b) suppose A arrives at a node u, if u is labeled with an element of $\Sigma \times Q$ (say (σ, q)) and A has memorized q, then goto (4) otherwise A determines which rule P should apply at u (note that A can do this without leaving u, it can use its string regular look-around to match unary patterns and negations of unary patterns: A guesses a rule checks whether the selection patterns matches at u and whether all rules of higher priority do not match); when A has determined which rule to apply it also knows which binary patterns have to be used to select the nodes that have to be processed next;

    (c) A non-deterministically picks one of these binary patterns, memorizes the associated state, non-deterministically runs to some node u' and checks whether it satisfies the binary pattern (for both up and down patterns this can be done while walking to u: no use of look-around is needed); go to (3b) with $u = u'$;

    This needs a number of states polynomial in the size of P.

4. Now A does the same starting from v and accepts if it returns again at v in state q. This needs a number of states polynomial in the size of P.

From Lemma 9 the result now follows. □

We next consider optimization of $\mathcal{DTL}^{\text{reg}}$ programs. A template rule r of a $\mathcal{DTL}$ program P is *useful* w.r.t. $\mathcal{D}$, when there exists a tree t in $L(\mathcal{D})$ such that P uses r at some node of t. A proof of the following proposition is similar to the proof of Theorem 8 (see also [9]).

Proposition 10. *Given a $\mathcal{DTL}^{\text{reg}}$ program P and a template rule r of P, deciding whether r is useful w.r.t. $\mathcal{D}$ is EXPTIME-complete.*

A template rule r of a $\mathcal{DTL}$ program P is *utterly useless* when no node of a tree in $L(\mathcal{D})$ matches the selection pattern of r.

Two unary patterns $p = u \cdot x \cdot d$ and $p' = u' \cdot x \cdot d'$ are *equivalent* w.r.t. $\mathcal{D}$ if for any tree $t \in L(\mathcal{D})$ and any node v of t: $(t, v) \in p$ iff $(t, v) \in p'$. If $L(\mathcal{D}) = T_\Sigma$, then p and p' are equivalent iff $L(u) = L(u')$ and $L(d) = L(d')$. This problem is known to be PSPACE-complete [22]. We show that it remains in PSPACE for arbitrary generalized DTDs. Two binary patterns p and p' are *equivalent* w.r.t. $\mathcal{D}$ if for any tree $t \in L(\mathcal{D})$ and any nodes v, v' of t: $(t, v, v') \in p$ iff $(t, v, v') \in p'$. We obtain:

Proposition 11. *1. Given a template rule r of P, it is decidable in PTIME whether or not r is utterly useless w.r.t. $\mathcal{D}$.*

2. Deciding whether or not two unary $\mathcal{DTL}^{\text{reg}}$ patterns are equivalent w.r.t. a generalized DTD is in PSPACE.

3. *Deciding whether or not two binary $\mathcal{DTL}^{\text{reg}}$ patterns are equivalent w.r.t. a generalized DTD is in* PSPACE.

Sketch of Proof: (1) Let $\mathcal{D}$ be a generalized DTD. Construct the non-deterministic finite-state automaton (NFA) $M^{\mathcal{D}}_{\text{branch}}$ with the following property can be constructed (details omitted): $w \in L(M^{\mathcal{D}}_{\text{branch}})$ if and only if there exists a tree $t \in L(\mathcal{D})$ such that w is a branch of t (i.e., w equals the sequence of symbols on a path from the root to a leaf). Moreover, the size of $M^{\mathcal{D}}_{\text{branch}}$ is polynomial in the size of $\mathcal{D}$ and $M^{\mathcal{D}}_{\text{branch}}$ can be constructed in time polynomial in the size of $\mathcal{D}$. For an NFA M define the language $M \leftarrow \# := \{w_1 \sigma \# \sigma w_2 \mid w_1 \sigma w_2 \in L(M)\}$. For two languages L and L', we denote by $L \# L'$ the language $\{w \sigma \# \sigma w' \mid w \sigma \in L, \sigma w' \in L'\}$. The pattern $p = u \cdot x \cdot d$ is utterly useless if $(M^{\mathcal{D}}_{\text{branch}} \leftarrow \#) \cap (L(u) \# L(d)) = \varnothing$. By standard techniques the latter can be shown to be in PTIME.

(2) Let $p = u \cdot x \cdot d$ and $p' = u' \cdot x \cdot d'$ be two unary patterns, and let $\mathcal{D}$ be a generalized DTD. They are equivalent with respect to $\mathcal{D}$ iff for every $w_1 \# w_2 \in M^{\mathcal{D}}_{\text{branch}} \leftarrow \#$, $w_1 \# w_2 \in L(u) \# L(d) \Leftrightarrow w_1 \# w_2 \in L(u') \# L(d')$. I.e., $L(u) \# L(d) \cap M^{\mathcal{D}}_{\text{branch}} \leftarrow \# = L(u') \# L(d') \cap M^{\mathcal{D}}_{\text{branch}} \leftarrow \#$. By standard techniques the latter can be shown to be in PSPACE.

(3) Let $p(x, y) \equiv x \cdot u \cdot d \cdot y$ and $p(x, y) \equiv x \cdot u' \cdot d' \cdot y$ be two binary patterns, and let $\mathcal{D}$ be a generalized DTD. For a tree t and $v, v' \in \text{Occ}(t)$ denote the set of common ancestors of v and v' by $\text{Anc}(v, v')$. Define the string language $\mathcal{D}_{\text{hook}}$ over $\Sigma \cup \{\#\}$ as $\{\text{path}(t, v, u) \# \text{path}(t, u, v') \mid t \in L(\mathcal{D}), v, v', u \in \text{Occ}(t), u \in \text{Anc}(v, v')\}$. Clearly, p and p' are equivalent with respect to $\mathcal{D}$ iff for every $w_1 \# w_2 \in \mathcal{D}_{\text{hook}}$, $w_1 \# w_2 \in L(u) \# L(d) \Leftrightarrow w_1 \# w_2 \in L(u') \# L(d')$.

It can be shown that $\mathcal{D}_{\text{hook}}$ is regular (details omitted). Moreover, the size of the NFA that accepts $\mathcal{D}_{\text{hook}}$ is polynomial in the size of $\mathcal{D}$ and can be constructed in time polynomial in the size of $\mathcal{D}$.

Now, p and p' are equivalent with respect to $\mathcal{D}$ iff $L(u) \# L(d) \cap \mathcal{D}_{\text{hook}} = L(u') \# L(d') \cap \mathcal{D}_{\text{hook}}$. By standard techniques the latter can be shown to be in PSPACE. $\square$

6 MSO as a Pattern Language for $\mathcal{DTL}$

We now consider a much more powerful instantiation of $\mathcal{DTL}$, where we use monadic second-order logic (MSO) formulas as a pattern language.

A tree $t \in \mathcal{T}_{\Sigma}$ can be viewed naturally as a finite relational structure (in the sense of mathematical logic [7]) over the binary relation symbols $\{E, <\}$ and the unary relation symbols $\{O_{\sigma} \mid \sigma \in \Sigma\}$. The domain of t, viewed as a structure, is the set of nodes of t. The edge relation E in t is the set of pairs (u, ui), where $u \in \text{Occ}(t)$ and $i \in [\text{rank}(t, u)]$. The relation $<$ in t is the set of pairs (ui, uj), where $u \in \text{Occ}(t)$, $i, j \in [\text{rank}(t, u)]$ and $i < j$. Finally, the set O_{σ} in t is the set of σ-labeled nodes of t. MSO allows the use of *set variables* ranging over sets of nodes of a tree, in addition to the individual variables ranging over the nodes themselves as provided by first-order logic (see, e.g., [7]). The satisfaction relation $\models$ is defined in the usual way.

Let $p = \varphi(x)$ and $p' = \varphi'(x, y)$, where φ and φ' are MSO formulas. Then for a tree s and nodes u and v:

- $(s, u) \in p$ iff $s \models \varphi[u]$; and
- $(s, u, v) \in p$ iff $s \models \varphi[u, v]$.

Denote the instantiation of $\mathcal{DTL}$ with MSO patterns by $\mathcal{DTL}^{mso}$. Clearly, any $\mathcal{DTL}^{reg}$ program can be simulated by a $\mathcal{DTL}^{mso}$ program.

7   Top-Down Document Transformations

In the remainder of this paper we study the natural fragment of $\mathcal{DTL}^{mso}$ that induces top-down transformations. Programs can, hence, no longer move up in the document and will always terminate.

Definition 12. A $\mathcal{DTL}^{mso}$ program $P = (\Sigma, \Delta, Q, q_0, R, \prec)$ belongs to $\mathcal{DTL}_d^{mso}$ if for every construction function f in a template rule in R, every $q \in Q$, and every input tree s with nodes u and v: if $(s, u, v) \in f(q)$, then $u \neq v$ and v is a descendant of u.

Note that $\mathcal{DTL}_d^{mso}$ is a decidable fragment of $\mathcal{DTL}^{mso}$.

7.1   A Computational Model

In this section we define top-down tree transducers with look-ahead which work over *unranked* trees (for short $\mathcal{TOP}^L$s). We first define the look-ahead which consists of forest regular languages as defined by Murata [18]:

Definition 13. A *non-deterministic bottom-up forest automaton* (NBFA) is a tuple $T = (Q, \Sigma, F, h)$, where Q is a finite set of states, Σ is an alphabet, $F \in \text{Reg}(Q)$, and h is a mapping $\Sigma \times Q \to \text{Reg}(Q)$. Define the semantics of T on a forest t inductively as follows: for $\sigma \in \Sigma$ and $n \geq 0$,

- $T(\sigma(t_1 \cdots t_n)) = \{q \mid q_1 \cdots q_n \in h(\sigma, q) \text{ and } q_i \in T(t_i) \text{ for } i \in [n]\}$,
- $T(t_1 \cdots t_n) = \{q_1 \ldots q_n \mid q_i \in T(t_i) \text{ for } i \in [n]\}$

A forest t is accepted by T if $T(t) \cap F \neq \varnothing$. A set of forests is *forest regular* if it is accepted by an NBFA.

Note that the forest regular languages are also obtained by adapting Definition 1 to forests, i.e., by simply dropping the condition on the start symbol.

For a tree t, we denote with $\hat{t}$ the tree obtained from t by replacing the root symbol $\sigma = t[\varepsilon]$ by $\hat{\sigma}$. A forest obtained from $t_1 \cdots t_n$ by changing a t_j into $\hat{t}_j$ for one $j \in [n]$ is a *pointed forest over* Σ. A *pointed forest regular language over* Σ, is a forest regular language of pointed forests over Σ. For a forest t and a node vj, we denote with $\text{point}(t, vj)$ the pointed forest $s_1 \cdots s_{j-1} \hat{s}_j s_{j+1} \cdots s_n$, where $s_i = t/vi$ for $i = 1, \ldots, n$; by convention $\text{point}(s, \varepsilon)$ denotes $\hat{s}$.

We now define $\mathcal{TOP}^L$s. The main difference to usual top-down tree transducers (over ranked trees) is the following. In the ranked case the right-hand side of a rule may contain (at leaves) recursive calls of the form $q(x_i)$, denoting the transformation of the ith subtree of the current node in state q. But i is unbounded in the case of unranked trees. Similar to (unranked) tree automata we use, instead of $q(x_i)$, regular string languages L over states (plus the special symbol 0). Intuitively, a string $w = q0q'$ in L means to process the first subtree of the current node in state q, *omit* the second, and process the third in state q' (i.e., the ith position $w(i)$ corresponds to x_i).

Definition 14. An *unranked top-down tree transducer M with look-ahead* is a tuple $(Q, \Sigma, \Delta, q_0, R)$, where Q is a finite set of *states*, Σ and Δ are alphabets of *input* and *output* symbols, respectively, $q_0 \in Q$ is the *initial state*, and R is a finite set of *rules* of the form $q(\sigma(\cdots)) \to \zeta \quad \langle F \rangle$, where ζ is in $\mathcal{F}_\Delta(\mathrm{Reg}(Q \cup \{0\}))$ and F is a pointed forest regular language over Σ; if $q = q_0$, then ζ is required to be a tree and $\zeta[\varepsilon] \notin \mathrm{Reg}(Q \cup \{0\})$.

For a forest $\zeta \in \mathcal{F}_\Delta(\mathrm{Reg}(Q \cup \{0\}))$ we denote by $\mathrm{ROcc}(\zeta)$ the set of all leaves of ζ which are labeled by elements in $\mathrm{Reg}(Q \cup \{0\})$, i.e., $\mathrm{ROcc}(\zeta) = \{\rho \in \mathrm{Occ}(\zeta) \mid \zeta[\rho] \in \mathrm{Reg}(Q \cup \{0\})\}$.

A rule r of the form $q(\sigma(\cdots)) \to \zeta \quad \langle F \rangle$ is called (q, σ)-rule, ζ is denoted by $\mathrm{rhs}(r)$ and F is denoted by F_r. For $q \in Q$, $\sigma \in \Sigma$, and $k \geq 0$ let $\mathrm{rins}_M(q, \sigma, k)$ denote the set of k-*instances of* (q, σ)-*rules*, that is, the set of all pairs (r, φ), where r is a (q, σ)-rule in R and φ is a mapping which assigns to every $\rho \in \mathrm{ROcc}(\mathrm{rhs}(r))$ a string of length k in the regular language $\mathrm{rhs}(r)[\rho]$. If for every $(r, \varphi_1), (r, \varphi_2) \in \mathrm{rins}_M(q, \sigma, k)$, $\varphi_1 = \varphi_2$, and for all distinct (q, σ)-rules r and r', $F_r \cap F_{r'} = \varnothing$, then M is *deterministic*. If not stated otherwise every $\mathcal{TOP}^L$ will be deterministic.

We are now ready to define the derivation relation realized by M. Intuitively, M starts processing in its initial state q_0 at the root node ε of the input tree s. This is denoted by $q_0(\varepsilon)$. Now a (q_0, σ) rule r of M can be applied, where $\sigma = s[\varepsilon]$ and $\mathrm{point}(s, \varepsilon) = \hat{s} \in F_r$. This means to replace $q_0(\varepsilon)$ by the right-hand side of r and to replace in r every regular language by the correct string of state calls (by "state call" we mean trees of the form $q(i)$). The latter is done by choosing with r a mapping φ such that $(r, \varphi) \in \mathrm{rins}_M(q_0, \sigma, k)$ (for deterministic $\mathcal{TOP}^L$s there is at most one such φ for each r), where k is the rank of the root of s.

Recall that for an occurrence $\rho \in \mathrm{ROcc}(\mathrm{rhs}(r))$, $\varphi(\rho)$ is a string w of length k over Q and 0, and that $w(i)$ denotes the i-th letter of w. For a string w, $w[s_1 \cdots s_k]$ denotes the forest $w(1)(s_1) \cdots w(k)(s_k)$, where $0(t) = \varepsilon$ for all trees t. Formally, the *derivation relation realized by M on s*, denoted by $\Rightarrow_{M,s}$, is the binary relation on $\mathcal{T}_{Q \cup \Delta}(\mathrm{Occ}(s))$ defined as follows. For $\xi, \xi' \in \mathcal{T}_{Q \cup \Delta}(\mathrm{Occ}(s))$, $\xi \Rightarrow \xi'$ iff there is an occurrence $u \in \mathrm{Occ}(\xi)$ such that

1. $\xi/u = q(v)$ with $q \in Q$ and $v \in \mathrm{Occ}(s)$,
2. there is a $(r, \varphi) \in \mathrm{rins}_M(q, \sigma, k)$, where $k = \mathrm{rank}(s, v)$ such that $\mathrm{point}(s, v) \in F_r$, $\xi' = \xi[u \leftarrow \zeta]$, and $\zeta = \mathrm{rhs}(r)[\rho \leftarrow \varphi(\rho)[v1 \cdots vk] \mid \rho \in \mathrm{ROcc}(\mathrm{rhs}(r))]$.

The *transformation realized by M*, denoted τ_M, is $\{(s, t) \in \mathcal{T}_\Sigma \times \mathcal{T}_\Delta \mid q_0(\varepsilon) \Rightarrow^*_M t\}$.

Example 15. Recall the $\mathcal{DTL}_d^{mso}$ program from Example 7. Now consider the $\mathcal{TOP}^L$ M consisting of the states q_0, q and of the following two rules.[5]

$$q_0(\sigma(\cdots)) \rightarrow \sigma(q^*) \qquad \langle F \rangle$$
$$q(\sigma(\cdots)) \rightarrow \sigma(q^*)\,q^* \qquad \langle F \rangle,$$

where F is the set of all pointed forests. Again consider the input tree $s = \sigma(\sigma(\sigma(\sigma)))$. In Figure 6 the corresponding derivation by M is shown. Note

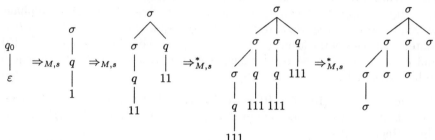

Fig. 6. Derivation of M on the input tree $s = \sigma(\sigma(\sigma(\sigma)))$

that M realizes the same transformation as P, even though the trees in the derivation of M are different from those of P. While in the $\mathcal{DTL}_d^{mso}$ program P one single pattern can select all descendants, the transducer M has to select these patterns while it moves top-down symbol by symbol through the input tree.

We obtain the following equivalence (proof omitted):

Theorem 16. *The transformations defined by $\mathcal{DTL}_d^{mso}$ programs are exactly those computed by deterministic $\mathcal{TOP}^L$s.*

The above Theorem states that $\mathcal{TOP}^L$s can be used as a natural implementation model for $\mathcal{DTL}_d^{mso}$. We next refine this result by showing that the look-ahead can be dispensed with.

Theorem 17. *Every $\mathcal{DTL}_d^{mso}$ program can be implemented by a bottom-up relabeling followed by a deterministic $\mathcal{TOP}^L$ without look-ahead.*

Essentially, the look-ahead information needed at each node is encoded by a bottom-up relabeling into the label of each node (proof omitted). A bottom-up relabeling is obtained from an NBFA A by simply relabeling every node u by the state of A that processes u.

7.2   Ranges

The *range* of a $\mathcal{DTL}_d^{mso}$ program P is defined as $\tau_P(\mathcal{T}_\Sigma) := \{t \mid \exists s \in \mathcal{T}_\Sigma : (s,t) \in \tau_P\}$ and can in general not be described by a generalized DTD. Consider, e.g.,

---

[5] Here, we denote regular languages by regular expressions.

the $\mathcal{DTL}_d^{\mathrm{mso}}$ program P_{copy} which takes as input XML documents consisting of a list $\mathrm{list}(a_{i_1} \cdots a_{i_n})$ of items $a_1, \ldots, a_k$ only; P_{copy} should transform this list into two lists consisting of the serial numbers and prices of $a_1, \ldots, a_k$, respectively. Thus, $s = \mathrm{list}(a_{i_1} \cdots a_{i_n})$ should be transformed into $t = \mathrm{out}(\mathrm{list}(b_{i_1} \cdots b_{i_n})$ $\mathrm{list}(p_{i_1} \cdots p_{i_n}))$, where the b_i are the corresponding numbers, and p_i the prices. The program P_{copy} has the rules: $r_1 = (q_0, \mathrm{root}(x), \mathrm{list}(f_1, f_2))$, where $\mathrm{root}(x)$ denotes the MSO formula which is true iff x is the root node and f_1 maps $q_\#$ to the MSO formula $E(x, y)$ (and the other states to $false$) and f_2 maps q_p to $E(x, y)$ (and the other states to $false$). Then for $q_\#$ and q_p there are rules $r_2 = (q_\#, O_{a_i}(x), b_i)$ and $r_3 = (q_p, O_{a_i}(x), p_i)$ for $i \in [k]$. Now, s is transformed by P_{copy} into t. Clearly, the range $\tau_{P_{\mathrm{copy}}}(\mathcal{T}_\Sigma)$ of P_{copy} cannot be generated by a generalized DTD, because the string of leaf labels from left to right is a non context-free string language (for $p_i = b_i$ it is $\{ww \mid w \in \{b_1, \ldots, b_n\}^*\}$).

We show, however, that the output of a $\mathcal{DTL}_d^{\mathrm{mso}}$ program can always be restricted to a (generalized) DTD. Similar results are known for ranked top-down tree transducers [24,8].

It follows from Theorem 16 and results of Fülöp [14], that it is even undecidable whether the output schema of a $\mathcal{DTL}_d^{\mathrm{mso}}$ (or even a $\mathcal{DTL}^{\mathrm{reg}}$) program can be described by a (generalized) DTD. We now exhibit some relevant optimization problems that are decidable: it is decidable whether or not the range of a $\mathcal{DTL}_d^{\mathrm{mso}}$ program is empty or finite.

Theorem 18. *The class of output languages of $\mathcal{DTL}_d^{\mathrm{mso}}$ programs is (1) closed under intersection with generalized DTD's and (2) has a decidable emptiness and finiteness problem.*

Sketch of Proof: The proof of (1) is left out; it is based on closure of extended DTDs under intersection and the fact that inverses of macro tree transducers (working on binary encodings of unranked trees) preserve regular tree languages (Theorem 7.4(1) of [13]). (2) It is well known that unranked forests can be coded by binary trees (see, e.g., [20]). Figure 7 shows the forest $t = \sigma(a_1 a_2(b_1 b_2) a_3) \delta(a_4)$ and its binary encoding $\mathrm{enc}(t)$. Here, the edges are labeled for clarity: γ-edges indicate the edges between nodes, while $<$-edges indicate the ordering of siblings. Intuitively, for every unranked forest s the first child of a node u in its encoding $\mathrm{enc}(s)$ is the first child of the corresponding node v in s (viz. a γ-edge), and the second child of u in $\mathrm{enc}(s)$ is the right sibling of v in s (viz. a $<$-edge). For technical reasons we only use binary labels in the encodings, plus the constant symbol nil. We will now show how to simulate a $\mathcal{TOP}^L$ M by a tree transducer N which works on the binary encodings, i.e., $\mathrm{enc}^{-1} \circ N \circ \mathrm{enc} = \tau_M$. Clearly, the range of M is finite (empty) iff the output language of N is finite (empty). Let us now discuss the tree transducer N. A (usual) top-down tree transducer over ranked trees is not sufficient, because in order to simulate a rule with right-hand side of the form $L_1 \cdots L_n$ with $L_i \in \mathrm{Reg}(Q \cup \{0\})$, the binary version must generate the translations of the L_i "on top" of each other, i.e., the corresponding root nodes are (rightmost) descendants of each other.

There is a tree transducer model which can simulate this kind of behaviour by the additional use of *parameters*: the *macro tree transducer* (with look-ahead)

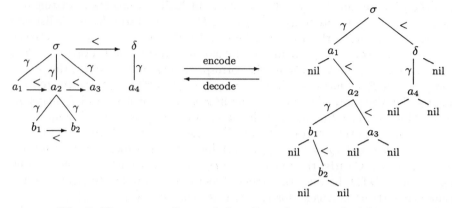

Fig. 7. Binary encoding and decoding of an unranked forest

(MTT) [13,10]. The idea is that for every regular language L in the right-hand side of a rule of M the MTT N has a state q_L which simulates this language. It must do this on descendants of the form $u12^*$. Each state (besides q_0) is of rank two which means that it has two parameters y_1 and y_2. An occurrence of $\langle q_L, x_i \rangle (t_1, t_2)$ in the right-hand side of an MTT means that q_L should process the ith son of the current node with t_1, t_2 as y_1, y_2, respectively (cf. [10]). By look-ahead (and the states of N) we can determine which state q of M should translate the current node. Thus, the right-hand side of a (q_L, σ)-rule with look-ahead q (on the rightmost input subtree) is obtained from the encoding of the right-hand side ζ of the (q, σ)-rule of M by replacing each regular language L' (which appears as $L'(\text{nil}, \text{nil})$ in $\text{enc}(\zeta)$) by $\langle q_{L'}, x_1 \rangle$. Additionally, replace the rightmost nil-labeled leaf by $\langle q_L, x_2 \rangle (\text{nil}, y_2)$.

If, e.g., $\zeta = L_1 \cdots L_n$, then we get for N a right-hand side of the form

$$\langle q_{L_1}, x_1 \rangle (\text{nil}, \langle q_{L_2}, x_1 \rangle (\text{nil}, \dots \langle q_{L_n}, x_1 \rangle (\text{nil}, \langle q_L, x_2 \rangle (\text{nil}, y_2)))).$$

Finally, since the first son of a state is always nil, we need rules $\langle q_L, \text{nil} \rangle (y_1, y_2) \to y_2$. The formal construction is straightforward. Then decidability of emptiness and finiteness follows from Lemma 3.14 and Theorem 4.5 of [6], respectively. □

7.3 Safe Transformations

We now define a dynamic restriction on $\mathcal{DTL}_d^{\text{mso}}$ programs that allows copying but nevertheless induces transformations of only linear size increase. We bound the number of times that any node u of an input tree s may be selected during the transformation of s. If k is such a bound (*copying bound*), then clearly the size of an output tree is bounded by $k \cdot \rho$ times the size of the input tree, where ρ is the size of the largest right-hand side. Hence, we get a linear size increase. A $\mathcal{DTL}_d^{\text{mso}}$ program for which there exists such a bound k is called *safe*. In terms of tree transducers this is the natural notion of *finite copying* (cf. [12]).

Consider the $\mathcal{DTL}_d^{\mathrm{mso}}$ program P_{copy} discussed in Section 7.2. Clearly P_{copy} is safe: it has copying bound 2. The program P of Example 7 is *not* safe: The leaf of the monadic input tree of height n is transformed 2^{n-1} times, i.e., there is no copying bound for P.

We note now, without proof, that safeness of $\mathcal{DTL}_d^{\mathrm{mso}}$ programs is decidable. The proof uses Theorem 18(2) and is similar to the proof of Lemma 3 in [11].

Theorem 19. *Safeness of $\mathcal{DTL}_d^{\mathrm{mso}}$ programs is decidable.*

Acknowledgment

We thank Joost Engelfriet and Jan Van den Bussche for many helpful comments on an earlier version of this paper. The second author thanks Geert Jan Bex for enlightening discussions on XML and XSL.

References

1. S. Abiteboul. On views and XML. In *Proceedings of the 18th ACM Symposium on Principles of Database Systems*, pages 1–9. ACM Press, 1999.
2. A. Bosworth. A proposal for an XSL query language. http://www.w3.org/TandS/QL/QL98/pp/microsoft-extensions.html.
3. A. Brüggemann-Klein, M. Murata, and D. Wood. Regular tree languages over non-ranked alphabets (draft 1). Manuscript, 1998.
4. J. Clark and S. Deach. Extensible stylesheet language (XSL). http://www.w3.org/TR/WD-xsl.
5. World Wide Web Consortium. Extensible Markup Language (XML). http://www.w3.org/XML/.
6. Frank Drewes and Joost Engelfriet. Decidability of finiteness of ranges of tree transductions. *Inform. and Comput.*, 145:1–50, 1998.
7. H.-D. Ebbinghaus and J. Flum. *Finite Model Theory*. Springer, 1995.
8. J. Engelfriet. Bottom-up and top-down tree transformations — a comparison. *Math. Systems Theory*, 9(3):198–231, 1975.
9. J. Engelfriet and G. Filè. Passes and paths of attribute grammars. *Inform. and Control*, 49:125–169, 1981.
10. J. Engelfriet and S. Maneth. Macro tree transducers, attribute grammars, and MSO definable tree translations. *Inform. and Comput.*, 154:34–91, 1999.
11. J. Engelfriet and S. Maneth. Characterizing and Deciding MSO-definability of Macro Tree Transductions. To appear in *Proc. STACS'00*.
12. J. Engelfriet, G. Rozenberg, and G. Slutzki. Tree transducers, L systems, and two-way machines. *J. of Comp. Syst. Sci.*, 20:150–202, 1980.
13. J. Engelfriet and H. Vogler. Macro tree transducers. *J. of Comp. Syst. Sci.*, 31:71–146, 1985.
14. Z. Fülöp. Undecidable properties of deterministic top-down tree transducers. *Theoret. Comput. Sci.*, 134:311–328, 1994.
15. M. Jazayeri, W. F. Ogden, and W. C. Rounds. The intrinsically exponential complexity of the circularity problem for attribute grammars. *Comm. ACM*, 18:697–706, 1975.

16. B. Ludäscher, Y.Papakonstantinou, P. Velikhov, and V. Vianu. View definition and DTD inference for XML. In *Proceedings of the Workshop on Query Processing for Semistructured Data and Non-Standard Data Formats*, 1999.
17. S. Maneth. The generating power of total deterministic tree transducers. *Inform. and Comput.*, 147:111–144, 1998.
18. M. Murata. Forest-regular languages and tree-regular languages. Manuscript, 1995.
19. F. Neven and T. Schwentick. Query automata. In *Proceedings of the 18th ACM Symposium on Principles of Database Systems*, pages 205–214. ACM Press, 1999.
20. C. Pair and A. Quere. Définition et etude des bilangages réguliers. *Information and Control*, 13(6):565–593, 1968.
21. Y. Papakonstantinou and V. Vianu. DTD Inference for Views of XML Data. To appear in *Proc. PODS'2000*. ACM Press, 2000.
22. L. J. Stockmeyer and A. R. Meyer. Word problems requiring exponential time: Preliminary report. In *Proc. STOC'73*, pages 1-9, 1973.
23. D. Suciu. Semistructured data and XML. In *Proceedings of International Conference on Foundations of Data Organization*, 1998.
24. J. W. Thatcher. Generalized^2 sequential machine maps. *J. of Comp. Syst. Sci.*, 4:339–367, 1970.

Extensions of Attribute Grammars for Structured Document Queries

Frank Neven*

Limburgs Universitair Centrum, Universitaire Campus, Dept. WNI, Infolab,
B-3590 Diepenbeek, Belgium
frank.neven@luc.ac.be

Abstract. Document specification languages like XML, model documents using extended context-free grammars. These differ from standard context-free grammars in that they allow arbitrary regular expressions on the right-hand side of productions. To query such documents, we introduce a new form of attribute grammars (extended AGs) that work directly over extended context-free grammars rather than over standard context-free grammars. Viewed as a query language, extended AGs are particularly relevant as they can take into account the inherent order of the children of a node in a document. We show that two key properties of standard attribute grammars carry over to extended AGs: efficiency of evaluation and decidability of well-definedness. We further characterize the expressiveness of extended AGs in terms of monadic second-order logic and establish the complexity of their non-emptiness and equivalence problem to be complete for EXPTIME. As an application we show that the Region Algebra expressions can be efficiently translated into extended AGs. This translation drastically improves the known upper bound on the complexity of the emptiness and equivalence test for Region Algebra expressions.

1 Introduction

Structured document databases can be seen as derivation trees of some grammar which functions as the "schema" of the database [2,4,19,20,22,32,36]. Document specification languages like, e.g., XML [12], model documents using *extended* context-free grammars. Extended context-free grammars (ECFG) are context-free grammars (CFG) having regular expressions over grammar symbols on the right-hand side of productions. It is known that ECFGs generate the same class of string languages as CFGs. Hence, from a formal language point of view, ECFGs are nothing but shorthands for CFGs. However, when grammars are used to model documents, i.e., when also the derivation trees are taken into consideration, the difference between CFGs and ECFGs becomes apparent. Indeed, compare Figure 1 and Figure 2. They both model a list of poems, but the CFG needs the extra non-terminals PoemList, VerseList, WordList, and LetterList to

---

* Research Assistant of the Fund for Scientific Research, Flanders.

R. Connor and A. Mendelzon (Eds.): DBPL'99, LNCS 1949, pp. 99–116, 2000.

allow for an arbitrary number of poems, verses, words, and letters. These non-terminals, however, have no meaning at the level of the logical specification of the document.

A crucial difference between derivation trees of CFGs and derivation trees of ECFGs is that the former are ranked while the latter are not. In other words, nodes in a derivation tree of an ECFG need not have a fixed maximal number of children. While ranked trees have been studied in depth [17,38], unranked trees only recently received new attention in the context of SGML and XML. Based on work of Pair and Quere [33] and Takahashi [37], Murata defined a bottom-up automaton model for unranked trees [26]. This required describing transition functions for an arbitrary number of children. Murata's approach is the following: a node is assigned a state by checking the sequence of states assigned to its children for membership in a regular language. In this way, the "infinite" transition function is represented in a finite way. We will extend this idea to attribute grammars. Brüggemann-Klein, Murata and Wood initiated an extensive study of tree automata over unranked trees [9].

The classical formalism of *attribute grammars*, introduced by Knuth [25], has always been a prominent framework for expressing computations on derivation trees. Therefore, in previous work, we investigated attribute grammars as a query language for derivation trees of CFGs [28,31,32]. Attribute grammars provide a mechanism for annotating the nodes of a tree with so-called "attributes", by means of so-called "semantic rules" which can work either bottom-up (for so-called "synthesized" attribute values) or top-down (for so-called "inherited" attribute values). Attribute grammars are applied in such diverse fields of computer science as compiler construction and software engineering (for a survey, see [14]).

Inspired by the idea of representing transition functions for automata on unranked trees as regular string languages, we introduce extended attribute grammars (extended AGs) that work directly over ECFGs rather than over standard CFGs. The main difficulty in achieving this is that the right-hand sides of productions contain regular expressions that, in general, specify infinite string languages. This gives rise to two problems for the definition of extended AGs that are not present for standard AGs:

(i) in a production, there may be an unbounded number of grammar symbols for which attributes should be defined; and

(ii) the definition of an attribute should take into account that the number of attributes it depends on may be unbounded.

We resolve these problems in the following way. For (i), we only consider unambiguous regular expressions in the right-hand sides of productions.[1] This means that every child of a node derived by the production $p = X \to r$ corresponds to exactly one position in r. We then define attributes uniformly for every position

---

[1] This is no loss of generality, as any regular language can be denoted by an unambiguous regular expression [7]. SGML is even more restrictive as it allows only *one*-unambiguous regular languages [8].

$$DB \rightarrow PoemList$$
$$PoemList \rightarrow Poem \ PoemList$$
$$PoemList \rightarrow Poem$$
$$Poem \rightarrow VerseList$$
$$VerseList \rightarrow Verse \ VerseList$$
$$VerseList \rightarrow Verse$$
$$Verse \rightarrow WordList$$
$$WordList \rightarrow Word \ WordList$$
$$WordList \rightarrow Word$$
$$Word \rightarrow LetterList$$
$$LetterList \rightarrow Letter \ LetterList$$
$$LetterList \rightarrow Letter$$
$$Letter \rightarrow a \mid \ldots \mid z$$

Fig. 1. A CFG modeling a list of poems

$$DB \rightarrow Poem^{+}$$
$$Poem \rightarrow Verse^{+}$$
$$Verse \rightarrow Word^{+}$$
$$Word \rightarrow (a + \cdots + z)^{+}$$

Fig. 2. An ECFG modeling a list of poems

in r and for the left-hand side of p. For (ii), we only allow a finite set D as the semantic domain of the attributes and we represent semantic rules as regular languages over D much in the same way tree automata over unranked trees are defined.

By carefully tailoring the semantics of inherited attributes, extended AGs can take into account the inherent order of the children of a node in a document. This makes extended AGs particularly relevant as a query language. Indeed, as argued by Suciu [36], achieving this capability is one of the major challenges when applying the techniques developed for semi-structured data [1] to XML-documents.

An important subclass of queries in the context of structured document databases, are the queries that select those subtrees in a document that satisfy a certain pattern [3,23,24,27]. These are essentially unary queries: they map a document to a set of its nodes. Extended AGs are especially tailored to express such unary queries: the result of an extended AG consists of those nodes for which the value of a designated attribute equals 1.[2]

The contributions of this paper can be summarized as follows:

1. We introduce extended attribute grammars as a query language for structured document databases defined by ECFGs. Queries in this query language can be evaluated in time quadratic in the number of nodes of the

---

[2] We always assume that D contains the values 0 and 1 (*false* and *true*).

tree. We show that non-circularity, the property that an attribute grammar is well-defined for every tree, is in EXPTIME. The latter is also a lower bound since deciding non-circularity for standard attribute grammar is already known to be hard for EXPTIME [25,21].

2. We generalize our earlier results on standard attribute grammars [5,32] by showing that extended AGs express precisely the unary queries definable in monadic second-order logic (MSO).

3. We establish the EXPTIME-completeness of the non-emptiness (given an extended AG, does there exist a tree of which a node is selected by this extended AG?) and of the equivalence problem of extended AGs.

4. We show that Region Algebra expressions (introduced by Consens and Milo [11]) can be simulated by extended AGs. Stated as such, the result is not surprising, since the former essentially corresponds to a fragment of first-order logic over trees while the latter corresponds to full MSO. We, however, exhibit an *efficient* translation, which gives rise to a drastic improvement on the complexity of the equivalence problem of Region Algebra expressions. To be precise, Consens and Milo first translate each Region Algebra expression into an equivalent first-order logic formula on trees and then invoke the known algorithm testing decidability of such formulas. Unfortunately, the latter algorithm has non-elementary complexity. That is, the complexity of this algorithm cannot be bounded by an elementary function (i.e., an iterated exponential $2^{\hat{}}(2^{\hat{}} \ldots (2^n))$) where n is the size of the input). This approach therefore conceals the real complexity of the equivalence test of Region Algebra expressions. Our efficient translation of Region Algebra expressions into extended AGs, however, gives an EXPTIME algorithm. The thus obtained upper bound more closely matches the coNP lower bound [11].

This paper is further organized as follows. In Section 2, we recall some basic definitions. In Section 3, we give an example introducing the important ideas for the definition of extended AGs introduced in Section 4. In Section 5, we obtain the exact complexity of the non-circularity test for extended AGs. In Section 6, we characterize the expressiveness of extended AGs in terms of monadic second-order logic. In Section 7, we establish the exact complexity of the emptiness and equivalence problem of extended AGs. We then use this result to improve the complexity of the emptiness and equivalence problem of Region Algebra expressions in Section 8. We present some concluding remarks in Section 9.

Due to space limitations, most proofs are omitted. They can be found in the author's Phd thesis [29].

2   Preliminaries

Let $\mathbf{N}$ denote the set of natural numbers. For a finite set S, we denote by $|S|$ the cardinality of S. For integers i and j, we denote by $[i,j]$ the set $\{i,\ldots,j\}$. In the following, Σ is a finite alphabet. If $w = a_1 \cdots a_n$ is a string over Σ then we denote a_i by $w(i)$ for $i \in \{1,\ldots,n\}$. We denote the length of w by $|w|$.

For a regular expression r over Σ, we denote by $L(r)$ the language defined by r and by $\text{Sym}(r)$ the set of Σ-symbols occurring in r. The *marking* $\tilde{r}$ of r is obtained by subscribing in r the first occurrence of a symbol of $\text{Sym}(r)$ by 1, the second by 2, and so on. For example, $a_1(a_2+b_3^*)^*a_4$ is the marking of $a(a+b^*)^*a$. We let $|r|$ denote the number of occurrences of Σ-symbols in r, while $r(i)$ denotes the Σ-symbol at the ith occurrence in r. Let $\widetilde{\Sigma}$ be the alphabet obtained from Σ by subscribing every symbol by all natural numbers, i.e., $\widetilde{\Sigma} := \{a_i \mid a \in \Sigma, i \in \mathbf{N}\}$. If $w \in \widetilde{\Sigma}^*$ then $w^{\#}$ denotes the string obtained from w by dropping the subscripts.

In the definition of extended AGs we shall restrict ourselves to unambiguous regular expressions defined as follows:

Definition 1. A regular expression r over Σ is *unambiguous* if for all $v, w \in L(\tilde{r})$, $v^{\#} = w^{\#}$ implies $v = w$.

That is, a regular expression r is unambiguous if every string in $L(r)$ can be matched to r in only one way. For example, the regular expression $(a + b)^*$ is unambiguous while $(aa + a)^*$ is not. Indeed, it is easily checked that the string aa can be matched to $(aa + a)^*$ in two different ways.

The following proposition, obtained by Book et al. [7], says that the restriction to unambiguous regular expressions is no loss of generality.

Proposition 2. *For every regular language R there exists an unambiguous regular expression r such that $L(r) = R$.*

If w is a string and r is an unambiguous regular expression with $w \in L(r)$, then $\tilde{w}_r$ denotes the unique string over $\widetilde{\Sigma}$ such that $\tilde{w}_r^{\#} = w$ and $\tilde{w}_r \in L(\tilde{r})$. For $i = 1, \ldots, |w|$, define $\text{pos}_r(i, w)$ as the subscript of the ith letter in $\tilde{w}_r$. Intuitively, $\text{pos}_r(i, w)$ indicates the position in r matching the ith letter of w. For example, if $r = a(b + a)^*$ and $w = abba$, then $\tilde{r} = a_1(b_2 + a_3)^*$ and $\tilde{w}_r = a_1b_2b_2a_3$. Hence,

$$\text{pos}_r(1, w) = 1, \quad \text{pos}_r(2, w) = 2, \quad \text{pos}_r(3, w) = 2, \text{ and } \text{pos}_r(4, w) = 3.$$

In the sequel, when we say *regular expression*, we always mean *unambiguous* regular expression.

Extended AGs are defined over extended context-free grammars which are defined as follows. An *extended context-free grammar* (ECFG) is a tuple $G = (N, T, P, U)$, where T and N are disjoint finite non-empty sets, called the set of *terminals* and *non-terminals*, respectively; $U \in N$ is the *start symbol*; and P is a set of *productions* consisting of rules of the form $X \to r$ where $X \in N$ and r is a regular expression over $N \cup T$ such that $\varepsilon \notin L(r)$ and $L(r) \neq \emptyset$. Additionally, if $X \to r_1$ and $X \to r_2$ belong to P then $L(r_1) \cap L(r_2) \neq \emptyset$.

A *derivation tree* $\mathbf{t}$ over an ECFG G is a tree labelled with symbols from $N \cup T$ such that the root of $\mathbf{t}$ is labelled with U; for every interior node $\mathbf{n}$ with children $\mathbf{n}_1, \ldots, \mathbf{n}_m$ there exists a production $X \to r$ such that $\mathbf{n}$ is labelled with X, for $i = 1, \ldots, m$, $\mathbf{n}_i$ is labelled with X_i, and $X_1 \cdots X_m \in L(r)$; we say that $\mathbf{n}$ is *derived* by $X \to r$; and every leaf node is labelled with a terminal. We denote by $\text{root}(\mathbf{t})$ the root node of $\mathbf{t}$.

Note that derivation trees of ECFGs are *unranked* in the sense that the number of children of a node need not be bounded by any constant and does not depend on the label of that node.

Throughout the paper we make the harmless technical assumption that the start symbol does not occur on the right-hand side of a production.

3 Example

We give a small example introducing the important ideas for the definition of extended attribute grammars in the next section.

First, we briefly illustrate the mechanism of attribute grammars by giving an example of a Boolean valued standard attribute grammar (BAG). The latter are studied by Neven and Van den Bussche [28,31,32]. As mentioned in the introduction, attribute grammars provide a mechanism for annotating the nodes of a tree with so-called "attributes", by means of so-called "semantic rules". A BAG assigns Boolean values by means of propositional logic formulas to attributes of nodes of input trees. Consider the CFG consisting of the productions $U \to AA$, $A \to a$, and $A \to b$. The following BAG selects the first A whenever the first A is expanded to an a and the second A is expanded to a b:

$$
\begin{aligned}
U \to AA & \quad select(1) := is\_a(1) \wedge \neg is\_a(2); \\
A \to a & \quad is\_a(0) := true \\
A \to b & \quad is\_a(0) := false
\end{aligned}
$$

Here, the 1 in $select(1)$ indicates that the attribute $select$ of the first A is being defined. Moreover, this attribute is true whenever the first A is expanded to an a (that is, $is\_a(1)$ should be true) and the second A is expanded to a b (that is, $is\_a(2)$ should be false). The following rules then define the attribute is_a in the obvious way. In the above, 0 refers to the left-hand side of the rule.

Consider the ECFG consisting of the sole rule $U \to (A + B)^*$. We now want to construct an attribute grammar selecting those A's that are preceded by an even number of A's and succeeded by an odd number of B's. Like above we will use rules defining the attribute $select$. This gives rise to two problems not present for BAGs : (i) U can have an unbounded number of children labelled with A which implies that an unbounded number of attributes should be defined; (ii) the definition of an attribute of an A depends on its siblings, whose number is again unbounded.

We resolve this in the following way. For (i), we just define $select$ uniformly for each node that corresponds to the first position in the regular expression $(A + B)^*$. For (ii), we use regular languages as semantic rules rather than propositional formulas. The following extended AG now expresses the above query:

$$
\begin{aligned}
U \to (A + B)^* \quad select(1) := \langle \sigma_1 = lab, \sigma_2 = lab; \\
R_{true} = (B^* AB^* AB^*)^* \# A^* BA^* (A^* BA^* BA^*)^*, \\
R_{false} = (A + B + \#)^* - R_{true} \rangle.
\end{aligned}
$$

The 1 in $select(1)$ indicates that the attribute $select$ is defined uniformly for every node corresponding to the first position in $(A + B)^*$. In the first part of the semantic rule, each σ_i lists the attributes of position i that will be used. Here, both for position 1 and 2 this is only the attribute lab which is a special attribute containing the label of the node. Consider the input tree $U(AAABBB)$. Then, to check, for instance, whether the third A is selected we enumerate the attributes mentioned in the first part of the rule and insert the symbol $\#$ before the node under consideration. This gives us the string

$$
\begin{array}{cccccc}
1 & 1 & 1 & 2 & 2 & 2 \\
\mathbf{A} & \mathbf{A} & \#\mathbf{A} & \mathbf{B} & \mathbf{B} & \mathbf{B} \\
1 & 2 & 3 & 4 & 5 & 6
\end{array}
$$

$\qquad$ position in $(A + B)^*$

$\qquad$ position in $AAABBB$

The attribute $select$ of the third child will be assigned the value $true$ since the above string belongs to R_{true}. Note that

$$(B^*AB^*AB^*)^* \text{ and } A^*BA^*(A^*BA^*BA^*)^*$$

define the set of strings with an even number of A's and with an odd number of B's, respectively. The above will be defined formally in the next section.

4   Attribute Grammars over Extended Context-Free Grammars

In this section we define extended attribute grammars (extended AGs) over ECFGs whose attributes can take only values from a finite set D. Hence, we leave the framework of only Booleans as attribute values. Nevertheless, we still have the equivalence with MSO as is shown in the next section.

Unless explicitly stated otherwise, we always assume an ECFG $G = (N, T, P, U)$. When we say tree we always mean derivation tree of G.

Definition 3. An *attribute grammar vocabulary* is a tuple $(D, A, \mathrm{Syn}, \mathrm{Inh})$, where

- D is a finite set of values called the *semantic domain*. We assume that D always contains the Boolean values 0 and 1;
- A is a finite set of symbols called *attributes*; we always assume that A contains the attribute lab;
- Syn and Inh are functions from $N \cup T$ to the powerset of $A - \{lab\}$ such that for every $X \in N$, $\mathrm{Syn}(X) \cap \mathrm{Inh}(X) = \emptyset$; for every $X \in T$, $\mathrm{Syn}(X) = \emptyset$; and $\mathrm{Inh}(U) = \emptyset$.

If $a \in \mathrm{Syn}(X)$, we say that a is a *synthesized attribute of* X. If $a \in \mathrm{Inh}(X)$, we say that a is an *inherited attribute of* X. We also agree that lab is an attribute of every X (this is a predefined attribute; for each node its value will be the label of that node). The above conditions express that an attribute cannot be a synthesized and an inherited attribute of the same grammar symbol, that terminal symbols do not have synthesized attributes, and that the start symbol does not have inherited attributes.

We now formally define the semantic rules of extended AGs. For a production $p = X \rightarrow r$, define $p(0) = X$, and for $i \in [1, |r|]$, define $p(i) = r(i)$. We fix some attribute grammar vocabulary $(A, D, \text{Syn}, \text{Inh})$ in the following definitions.

Definition 4.   1. Let $p = X \rightarrow r$ be a production of G and let a be an attribute of $p(i)$ for some $i \in [0, |r|]$. The triple (p, a, i) is called a *context* if $a \in \text{Syn}(p(i))$ implies $i = 0$, and $a \in \text{Inh}(p(i))$ implies $i > 0$.

2. A *rule in the context* (p, a, i) is an expression of the form

$$a(i) := \langle \sigma_0, \ldots, \sigma_{|r|}; (R_d)_{d \in D} \rangle,$$

where
- for $j = [0, |r|]$, σ_j is a sequence of attributes of $p(j)$;
- if $i = 0$ then, for each $d \in D$, R_d is a regular language over the alphabet D; and
- if $i > 0$ then, for each $d \in D$, R_d is a regular language over the alphabet $D \cup \{\#\}$.

For all $d, d' \in D$, if $d \neq d'$ then $R_d \cap R_{d'} = \emptyset$. Further, if $i = 0$ then $\bigcup_{d \in D} R_d = D^*$. If $i > 0$ then $\bigcup_{d \in D} R_d$ should contain all strings over D with exactly one occurrence of the symbol $\#$. Note that a R_d is allowed to contain strings with several occurrences of $\#$. We always assume that $\# \notin D$.

An extended AG is then defined as follows:

Definition 5. An *extended attribute grammar (extended AG)* $\mathcal{F}$ consists of an attribute grammar vocabulary, together with a mapping assigning to each context a rule in that context.

It will always be understood which rule is associated to which context. We illustrate the above definitions with an example.

Example 6. In Figure 3 an example of an extended AG $\mathcal{F}$ is depicted over the ECFG of Figure 2. Recall that every grammar symbol has the attribute *lab*; for each node this attribute has the label of that node as value. We have $\text{Syn}(\text{Word}) = \{king, lord\}$, $\text{Syn}(\text{Verse}) = \{king\_lord\}$, $\text{Syn}(\text{Poem}) = \{result\}$, and $\text{Inh}(\text{Poem}) = \{first\}$. The grammar symbols DB, a, ..., z, Verse, and Word have no attributes apart from *lab*. The semantics of this extended AG will be explained below. Here, $D = \{0, 1, a, \ldots, z, \text{DB}, \text{Poem}, \text{Verse}, \text{Word}\}$. We use regular expressions to define the languages R_1; for the first rule, R_0 is defined as $(D \cup \{\#\})^* - R_1$; for all other rules, R_0 is defined as $D^* - R_1$; those R_d that are not specified are empty; ε stands for the empty sequence of attributes.   □

The semantics of an extended AG is that it defines attributes of the nodes of derivation trees of the underlying grammar G. This is formalized next.

$$\text{DB} \to \text{Poem}^+ \qquad \textit{first}(1) := \langle \sigma_0 = \textit{lab}, \sigma_1 = \textit{lab}; R_1 = \text{DB}\#\text{Poem}^+ \rangle$$

$$\text{Poem} \to \text{Verse}^+ \qquad \textit{result}(0) := \langle \sigma_0 = \textit{first}, \sigma_1 = \textit{king\_lord};$$
$$R_1 = 1(1+0)^* + 0(1(1+0))^*(1+\varepsilon) \rangle$$

$$\text{Verse} \to \text{Word}^+ \qquad \textit{king\_lord}(0) := \langle \sigma_0 = \varepsilon, \sigma_1 = (\textit{king}, \textit{lord});$$
$$R_1 = (0+1)^* + 1 + (0+1)^* \rangle$$

$$\text{Word} \to (a + \ldots + z)^+ \quad \textit{king}(0) := \langle \sigma_0 = \varepsilon, \sigma_1 = \textit{lab}, \ldots, \sigma_{26} = \textit{lab}; R_1 = \{\text{king}\} \rangle$$
$$\textit{lord}(0) := \langle \sigma_0 = \varepsilon, \sigma_1 = \textit{lab}, \ldots, \sigma_{26} = \textit{lab}; R_1 = \{\text{lord}\} \rangle$$

Fig. 3. Example of an extended AG

Definition 7. If t is a derivation tree of G then a *valuation* v *of* t is a function that maps each pair (n, a), where n is a node in t and a is an attribute of the label of n, to an element of D, and that maps for every n, $v((\textit{lab}, n))$ to the label of n.

In the sequel, for a pair (n, a) as above we will use the more intuitive notation $a(n)$. To define the semantics of $\mathcal{F}$ we first need the following definition. If $\sigma = a_1 \cdots a_k$ is a sequence of attributes and n is a node of t, then define $\sigma(n)$ as the sequence of attribute-node pairs $\sigma(n) = a_1(n) \cdots a_k(n)$.

Definition 8. Let t be a derivation tree, n a node of t, and a an attribute of the label of n.

Synthesized Let $n_1, \ldots, n_m$ be the children of n derived by $p = X \to r$, and let $\langle \sigma_0, \ldots, \sigma_{|r|}; (R_d)_{d \in D} \rangle$ be the rule associated to the context $(p, a, 0)$. Define for $l \in [1, m]$, $j_l = \text{pos}_r(l, w)$, where w is the string formed by the labels of the children of n. Then define $W(a(n))$ as the sequence

$$\sigma_0(n) \cdot \sigma_{j_1}(n_1) \cdots \sigma_{j_m}(n_m).$$

For each d, we denote the language R_d associated to $a(n)$ by $R_d^{a(n)}$.

Inherited Let $n_1, \ldots, n_{k-1}$ be the left siblings, $n_{k+1}, \ldots, n_m$ be the right siblings, and n_0 be the parent of n. Let n_0 be derived by $p = X \to r$, and define for $l \in [1, m]$, $j_l = \text{pos}_r(l, w)$, where w is the string formed by the labels of the children of n_0. Let $\langle \sigma_0, \ldots, \sigma_{|r|}; (R_d)_{d \in D} \rangle$ be the rule associated to the context (p, a, j_k). Now define $W(a(n))$ as the sequence

$$\sigma_0(n_0) \cdot \sigma_{j_1}(n_1) \cdots \sigma_{j_{k-1}}(n_{k-1}) \cdot \# \cdot \sigma_{j_k}(n) \cdots \sigma_{j_{k+1}}(n_{k+1}) \sigma_{j_m}(n_m).$$

For each d, we denote the language R_d associated to $a(n)$ by $R_d^{a(n)}$.

If v is a valuation then define $v(W(a(n)))$ as the string obtained from $W(a(n))$ by replacing each $b(m)$ in $W(a(n))$ by $v(b(m))$. Note that the empty sequence is just replaced by the empty string.

We are now ready to define the semantics of an extended AG $\mathcal{F}$ on a derivation tree.

Definition 9. Given an extended AG $\mathcal{F}$ and a derivation tree $\mathbf{t}$, we define a sequence of partial valuations $(\mathcal{F}_j)_{j \geq 0}$ as follows:

1. $\mathcal{F}_0(\mathbf{t})$ is the valuation that maps, for every node $\mathbf{n}$, $lab(\mathbf{n})$ to the label of $\mathbf{n}$ and is undefined everywhere else;
2. for $j > 0$, if $\mathcal{F}_{j-1}(\mathbf{t})$ is defined on all $b(\mathbf{m})$ occurring in $W(a(\mathbf{n}))$ then $\mathcal{F}_j(\mathbf{t})(a(\mathbf{n})) = d$ where $\mathcal{F}_{j-1}(W(a(\mathbf{n}))) \in R_d^{a(\mathbf{n})}$. Note that this is well defined.

If for every $\mathbf{t}$ there is an l such that $\mathcal{F}_l(\mathbf{t})$ is totally defined (this implies that $\mathcal{F}_l(\mathbf{t}) = \mathcal{F}_{l-1}(\mathbf{t})$) then we say that $\mathcal{F}$ is *non-circular*. Obviously, non-circularity is an important property. In the next section we show that it is decidable whether an extended AG is non-circular. Therefore, in the sequel, we always assume an extended AG to be non-circular.

Definition 10. The valuation $\mathcal{F}(\mathbf{t})$ equals $\mathcal{F}_l(\mathbf{t})$ with l such that $\mathcal{F}_l(\mathbf{t}) = \mathcal{F}_{l+1}(\mathbf{t})$.

We will use the following definition of a query:

Definition 11. A *query* is a function mapping each derivation tree to a set of its nodes.

An extended AG $\mathcal{F}$ can be used in a simple way to express queries. Among the attributes in the vocabulary of $\mathcal{F}$, we designate some attribute *result*, and define:

Definition 12. An extended AG $\mathcal{F}$ expresses the query $\mathcal{Q}$ defined by

$$\mathcal{Q}(\mathbf{t}) = \{\mathbf{n} \mid \mathcal{F}(\mathbf{t})(result(\mathbf{n})) = 1\},$$

for every tree $\mathbf{t}$.

Example 13. Recall the extended AG $\mathcal{F}$ of Figure 3. This extended AG selects the first poem and every poem that has the strings king or lord in every other verse starting from the first one. In Figure 4 an illustration is given of the result of $\mathcal{F}$ on a derivation tree $\mathbf{t}$. At each node $\mathbf{n}$, we show the values $\mathcal{F}(W(a(\mathbf{n})))$ and $\mathcal{F}(\mathbf{t})(a(\mathbf{n}))$. We abbreviate $a(\mathbf{n})$ by a, *king* by k, *lord* by l, and *king_lord* by k_l.

The definition of the inherited attribute *first* indicates how the use of # can distinguish in a uniform way between different occurrences of the grammar symbol Poem. This is only a simple example. In the next section we show that extended AGs can express all queries definable in MSO. Hence, they can also specify all relationships between siblings definable in MSO.

The language R_1 associated to *result* (cf. Figure 3), contains those strings representing that the current Poem is the first one, or representing that for every other verse starting at the first one the value of the attribute *king_lord* is 1.   □

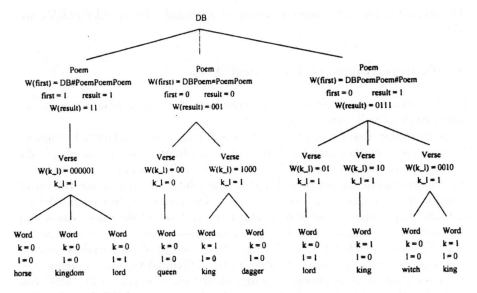

Fig. 4. A derivation tree and its valuation as defined by the extended AG in Figure 3

5   Deciding Non-circularity Is in EXPTIME

In this section we show that it is decidable whether an extended AG is non-circular. In particular, we show that deciding non-circularity is in EXPTIME. As it is well known that deciding non-circularity of *standard* AGs is complete for EXPTIME [21], going from ranked to unranked does not increase the complexity of the non-circularity problem.

A naive approach to testing non-circularity is to transform an extended AG $\mathcal{F}$ into a standard AG $\mathcal{F}'$ such that $\mathcal{F}$ is non-circular if and only if $\mathcal{F}'$ is non-circular and then use the known exponential algorithm on $\mathcal{F}'$. We can namely always find an integer N (polynomially depending on $\mathcal{F}$) such that we only have to test non-circularity of $\mathcal{F}$ on trees of rank N. Unfortunately, this approach exponentially increases the size of the AG. Indeed, a production $X \rightarrow (a + b) \cdots (a+b)$ (n times), for example, has to be translated to the set of productions $\{X \rightarrow w \mid w \in \{a, b\}^* \land |w| = n\}$. So, the complexity of the above algorithm is double exponential time. Therefore, we abandon this approach and give a different algorithm whose complexity is in EXPTIME.

To this end, we generalize the tree walking automata of Bloem and Engelfriet [6] to unranked trees. We then show that for each extended AG $\mathcal{F}$, there exists a tree walking automata $W_{\mathcal{F}}$ such that $\mathcal{F}$ is non-circular if and only if $W_{\mathcal{F}}$ does not cycle. Moreover, the size of $W_{\mathcal{F}}$ is polynomial in the size of $\mathcal{F}$. We then obtain our result by showing that testing whether a tree walking automaton cycles is in EXPTIME. We omit the details.

Theorem 14. *Deciding non-circularity of extended AGs is EXPTIME-complete.*

6   Expressiveness of Extended AGs

In this section we characterize the expressiveness of extended AGs as the queries definable in monadic second-order logic.

A derivation tree **t** can be viewed naturally as a finite relational structure (in the sense of mathematical logic [16]) over the binary relation symbols $\{E, <\}$ and the unary relation symbols $\{O_a \mid a \in N \cup T\}$. The domain of **t**, viewed as a structure, equals the set of nodes of **t**. The relation E in **t** equals the set of pairs $(\mathbf{n}, \mathbf{n}')$ such that $\mathbf{n}'$ is a child of **n** in **t**. The relation $<$ in **t** equals the set of pairs $(\mathbf{n}, \mathbf{n}')$ such that $\mathbf{n}' \neq \mathbf{n}$, $\mathbf{n}'$ and **n** are children of the same parent and $\mathbf{n}'$ is a child occurring after **n**. The set O_a in **t** equals the set of a-labeled nodes of **t**. *Monadic second-order logic* (MSO) allows the use of *set variables* ranging over sets of nodes of a tree, in addition to the individual variables ranging over the nodes themselves as provided by first-order logic (see, e.g., [16]). MSO can be used in the standard way to define queries. If $\varphi(x)$ is an MSO-formula, then φ defines the query $\mathcal{Q}$ defined by $\mathcal{Q}(\mathbf{t}) := \{\mathbf{n} \mid \mathbf{t} \models \varphi[\mathbf{n}]\}$.

We obtain:

Theorem 15. *A query is expressible by an extended AG if and only if it is definable in MSO.*

The proof of the above theorem is similar to the proof relating BAGs to MSO [32]. In MSO we can use set variables to represent assignment of values to attributes. For the other direction we make use of the ability of extended AGs to compute MSO-types of trees. The only complication arises from the fact that trees are unranked. See [29] for more details.

7   Optimization

We now obtain the exact complexity of some relevant optimization problems for extended AGs. These results will be used in the next section to obtain a new upper bound for deciding equivalence of Region Algebra expressions introduced by Consens and Milo [11]. We represent the regular languages R_d in the semantic rules by nondeterministic finite acceptors (NFAs). The size of an extended AG is the size of the attribute grammar vocabulary plus the size of the NFAs in the semantic rules. Consider the following optimization problems:

- NON-EMPTINESS: Given an extended AG $\mathcal{F}$, does there exists a tree **t** and a node **n** of **t** such that $\mathcal{F}(\mathbf{t})(result(\mathbf{n})) = 1$?
- EQUIVALENCE: Given two extended AGs $\mathcal{F}_1$ and $\mathcal{F}_2$ over the same grammar, do $\mathcal{F}_1$ and $\mathcal{F}_2$ express the same query?

We obtain:

Theorem 16. NON-EMPTINESS *and* EQUIVALENCE *are EXPTIME-complete.*

We outline the proof. Hardness is shown by a reduction from TWO PLAYER CORRIDOR TILING [10]. To show membership, we transform a finite AG $\mathcal{F}$ into a non-deterministic bottom-up automaton $M_{\mathcal{F}}$ (NBTA) over unranked trees such that $M_{\mathcal{F}}$ accepts a tree if and only if $\mathcal{F}$ is non-empty. The size of $M_{\mathcal{F}}$ is exponential in the size of $\mathcal{F}$ and the non-emptiness test of NBTAs can be done in PTIME. Hence, testing non-emptiness of extended AGs can be done in EXPTIME. Further, it can be shown that equivalence can be reduced to non-emptiness in polynomial time.

8 An Application of Extended AGs: Optimization of Region Algebra Expressions

The region algebra introduced by Consens and Milo [11] is a set-at-a-time algebra, based on the PAT algebra [35], for manipulating text regions. In this section we show that any Region Algebra expression can be simulated by an extended AG of polynomial size. This then leads to an EXPTIME algorithm for the equivalence and emptiness test of Region Algebra expressions. The algorithm of Consens and Milo is based on the equivalence test for first-order logic formulas over trees which has a non-elementary lower bound. Our algorithm therefore drastically improves the complexity of the equivalence test for the Region Algebra and matches more closely the coNP lower bound [11].

It should be pointed out that our definition differs slightly from the one in [11]. Indeed, we restrict ourselves to regular languages as patterns, while Consens and Milo do not use a particular pattern language. This is no loss of generality since

- on the one hand, regular languages are the most commonly used pattern language in the context of document databases; and,
- on the other hand, the huge complexity of the algorithm of [11] is not due to the pattern language at hand, but is due to quantifier alternation of the resulting first-order logic formula, induced by combinations of the operators '−' (difference) and $<$, $>$, $\subset$, and $\supset$.

A *region index schema* $\mathcal{I} = (S_1, \ldots, S_n, \Sigma)$ consists of a set of region names $S_1, \ldots, S_n$ and a finite alphabet Σ. If N is a natural number, then a *region over* N is a pair (i, j) with $i \leq j$ and $i, j \in \{1, \ldots, N\}$. An *instance* I of a region index schema $\mathcal{I}$ consists of a string $I(\omega) = a_1 \ldots a_{N_I} \in \Sigma^*$ with $N_I > 0$, and a mapping associating to each region name S a set of regions over N_I.

We abbreviate $r \in \bigcup_{i=1}^n I(S_i)$ by $r \in I$. We use the notation $L(r)$ (respectively $R(r)$) to denote the location of the left (respectively right) endpoint of a region r and denote by $\omega(r)$ the string $a_{L(r)} \ldots a_{R(r)}$.

Example 17. Consider the region index schema $\mathcal{I} = (\textbf{Proc}, \textbf{Func}, \textbf{Var}, \Sigma)$. In Figure 5 an example of an instance over $\mathcal{I}$ is depicted. Here, $N_I = 16$, $I(\omega) =$

abcdefghijklmnop, $I(\mathbf{Proc}) = \{(1,16),(6,10)\}$, $I(\mathbf{Func}) = \{(12,16)\}$ and
$I(\mathbf{Var}) = \{(2,3),(6,7),(12,13)\}$. □

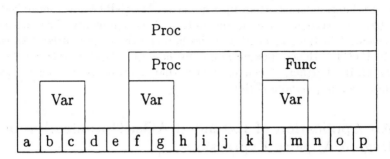

Fig. 5. An instance I over the region index schema of Example 17

For two regions r and s in I define:

– $r < s$ if $R(r) < L(s)$ (r *precedes* s); and
– $r \subset s$ if $L(s) < L(r)$ and $R(r) \le R(s)$, or $L(s) \le L(r)$ and $R(r) < R(s)$ (r is *included in* s).

We also allow the dual operators $r > s$ and $r \supset s$ which have the obvious meaning. An instance I is *hierarchical* if

– $I(S) \cap I(S') = \emptyset$ for all region names S and S' in $\mathcal{I}$, and
– for all $r, s \in I$, one of the following holds: $r < s$, $s < r$, $r \subset s$ or $s \subset r$.

The last condition simply says that if two regions overlap then one is strictly contained in the other. The instance in Figure 5 is hierarchical. Like in [11], we only consider hierarchical instances. We next define the Region Algebra.

Definition 18. *Region Algebra expressions over* $\mathcal{I} = (S_1, \ldots, S_n, \Sigma)$ *are inductively defined as follows:*

– every region name of $\mathcal{I}$ is a Region Algebra expression;
– if e_1 and e_2 are Region Algebra expressions then $e_1 \cup e_2$, $e_1 - e_2$, $e_1 \subset e_2$, $e_1 < e_2$, $e_1 \supset e_2$, and $e_1 > e_2$ are also Region Algebra expressions;
– if e is a Region Algebra expression and R is a regular language then $\sigma_R(e)$ is a Region Algebra expression.

The semantics of a Region Algebra expression on an instance I is defined as follows:

$$
\begin{aligned}
[\![S]\!]^I &:= \{r \mid r \in I(S)\}; \\
[\![\sigma_R(e)]\!]^I &:= \{r \mid r \in [\![e]\!]^I \text{ and } \omega(r) \in R\}; \\
[\![e_1 \cup e_2]\!]^I &:= [\![e_1]\!]^I \cup [\![e_2]\!]^I; \\
[\![e_1 - e_2]\!]^I &:= [\![e_1]\!]^I - [\![e_2]\!]^I;
\end{aligned}
$$

and for $\star \in \{<, >, \subset, \supset\}$:

$$[\![e_1 \star e_2]\!]^I := \{r \mid r \in [\![e_1]\!]^I \text{ and } \exists s \in [\![e_2]\!]^I \text{ such that } r \star s\}.$$

As an example consider the Region Algebra expression

$$\mathbf{Proc} \supset \sigma_{\Sigma^* \text{start} \Sigma^*}(\mathbf{Proc})$$

defining all the **Proc** regions which contain a **Proc** region that contains the string start.

An important observation is that for any region index schema $\mathcal{I} = (S_1, \ldots, S_n, \Sigma)$ there exists an ECFG $G_\mathcal{I}$ such that any hierarchical instance of $\mathcal{I}$ 'corresponds' to a derivation tree of $G_\mathcal{I}$. This ECFG is defined as follows: $G_\mathcal{I} = (N, T, P, U)$, with $N = \{S_1, \ldots, S_n\}$, $T = \Sigma$, and where P consists of the rules

$$
\begin{aligned}
p_0 &:= U \rightarrow (S_1 + \ldots + S_n + \Sigma)^+; \\
p_1 &:= S_1 \rightarrow (S_1 + \ldots + S_n + \Sigma)^+; \\
&\;\;\vdots \\
p_n &:= S_n \rightarrow (S_1 + \ldots + S_n + \Sigma)^+.
\end{aligned}
$$

For example, the derivation tree $\mathbf{t}_I$ of $G_\mathcal{I}$ representing the instance I of Figure 5 is depicted in Figure 6. Regions in I then correspond to nodes in $\mathbf{t}_I$ in the obvious way. We denote the node in $\mathbf{t}_I$ that corresponds to the region r by $\mathbf{n}_r$.

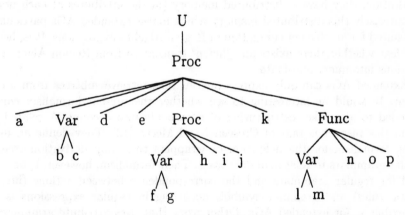

Fig. 6. The tree $\mathbf{t}_I$ corresponding to the instance I of Figure 5

Since extended AGs can store results of subcomputations in their attributes, they are naturally closed under composition. It is, hence, no surprise that the translation of Region Algebra expressions into extended AGs proceeds by induction on the structure of the former.

Lemma 19. *For every Region Algebra expression e over $\mathcal{I}$ there exists an extended AG $\mathcal{F}_e$ over $G_\mathcal{I}$ such that for every hierarchical instance I and region*

$r \in I$, $r \in [\![e]\!]^I$ *if and only if* $\mathcal{F}_e(\mathbf{t}_I)(result_e(\mathbf{n}_r)) = 1$. *Moreover, $\mathcal{F}_e$ can be constructed in time polynomial in the size of e.*

We need the following notion to state the main result of this section. A Region Algebra expression e over $\mathcal{I}$ is *empty* if for every hierarchical instance I over $\mathcal{I}$, $[\![e]\!]^I = \emptyset$. Two Region Algebra expressions e_1 and e_2 over $\mathcal{I}$ are *equivalent* if for every hierarchical instance I over $\mathcal{I}$, $[\![e_1]\!]^I = [\![e_2]\!]^I$.

Theorem 20. *Testing emptiness and equivalence of Region Algebra expressions is in* EXPTIME.

9 Discussion

In other work [30], Schwentick and the present author defined query automata to query structured documents. Query automata are two-way automata over (un)ranked trees that can select nodes depending on the current state and on the label at these nodes. Query automata can express precisely the unary MSO definable queries and have an EXPTIME-complete equivalence problem. This makes them look rather similar to extended AGs. The two formalisms are, however, very different in nature. Indeed, query automata constitute a procedural formalism that has only local memory (in the state of the automaton), but which can visit each node more than a constant number of times. Attribute grammars, on the other hand, are a declarative formalism, whose evaluation visits each node of the input tree only a constant number of times (once for each attribute). In addition, they have a distributed memory (in the attributes at each node). It is precisely this distributed memory which makes extended AGs particularly well-suited for an efficient simulation of Region Algebra expressions. It is, hence, not clear whether there exists an *efficient* translation from Region Algebra expressions into query automata.

Extended AGs can only express queries that retrieve subtrees from a document. It would be interesting to see whether the present formalism can be extended to also take restructuring of documents into account. A related paper in this respect is that of Crescenzi and Mecca [13]. They define an interesting formalism for the definition of wrappers that map derivation trees of regular grammars to relational databases. Their formalism, however, is only defined for regular grammars and the correspondence between actions (i.e., semantic rules) and grammar symbols occurring in regular expressions is not so flexible as for extended AGs. Other work that uses attribute grammars in the context of databases includes work of Abiteboul, Cluet, and Milo [2] and Kilpeläinen et al. [22].

Acknowledgement

This paper is inspired by the work of Brüggemann-Klein, Murata and Wood. I thank them for providing me with a first draft of [9]. I thank Jan Van den Bussche and Dirk Van Gucht for helpful discussions on topics treated in this paper.

References

1. S. Abiteboul, P. Buneman, and D. Suciu. *Data on the Web : From Relations to Semistructured Data and XML.* Morgan Kaufmann, 1999.
2. S. Abiteboul, S. Cluet, and T. Milo. A logical view of structured files. *VLDB Journal,* 7(2):96–114, 1998.
3. R. Beaza-Yates and G. Navarro. Integrating contents and structure in text retrieval. *ACM SIGMOD Record,* 25(1):67–79, March 1996.
4. C. Beeri and T. Milo. Schemas for integration and translation of structured and semi-structured data. In P. Buneman C. Beeri, editor, *Database Theory – ICDT99,* volume 1540 of *Lecture Notes in Computer Science,* pages 296–313. Springer-Verlag, 1998.
5. R. Bloem and J. Engelfriet. Characterization of properties and relations defined in monadic second order logic on the nodes of trees. Technical Report 97-03, Rijksuniversiteit Leiden, 1997.
6. R. Bloem and J. Engelfriet. Monadic second order logic and node relations on graphs and trees. In J. Mycielski, G. Rozenberg, and A. Salomaa, editors, *Structures in Logic and Computer Science,* volume 1261 of *Lecture Notes in Computer Science,* pages 144–161. Springer-Verlag, 1997.
7. R. Book, S. Even, S. Greibach, and G. Ott. Ambiguity in graphs and expressions. *IEEE Transactions on Computers,* c-20(2):149–153, 1971.
8. A. Brüggemann-Klein and Wood D. One unambiguous regular languages. *Information and Computation,* 140(2):229–253, 1998.
9. A. Brüggemann-Klein, M. Murata, and D. Wood. Regular tree languages over non-ranked alphabets (draft 1). Unpublished manuscript, 1998.
10. B. S. Chlebus. Domino-tiling games. *Journal of Computer and System Sciences,* 32(3):374–392, 1986.
11. M. Consens and T. Milo. Algebras for querying text regions: Expressive power and optimization. *Journal of Computer and System Sciences,* 3:272–288, 1998.
12. World Wide Web Consortium. Extensible Markup Language (XML). http://www.w3.org/XML/.
13. V. Crescenzi and G. Mecca. Grammars have exceptions. *Information Systems – Special Issue on Semistructured Data,* 23(8):539–565, 1998.
14. P. Deransart, M. Jourdan, and B. Lorho. *Attribute Grammars: Definition, Systems and Bibliography,* volume 323 of *Lecture Notes in Computer Science.* Springer, 1988.
15. A. Deutsch, M. Fernandez, D. Florescu, A. Levy, and D. Suciu. XML-QL: a query language for XML. In *Proceedings of the WWW8 Conference,* Toronto, 1999.
16. H.-D. Ebbinghaus and J. Flum. *Finite Model Theory.* Springer, 1995.
17. F. Gécseg and M. Steinby. Tree languages. In Rozenberg and Salomaa [34], chapter 1.
18. N. Globerman and D. Harel. Complexity results for two-way and multi-pebble automata and their logics. *Theoretical Computer Science,* 169(2):161–184, 1996.
19. G. H. Gonnet and F. W. Tompa. Mind your grammar: a new approach to modelling text. In *Proceedings 13th Conference on VLDB,* pages 339–346, 1987.
20. M. Gyssens, J. Paredaens, and D. Van Gucht. A grammar-based approach towards unifying hierarchical data models. *SIAM Journal on Computing,* 23(6):1093–1137, 1994.
21. M. Jazayeri, W. F. Ogden, and W. C. Rounds. The intrinsically exponential complexity of the circularity problem for attribute grammars. *Communications of the ACM,* 18(12):697–706, 1975.

22. P. Kilpeläinen, G. Lindén, H. Mannila, and E. Nikunen. A structured text database system. In R. Furuta, editor, *Proceedings of the International Conference on Electronic Publishing, Document Manipulation & Typography*, The Cambridge Series on Electronic Publishing, pages 139–151. Cambridge University Press, 1990.

23. P. Kilpeläinen and H. Mannila. Retrieval from hierarchical texts by partial patterns. In *Proceedings of the Sixteenth International Conference on Research and Development in Information Retrieval*, pages 214–222. ACM Press, 1993.

24. P. Kilpeläinen and H. Mannila. Query primitives for tree-structured data. In M. Crochemore and D. Gusfield, editors, *Proceedings of the fifth Symposium on Combinatorial Pattern Matching*, pages 213–225. Springer-Verlag, 1994.

25. D. E. Knuth. Semantics of context-free languages. *Mathematical Systems Theory*, 2(2):127–145, 1968. See also *Mathematical Systems Theory*, 5(2):95–96, 1971.

26. M. Murata. Forest-regular languages and tree-regular languages. Unpublished manuscript, 1995.

27. A. Neumann and H. Seidl. Locating matches of tree patterns in forests. In V. Arvind and R. Ramanujam, editors, *Foundations of Software Technology and Theoretical Computer Science*, Lecture Notes in Computer Science, pages 134–145. Springer, 1998.

28. F. Neven. Structured document query languages based on attribute grammars: locality and non-determinism. In T. Ripke T. Polle and K.-D. Schewe, editors, *Fundamentals of Information Systems*, pages 129–142. Kluwer, 1998.

29. F. Neven. *Design and Analysis of Query Languages for Structured Documents — A Formal and Logical Approach*. Doctor's thesis, Limburgs Universitair Centrum (LUC), 1999.

30. F. Neven and T. Schwentick. Query automata. In *Proceedings of the Eighteenth ACM Symposium on Principles of Database Systems*, pages 205–214. ACM Press, 1999.

31. F. Neven and J. Van den Bussche. On implementing structured document query facilities on top of a DOOD. In F. Bry, R. Ramakrishnan, and K. Ramamohanarao, editors, *Deductive and Object-Oriented Databases*, volume 1341 of *Lecture Notes in Computer Science*, pages 351–367. Springer-Verlag, 1997.

32. F. Neven and J. Van den Bussche. Expressiveness of structured document query languages based on attribute grammars. In *Proceedings of the Seventeenth ACM Symposium on Principles of Database Systems*, pages 11–17. ACM Press, 1998.

33. C. Pair and A. Quere. Définition et etude des bilangages réguliers. *Information and Control*, 13(6):565–593, 1968.

34. G. Rozenberg and A. Salomaa, editors. *Handbook of Formal Languages*, volume 3. Springer, 1997.

35. A. Salminen and F. Tompa. PAT expressions: an algebra for text search. *Acta Linguistica Hungarica*, 41:277–306, 1992.

36. D. Suciu. Semistructured data and XML. In *Proceedings of the 5th International Conference on Foundations of Data Organization and Algorithms*, 1998.

37. M. Takahashi. Generalizations of regular sets and their application to a study of context-free languages. *Information and Control*, 27(1):1–36, 1975.

38. W. Thomas. Languages, automata, and logic. In Rozenberg and Salomaa [34], chapter 7.

39. M. Y. Vardi. Automata theory for database theoreticians. In *Proceedings of the Eighth ACM Symposium on Principles of Database Systems*, pages 83–92. ACM Press, 1989.

An Overview of Souk Nets: A Component-based Paradigm for Data Source Integration

William J. McIver, Jr.[1], Karim Keddara[2], Christian Och[2], Roger King[2],
Clarence A. Ellis[2], John Todd[2], Nathan Getrich[2], Richard M. Osborne[2], Brian Temple[2]

[1] Department of Computer Sciences, Purdue University, West Lafayette, Indiana
47907-1398, USA.

mciver@cs.purdue.edu

[2] Department of Computer Science, University of Colorado, Boulder, Colorado
80309-0430 USA

{karim, och, roger, skip, toddjr, getrich, rick,
temple}@cs.colorado.edu

Abstract. Construction of complex software systems with off-the-shelf components has become a reality. Component-based frameworks tailored specifically for the domain of database integration are lacking, however. To use an existing component framework, data integrators must construct custom components specialized to the tasks of the data integration problem at hand. This approach allows other components provided by the framework to be reused, but is overly tedious and requires the integrator to employ the programming paradigms assumed by the component framework for interconnection and intercommunication between components, and manipulation of data provided by them. An alternate approach would employ a framework containing components tailored to data integration and which allows them to be interconnected using programming methods that are more natural to the domain of data integration. Souk is a language-independent, component-based paradigm for data integration. It is designed to allow the rapid construction of data integration solutions from off-the-shelf components, and to allow flexible evolution. This paper gives an overview of this paradigm.

1 Introduction

This work addresses database, or data source, integration specifically through the use of a component-based framework and programming paradigm specifically designed to support the rapid construction of data integration solutions in the context of distributed object environments, and which can be easily adapted to evolve in the face of changes to the underlying local data sources and changing client requirements.

---

1. This work is supported by NSF grant 9806829 under the Experimental Systems Program.

R. Connor and A. Mendelzon (Eds.): DBPL'99, LNCS 1949, pp. 117-128, 2000.

The main goal of *database integration* is to create a *global database* which incorporates and encapsulates data from a community of discrete, possibly heterogeneous, *local databases*; and which can accept requests from clients to retrieve or update data managed by the community of local databases without regard to their location in a network of data sources, representation, data model, access methods, or languages required to properly specify the requests of the individual local databases [4]. Thus, in meeting this goal, the global database might be required to accept a query expression from a client, manage its translation into several sub-queries in different query languages or method invocations, retrieve the results, and convert them into the representation and data model required by the client. Furthermore, the global database is most likely constrained to respect the separate and independent design, control, and administration of the local databases with which it interacts in order to service client requests. For example, the global database may be required to adapt to independently initiated schema design changes to a local database, or the global database may not be able to implement global transaction semantics by accessing information about the transaction schedules of local data sources. This separate and independent design, control, and administration is called *local autonomy*. We will refer to local databases from now on using the more general term, *local data source,* to indicate that data to be integrated may not be managed by a proper database management system, but may be some other type of system, such as a file system or an application.

There are several classical approaches to data source integration. First, the schemas from all local data sources are integrated into a *common data model* to form a *global schema*, and then queries in a corresponding *common query language* are performed against this global schema [2]. This approach becomes intractable when the number of local data sources becomes large. Second, the intractability of global schema integration can be dealt with by performing integration on only those parts of local schemas that are exported by local data sources [16]. Third, schema integration can be avoided altogether in lieu of a system that can accept requests in the form of global query language expressions or method invocations and translate them accordingly into the query languages or method invocations corresponding to the underlying local data sources required to satisfy the requests [7]. Finally, highly customized point solutions can be constructed based on the particularities of the local data sources to be integrated. These are costly and often not easy to adapt to evolution of the local data sources.

2 Our approach

Our approach to data integration is orthogonal to those discussed above: construction of data integration solutions using a component-based framework, but using a programming or modeling paradigm that allows methods that are more natural to the domain of data integration. Current component-based frameworks force the data integrator to use tedious, imperative programming techniques and tedious procedures for binding and communicating with other components or objects in the framework. The complimentary and problematic nature of data integrator needs and distributed object environments is being recognized by industrial data integration providers such as Cohera [10]. The collection of components in our framework allow the modularization of functionality used in well-known approaches to data integration, such as view construction, set operations, and data transformations. There is considerable overlap in the issues that must be addressed in each of the existing data integration approaches, including schema integration and translation, query decomposition and query language translation, maintenance of consistency and dependency constraints across local data sources, and global transaction processing. Data sources can and are now being wrapped or constructed using mature distributed object and component-based software systems. These realities can be factored to produce a covering set of components, and a paradigm for communication and coordination between them. The result can be a covering set of components which allow the data integrator to rapidly construct solutions taking one of the dominant approaches discussed above.

2.1   Component-based Software

Szyperski defines software components as binary units of independent production, acquisition, and deployment that interact to form a functioning system [27]. Independence allows for multiple independent developers, and the ability to integrate at the binary level ensures robust integration. Our definition of components are units which define specialized, prefabricated functionality whose instances can be combined with other components to construct solutions to data integration problems involving multiple, distributed data sources. Data sources may or may not be traditional database management systems. Data sources in this context are assumed to be wrapped using a technology such as CORBA [22].

We have identified an additional set of requirements that we think a component language must meet to support data integration. A component language for data integration must provide features or constructs that are: tailored to data definition, manipulation, and integration; interface manipulation; amenable to component evolution analysis; capable of expressing event subscription, event notification and fault tolerance logic; capable of expressing global constraints; amenable to dynamic interface discovery or "trading" in CORBA paralance [?]; and, finally, it must be amenable to highly scalable methods of composition, such as pattern-based software construction. The work described in this paper seeks to address meta-language issues around component interaction, data manipulation, event handling, and pattern-based integration.

3   Perspectives on Modeling Data Integration Solutions

The overriding requirement for our paradigm is that it should support programming approaches that are at or near the level of a data manipulation language. Existing component languages do not allow this.

Carriero and Geletner's [8] taxonomy of conceptual classes of parallel programming approaches provide a useful start here. We can envision the development of a data integration in terms of the *results* of the data integration process, the agenda of tasks that must be performed to achieve integration, or the *ensemble of specialists* required to perform data integration. We believe that these three paradigms are relevant classifications for the predominant data integration approaches described above. We do not suggest that each data integration approach falls squarely within one of these parallel programming approaches; rather, different aspects of each data integration approach are similar enough to be useful to us here.

Global database query languages provide result-oriented solutions. They allow a more "natural" means of expressing desired results solutions than do imperative programing languages. Schema integration and federation can be naturally articulated as an agenda of tasks that must be executed to achieve the desired integration. Customized data integration approaches and some aspects of the other data integration approaches require ensembles of specialists for certain parts of the solution.

Our work has been influenced in various ways by a number of research efforts involving modular or component-based data integration. These include *a la Carte* [12], *COMANDOS* [3], *Garlic* [25], *InterBase* [6], *MIND* [11], *Pegasus* [26], and *TSIMMIS* [14]. These projects variously addressed aspects of componentization of multidatabase systems from transaction management to query processing, the use of standard distributed object technologies, and the use of mediators [30] as the unit of componentization. InterBase, Garlic, and Pegasus provide fairly complete decompositions of the overall problem space of distributed data integration. Our work is focused in particular on tailoring current component-based software construction approaches, embodied in technologies such as *Enterprise Java Beans* [28], to the domain of distributed data integration. Mediators are to provide the containers for our components.

The paradigm we are developing is intended to support the three programming or modeling approaches of expressing: result-oriented solutions, agenda-based solutions, and solutions based on the use of ensembles of specialists. Just as important, our paradigm must also provide a bridge between existing component-based programming paradigms and environments, because the reality is that while technologies like CORBA provide "glue" for components in such systems, but once they are glued together a programming paradigm that is not natural to database programming is required to exchange and manipulate data that are exchanged between the components. For example, the tasks of locating object references and performing object binding is still relatively low-level, tedious and technology dependent. Data-oriented tasks, such as the submitting of queries and the retrieval of result sets using technologies such as JDBC [31] must also be implemented in a way that is low-level, brittle with respect to the evolution of data integration solutions, and imperative, usually in great contrast to the underlying query expressions being passed from client to server. Component-based frameworks such as *Enterprise Java Beans* provide powerful mechanisms such as reflection and contracts for addressing these problems, but components therein must ultimately be manipulated in ways that are at odds (e.g. imperative and low-level) with conceptual models of distributed data integration solutions.

Our hypothesis is that Petri net graphs can provide a useful modeling tool for data integration in this context. They provide an abstract and formal way of modeling: data flow and control problems seen in data integration, concurrent and asynchronous behavior often extant and useful in distributed and database systems, and event detection and temporality. Petri nets offer many analysis techniques applicable to data integration, including reachability, coverability, and boundedness [23]. Variants of the general Petri net model have proven useful for the modeling of composite event detection and active database systems architectures [15, 19], and the specification and verification of distributed databases and software systems [5, 29]. The particular variant of Petri nets we use has the added benefit of being able to analyze and model dynamic changes to a network. We expect to apply these capabilities to model the handling of changes in data integration requirements and fault tolerance of a running data integration solution.

4   The Souk Network Specification Model

Our specification model for data integration is the *Souk Net (SNet)*, a variant of *WorkFlow Nets* (WoFNets) designed to model data integration process flows. WoFNets are a class of Colored Petri nets [23]. This class of Petri nets has been used by Ellis and Keddara to model workflow processes and dynamic change in them [13]. An *SNet* is a bi-partite net with two kinds of nodes, *places* and *transitions*. They are colored in the sense that the tokens in an SNet can be assigned color types to indicate what type of information they carry: data type, control type (e.g. parameters), or combinations of both. The distribution of tokens in the *SNet* represent its state. Tokens may be distributed over places and transitions.

Each transition in an SNet is associated with one of several types of data integration components. A component is executed when the associated transition *fires*. The association between transitions and components is injective (i.e. each instance of a component type is uniquely associated with a transition). Each transition has at least one input place and at least one output place. A transition's connectors are associated with the ports of its associated component through a total and injective labeling over port names.

Each SNet has a single entry place and a single exit place. A net is connected, and each node in the net is reachable from the entry and may lead to the exit place. The firing of an AFN starts the moment a token is injected into its entry place, and completes when a token is produced into its exit place. Below, we discuss the modeling elements of our variant of WoFNets.

4.1   The Modeling Elements

A Souk process (S-process) is a procedure where data and control objects are passed between Souk-components (S-components) according to a well-defined set of semantics to achieve or contribute to an overall set of data integration goals. Each S-process is defined in the context of a container. It will normally be the case that the container for an S-process is a method in the object-oriented sense, and that collections of these methods will be implemented within a mediator or some other type of distributed object. Thus, each S-process constitutes all or part of an implementation of a method defined in the mediator's interface.

Each S-process defines a configuration of interconnected S-components and data places, and the flow of control and data among these network entities. An S-component (*figure 1*) may be one of several types, each type designed to perform specific operations on data object sets or control information. Operations on the elements of a data object set may be at either or both the semantic or structural levels. The flow of an S-process is specified by interconnecting its component using connectors (i.e. edges).

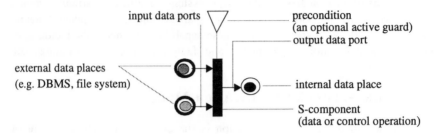

Fig. 1   The basic structure of an S-component.

Data places may be internal or external to an S-process. An *internal data place* is declared, created, and managed as part of an S-process. Internal data places are repositories that behave like Linda tuple spaces [8], except that they may only hold one token and the data contained therein may be complex objects. An *external data place* is a local data source whose existence and operation may be independent and autonomous of the S-process. A local data source can be a proper database management systems, a file system, or an application program. Each local data source is encapsulated by a *server object*. These server objects are assumed to be objects in some distributed environment such as CORBA[22] or DCOM[18]. Each local data source involved in an S-process is accessed through the *interface* of its associated *server object*. S-processes manipulate sets of data which originate from and are ultimately stored in local data sources.

S-processes make no assumptions about the structure of the data objects on which they operate. To support data integration data objects in our model must be able to represent arbitrarily complex data, including 1NF tuples, structurally complex objects, nested relations, text streams, and byte streams. We have, therefore, chosen as our *global data model* the data type system for set forth by CORBA IDL [22]. Thus, data objects may be of any type expressible in IDL and data object sets are IDL sequences having data objects as their elements.

An S-component is modeled using a black box approach with respect to the structure of the data object sets it processes. Room prevents us from discussing the intricacies of S-component firings here. It suffices to say that the general firing process of an S-component has three phases:

Phase 1: the S-component consumes one token from each of its input places.

Phase 2: the S-component performs its specified operation based on the information contained in the tokens it has consumed;

Phase 3: the S-component produces one new token for each of its output places.

S-components may be broadly classified as:

Filters: components that alter the membership of a data object set according to criteria specified by the modeler of the S-process. Filters support the database notion of *selection*. They do not alter the structure of their input data object sets. The filtering criteria are referred to as the *filtering guards* and are specified by a logical expression (e.g. in some predicate calculus or algebra). Each filter has one input data port and one output data port.

Transforms: components that perform specific structural or semantic (e.g. data value) transformations on a single input data object set. Transforms support the database notions of view construction and schema modification. Each transform has one single input data port and one single output data port.

Blenders: components that combine several data inputs into one single data output. The blending may be structural, elemental, or both. A structural blending is used to perform *view construction* over multiple data sources. Element-wise blendings are essentially set-based operations and support such operations as union, intersection, set difference, set division, Cartesian product, and join.

Controllers: components that manage the routing of tokens in an S-process. Controllers support the global database notion of global query decomposition, where a query is split into several sub-queries, each sent to a specific local data source. A controller may also be used to combine or decompose parameter values coming from different components.

A *data port* provides a conduit for transferring tokens between an S-component and one of its data places. An S-component transfers data object sets between its data places and itself using the methods *produce* and *consume*, which are defined for all *data ports* in attached to an S-component. If the methods *produce* or *consume* are to be invoked on a data port to or from an internal data place, a built-in implementation of these methods can be used.

To achieve *data object set* transfers between an S-component and an external data place, however, the implementations of the *produce* and *consume* methods must be overridden because we cannot assume which methods in the interface of the server object that wraps that external data place must be invoked to transfer data to and from it. This must be done for each data port attached to an external data place.

The usual Petri net semantics of token consumption will not usually apply for external data places, as the corpus of data in local data source will not likely be entirely removed during a query. Rather, data contained in the token that represents the contents of a local data source will either be copied, augmented or removed, but the token itself will remain. These special semantics for external data places allow us to retain the usual firing semantics for interior of an S-process since an S-component connected to an external data place needs only to receive a control token (e.g. a request involving the external data place) to be enabled. We simplify our graphical notation by using a double arrow for a data port if both updates and retrievals are possible from an external data place.

The server objects that wrap external data places provide two fundamental ways of transferring data object sets across their interfaces, using *parameterized accessors* or *cursor-based accessors*. Parameterized accessors provide for the retrieval data object sets via *out* or *in out* parameters. Iterative accessors provide for the retrieval of data object sets, first, using an initialize method which returns a cursor, and then repeated invocations of an iterator method to extract each element of the data object set resulting from the initialize method invocation. Thus, the data object sets transferred by parameterized accessors can be scalar values or sequences, and those transferred by iterative accessors are individual data objects which are aggregated into a sequence one at a time.

We give an example in *figure 2* of the handling of a global query, its decomposition into subqueries for each of the mediator's constituent local data sources, and the return of the results. This S-process accepts as input a token from place P_{in} in the form of a global query expression, $query_g$. S-component C_1 is a *transform* created such that it can parse and decompose $query_g$ into query expressions in the dialects or languages required by external data sources EP_1 and EP_2. The resulting expressions are $query_1$ and $query_2$. Once the tokens containing $query_1$ and $query_2$ reach data places P_1 and P_3 respectively, the *controller* components responsible for interacting with the external data sources, C_2 and C_3, are enabled and fire. S-component C_4, a *blender*, then combines the results, $result_1$ and $result_2$, in some way meaningful to the data integrator to produce $result_g$. If a global query involves only one external data place, component C_1 will generate a null query for the other external data place, a *no-op* that is ignored by the controller that receives it.

4.2   Event Subscription and Notification

Each S-component may *observe events* and may perform *event notifications* [9, 24]. Rules are declared, in the form of an S-process, for execution when a component observes an event to which it has *subscribed* and that event indicates a specified *condition*. Events in our model support the notion of global database constraints and the specification of a course of action if constraints are violated. Rules may themselves subscribe to other events and perform event notifications to handle events that are triggered during the execution of the rules. An event subscription is represented as a *precondition* which adorns an S-component, depicted using a triangle. It should be noted that the use of a Petri net approach allows us to readily apply the efficient composite event detection approach developed by Gatziu and Dittrich [15].

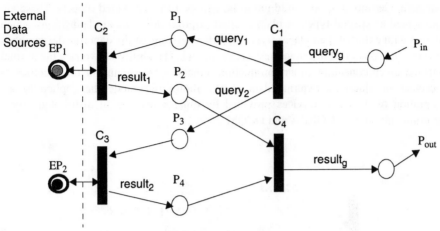

Fig. 2 An Example

Suppose in the example shown in *figure 2*, we are required to update an ADDRESS attribute value in EP_2 whenever an ADDRESS update is sent to EP_1. This event subscription and corresponding rule can be specified as shown in *figure 3*. The event subscription is the expression written over the triangle. It specifies that whenever component C_1, in figure 2, generates a *query₁* token that is an update, this rule should be fired. The *guard* on component C5 of the rule tests if the update is to ADDRESS. If it is, an ADDRESS update is generated for EP2 and sent to data place P_4 to replace the no-op token that would have been generated by C_1. The S-process in *figure 2* then resumes with the new query token that has been placed in P_4. If the *guard* is false, then the rule ends.

Modular design is further supported in Souk Networks through the use of Souk-macros (S-macro). An S-macro is an S-component that references another S-process. We call this type of S-process an S-subprocess. The S-subprocess is executed whenever the macro starts. The S-process may in turn contain S-macros and so on. Thus, arbitrary process nestings can be achieved.

5   Conclusion

We have presented a new component-based paradigm that is designed to support a more natural programming paradigm for data integration than provided by existing component-based frameworks and the use of distributed objects external to our framework. The programming paradigm is supported through the use of a special variant of Petri nets, called *SoukNets*. The SoukNet model contains special types of *transitions* called *S-components* which modularize common or custom data integration operations, such as query translation and decomposition, set operations, and view construction. Data to be integrated are transferred among components in our framework as *tokens*. Control information such as query expressions and parameters are passed in tokens as well. We support a global data model which can be used to represent data coming from local data sources of virtually any complexity and structure. Local data sources are assumed in our paradigm to be wrapped by distributed objects. These are represented as special types of places called *external data places*. Transitions which interact with external data places use *overridden* versions of the data transfer methods *produce* and *consume* built in to the *SoukNet* model. The ability to override the normal Petri net token consumption and production semantics to account for the specifics of interfaces provided by external data places allows our model be applied to the integration of data and services provided by objects resident in distributed object environments such as CORBA and DCOM.

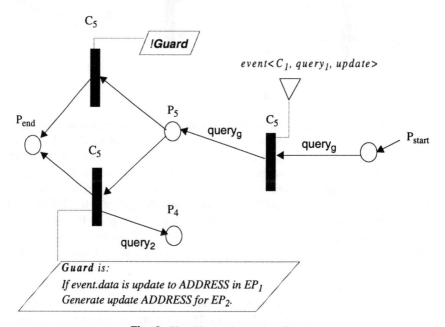

Fig. 3 Handling update constraints

SoukNet articulates a model and a modeling paradigm not a specific database programming language. It is a meta-language. We are in the process of developing a database programming and integration language called *COIL* which is an instance of the SoukNet meta-language [20].

SoukNets are based on *WoFNets* which are designed to be adaptive [13]. That is, they can be used to analyze and model dynamic changes to a Petri net. We expect to apply these capabilities to model the handling of changes in data integration requirements and fault tolerance of a running data integration solution. Finally, we are addressing the modeling in *SoukNet* of global transactions, environment-wide mediator coordination [1], and the specification of inter-mediator and inter-object behavioral constraints [17].

References

1. Jean-Marc Andreoli and Francois Pacull. "A Quick Overview of the CLF." Xerox Research Centre Europe. Grenoble, France. (Web site). December 10, 1997.

2. C. Batini, M. Lenzerini, and S.B. Navathe. "A Comparative Analysis f Methodologies for Database Schema Integration." ACM Computing Surveys. Vol 18, No. 4, December 1986. pp. 324-364.

3. Elisa, Bertino, Mauro Negri, and Licia Sbattella. "An Overview of the Comandos Integration System." in *Object-Oriented Multidatabase Systems: A Solution for Advanced Applications*. Omran A. Bukhres and Ahmed K. Elmagarmid (eds). Prentice Hall. 1996.

4. Athman Bouguettaya, Boualem Benatallah, and Ahmed Elmagarmid. "An Overview of Multidatabase Systems: Past and Present." in Management of Heterogeneous and Autonomous Database Systems. Ahmed Elmagarmid, Marek Rusinkiewicz, Amit Sheth editors. Morgan Kaufmann. 1999.

5. G. Bruno and G. Marchetto. "Process-translatable Petri nets for the rapid prototyping of process control systems." IEEE Transactions on Software Engineering. Vol 12, No. 2. February 1986.

6. Omran A. Bukhres, Jiansan Chen, Weimin Du, Ahmed K. Elmagarmid, Rob Pezzoli. "InterBase: An Execution Environment for Heterogeneous Software Systems." *IEEE Computer.* 26(8): 57-69 (1993) .

7. O. Bukhres, A. K. Elmagarmid, and E. Kuhn. Advanced Languages for Multidatabase Systems. Chapter in "Object-Oriented Multidatabase Systems", A.K. Elmagarmid, O. Bukhres (eds), Prentice-Hall. 1996

8. Nicholas Carriero and David Gelertner. "How to Write Parallel Programs: A Guide to the Perplexed." ACM Computing Surveys. Vol 21, No 3. September 1989. pp 323-357.

9. Antonio Carzaniga, Elisabetta Di Nitto, David S. Rosenblum and Alexander L. Wolf . "Issues in Supporting Event-Based Architectural Styles." Third International Software Architecture Workshop, Orlando, Florida, November 1998, pp. 17-20.

10. Cohera Corporation. " 'Comming to Terms' with Distributed Computing." http://www.cohera.com. 1999.

11. A. Dogac, C.Dengi, and M.T. Öszu. "Distributed Object Computing Platforms." *Communications of the ACM*. September 1998, Vol. 41. No. 9.

12. Pamela Drew, Roger King, Dennis Heimbigner: A Toolkit for the Incremental Implementation of Heterogeneous Database Management Systems. VLDB Journal 1(2): 241-284 (1992).

13. Clarence Ellis and Karim Keddara. "ML-DEWS: A Meta-Language to Support Dynamic Evolution of Workflow System." to appear in the Journal of CSCW Special Issue on Adaptive Workflow. 1999.

14. H. Garcia-Molina , Y. Papakonstantinou , D. Quass , A. Rajaraman , Y. Sagiv , J. Ullman , V. Vassalos, J. Widom . "The TSIMMIS approach to mediation: Data models and Languages." Journal of Intelligent Information Systems. 1997.

15. Stella Gatziu and Klaus R. Dittrich. "Detecting Composite Events in Active Database Systems Using Petri Nets." in *Proceedings of the 4th International Workshop on Research Issues in Data Engineering: Active Database Systems*. Houston, Texas. February 1994.

16. D. Heimbigner and D. McLeod. A federated architecture for information management. ACM Trans. on Office Information Systems, 3(3), pages 253-278. July 1985.

17. P. Inverardi and A.L. Wolf. Formal Specification and Analysis of Software Architectures Using the Chemical Abstract Machine Model. IEEE Transactions on Software Engineering. Vol. 21, No. 4, April 1995.

18. Microsoft Corporation. Distributed Component Object Model Protocol -- DCOM/1.0. http://www.microsoft.com. January 1998.

19. Waseem Naqvi and Mohamed T. Ibrahim. "REFLEX Active Database Model: Application of Petri-Nets." in *Proceedings of 4th International Database and Expert Systems Applications Conference (DEXA'93)*. Prague, Czech Republic. September 1993.

20. W. J. McIver, Jr., R. King, R.M. Osborne, and C. Och. The COIL Project: A Common Object Interconnection Language to Support Database Integration and Evolution. Proceedings fo the Third International Baltic Workshop on Databases and Information Systems. Riga, Latvia. April 15-17, 1998.

21. Gary Nutt. *Operating Systems: A Modern Prespective*. Addison-Wesley. 1997.

22. Object Management Group. *The Common Object Request Broker: Architecture and Specification.*
July 7, 1998.

23. James L. Peterson. *Petri Net Theory and The Modeling of Systems*. Prentice-Hall: Englewood Cliffs, NJ. 1981.

24. David S. Rosenblum and Alexander L. Wolf . "A Design Framework for Internet-Scale Event Observation and Notification." 6th European Software Engineering Conference (held jointly with SIGSOFT '97: Fifth International Symposium on the Foundations of Software Engineering), Lecture Notes in Computer Science 1301, Springer, Berlin, 1997, pp. 344-360.

25. Mary Tork Roth, Manish Arya, Laura M. Haas, Michael J. Carey, William F. Cody, Ronald Fagin, Peter M. Schwarz, Joachim Thomas II, Edward L. Wimmers. "The Garlic Project." *Proceedings of SIGMOD Conference 1996*. p. 557.

26. Ming-Chien Shan, Rafi Ahmed, Jim Davis, Weimin Du, William Kent. "Pegasus: A Heterogeneous Information Management System." *Modern Database Systems: The Object Model, Interoperability, and Beyond*. Won Kim (Ed.). ACM Press and Addison-Wesley. 1995. pp. 664-682.

27. Szyperski, C. Component Software: Beyond Object-Oriented Programming. *Addison-Wesley*. 1999.

28. Anne Thomas. "Enterprise Javabeans Technology: Server Component Model for the Java Platform." *Patricia Seybold Group (Prepared for Sun Microsystems, Inc.)*. December 1998. (www.javasoft.com).

29. Klaus Voss. "Using Predicate/Transition-Nets to Model and Analyze Distributed Database Systems." IEEE Transactions on Software Engineering. Vol. SE-6, No. 6, November 1980.

30. Gio Wiederhold. "Mediators in the architecture of future information systems." IEEE Computer. Vol 25, No. 3. 1992.

31. Seth White, Maydene Fisher, R. G. G. Cattell, Graham Hamilton, Mark Hapner. *JDBC[tm] API Tutorial and Reference, Second Edition: Universal Data Access for the Java[tm] 2 Platform*. Addison Wesley Longman. 1999.

Defining and Handling Transient Fields in PJama

Tony Printezis[1], Malcolm P. Atkinson[1], and Mick Jordan[2]

[1] Department of Computing Science, University of Glasgow,
17 Lilybank Gardens, Glasgow G12 8RZ, Scotland
{tony,mpa}@dcs.gla.ac.uk
[2] Sun Microsystems Laboratories,
901 San Antonio Road, MS UMTV29-110, Palto Alto, CA 94043, USA
mick.jordan@eng.sun.com

Abstract. The `transient` keyword of the Java™ programming language was originally introduced to prevent specific class fields from being stored by a persistence mechanism. In the context of orthogonal persistence, this is a particularly useful feature, since it allows the developer to easily deal with state that is external to the system. Such state is inherently transient and should not be stored, but instead re-created when necessary. Unfortunately, the Java Language Specification does not accurately define the semantics and correct usage of the `transient` keyword. This has left it open to misinterpretation by third parties and its current meaning is tied to the popular Java Object Serialisation mechanism. In this paper we explain why the currently widely-accepted use of the `transient` keyword is not appropriate in the context of orthogonal persistence, we present a more detailed definition for it, and we show how the handling of transient fields can be efficiently implemented in an orthogonally persistent system, while preserving the desired semantics.

1 Introduction

When programming in PJama, an orthogonally persistent system for the Java™ programming language [5,3], it is often necessary to mark fields of objects as transient so that the system does not write their contents to disk. This is crucial when dealing with state external to the system, that inherently cannot be stored on disk, but instead must be re-created when necessary (this is an important requirement for all open persistent systems — see Section 3).

In the context of the Java language, the natural way to mark such fields as transient would have been to use the `transient` keyword. Unfortunately, the Java Language Specification [14] gives a very loose definition of the semantics and the correct usage of `transient`. This has allowed third parties to misinterpret it and tie it to the popular and widely-used Java Object Serialisation mechanism [32]. Since this mechanism is part of the Java platform, this use of `transient` has become a de-facto standard and has been propagated to the platform's standard libraries [33].

R. Connor and A. Mendelzon (Eds.): DBPL'99, LNCS 1949, pp. 129–151, 2000.

In this paper we argue that the current use of the `transient` keyword is overloaded with two different meanings, one of which is not fully compatible with persistence. This has forced both the PJama team and GemStone Inc. to introduce in their persistent systems ad-hoc ways for ignoring some occurrences of `transient` in the standard libraries of the JDK platform (see Section 4.3 and 4.4 respectively).

We believe that the correct interpretation of the `transient` keyword is an issue that should be addressed by the designers of the Java language, since it can ultimately apply to the majority of systems that provide persistence for the Java language, not only the orthogonal ones.

1.1   Paper Overview

Section 2 gives a brief overview of the PJama system and its architecture. Section 3 establishes the need for transient data in open orthogonally persistent systems. Section 4 includes an overview of the current interpretations of the `transient` keyword, gives concrete examples from the standard classes of the Java platform that show that its use is overloaded, and presents the reasons why PJama and GemStone Inc. have to ignore some occurrences of `transient` for the purposes of their storage systems. Section 5 describes the way transient fields are handled in the PJama system. Finally, Section 6 concludes the paper.

2   Overview of PJama

Orthogonal Persistence [6] is a language-independent model of persistence defined by the following three principles [19,4].

- **Type Orthogonality.** Persistence is available for all data, irrespective of type.
- **Persistence By Reachability**[1]**.** The lifetime of all objects is determined by reachability from a designated set of root objects.
- **Persistence Independence.** It is indistinguishable whether code is operating on short-lived or long-lived data.

PJama [5,3,22] is a system that provides orthogonal persistence for the Java programming language [14,1]. It was developed collaboratively between the Department of Computing Science at the University of Glasgow and the Research Laboratories of Sun Microsystems. It conforms to the three principles of orthogonal persistence since

- instances of *any* class can persist (this includes the classes themselves, as they are instances of the class `Class`, and their static fields),
- all objects reachable from a set of declared roots become persistent, unless explicitly specified as transient (see Section 4.3), and

---

[1] This is also referred to as *Transitive Persistence*.

– code that operates over transient data can also operate over persistent data, with no changes to the original source or post-processing of the bytecodes being necessary.

An additional requirement for the PJama system was to implement all the above without introducing any new constructs to or changing the syntax of the Java language. This way, third-party classes (even ones developed for the "vanilla" Java language) can persist[2] using PJama, without requiring any changes to the original sources (i.e. .java files) or the compiled bytecodes (i.e. .class files) [5,3]. We have achieved this by introducing a small number of PJama-specific classes that encompass the (minimal) API needed by the programmers to access the persistence facilities of PJama [35,20]. Some of these classes provide wrappers to native calls inside our customised interpreter (see Section 2.1). This approach also allows us to use the standard Java compiler (javac) *unchanged* in order to compile PJama-specific classes.

Unfortunately, our claim of complete type orthogonality is not yet entirely true. Even though the majority of classes can persist unchanged, there is a small number of them that either require some changes in order to persist or cannot persist at all. Examples of classes that require changes are ones that use the **transient** keyword in a manner incompatible with orthogonal persistence (see Section 4.3 for a lengthier explanation) or depend on static initialisers to load dynamic libraries[3]. Examples of classes that cannot persist at all are those tied closely to the implementation of the Virtual Machine (VM) (**Thread**, **Exception**, etc.). The issues of type orthogonality in the Java language are discussed in more detail by Jordan and Atkinson [18,19,4].

PJama has taken a much more aggressive approach than any other project that provides persistence for the Java language that we are aware of (this includes systems that conform to the ODMG standard [8], GemStone/J [13], etc.) in order to achieve complete type orthogonality. However, we believe that the issues concerning the **transient** keyword, raised in the context of PJama, and hence the Java language, are significant for any other language that aspires to persistence. Many systems adopt partial persistence, i.e. only some classes can persistent (e.g. Java Object Serialisation [32]). For these systems a correct treatment of **transient** is essential, as it is the only way in which application programmers can specify how references to non-persistable objects can be dealt with. Our discussion, suggested semantics, and implementation are therefore of relevance to the design of future persistent languages and to all forms of persistence for the Java language.

---

[2] In this paper, by "a class can persist" we imply that its instances can also persist.

[3] In PJama, the static initialiser of a class is invoked once, when the class is first loaded, and not every time it is fetched from the store by a new invocation of the VM. If some operations need to take place when a class is fetched from the store (e.g. dynamic library loading), this is done by the *Global Runtime Events*, as described in the Orthogonal Persistence for the Java Platform Proposal [20].

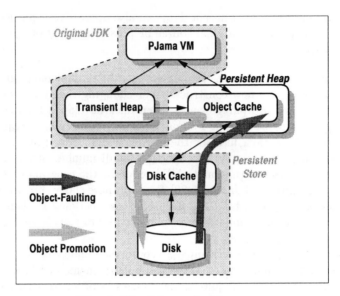

Fig. 1. The PJama Architecture

2.1 The PJama Architecture

This section provides a brief overview of the low-level architecture of the PJama system. It is included here, as it will be referred to in Section 5.

PJama achieves the three principles of orthogonal persistence, mentioned in the previous section, by requiring changes to the VM. It can be argued that this is the only way to make some classes persistent (e.g. `Class`, `Thread`), since their state cannot be accessed from inside a Java program, hence a solution written entirely in the Java language would be inappropriate. In fact, GemStone Inc. have taken a similar approach for their GemStone/J product [13].

The current PJama implementation is based on Sun's Classic JDK™ Platform. A high-level illustration of its architecture is given in Figure 1. The original JDK platform comprises the VM and the *Transient Heap*[4], where objects are allocated and manipulated. PJama extends this by adding the *Object Cache*, where persistent objects are cached and manipulated. Objects in the transient heap and in the object cache appear the same to the VM; therefore the combination of the transient heap and the object cache can be viewed as a single *Persistent Heap*. In fact, these two components might be unified in future implementations of PJama.

When an object in the transient heap becomes persistent (i.e. when there is a reference to it from a persistent object in the object cache), it is moved to the object cache and an image of it is written to disk, via the *Disk Cache* of the persistent store (this operation is called *Object Promotion* and is illustrated in Figure 1). When an object needs to be fetched from disk, the buffer

---

[4] This is also known as the *Garbage Collected Heap*.

where it resides is copied to the disk cache and then the object is copied to the object cache (this operation is called *Object-Faulting* and is also illustrated in Figure 1). At this point, all the references in it are PIDs[5]. The VM will detect when one of these is dereferenced and will fetch the appropriate object from disk. More information on the memory management of PJama is given by Daynès and Atkinson [9].

The above architecture and the tight coupling between the components allows the performance of the PJama system to be very good, since all the object-fetching and dirty object-tracking is done entirely inside the runtime system. In fact, performance evaluation experiments by Ridgway et al. show PJama faster than all the approaches, written entirely in the Java language, that map objects to relational or object-oriented databases [28].

3   The Need for Transient Data in Orthogonally Persistent Systems

Modern programming languages typically include a large number of standard facilities, such as commonly-used utilities and bindings to external resources. One of the trends in programming language design is to keep the core and syntax of the language minimal and bundle most of the required facilities as libraries. This allows the language to be left unchanged, when new facilities are added to it, and makes third-party library additions and experimentation easier. Examples of this trend are the C++ platform [15] and the still-expanding Java platform [14,33].

In contrast, early orthogonally persistent languages, like PS-algol [2] and Napier88 [21], were designed as closed systems. This allowed their implementers to achieve complete type orthogonality, since the state of all the data that needed to persist was known to the system. This approach proved the feasability of orthogonal persistence. However, it was very limiting, as the addition of any new facilities to the system, which had to communicate with external resources and therefore could not be written in the language itself, had to be incorporated inside the core of the system and could not be bundled as external libraries. This was the case, for example, for the windowing system and sockets. This limitation has been one of the biggest criticisms of orthogonally persistent systems.

The above has sparked an interest in orthogonally persistent systems that can handle external state through a well-defined interface. Such systems are called *open*. A severe complication arises however when an open persistent system attempts to make external state persistent. When it re-instates it, it will not know how to perform any required initialisation as it does not know the data contents, layout, and interpretation. The only way that this can be achieved in a generic manner is to delegate to a library, which manages the external state, the identification of which data should not be put into the store and how its re-initialisation should be handled.

---

[5] *Persistent Identifiers*, the equivalent of references in the persistent store that uniquely identify persistent objects [26].

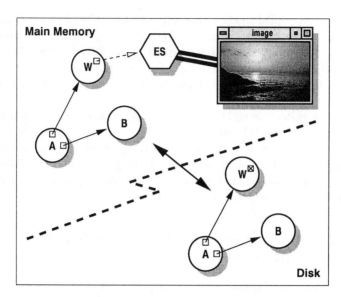

Fig. 2. Handling External State in a Persistent System

We will call data that the application or library chooses not to allow to become persistent, *transient*. An open persistent system should have a well-defined way of allowing users to mark data as transient and restore it to well-defined values, when moving it to disk, so that the next access to it can be detected and any necessary re-initialisation code run.

The handling of external state using transient data is illustrated in Figure 2. Object **W** in memory contains the state of the image window in a format that the persistent system can understand and manipulate. Any changes to **W** are propagated, via calls to the appropriate library, to object **ES** that is the window state inside the windowing toolkit and is external to the persistent system. The reference from **W** to **ES** has been marked transient, hence the dashed arrow (notice that it is the reference field in object **W** that needs to be marked transient, *not* object **ES** itself). When object **W** is stored on disk, that reference will be cut and set to a default value. This will be detected, when **W** is re-activated, and the re-initialisation of **ES** will be triggered with a call to the windowing library.

An interesting question, which arises in the above example, is what happens when object **W** is written to disk and then accessed shortly afterwards, within the same activation of the system. Obviously, we do not want the reference to **ES** to be cut, since this will force the image window to be re-created every time its state is written to disk. We believe that, during the same activation of the system, the reference to **ES** should be retained in memory, but cut every time it is written to disk. On a new activation of the system, only the *first* access to **W** will detect that the reference had been cut; this will force an equivalent of **ES** to be re-created[6] and a reference to it stored in **W**.

Past experience with using persistent systems has shown that there are three cases where programmers need to mark data as transient.

- **For Handling External State.** As explained in the previous section, data that contains external state, which the system cannot handle, should not be written to the store but should be re-initialised when faulted-in. An example of this is the state of GUI components, which typically can only be interpreted by the windowing library.
- **As a Model of Resumable Programming.** Apart from external state, there are other categories of data that need to be re-initialised when read by a new invocation of the VM. If the system sets them to a default value when it puts them to disk, the application can later detect that this has happened and re-initialise them. An example of this is a string containing the name of the machine on which the application is running, that has to be reset every time the application starts up.
- **For Efficiency.** There are cases when it is more efficient to re-create data, rather than store it on disk. For example, application developers might choose to store rarely accessed data in a compressed format and re-create it upon use, in order to save space on disk. This technique is of course strictly an optimisation and it can be argued that it breaks the rules of type orthogonality, as defined in Section 2. However, developers might choose to use it to tune their applications.

We can now give the following definition.

Definition 1 *Transient data, in an open persistent system, is data that is not written to the persistent store, keeps its value throughout the same activation of the system, and is reset to a well-known default value, upon its first use in a new activation of the system.*

4   Defining Transient Data in the Java Language

The Java programming language has a standard keyword called `transient` that was introduced to be used in situations similar to the ones presented in Section 3. However, its semantics have not been accurately defined and its current use in the standard libraries of the JDK platform is not completely compatible with Definition 1. The issues raised by this are discussed in this section.

---

[6] Since the Java language is platform-independent, the next activation can be on a different architecture/OS/windowing environment, thus an equivalent rather than identical object is needed.

4.1 The transient Keyword in the Java Language

In the Java Language Specification (JLS) version 1.0 [14, page 147], the transient keyword is defined as follows.

Definition 2 *"Variables may be marked* transient *to indicate that they are not part of the persistent state of an object. If an instance of the class* Point*:*

```
class Point {
    int x, y;
    transient float rho, theta;
}
```

were saved to persistent storage by a system service, then only the fields x *and* y *would be saved. This specification does not yet specify details of such services; we intend to provide them in a future version of this specification."*

Even though the above definition loosely describes that transient fields should not be made persistent, it does not accurately define the following.

- What the persistent state of an object is.
- Under what circumstances a field should not be placed in persistent storage.
- What values the transient fields are set to when the object is re-activated from persistent storage.
- Whether transient fields retain their value, when an object is evicted from memory to disk and then re-read, within the same invocation of the VM.

It turns out that the above details are very important when interpreting transient fields in the context of an orthogonally persistent system. In fact, if they are misinterpreted, they can negatively affect the programming model and break, in many cases, transparency and orthogonality. This will become apparent in later sections of the paper.

4.2 Java Object Serialization

Java Object Serialization (JOS) [32] is a mechanism that provides facilities to translate an object graph to and from a byte-stream. It was originally developed as part of the *Java Remote Method Invocation* (RMI) [34] framework[7], which allows object graphs to be moved between different hosts. However, since a byte-stream can be stored on disk and then retrieved at a later time, it is easy to see how JOS can also be used as a persistence mechanism.

Since the 1.1 release of the Java platform, JOS has been part of the standard java.io package, accessed via the ObjectInputStream and the ObjectOutputStream classes [33]. Apart from RMI, it is also used extensively

---

[7] Ken Arnold of Sun Microsystems, personal communication.

for persistence facilities in the JavaBeans™ [30] and JavaSpaces™ [31] frameworks. Since these frameworks are very high-profile and widely used, *"JOS has effectively become the default persistence mechanism for the Java platform"* [19].

We believe that there are numerous problems with using JOS as a persistence mechanism for production-quality code. These are presented in detail by Evans [10] and Jordan [17] and they are beyond the scope of this paper. We will concentrate instead on the `transient` keyword in the context of JOS.

The `transient` Keyword and JOS For reasons similar to the ones presented in Section 3, a way of specifying that some fields of a class should not be serialised was necessary for JOS. Starting with the 1.1 release of the Java platform, the `transient` keyword has been used for this purpose. The JOS specification defines it as follows [32, pages 10–11].

Definition 3 *"Transient fields are not persistent and will not be saved by any persistence mechanism. Marking the field will prevent the state from appearing in the stream and from being restored during deserialization."*

A definition similar to the above is also included in the Java Platform 1.2 Core API Specification [33, class `java.io.ObjectOutputStream`].

Definition 4 *"The default serialization mechanism for an object writes the class of the object, the class signature, and the values of all non-transient and non-static fields. References to other objects (except in transient or static fields) cause those objects to be written also."*

From the above two quotes, it is clear that the de-facto definition of the `transient` keyword is "not serialisable by JOS". However, the JLS [14] does not include any changes to the Java programming language, which were introduced in version 1.1 onwards, and hence does not "officially" embrace this definition. We are expecting however that its next edition will.

Concrete Example: `java.awt.Component` The `transient` keyword is used extensively in the standard libraries of the JDK platform, in classes that can be serialised. The example below is from the `Component` class of the `java.awt` package [33].

```
package java.awt;

public abstract class Component
   implements java.io.Serializable, ...
{
    transient ComponentPeer peer;
    ...
}
```

All AWT component classes extend this class and **peer** is the architecture/OS-dependent state of each component. It is marked **transient** so that it is re-created when the object is deserialised on another machine. This, in fact, is very similar to the situation illustrated in Figure 2, if we assume that object **W** in that figure is the **Component** object and object **ES** is the **peer** object.

An interesting observation is that, even though a method that intialises the peer object exists, there is no mechanism to call it after deserialisation, as seems natural. Instead, every method of the **Component** class checks whether **peer** is null and, if it is, it then calls the initialisation method. This requirement for an explicit check before every use is extremely tedious, confusing, and error-prone.

Concrete Example: java.util.Hashtable Another example we will consider is the **Hashtable** class of the **java.util** package [33].

```
package java.util;

public class Hashtable
   extends Dictionary
   implements Cloneable, java.io.Serializable
{
    private transient HashtableEntry table[];
    ...
}
```

According to the above, the array that contains the hash table entries has been marked **transient** and will not be automatically serialised. At first sight, this indicates that the contents of a hashtable will not be saved and restored. In fact, it is an idiom which means that class **Hashtable** should provide special marshalling code (e.g. the **writeObject** and **readObject** methods [33]) to put the hashtable entries in the byte-stream and to retrieve them later. Effectively, the hashtable is "manually" serialised and re-created when deserialised.

There are two reasons behind this "strange" behaviour. The first one is optimisation. Assuming that hashtables are sparsely populated, serialising only their entries, rather than the table itself and all auxiliary objects, generates a smaller byte-stream. This is important since, as mentioned above, the original use of JOS was in RMI and smaller byte-streams are transmitted more efficiently over the network. For the same reasons, there are many collection classes, in the standard libraries of the JDK platform 1.2, that also have their principle data fields marked with **transient**. Examples include **LinkedList**, **TreeMap**, and **TreeSet** [33].

The second reason is that the location of each entry in the table depends on the entry's hashcode. However, the JLS defines the **hashCode** method as follows [14, pages 459–460].

Definition 5 *"Whenever it is invoked on the same object more then once during an execution of a Java application, **hashCode** must consistently return the same* *integer. The integer may be positive, negative, or zero. This integer does not, however, have to remain consistent from one Java application to another, or from one execution of an application to another execution of the same application."*

According to the above definition, when a byte-stream is deserialised, possibly on a different machine, the new copies of the objects that are created might have different hashcodes. This forces the hashtable to have to be re-created, so that each of its entries is inserted in the correct slots, specified by its (possibly different) hashcode[8].

Concrete Example Summary The two concrete examples above illustrate that the `transient` keyword is overloaded by JOS with the following two meanings.

- **Not Serialisable.** This means that the field should not be serialised and should be reset to its default value in the serialised byte-stream. This is the case for the `Component` example.
- **Special Marshalling Required.** This means that the field should not be serialised "as is", but special code should be run instead to serialise/deserialise it. This is the case for the `Hashtable` example.

It is worth emphasising here that the second case above directly contradicts Definition 3, which states that *"transient fields will not be saved by any persistent mechanism"*, since it *does* allow data in transient fields to be serialised; this just happens by a different mechanism, namely the `writeObject` method [33].

The `serialPersistentFields` Mechanism In addition to the `transient` keyword, a new mechanism was introduced in the JDK1.2 platform that can be used to specify which fields should be serialised by JOS. An array with name `serialPersistentFields` and signature `static final private ObjectStreamField[]` can be introduced in a class to specify which fields of that class should be serialised [32, pages 4–5] (notice that this is the inverse of the `transient` keyword, which specifies the fields that should *not* be serialised). Its entries are instances of class `ObjectStreamField`, each of which represents a field of a given name and type. The use of this mechanism is illustrated in the following example[9].

```
class Point {
   int x, y;
   float rho, theta;
```

---

[8] This is an example where internal state has been allowed to become external, in order to free implementers from constraints; erroneously in our opinion [19].

[9] The expression `Integer.TYPE` in the example denotes the class of the primitive type `int`.

```
static final private ObjectStreamField[]
  serialPersistentFields = {
  new ObjectStreamField("x", Integer.TYPE),
  new ObjectStreamField("y", Integer.TYPE)
  };
}
```

According to the above, when an instance of class Point is serialised, only the fields x and y will be written to the generated byte-stream; the fields rho and theta will be considered transient. In fact, for the purposes of JOS, the above class will behave in an identical way to the one included in Definition 2, the latter using transient instead of serialPersistentFields.

We believe that the use of serialPersistentFields is unecessarily awkward and verbose (e.g. compare the source of class Point above to the one included in Definition 2). Unfortunately, it is also unsafe because, even though the setPersistentFields field itself must be declared final and hence cannot be updated, its contents are *not* (in fact, they cannot be, according to the Java programming language [14]). By assigning new instances of ObjectStreamField to the array slots, one can arrange for different fields to be serialised at different times, with confusing consequences. Finally, using serialPersistentFields is also error-prone. A mispelling of its name or a small difference in signature will allow JOS to "quietly" ignore it, creating a very subtle debugging problem for the developer. This, in fact, happened to us when we were evaluating its use; it took us over 30 mins to spot the error.

Even though it has shortcomings, this mechanism could ultimately eliminate the use of the transient keyword for the purposes of JOS. This will make it "available" for use exclusively in the context of persistence. However, at least for now, this is not possible, as all but three classes in the standard libraries of the JDK platform 1.2 use the transient keyword in favour of serialPersistentFields.

4.3   Defining Transient Fields in PJama

In an ideal implementation of the PJama system, we would like the transient keyword to follow Definition 1. However, since we have built PJama on top of the JDK platform, we have also inherited the platform's standard libraries, where transient meets the needs of JOS, as explained in Section 8. There are two issues that should be considered.

- Persistent objects in PJama retain the same hashcode across multiple invocations of the system (this is basically an extra constraint on Definition 5).
- Specially encoding object graphs is not desirable in PJama since it will complicate its incremental object-fetching operation, it will break the concept of persistence independence, and the bandwidth issue, present in a distributed context, is less significant for persistence.

It follows that PJama should ignore, for the purposes of persistence, some occurrences of the `transient` keyword in the standard libraries of the JDK platform (in classes that it can deal with, e.g. `Hashtable` and other collections), but not all of them (in classes that contain external state that PJama cannot deal with, e.g. `Component`). One solution to this would have been to remove the inappropriate occurences of `transient`. Unfortunately, this is not possible, since PJama uses JOS in the context of RMI [29] and JOS would not then operate correctly over such classes.

This forced us to implement an alternative way of marking fields transient, which are considered as such only by PJama in the context of persistence, that does not interfere with JOS. By default, the `transient` keyword is ignored by the PJama system and the following method

```
public static final void
markTransient (String fieldName);
```

has been introduced in the PJSystem PJama-specific class [35]. This method can only be called inside the static initialiser of a class and notifies the PJama system that the static or instance field of that class with name `fieldName` should not be stored on disk[10].

A concrete example of the use of `markTransient` is included below. It presents the `Component` class of the `java.awt` package (see Section 7), after it was modified for use in PJama (it is worth pointing out that, even though we had to modify a few more of the standard classes of the JDK platform in a similar way, their public API remained the same, allowing all existing, even non PJama-specific, Java programs to operate unchanged).

```
package java.awt;
import org.opj.utilities.PJSystem;

public abstract class Component
  implements java.io.Serializable, ...
{
    transient ComponentPeer peer;
    transient Container parent;
    ...
    static {
        PJSystem.markTransient("peer");
    }
}
```

When a `Component` object is written to the store, the `peer` field, which contains the external state of the component, will be set to the `null` value, since `markTransient` has been called on it. However, the `parent` field *will* be saved

---

[10] Naturally, appropriate exceptions will be thrown if `markTransient` is not called inside a static initialiser or the field name is invalid.

to disk, even though it has the modifier `transient` (this is desirable since in PJama we want to make the structure of a GUI persistent and the `parent` object is part of it). Since the above example can be slightly misleading, it is worth pointing out that the `markTransient` method can be called on fields that are not tagged with `transient`, if necessary.

Even though the introduction of the `markTransient` method is not particularly elegant, it is functional, straightforward to use, and allows the information on the transience of fields to be kept inside the class source, rather than somewhere else. It is also safe, since instances of a class can only be created after its static initialiser has been invoked [14]. This ensures that, when a new instance is allocated, PJama has already been notified about which fields must be considered as transient.

It is worth emphasising that our approach directly contradicts Definition 3, which states that *"transient fields are not persistent and will not be saved by any persistence mechanism"*, since PJama stores transient fields on disk by default, unless the method `markTransient` has been called on them. Though clearly undesirable, this is necessary because of the overloaded meaning of the `transient` keyword, as explained in Section 8.

4.4 GemStone's Approach

GemStone Inc. also had to define a way to deal with the overloaded meaning of the `transient` keyword in their GemStone/J product [13]. The resulting technique is more restrictive than the one adopted by PJama, described in Section 4.3. By default GemStone/J obeys the `transient` keyword. However, when the GemStone/J's default repository (i.e. store) is built [12], the transient attribute for some standard classes (e.g. `Hashtable`, `Date`) is internally cleared for the purposes of the persistent object manager. This facility is internal and not available to users[11].

The above is the opposite to the approach taken by PJama: GemStone/J obeys the `transient` keyword, unless otherwise specified, as opposed to PJama that ignores the `transient` keyword, unless otherwise specified. However, the final outcome is the same in both cases: some fields prefixed with `transient` in the standard libraries are not treated as such by the storage mechanism.

4.5 An Alternative Proposal

A more radical way to deal with the overloaded meaning of `transient` is included in the Orthogonal Persistence for the Java Platform Proposal [20] and was originally proposed by GemStone Inc. It involves extending the Java programming language with the introduction of the sub-modifiers `serial` and `storage`, that augment the `transient` keyword. Their meaning is as follows.

- `transient serial` only means "not serialisable" (i.e. only transient in the context of JOS).

---

[11] Allen Otis and Venkatesh Ram of GemStone Inc., personal communication.

- **transient storage** only means "not persistent" (i.e. only transient in the context of the persistence mechanism, in our case PJama).
- **transient** on its own is the combination of both of the above, i.e. "not serialisable" *and* "not persistent".

The meaning of **transient** on its own does not differ from its current interpretation in the JDK platform (see Section 8), as it encompasses both **serial** and **storage**. This allows for backward compatibility, since existing classes that use **transient** will still operate correctly unchanged. Only if one of the sub-modifiers is introduced into a class, may changes to its methods be necessary to reflect the change in semantics.

A concrete example of their use is given below. It is the **Component** class, presented in Section 4.3, amended appropriately.

```
package java.awt;

public abstract class Component
  implements java.io.Serializable, ...
{
    transient ComponentPeer peer;
    transient serial Container parent;
    ...
    /* no markTransient is required */
}
```

In the above, the **parent** field is marked **transient serial**, while the **peer** field remains marked **transient**. This allows for the correct handling of these fields by both PJama and JOS, eliminating the need for the **markTransient** method.

It is worth emphasising that the **serialPersistentFields** mechanism, in conjuction with the **transient** keyword being used only for persistence, can also provide a way of distinguishing between transience for persistence and transience for JOS (see Section 8). However, we believe that the **transient serial** and **transient storage** sub-modifiers provide a much more compact, safer, clearer, and less error-prone way of doing so.

4.6   A Note on Persistence vs. Distribution

Earlier sections have explained why it is necessary to introduce a new way of marking fields transient for the purposes of persistence and how this should not interfere with JOS. Both PJama and GemStone Inc. have adopted ad-hoc solutions and the proposal for the **serial** and **storage** sub-modifiers attempts to introduce a consistent way of dealing with this. However, there is another related issue that should also be considered.

As mentioned in an Section 4.2, JOS is used for both persistence (e.g. JavaSpaces) and distribution (e.g. RMI) in the Java platform. However, the trade-offs of persistence and distribution are radically different, mainly due to differences in bandwidth[12]. For example, it is typically more efficient to minimise the size of a byte-stream, generated when serialising an object graph, so it is transmitted quicker over the network. This optimisation is not really necessary in the context of persistence, since the local disk of a machine can usually be accessed very efficiently[13].

Apart from efficiency reasons, there is also the distinction between data that is allowed to persist but not be transmitted and vice versa. An example of the former is sensitive information (e.g. password) that the user/programmer would trust the local disk to store but would not trust the network to transmit. Examples of the latter are more subtle. However they do exist in the internals of PJRMI, the PJama-specific extensions to RMI [29].

Given the above, we believe that any definition of transience should deal with the persistence/distribution separation (Evans also reaches the same conclusion [10]). Ideally, in an orthogonally persistent system, JOS should only be used in the context of RMI and not to provide any persistence facilities. In this case, the proposed serial and storage sub-modifiers will be interpreted as *not transmittable* and *not persistent*, respectively.

5   Handling Transient Fields in a Persistent System

This section overviews implementation techniques for handling transient fields in persistent systems, while preserving the semantics of Definition 1. Section 5.1 deals with issues raised when propagating updates to the persistent store and Section 5.2 covers issues concerning object eviction.

5.1   Updating Objects

Typically, persistent systems need to keep track of which persistent objects are updated (dirtied) during program execution, in order to propagate these updates to the persistent store. The accuracy of the dirtying information (i.e. object-grain or field-grain) is a trade-off between run-time performance (i.e. how fast it can be recorded), space requirements (i.e. how much space is required to record it), and stabilisation operation efficiency (i.e. how fast the system can detect which objects have been updated and propagate the changes to disk).

In the current release of PJama (based on the JDK classic platform), the dirtying information is object-grain. Each persistent object has a dirty flag on its header, which is set when an update to it occurs. The stabilisation operation discovers which objects have their dirty flag set and updates their disk image. This works efficiently for small objects (i.e. most class instances), since they are

---

[12] Thanks to Alex Garthwaite for this observation.

[13] Interestingly enough, there are situations where it is more efficient to access the memory of another machine through a LAN rather than the local disk [11]. Such techniques however are still at an experimental stage and normally require special operating system support. But much of the traffic carried by RMI is over much slower WANs.

very likely to reside on a single disk page. In this case, the I/O operation will always dwarf the memory copying operation from the object cache to the disk cache (see Figure 1). Large arrays are associated with a card table [16], which specifies which parts of the array are updated, in an attempt to minimise disk traffic. The mechanism is explained in more detail by Daynès and Atkinson [9].

The fact that persistent objects are updated in their entirety, rather than on a field-by-field basis, introduces a potential problem for objects which contain transient fields. Such fields have to be set to a default value, when they are written to the store, but their in-memory value has to be retained (as specified by Definition 1). An obvious approach to propagating updates to the store is to translate each object into store format in-place in the object cache (this involves translating all the references in it to PIDs and resetting the transient fields — this operation is called *unswizzling*), copy these modified contents to the disk cache, and translate the original object image back to VM format. However, this actually discards the values of the transient fields, as they are overwritten with the default values, and it does not allow them to be restored at the end of the stabilisation operation, as required by Definition 1[14]. Even though auxiliary data structures could be temporarily set up to hold the overwritten values, this would complicate the implementation and require extra space to be reserved.

A more elegent solution is given here. Notice that for an object to be updated on disk, its image has to be copied from the object cache to the disk cache. This presents an opportunity to perform all the necessary translations in the disk-cache buffer, while leaving the original image of the object unchanged. This way, the transient fields will only be overwritten with the appropriate default values on the disk-cache buffer and not in the object cache, eliminating the problem mentioned above.

In order for this to be possible, it is necessary for a well-defined interface to be defined between the persistent heap manager and the persistent store that allows the former to access the disk cache. Such an interface has been introduced in Sphere, the new persistent object store from Glasgow University that will be used in the next version of PJama [26,27,25], in the form of the *Unswizzling Callbacks* [23]. Every time an object-update call is invoked, Sphere performs an up-call (the unswizzling callback) to the persistent heap manager, providing it with the address of the object image in the disk-cache buffer, so that the necessary translations can be performed.

The operation of the unswizzling callbacks is explained in more detail by Printezis and Atkinson [24]. Apart from handling transient fields, they can also be used to unswizzle references directly on the disk cache. This avoids the unecessary in-place translation of each object mentioned above.

Their use will be illustrated using a concrete example. Figure 3 shows the initial state of the system. Object **A** is a persistent object, cached in memory, with PID P_A (for the purposes of this example, the PID of each cached persistent

---

[14] The same problem does not apply to the unswizzled references, since there is a one-to-one mapping between the address of a persistent object and its PID, therefore translating between them is always possible.

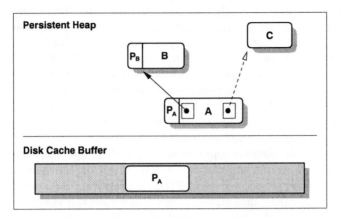

Fig. 3. Updating Object **A** — Initial

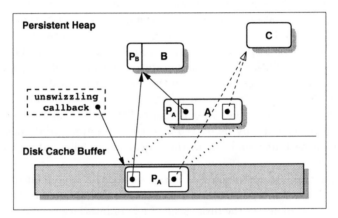

Fig. 4. Updating Object **A** — Copying

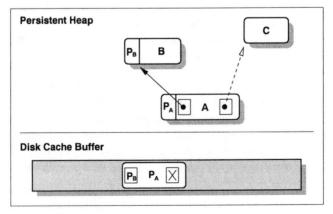

Fig. 5. Updating Object **A** — Unswizzling

object is stored in its header). It contains two references: one to object **B**, which is also persistent and has PID P_B, and a transient one (hence the dashed line) to object **C**.

The first step in updating object **A** is illustrated in Figure 4. The object's image is copied to the disk-cache buffer "as is", with its reference fields still containing memory addresses. Then the unswizzling callback is invoked, accepting as a parameter the address of the object on the disk-cache buffer.

Figure 5 illustrates the state of the system after the unswizzling callback has finished its operation. The reference to object **B** has been replaced by the object's PID (i.e. P_B) and the reference to object **C** has been set to null, as it is transient. Finally, notice that during this entire operation, the in-memory image of object **A** remained unchaged.

The current PJama system is using a scheme very similar to this to unswizzle objects. However, this has been achieved without the use of proper interfaces, which resulted in the abstractions within the system collapsing. We believe that the introduction of the unswizzling callbacks provides an elegant solution to this problem, while keeping the two components (i.e. the object cache and the store layer) well separated.

Finally, it is worth pointing out that this implementation technique is not only applicable to systems with a one-to-one tight coupling between the virtual machine and the store (like PJama, as illustrated in Figure 1), but also to client-server architectures. In this case, on the client side, the unswizzling can take place on the buffer that will be used to transfer the data to the server.

5.2   Evicting Objects

In the context of PJama, *Object Eviction* is the operation that removes persistent objects from the object cache (see Figure 1), in order to make space for others to be faulted in[15]. It is implemented entirely inside the memory management of the customised interpreter and is transparent to the programmer. Because of this, the eviction mechanism should not violate Definition 1.

However, an evicted object can be faulted in by either the same invocation of the system that evicted it or a different one at a later time. This definition raises some interesting issues when considering eviction of objects that contain transient fields. In particular, when such an object is evicted, it is unclear what values the transient fields in its disk image should be set to.

- If they are set to the default values, as it is natural, and the object is refetched within the same invocation of the system, the transient fields will be reset. This clashes with Definition 1.
- If they are set to the values that they contained in memory, when the object was evicted, and the object is fetched in a different invocation of the system,

---

[15] It should not be confused with the page eviction operation of a virtual memory system. Such pages can only be evicted and fetched by the same invocation of a process and are discarded after that process has finished execution.

the value of the fields will most likely be invalid. This is especially severe if the transient fields happen to contain memory addresses, as it will introduce "dangling" references.

One solution to the above problem is to always pin in the object cache all persistent objects containing transient fields and not allow them to be evicted. This should work well since, in theory, only a small portion of objects have transient fields. However, it might impose scalability problems for some applications. The obvious alternative of storing the values of the transient fields in auxialiary data structures, before the object is evicted, can introduce scalability problems as well.

A refinement is to evict an object, only when its transient fields (if any) already contain the default values. This will mean that either the object has not been used or any external resources, which it pointed to, have been explicitly disposed of by the application and its transient fields have been reset. In either case, it is safe to evict the object, since its state will be valid, if it is faulted in by the same or a different invocation of the system.

6   Conclusions

This paper raises several issues concerning the interpretation and use of the transient keyword in the Java programming language, in the Java platform standard libraries, and in an orthogonally persistent environment such as PJama. We hope that, using concrete examples from the JDK platform and PJama libraries, we have convincingly shown that

- the transient keyword has not been defined sufficiently accurately in the JLS,
- its current usage in the standard libraries of the JDK platform is inconsistent with the existing JLS definition,
- its currently overloaded meaning requires persistence mechanisms to adopt ad-hoc workarounds,
- the fundamental distinction between its use in a persistent and distributed context is not addressed, and
- it is feasible to implement efficiently the handling of transient fields, while obeying Definition 1.

We have proposed a definition, Definition 1, that clarifies the semantics of transient in a way which we believe appropriate for providing persistence to Java and other languages and have shown that this is practically feasible. We would like to see some of the issues presented in this paper included in future versions of the JLS and propagated to the standard libraries of the JDK platform.

It is currently unclear whether the serialPersistentFields mechanism will eventually be adopted by the whole JOS community. The wide use of the transient keyword, in the context of JOS, and the requirements for backward compatibility, might inhibit this. In this case, the proposal for the introduction of the `serial` and `storage` sub-modifiers would be a compromise that yields a more elegant solution. However, if we could change history, we would have adopted the following three keywords instead:

- `transient` to mean not storable,
- `local` to mean not transmittable, and
- `special` to mean "special marshalling required".

We believe that future programming languages should include persistence and that this requires more care of the definition of transience. The management of the interplay between persistence and transience becomes important as we move towards open systems.

Acknowledgements

This work is funded by the British Engineering and Science Research Council, grant number GR/K87791, and by a collaborative research grant from Sun Microsystems Inc. The authors would like to thank the following people: Susan Spence for her very constructive input on this paper, Huw Evans for his, as always, detailed comments and for providing early access to his paper, Peter Dickman and Craig Hamilton for their encouraging feedback, Allen Otis and Venkatesh Ram of GemStone Inc. for their useful information on GemStone/J. Bernd Mathiske implemented the PJama Action Handlers and the handling of the `markTransient` method. Laurent Daynès implemented most of the memory management and store layer of the current PJama system. The authors are also grateful to the rest of the PJama team, both at Sun Labs and at the University of Glasgow, for their help, comments, and support.

Trademarks

Sun, Java, JavaSpaces, JavaBeans and JDK are trademarks or registered trademarks in the United States and other countries.

References

1. K. Arnold and J. Gosling. *The Java Programming Language.* Addison-Wesley, 1996.
2. M. P. Atkinson, K. J. Chisholm, and W. P. Cockshott. PS-algol: an Algol with a Persistent Heap. *ACM SIGPLAN Notices*, 17(7):24–31, July 1982.
3. M. P. Atkinson, L. Daynès, M. J. Jordan, T. Printezis, and S. Spence. An Orthogonally Persistent Java. *SIGMOD Record (ACM Special Interest Group on Management of Data)*, 25(4):68–75, December 1996.
4. M. P. Atkinson and M. J. Jordan. Issues Raised by Three Years of Developing PJama: An Orthogonally Persistent Platform for Java™. In *Proceedings of ICDT'99*, Jerusalem, Israel, January 1999.

5. M. P. Atkinson, M. J. Jordan, L. Daynès, and S. Spence. Design Issues for Persistent Java: a Type-Safe Object-Oriented Orthogonally Persistent System. In *Proceedings of POS'7*, Cape May, New Jersey, USA, May 1996.

6. M. P. Atkinson and R. Morrison. Orthogonal Persistent Object Systems. *VLDB Journal*, 4(3), 1995.

7. M. P. Atkinson and R. C. Welland, editors. *Fully Integrated Data Environments*. Springer-Verlag, 1999.

8. R. G. G. Cattell, editor. *The Object Database Standard: ODMG 2.0*. Morgan Kaufmann Publishers, 1997.

9. L. Daynès and M. P. Atkinson. Main-Memory Management to support Orthogonal Persistence for Java. In *Proceedings of the Second International Workshop on Persistence and Java (PJW2)*, Half Moon Bay, CA, USA, August 1997.

10. H. Evans. Why Object Serialization is Inappropriate for Providing Persistence in Java. Technical report, Department of Computing Science, University of Glasgow, Scotland, 2000. *In Preparation*.

11. M. J. Feeley, W. E. Morgan, F. H. Pighin, A. R. Karlin, and H. M. Levy. Implementing Global Memory Management in a Workstation Cluster. In *Proceedings of the 15th ACM Symposium on Operating Systems Principles (SOSP-15)*, pages 201–212, Copper Mountain Resort, CO, USA, December 1995. ACM Press.

12. GemStone Systems Inc. *GemStone/J™ Administration for Unix*, March 1998. Version 1.1.

13. GemStone Systems Inc. *GemStone/J™ Programming Guide*, March 1998. Version 1.1.

14. J. Gosling, B. Joy, and G. Steele. *The Java Language Specification*. Addison-Wesley, 1996.

15. ISO. Working Paper for Draft Proposed International Standard for Information Systems — Programming Language C++, 1998. ISO/IEC 14882-1998.

16. R. E. Jones. *Garbage Collection: Algorithms for Automatic Dynamic Memory Management*. John Wiley & Sons, Ltd, 1996. With a chapter on Distributed Garbage Collection by R. Lins.

17. D. Jordan. Serialisation is not a database substitute. *Java™ Report*, pages 68–79, July 1999.

18. M. J. Jordan. Early Experiences with Persistent Java. In *Proceedings of the First International Workshop on Persistence and Java (PJW1)*, Drymen, Scotland, September 1996.

19. M. J. Jordan and M. P. Atkinson. Orthogonal Persistence for Java — A Mid-term Report. In *Proceedings of the Third International Workshop on Persistence and Java (PJW3)*, pages 335–352, Tiburon, California, September 1998.

20. M. J. Jordan and M. P. Atkinson, editors. Orthogonal Persistence for the Java™ Platform — Draft Specification. Technical report, Sun Microsystems Inc, 1999.

21. R. Morrison, R. C. H. Connor, Q. Cutts, G. N. C. Kirby, D. S. Munro, and M. P. Atkinson. The Napier88 Persistent Programming Language and Environment. In Atkinson and Welland [7], chapter 1.1.3, pages 98–154.

22. T. Printezis. Orthogonal Persistence: The Future for Storing Objects? In *Proceedings of the Practical Applications for Java Conference 1999 (PAJava'99)*, pages 5–17, London, UK, April 1999. *Invited Paper*.

23. T. Printezis. The Sphere User's Guide. Technical Report TR-1999-47, Department of Computing Science, University of Glasgow, Scotland, July 1999.

24. T. Printezis and M. P. Atkinson. An Efficient Object Promotion Algorithm for Persistent Object Systems, 2000. Accepted for publication at *Software – Practice and Experience*.

25. T. Printezis, M. P. Atkinson, and L. Daynès. The Implementation of Sphere: a Scalable, Flexible, and Extensible Persistent Object Store. Technical Report TR-1998-46, Department of Computing Science, University of Glasgow, Scotland, May 1998.

26. T. Printezis, M. P. Atkinson, L. Daynès, S. Spence, and P. J. Bailey. The Design of a new Persistent Object Store for PJama. In *Proceedings of the Second International Workshop on Persistence and Java (PJW2)*, Half Moon Bay, CA, USA, August 1997. Published as SunLabs Technical Report TR-97-63.

27. T. Printezis, M. P. Atkinson, L. Daynès, S. Spence, and P. J. Bailey. The Design of Sphere: a Scalable, Flexible, and Extensible Persistent Object Store. Technical Report TR-1997-45, Department of Computing Science, University of Glasgow, Scotland, August 1997.

28. J. V. E. Ridgway, C. Thrall, and J. C. Wileden. Towards Assessing Approaches to Persistence for Java. In *Proceedings of the Second International Workshop on Persistence and Java (PJW2)*, Half Moon Bay, CA, USA, August 1997.

29. S. Spence. *Persistent RMI*. Department of Computing Science, University of Glasgow, Scotland, March 1998.

30. Sun Microsystems Inc. *JavaBeans*™, July 1997. Version 1.01.

31. Sun Microsystems Inc. *JavaSpaces*™ *Specification*, July 1998. Revision 1.0 Beta.

32. Sun Microsystems Inc. *Java*™ *Object Serialization Specification — JDK*™ *1.2*, November 1998. Revision 1.43.

33. Sun Microsystems Inc. *Java*™ *Platform 1.2 Core API Specification*, 1998.

34. Sun Microsystems Inc. *Java*™ *Remote Method Invocation Specification*, October 1998. Revision 1.5.

35. Sun Microsystems Inc and The University of Glasgow. *PJama API*, 1998. Release 0.5.7.13.

A Framework for Optimizing Distributed Workflow Executions

Guozhu Dong[1], Richard Hull[2], Bharat Kumar[2], Jianwen Su[3], and Gang Zhou[2]

[1] Department of Computer Science and Engineering, Wright State University, Dayton, Ohio 45435. gdong@cs.wright.edu
[2] Bell Laboratories, Lucent Technologies, 600 Mountain Ave., Murray Hill, NJ 07974. {hull,bharat,gzhou}@research.bell-labs.com
[3] Department of Computer Science, University of California, Santa Barbara, CA 93106. su@cs.ucsb.edu

Abstract. A central problem in workflow concerns optimizing the distribution of work in a workflow: how should the execution of tasks and the management of tasks be distributed across multiple processing nodes (i.e., computers). In some cases task management or execution may be at a processing node with limited functionality, and so it is useful to optimize translations of (sub-)workflow schemas into flowcharts, that can be executed in a restricted environment, e.g., in a scripting language or using a flowchart-based workflow engine.

This paper presents a framework for optimizing the physical distribution of workflow schemas, and the mapping of sub-workflow schemas into flowcharts. We provide a general model for representing essentially any distribution of a workflow schema, and for representing a broad variety of execution strategies. The model is based on families of "communicating flowcharts" (CFs). In the framework, a workflow schema is first rewritten as a family of CFs that are essentially atomic and execute in parallel. The CFs can be grouped into "clusters". Several CFs can be combined to form a single CF, which is useful when executing a sub-schema on a limited processor. Local rewriting rules are used to specify equivalence-preserving transformations. We developed a set of formulas to quantify the metrics used for choosing a near optimal set of CF clusters for executing a workflow. The current paper focuses primarily on ECA-based workflow models, such as Flowmark, Meteor and Mentor, and condition-action based workflow models, such as ThinkSheet and Vortex.

1 Introduction

A workflow management system provides a framework and mechanism for organizing the execution of multiple tasks, typically in support of a business or scientific process. A variety of workflow models and implementation strategies have been proposed [GHS95,WfM99]. Several recent projects have focused on developing architectures and systems that support distributed execution of workflows [AMG+95,DKM+96,WW97,BMR96]. A central problem concerns how to optimally distribute a workflow, i.e., how should the management and execution of tasks be distributed across multiple processing nodes? For example, while communication costs may increase with distribution, execution of task management on the same node that that executes the tasks may reduce communication costs and overall execution time. In some cases, the processing node for executing a sub-workflow may have limited functionality. For this reason, it is useful to optimize translations of some sub-schemas into flowcharts, that can be executed in a restricted environment, e.g., in a scripting language or using a flowchart-based workflow engine. This paper

R. Connor and A. Mendelzon (Eds.): DBPL'99, LNCS 1949, pp. 152-167, 2000.
© Springer-Verlag Berlin Heidelberg 2000

presents a framework and techniques for optimizing distributed execution of work-flows that includes the physical distribution of workflow schemas, and the mapping of sub-workflow schemas into flowcharts.

The framework developed is similar to the framework used in relational database query optimization. In particular, it provides an abstract model for representing "log-ical execution plans" for workflow schemas. These plans give a partitioning of a workflow schema, indicate data and control flow dependencies between the par-titions, and also indicate how the workflow sub-schemas should be implemented. Analogous to the relational algebra, this model is not intended for end-users or workflow designers. Rather it captures relevant features concerning distribution and execution of many workflow models, including those based on flowcharts, on petri-nets (e.g., ICN [Ell79]), on an event-condition-action (ECA) paradigm (e.g., Flow-mark [LR94], Meteor [KS95], Mentor [WWWD96]), and on a condition-action (CA) paradigm (e.g., ThinkSheet [PYLS96], Vortex [HLS$^+$99a]). Furthermore, the model is closed under a variety of equivalence-preserving transformations and re-writing rules. This permits the exploration of a broad space of possible implemen-tation strategies for a given workflow schema.

The abstract model is based on families of "communicating flowcharts" (CFs); these are flowcharts with specialized mechanisms to support inbound and outbound data flow, and to track control flow information. In the framework, a workflow schema is first rewritten as a family of CFs which are essentially atomic. These can be viewed as executing in parallel, while satisfying the synchronization constraints implied by the original workflow schema. The CFs can be grouped into "clusters"; in one approach to implementation each cluster is executed on a separate process-ing node, and data can be shared with minimal cost between the CFs in a cluster. These parts of the framework are useful in studying the costs and benefits of dif-ferent distributions of the execution of a workflow schema, assuming that each of the processing nodes provides a workflow engine that supports parallel execution of workflow tasks within a single workflow instance.

In some applications, it may be appropriate to execute a sub-workflow on a processing node that does not support a general-purpose workflow engine. One mo-tivation for this is to put task management on the same platform as task executions, e.g., if several related tasks are executed on the same platform. In such cases, the processing node might be a legacy system that does not support full-fledged parallel workflow execution. Indeed, the processing node might be part of a very limited legacy system, such as a component of a data or telecommunications network. A sub-workflow might be executed on such systems by translating it into a script, which is structured as a flowchart and invokes tasks in a synchronous fashion.

In other applications, it may be desirable to execute a sub-workflow on a re-stricted, flowchart-based workflow engine, in order to take advantage of existing in-terfaces to back-end components, rather than installing a general-purpose workflow engine and building new interfaces. (The customer-care focused workflow system Mosaix [Mos] is one such example.) In the abstract model presented in the current paper, several communicating flowcharts can be composed to form a single commu-nicating flowchart; these are suitable for execution on limited processing nodes.

To summarize, there are three main components in the abstract model:

(a) The use of one or more flowcharts, executing in parallel, to specify the internal operation of a workflow schema;

(b) A coherent mechanism for describing how these flowcharts communicate with each other, including both synchronization and data flow; and

(c) An approach that permits data flow and control flow dependencies to be treated in a uniform manner.

In addition, the paper presents a first family of rewriting rules that can express a broad family of transformations on logical execution plans.

So far we have discussed logical execution plans, which are high-level representations of how a workflow can be distributed. Our framework also includes the notion of "physical execution plan", which incorporates information about what processing nodes different clusters will be executed on, what networks will be connecting them, and how synchronization and data flow will be handled. We have also developed formulas for computing the costs of different physical execution plans, based on the key factors of response time and throughput.

The key difference between our framework and that for query optimization is that Our framework is based on a language for coordinating tasks, rather than a language for manipulating data. As a result, the major cost factors and optimization techniques are different, and related to those found in distributed computing and code re-writing in compilers.

The focus of this paper is on the presentation of a novel framework for optimizing the distribution and execution of workflow schemas. Due to space limitations, the paper does not explore in depth the important issue of mechanisms to restrict or otherwise help in exploring the space of possible implementations. The techniques used in query optimization may be an appropriate starting point on this problem.

In this paper we focus on compile-time analysis of workflow schemas, and mapping of parallel workflows into flowcharts. However, we expect that the framework and principles explored here are also relevant to other situations. For example, decisions concerning the distribution of work for an individual instance of a workflow schema could be performed during runtime. Specifically, at different stages of the execution of the instance, the remaining portions of a workflow schema could be partitioned and distributed to different processors. Further, if required by some of the processors, selected sub-workflows could be translated into flowcharts. The specific partitioning, and the optimal flowcharts, will typically be dependent on the data obtained from the processing of the workflow instance that has already occurred.

Related Work: The area of optimization of workflow executions is a relatively new field, and few papers have been written on the topic. Distribution is clearly advantageous to support scalability, which is becoming a serious issue as more and more users access popular web interfaces for digital libraries and online shopping etc. As noted above, several projects have developed distributed workflow systems [AMG+95,DKM+96,WW97,BMR96], but to our knowledge the literature has not addressed the issue of optimal distributions of workflows.

A family of run-time optimizations on centralized workflows is introduced in [HLS+99b,HKL+99], and studied in connection with the Vortex workflow model.

One kind of optimization is to determine that certain tasks are *unneeded* for successful execution of a workflow instance. This is especially useful in contexts where the workflow is focused on accomplishing specified "target" activities, and where intermediate activities can be omitted if not needed. Another kind of optimization, useful when parallel task execution is supported, is to support eager parallel execution of some tasks in order to reduce overall response time. References [HLS+99b,HKL+99] explore how these and other optimizations can be supported at *runtime*. The current paper provides a complementary approach, focusing on the use of these and related ideas for optimizations used primarily at *compile-time*.

Our model of CFs is closely related to that of communicating sequential processes (CSP) with two main differences: (1) in our model, a set of flowcharts (processes) starts at the beginning and they will not spawn new processes, and (2) we carefully distinguish between communications of getting an attribute value instantaneously and that of getting the value only after it has been defined.

Organization: §2 presents some motivating examples. §3 introduces a formal model of CFs, and describes approaches for implementing the model. §4 presents a physical model for distributed workflows and analyzes key cost factors for them. §5 presents a representative family of rules and transformations on clusters of CFs. §6 offers brief conclusions.

2   Motivating Examples

We provide a brief introduction to the framework for workflow distribution, including: (a) the abstract model used to represent distributed workflow schemas; (b) the basic approach to partitioning workflow schemas across different nodes; and (c) techniques for creating and manipulating flowcharts which can execute workflow subschemas on limited processing nodes. §3 gives a formal presentation of the abstract model, and §3 and §4 discuss different options for implementing the model.

Fig. 1 shows a workflow schema with 5 tasks (shown as rectangles). We assume that each task has the form $A = f(A_{i_1}, ..., A_{i_n})$, where f is a function call that returns a value for attribute A, and may have side-effects. As typical with many workflow models, there are two activities with each task: task *management* and task *execution*. In a centralized WFMS all tasks (and associated data management) are managed by one node, and the task executions are carried out by

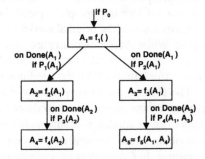

Fig. 1. Example ECA workflow schema

one or more other nodes. In our framework, the task management and execution may be performed by the same or different nodes. We generally assume in this paper that the data management associated with a task is performed by the node that is performing the task management, but this assumption can be relaxed.

In workflow specifications, the attribute names have global scope, and so data flow is expressed implicitly, rather than using explicit data channels. This follows

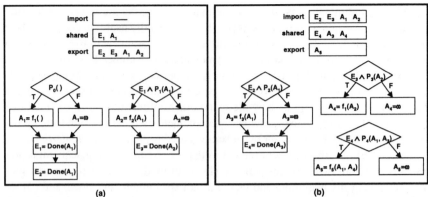

(a)   (b)

Fig. 2. Decomposition of schema into flowcharts, and partition onto two processing nodes

ThinkSheet and Vortex, and contrasts with the syntax of models such as FlowMark or Meteor. The use of global attributes or explicit data channels does not affect the expressive power of the models.

In Fig. 1 the edges indicate control flow. Except for A_1, the conditions include both events and predicates. In this example the events have the simple form "Done(A)", but other kinds of events can be incorporated. Data flow in this schema is indicated by how attributes are used in tasks; e.g. attribute A_4 is used for the task of computing A_5. The semantics of this workflow schema follows the spirit of ECA-style workflow models, such as Flowmark, Meteor, Mentor. A task (rectangle node) should be executed if its enabling condition is true, i.e., if the event in that condition is raised, and if subsequently the propositional part of the condition is satisfied.

We now use Fig. 2 to introduce key elements of the abstract model and our framework. First, focus on the 5 "atomic" flowcharts (ignore the two large boxes). Each corresponds to a single task in the schema of Fig. 1. These are *communicating flowcharts* (CFs). In principle, a parallel execution of these flowcharts is equivalent to an execution of the original workflow schema using a generic, parallel workflow engine. When these flowcharts are executed, attributes will be assigned an actual value if the corresponding enabling condition is true, and will be assigned the null value ω (for "disabled") if the condition is evaluated and found to be false.

The abstract model supports two different perspectives on attributes, that correspond to how attributes are evaluated in ECA models (e.g., FlowMark, Meteor, Mentor) vs. in condition-action models (e.g., ThinkSheet, Vortex). In ECA models, an attribute is read "immediately" when its value is needed, for this we use $read(A)$ operations. In CA models an attribute is read only after the attribute has been initialized, either by executing a task and receiving an actual value, or by determining that the attribute is disabled and receiving value ω. We use the operation $get(A)$ to indicate that the value of A is to be read only after it is initialized.

In addition to permitting support for different kinds of workflow models, the use of two perspectives on attribute reads permits us to treat events as a special kind of attribute. In Fig. 2 the events are represented as attributes E_i, using the *get* semantics; an attribute E is considered to remain uninitialized until some flowchart gives

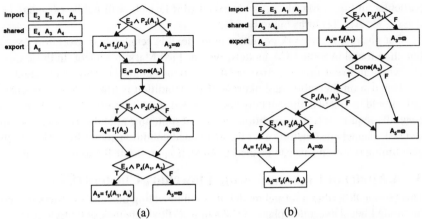

(a)   (b)

Fig. 3. Two flowcharts, each equivalent to the three flowcharts of Fig. 2(b)

it a value. (The launching of a flowchart for a given workflow is not represented explicitly in the abstract model, and different implementations of this are possible.)

In Fig. 2, each large square denotes a cluster of atomic flowcharts. Each cluster could be executed on a different node. The cluster includes a listing of attributes that are imported by the cluster, exported by it, or used internally (i.e., shared by the CFs within the cluster). We typically assume that each node has a *data repository* that maintains this data, which includes asynchronously receiving import data as it becomes available, and transmitting export data to the appropriate places.

Fig. 2 shows one execution plan for the initial workflow schema of Fig. 1, where tasks A_1 and A_2 are executing on one node, and tasks A_3, A_4, and A_5 are executing on another node. Another execution plan is formed by moving the flowchart for task A_3 from the second node to the first (and adjusting the schemas of the data repositories accordingly). What is the difference in the costs of these two execution plans (call them P_1 and P_2)? There are various factors, including communication costs between the two clusters (an important issue here is the relative sizes of expected values for A_2 and A_4, and between the clusters and the location of task executions). Another factor, that may arise if one of the clusters is on a limited node, concerns the overall CPU and data management load that the cluster imposes on that node.

Fig. 3 shows two ways that the three atomic CFs of Fig. 2(b) can be combined to form larger CFs. Fig. 3(a), shows one way to combine the three CFs into a single flowchart. This corresponds to a topological sort of the sub-schema of Fig. 1 involving A_3, A_4, A_5. An analogous flowchart could be constructed using the order A_4, A_3, A_5. If tasks A_3 and/or A_4 has a side-effect, then executing in one or the other order may be preferable, e.g., to have the side-effect occur as quickly as possible.

Assume now that in the initial workflow tasks A_1, A_3, and A_5 are "target" tasks, but that the other two are for internal purposes only. In this case it would be desirable, for a given workflow instance, to omit execution of A_4 if it is not needed for successful completion of the target tasks for that instance. Fig. 3(b) shows CF that is equivalent to that of Fig. 3(a). (§5 describes how the first CF can be transformed into the second one using a sequence of equivalence preserving rewrite rules.) In particular, in Fig. 3(b) task A_4 is not executed if task A_5 will not be executed, i.e., if $E_4 \wedge P_4(A_1, A_3)$ turns out to be false.

Our abstract framework permits a more flexible semantics of workflow execution than found in some ECA models, such as FlowMark or Meteor. In those models, when an event fires the associated conditions should be queued immediately and tested soon thereafter, and likewise if the condition is true then the associated task should be queued immediately and launched soon thereafter. In our model, we generally require only that conditions are tested sometime after the associated event, and tasks launched sometime after the associated condition comes true. More stringent timing requirements can be incorporated, if appropriate for some application.

3   A Model of Communicating Flowchart Clusters (CFC)

This section describes a formal model of communicating flowchart clusters for representing logical execution plans of tasks in workflow schemas, and discusses some implementation issues.

We assume the existence of attributes (and domains). A *task* is an expression $A = f(A_1, ..., A_n)$ where f is an (uninterpreted) function (procedure) name, A_i's are input attributes and A is an output attribute (*defined* by the task). In general we treat tasks as black boxes, i.e., the functions are uninterpreted. However, we note that a task may have "side-effects".

A *condition* over attributes $A_1, ..., A_k$ is a Boolean combination of predicates involving $A_1, ..., A_k$ and constants in their respective domains; the attributes used in the condition are also called the input attributes to the condition.

Definition.   A *flowchart* is a tuple $f = (T, C, E, s, L, I, O)$ where (1) T is a set of (attribute or task) nodes, (2) C is a set of (condition) nodes disjoint from T; (3) $s \in T \cup C$ is the *entry* node; (4) $E \subseteq (T \cup C) \times (T \cup C)$ such that (a) each $t \in T$ has at most one outgoing edge, (b) each $c \in C$ has at most two outgoing edges, and (c) every $x \in T \cup C - \{s\}$ is reachable from s; (5) L maps each task node to a task and each condition node to a condition; (6) I is a set of import attributes used by some tasks in f; and (7) O is a set of export attributes defined in f. Moreover, the flowchart f is *trivial* if $T \cup C = \{s\}$ and E is empty.

Let $f = (T, C, E, s, L, I, O)$ be a flowchart. We denote import and export attributes of f as $in(f) = I$ and $out(f) = O$. In this paper we focus on "acyclic" flowcharts: A flowchart (T, C, E, s, L, I, O) is *acyclic* if the graph $(T \cup C, E \cup D)$ has no cycles, where $D = \{(u, v) \mid u$ defines an attribute used by $v \}$.

Example 1. *Fig. 2(a) shows two flowcharts. The one in the left-hand side can be described as* $f_1 = (T, C, E, c, L, \emptyset, \{A_1, E_1, E_2\})$*, where* $T = \{a_1, ..., a_4\}$*,* $C = \{c_2\}$*,* a_1, a_2 *(resp.* a_3, a_4*) are two nodes defining attribute* A_2 *(resp.* E_1, E_2*),* c_2 *the entry condition node and* $E = \{(c_2, a_1), (c_2, a_2), (a_1, a_3), (a_2, a_3), (a_3, a_4)\}$*. In fact,* f_1 *is acyclic.*

Semantics (or *execution*) of a flowchart is defined in the straightforward way with the exception of acquiring values for import attributes. Initially all attributes have the null value $\perp$ (stands for "uninitialized"). One method of acquiring a value for an import attribute A, called *immediate read* and denoted as $read(A)$, is to re-trieve the current value of the attribute, regardless of whether A has a proper value or the null value. This method is used in many workflow systems such as FlowMark and Meteor. Immediate read is however undesirable sometimes because the timing of tasks and external events may cause delays in computing attribute values which may cause nondeterministic behaviors of the workflow system.

In acyclic flowcharts, a task may be executed at most once. This allows an al-ternative method, called *proper read*, which does the following. When a value for an import attribute A is requested, if A has a proper value (non-$\perp$), the value is fetched; if A currently has the value $\perp$, the task requesting A waits until A is as-signed a proper value, and then the new value is fetched. We denote this operation as $get(A)$. This operation is used in the Vortex paradigm which provides a declarative workflow specification language.

From now on, we assume that each input attribute of every task must be specified with either a *read* or *get* operation. Although *get* operations provide a clean interac-tion between tasks, they may cause the execution of CFCs to "stall". For instance, if there are no tasks defining A prior to a $get(A)$ operation in a single flowchart, the *get* operation will be blocked forever. We assume that the flowcharts will never stall.

Proper read operations alone do not guarantee determinism. A flowchart $f = (T, C, E, s, L, I, O)$ is said to be *write-once* if in each execution of f, each attribute will be assigned a non-$\perp$ value at most once. It can be verified that every write-once flowchart with only proper read operations for all import attributes has a determin-istic behavior. The complexity of checking the write-once property of flowcharts depends on the condition language.

Definition. A *communicating flowchart cluster (CFC)* is a quadruple (F, I, S, O) where F is a set of flowcharts with pairwise disjoint sets of nodes, I (resp. O) a set of import (resp. export) attributes for flowcharts in F such that $I \subseteq \cup_{f \in F} in(f)$ $(O \subseteq \cup_{f \in F} out(f))$, and $S = (\cup_{f \in F} in(f)) \cap (\cup_{f \in F} out(f))$ a set of attributes defined and used by different flowcharts in F.

Example 2. *Fig. 2(b) shows a single CFC that includes three flowcharts, where the import/export/shared attributes are listed in the top.*

Definition. Let $\mathbf{F}$ be a set of CFCs and Tg a set of attributes (called the target attributes of the CFCs). $\mathbf{F}$ is said to be *well-formed* w.r.t. Tg if (a) for each CFC $F \in \mathbf{F}$ and each import attribute A in F, there is a CFC $F' \in \mathbf{F}$ which exports A, and (b) each attribute of Tg is exported by some CFC in $\mathbf{F}$.

For each well-formed set $\mathbf{F}$ of CFCs, we define a *dependency graph* $G_{\mathbf{F}}$ which characterizes the dependencies of control and data flows within flowcharts within $\mathbf{F}$. Specifically, $G_{\mathbf{F}} = (V, E)$ where V is the union of all flowchart nodes in CFCs of $\mathbf{F}$, and E contains all flowchart edges in CFCs of $\mathbf{F}$ and all edges (u, v) such that u defines an attribute that is used in v. A well-formed set $\mathbf{F}$ of CFCs is said to be *acyclic* if $G_{\mathbf{F}}$ has no cycles. The set of two CFCs in Fig. 2 is acyclic.

Finally we discuss some key issues in developing implementation models for CFCs. Clearly, the control structures of flowcharts are very simple and generally available in a variety of script languages; even a direct implementation (of the control structures) is also straightforward. There are, however, three decisions that need further discussion. The first issue is the mapping from flowcharts to processors. The conceptual model of CFCs assumes that each processor may be capable of executing multiple flowcharts concurrently. Thus the mapping is simply to assign each CFC to a processor. The second issue is about how the flowcharts in a set of CFCs are invoked. This can be done by having a single entry to the CFC, that will spawn all flowcharts in the CFC (e.g., through remote procedure calls).

The third issue is related to communication, i.e., passing attribute values between tasks. There are three different ways an attribute value can be sent around. (1) The attribute is defined and used in the same flowchart. If the attribute is accessed through a *read* operation, we just need to provide some storage space local to a flowchart for storing the attribute value. For acyclic flowcharts, since each *get* operation of an attribute is required to follow the task defining the attribute, *get* and *read* operations are effectively the same. (2) The attribute is defined and used in different flowcharts in the same CFC. In this case, we need to provide a common buffer (write exclusive) for all flowcharts (processes) involved. While *read* operations do not require extra support, *get* operations would require a list to be maintained for each attribute that have not received a proper value. (3) In the most general case, the attribute is defined in one CFC and used in another. There are many ways to implement *read* and *get*. For example, both "producer" and "consumer" processors maintain a buffer for holding the attribute value. Passing the value from the producer buffer to the consumer buffer can be done by push or pull. Similar to case (2), *get* operations still rely on maintaining a list of requests. One possible architecture for handling communications is through a data repository.

4   Optimization Issues in Choosing Execution Plans

In this section we present a physical model for workflow distribution that extends the logical model of the previous section. We identify key cost factors in the physical model, and illustrate how they affect the cost of different physical execution plans. We then develop a very preliminary cost model, by presenting formulas that can be used to give bounds on the costs of physical execution plans. The two bounds we consider are: total running time for processing a workflow instance, maximum throughput, i.e., maximum number of instances processed in a time unit, and total network load resulted from transferring data between CFCs.

4.1   A Physical Model for Executing Communicating Flowcharts

We assume that each CFC is executed on a separate processing node. The exchange of attribute values between the CFCs can use push or pull approaches. The execution of tasks in a CF may involve accessing data at a data repository on either the local or a remote processing node. To capture the costs for transferring attribute values between a task manager and the task execution in a uniform way, we conceptually replace the task node in a CFC by three nodes: an entry node, a node for data retrieval at the task execution machine, and an exit node. The in-edges of the original node are now in-edges of the entry node, while the out-edges of the original node are now out-edges of the exit node. There is an edge from the entry node to the data retrieval node and one from there to the exit node. If the data repository is local, the data retrieval node remains in the same CFC. Otherwise, this node will reside in a separate CFC.

When a new workflow instance is created, we assume for simplicity all the CFs are invoked for this instance at the same time. If an execution step in a CF depends on attribute(s) which have not been defined, the CF waits for the definition of the attribute(s), i.e., until a true value or null value ω is present.

Processing in a flowchart for a given workflow instance terminates when a leaf node of the flowchart completes.

4.2 Comparing Alternative CFCs

We give two examples here to illustrate the differences in performance and cost that alternative execution plans for the same workflow schema may have. We first show the difference in terms of response time and network load. Recall the example in Fig. 2 (a) and (b). Suppose that computing attribute A_3 (in CFC(b)) requires retrieving data from a different processing node where CFC(a) resides. A data retrieval node for A_3 is then created in CFC(a) with two edges crossing the CFC boundary leading to the CFC(b) cluster. If we move the CF for computing A_3 to CFC(a), these two edges will be eliminated, which most likely reduces network load and response time. This effect will be shown in our formulas presented in the next section.

The second example concerns Fig. 3. We show that we can transform the CFCs to eliminate unneeded evaluation of attributes during the execution of certain workflow instances. In Fig. 3 (a), the node $A_5 = \omega$ is moved much "closer" to the root node of the CF. In the cases when A_5 is evaluated to ω, we can avoid an unneeded execution of task A_4.

4.3 Cost Factors

The logical model of CFCs permits the management of tasks and actual execution of tasks to be on two distinct clusters. For ease of reasoning, we assume that task management nodes and task execution nodes are explicitly specified in a flowchart plan f. The notion of clusters is thus generalized, since all nodes (management or execution) need to be on some processing node. In the rest of this section, we do not distinguish between the two types of management and execution nodes, and refer to them simply as flowchart nodes.

We first define some notation. Let F_A represent the CFC in which an attribute A is computed. Let $|A|$ denote the expected size of A in number of bytes (this includes cases where the transmitted value of A is ω or $\perp$, which is viewed as having a size of one). Let $P_u(F, A)$ denote the probability of attribute A being used in the CFC F. $P_d(A)$ denotes the probability of attribute A being computed. We also use $P_d(X)$ to refer to the probability of any flowchart node X being executed, rather than simply the probability of an attribute being computed. For example, even condition nodes have probabilities associated with them, and reflect the probability of the condition node being evaluated (not the value of the condition being true or false). The actual meaning of X in $P_d(X)$ should be evident from the context.

We now derive bounds on response time and achievable throughput. These bounds depend on the cost associated with executing a workflow instance, which can primarily be broken down into two parts: 1) processing cost of executing flowchart nodes within clusters, and 2) communication cost of passing data between clusters.

Let $Work(A)$ denote the expected number of units of work required to compute node A for one workflow instance. Let $Nodes(F)$ denote the set of nodes in cluster F. $Work(F)$ denotes the total processing cost of cluster F for one workflow instance, and is given by: $Work(F) = \sum_{A \in Nodes(F)} (P_d(A) \cdot Work(A))$.

Communication cost depends on the amount of data transferred between clusters, the effective network bandwidth on the communication link between the clusters, and the method of communication between the clusters. We consider two possible methods of communication, namely, *push* and *pull*.

In the push mode, the value of an output attribute A is pushed to all the clusters F which may use that value, i.e., where $A \in in(F)$. This can result in a reduction of response time by hiding communication latency, since the target attribute does not have to wait for a source attribute value to be delivered when required. Moreover, efficient multicast algorithms are available for distributing a value from a single source to multiple targets. However, one drawback of the push model is that it results in increased network load, since the source value is distributed to clusters which may not use the value in the actual execution.

The pull mode defers communication until it is necessary. When a flowchart node is being computed that requires attribute values from other clusters, communication is initiated to retrieve those values at that point. The advantage of this model is reduced network load, however, reduction in communication latency (as in the push mode) is not achieved. We only consider the pull mode in deriving expressions for communication costs. The costs for the push mode can be derived similarly.

We assume we are given a function $Comm_{F_i,F_j}(d)$ that denotes the communication cost of transferring d bytes of data from cluster F_i to F_j. An example of this function would be: $Comm_{F_i,F_j}(d) = ts_{F_i,F_j} + tb_{F_i,F_j}d$. where ts_{F_i,F_j} (resp. tb_{F_i,F_j}) denotes the startup time (resp. byte transfer rate) for the communication between clusters F_i and F_j. However, any appropriate cost model can be chosen instead of the above. The total communication cost $Comm$ is then given by: $Comm = \sum_{F \in f} \sum_{A \in in(F)} P_u(F,A) \cdot Comm_{F_A,F}(|A|)$

We use the term *network load* to refer to the total amount of data transferred between the clusters during the execution of a workflow instance. As we explain later, network load is an important concept used for determining the maximum throughput. The total network load NL is given by: $NL = \sum_{F \in f} \sum_{A \in in(F)} P_u(F,A) \cdot |A|$

Response Time: We now give present some worst case bounds on average instance response time for a particular flowchart plan f. We assume that the time for computing attributes, and communicating attribute values between clusters, dominates the execution time. We assume that the source attributes for f are available at time $= 0$. We compute the expected response time of f by recursively computing the finish times of each flowchart node, by starting from the source nodes and proceeding in a topological sort order until the target nodes are reached.

Let T_A denote the finish time of the node A. Let $pred(A)$ denote the predecessor set of node A in F_A, and $input(A)$ denote the set of input attributes for node A. Let $Tenabled_A$ denote the expected time instant when it is the turn of A to execute (note that the inputs of A might not be ready at this time). Then, $Tenabled_A = \sum_{B \in pred(A)} (P_d(B) \cdot T_B)$ Now, let $Tready_A$ denote the time when the inputs to A are also ready. The set of inputs to A can be broken down into two categories, 1) those that are computed in the same CFC, and 2) those computed in other CFCs. Note that the acyclicity property of the CFCs implies that the first set of inputs will always be computed by time $Tenabled_A$. For the second set of inputs, assuming actual read, the execution of A is delayed until those inputs are pulled from the corresponding CFCs. Hence,

$Tready_A = \max[Tenabled_A, \max_{B \in (input(A) \cap (F_A))} (T_B + Comm_{F_B,F_A}(|B|))]$.

Note: for immediate read, the term T_B in this expression would not be present. If $Time(A)$ represents the expected processing time of A, we get $T_A = Tready_A + Time(A)$. The expected response time for the entire workflow is then given by $\max_{A \in Tg}(T_A)$. The above analysis gives an approximation of the response time. To be more accurate, we should incorporate the value for the expected load on the processing nodes, since that impacts the processing time of each node.

Throughput: The maximum achievable throughput is bounded by two factors: 1) processing power of the processing nodes, and 2) network bandwidth between the processing nodes.

Let Cap_F denote the processing capacity (in terms of number of processing units per unit time) of the processing node that executes cluster F. Assuming infinite network bandwidth, the maximum throughput achievable for a given processing node is given by the processing capacity of that node divided by the amount of work to be performed by the corresponding cluster. We denote this by $Throughput_F$:
$Throughput_F = \frac{Cap_F}{Work(F)}$. Similarly, we assume that the bandwidth of the link between two processing nodes (clusters) F_i and F_j is $Bandwidth_{F_i,F_j}$. The set of attributes whose value may be transferred from F_i and F_j is $(I_{F_i} \cap O_{F_j})$, and those from F_j to F_i is $(I_{F_j} \cap O_{F_i})$. The maximum throughput achievable due to this link (denoted by $Throughput_{F_i,F_j}$) is given by the link bandwidth divided by the network load generated due to traffic on this link. Assuming a pull mode, we get $Throughput_{F_i,F_j} = \frac{Bandwidth_{F_i,F_j}}{(\Sigma_{A \in (I_{F_i} \cap O_{F_j})}(P_u(F_i,A) \cdot |A|)) + (\Sigma_{A \in (I_{F_j} \cap O_{F_i})}(P_u(F_j,A) \cdot |A|))}$.

Hence, given a flowchart plan, the maximum achievable throughput is given by:
$Throughput = \min(\min_{F \in f}(Throughput_F), \min_{F_i,F_j \in f}(Throughput_{F_i,F_j}))$

Note that the above analysis presents upper bounds on the throughput. Actual throughput would vary depending on the expected network load.

5   Representative Transformations and Rewriting Rules

We now present some representative transformations and rewriting rules on logical execution plans. The first rule covers moving flowcharts between clusters, and the others focus on manipulating one or two CFs within a cluster. The application of these transformations should be guided by optimization goals and heuristics. These transformations are intended to be illustrative, but not necessarily complete.

The transformations rules take as input a logical execution plan, i.e., a family of CFCs, and produce as output another logical execution plan. To get started, given a workflow schema, we assume that an atomic CF is created for each task in that schema, and that a separate cluster is created for each CF. (An alternative would be to put all of the atomic CFs into a single cluster.)

For this section we assume that all condition nodes have two outgoing edges, one for true and one for false, and that all tasks eventually finish (or are determined to be "dead"). These assumptions ensure that all possible executions of a flowchart will eventually reach a terminal node.

5.1   Moving Flowcharts between Clusters

We can move flowcharts from one cluster to another, using the move transformation.

Move: This transformation moves a flowchart f from one CFC F_1 to another CFC F_2. In addition to removing f from F_1 and adding f to F_2, we also modify the sets of import, export and shared attributes of the two clusters to reflect the move: We remove those import attributes that are only used by f from the set of import attributes of F_1, and remove the attributes defined by f from the set of export attributes of F_1. Appropriate actions are also needed for F_2.

For example, consider Fig. 2. If we move the flowchart for task A_4 from the CFC of (b) to that of (a), we need to (i) remove E_3 and A_2 from the imports of (b), (ii) remove A_4 from the shared attributes of (b), (iii) add A_4 to the imports of (b), (iv) add A_4 to the exports of (a), (v) add E_3 and A_2 to the shared attributes of (a), and (vi) remove E_3 and A_2 from the exports of (a).

5.2   Combining and Decomposing Flowcharts

There is one rule for combining flowcharts, and one for decomposing them.

Append: This transformation appends a flowchart f_2 to another f_1 to produce a third f, provided that f_1 does not use any attribute defined in f_2: the node set and edge set of f are the union of the respective sets of f_1 and f_2, and moreover f has the edge (u, v), for each terminal node u of f_1 and the entry node v of f_2.

For example, consider Fig. 2. If we append the flowchart f_2 for task A_5 as entry node to the flowchart f_1 with for task A_3 then we add an edge from $E_4 = Done(A_3)$ to the root of f_2. Observe that we cannot append these two flowcharts in the other order because of the data flow dependency between them.

By combining the Append rule with the Reorder rules (given below) it is possible to achieve other ways of combining flowcharts. As a simple example, given two linear flowcharts with no data flow dependencies between them, one can form a flowchart interleaves the tasks of the two flowcharts in an arbitrary manner.

Split: This is the inverse of append; it splits one flowchart f into two flowcharts, f_1 and f_2. Splitting of f can be done at any node v which is a node cut of f (viewed as a graph): We invent a new (event) attribute E_{f_v}. f_1 consists of everything of f except the branch of f starting from v; furthermore, the edge leading to v now points to a new node with the assignment task $E_{f_v} = True$. f_2 consists of the branch of f starting from v, plus a new condition node "$E_{f_v} = True$" whose outgoing True edge goes to v, and outgoing False edge goes to a no-op terminal node. (We can avoid the use of E_{f_v}, if the branch from v does not depend on the rest of f.)

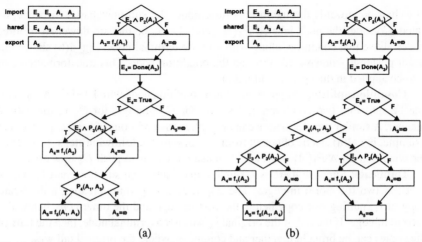

(a)   (b)

Fig. 4. Flowcharts arising at intermediate points in transformation from Fig. 3(a) to Fig. 3(b)

Split can also be performed using larger node cuts, although it is more complicated. First, we need to create several exit events, one for each element of the node cut. Second, we have to construct series of condition nodes, that essentially perform a case statement that checks which event is true in order to start processing at the correct part of the split-off flowchart.

5.3 Modifying a Flowchart

We now present several representative rules for modifying individual flowcharts. These are essentially equivalent to transformations that are used for code rewriting in compiler optimization. We shall illustrate some of the transformations using Fig. 4, which shows two flowcharts that arise when transforming the flowchart of Fig. 3(a) into the flowchart of Fig. 3(b).

A flowchart is said to be *single-entry-single-exit* if it has exactly one entry and one exit node. Observe that a singleton node is a single-entry-single-exit subflowchart. For the sake of simplifying the discussion, we assume without loss of generality that the single exit node is a no-op terminal node, by appending one such node if necessary. Observe that this no-op terminal node is always absorbed by the subsequent entry node in the examples.

Reorder: This transformation changes the ordering of two single-entry-single-exit sub-flowcharts f_1 and f_2 when there is no data dependency between them. More specifically, let f_1 and f_2 be two single-entry-single-exit sub-flowcharts of a flowchart such that (i) the exit node of f_1 goes to the entry node of f_2, (ii) there are no other edges leaving f_1, and (iii) there are no other edges entering f_2. This transformation will then exchange the ordering of f_1 and f_2.

For example, consider Fig. 3a. Let the four nodes headed by $E_2 \wedge P_2(A_1)$ be f_1, and the three nodes headed by $E_3 \wedge P_3(A_2)$ plus a no-op terminal node be f_2. Then the ordering of f_1 followed by f_2 can be changed to f_2 followed by f_1.

Reorder through condition: In some cases, it is useful to push a single-entry-single-exit sub-flowchart through a condition node. In the case of pushing a sub-flowchart downwards through a condition node, the sub-flowchart will be duplicated. Consider the node labeled $P_4(A_1, A_3)$. Let f_1 be the sub-flowchart of three nodes above that condition, along with a no-op terminal node. Fig. 4(b) shows the result pushing f_1 downwards through the condition node. This transformation can also be applied in the opposite direction.

Condition splitting: Suppose there is a condition node with label $C_1 \wedge C_2$. This can be split into two condition nodes, one for C_1 and one for C_2 in the natural manner. A similar transformation can be applied to conditions of form $C_1 \vee C_2$. For example, Fig. 4(a) can be obtained from Fig. 3(a) by the following steps. First, split the condition $E_4 \wedge P_4(A_1, A_3)$, and then use reordering to push E_4 upwards.

Duplicate: Suppose there is a single-entry-single-exit sub-flowchart f_1 whose root has two (or more) in-edges. The duplicate rule permits creating a duplicate copy of f_1, putting one copy below the first in-edge and the other copy below the second in-edge. If the tail of the original f_1 was not a terminal node, then the tails of the copies can be brought together and connected where the original tail was.

Delegate: Intuitively, this transformation works as if it is delegating the task of a node to a different processor. This can be used to increase parallelism. For this to work correctly, we must ensure that the dependencies are taken care of properly. Formally, we replace the old task node with a chain of two nodes: the first one spawns the action of the old task node (e.g., with keyword $spawn(A)$), and the second one is the action of waiting for that task to finish (e.g., by $get(A)$). Reordering can then be used to push the $get(A)$ node downwards in the flowchart.

Remove Unneeded: If a workflow schema has specified target and non-target tasks, then in some cases unneeded tasks can be detected an eliminated from flowcharts. For example, in Fig. 4(b) the two right-most tasks assigning A_4 are not needed anywhere below. As a result, these tasks, and the condition node above, can be deleted. This shows how Fig. 4(b) can be transformed into Fig. 3(b).

Other transformations (e.g.the unduplicate transformation) are also possible.

6   Conclusions

Our paper has focused on distributing workflow tasks among a set of processing nodes and on optimizing execution of the tasks. We developed a general framework for representing logical execution plans using communicating flowchart clusters and an initial set of transformations on logical executions plans. With intuitive examples from a simple workflow schema that can be defined in many workflow systems, we illustrated some heuristics of applying the rewrite rules in optimizing execution plans. We also presented the main components of a model of physical execution plans, along a preliminary analysis of key cost factors.

The technical results reported in this paper are preliminary; there are many interesting questions that deserve further investigation, ranging from theoretical foundation to practical application. In one extreme, there are many decision problems arising from this, such as: Is there a (sound and) complete set of rewrite rules? What is the complexity of testing if a set of CFCs have deterministic behavior? In the other extreme, it is fundamental to investigate further the issue of cost models, and heuristics for identifying efficient physical execution plans. It is also unclear how this kind of compile-time optimization techniques compares with the ones based on adaptive scheduling such as [HLS+99b,HKL+99].

Acknowledgment Part of work by Jianwen Su was supported by NSF grants IRI-9411330, IRI-9700370, and IIS-9817432.

References

[AMG+95] G. Alonso, C. Mohan, R. Gunther, D. Agrawal, A. El Abbadi, & M. Kamath. Exotica/FMQM: A persistent message-based architecture for distributed workflow management. In *Proc. IFIP WG8.1 Working Conf. on Information Systems for Decentralized Organizations*, 1995.

[BMR96] D. Barbara, S. Mehrotra, & M. Rusinkiewicz. INCAs: Managing dynamic workflows in distributed environments. *Journal of Database Management, Special Issue on Multidatabases*, 7(1), 1996.

[DKM+96] S. Das, K. Kochut, J. Miller, A. Sheth, & D. Worah. Orbwork: A reliable distributed corba-based workflow enactment system for meteor$_2$. Technical Report UGA-CS-TR-97-001, Department of Computer Science, University of Georgia, 1996.

[Ell79] C. A. Ellis. Information control nets: A mathematical model of office information flow. In *ACM Proc. Conf. Simulation, Modeling & Measurement of Computer Systems*, pp225–240, Aug 1979.

[GHS95] D. Georgakopoulos, M. Hornick, & A. Sheth. An overview of workflow management: From process modeling to workflow automation infrastructure. *Distributed & Parallel Databases*, 3(22):119–154, April 1995.

[HKL+99] R. Hull, B. Kumar, F. Llirbat, G. Zhou, G. Dong, & J. Su. Optimization techniques for data-intensive decision flows. Technical report, Bell Laboratories, Lucent Technologies, 1999. see http://www-db.research.bell-labs.com/projects/vortex.

[HLS+99a] R. Hull, F. Llirbat, E. Simon, J. Su, G. Dong, B. Kumar, & G. Zhou. Declarative workflows that support easy modification & dynamic browsing. In *Proc. of Intl. Joint Conf. on Work Activities Coordination & Collaboration (WACC)*, pp69–78, Feb 1999.

[HLS+99b] R. Hull, F. Llirbat, J. Su, G. Dong, B. Kumar, & G. Zhou. Adaptive execution of workflow: Analysis & optimization. Technical report, Bell Laboratories, Lucent Technologies, 1999. see http://www-db.research.bell-labs.com/projects/vortex.

[KS95] N. Krishnakumar & A. Sheth. Managing heterogeneous multi-systems tasks to support enterprise-wide operations. *Distributed & Parallel Databases*, 3(2), 1995.

[LR94] F. Leymann & D. Roller. Business process management with FlowMark. In *Proc. of IEEE Computer Conference*, pp230–234, 1994.

[Mos] Mosaix, Incorporated. 1999. http://www.aiim.org/wfmc.

[PYLS96] P. Piatko, R. Yangarber, D. Lin, & D. Shasha. Thinksheet: A tool for tailoring complex documents. In *Proc. ACM SIGMOD*, page 546, 1996.

[WfM99] Workflow management coalition, 1999. http://www.aiim.org/wfmc.

[WW97] D. Wodtke & G. Weikum. A formal foundation for distributed workflow execution based on state charts. In *Proc. of Intl. Conf. on Database Theory*, pages 230–246, 1997.

[WWWD96] D. Wodtke, J. Weissenfels, G. Weikum, & A. K. Dittrich. The Mentor project: Steps towards enterprise-wide workflow management. In *Proc. of IEEE Intl. Conf. on Data Engineering*, New Orleans, 1996.

Querying Semistructured Data
Based on Schema Matching

André Bergholz[***]
and Johann Christoph Freytag

Humboldt-University Berlin
{bergholz,freytag}@dbis.informatik.hu-berlin.de

Abstract. Traditional database management requires design and ensures declarativity. In the context of semistructured data a more flexible
approach is appropriate due to missing schema information. In this paper we present a query language based on schema matching. Intuitively,
a query is a pair consisting of what we want and how we want it. We
propose that the former can be achieved by matching a (partial) schema
and the latter by specifying additional operations. We describe in some
detail our notion of schema covering various concepts typically found
in query languages, such as predicates, variables and paths. We outline
the optimization potential that this modular approach offers and discuss
how we use constraints for query processing.

1 Introduction

Traditional database management requires design and ensures declarativity. Semistructured data, "data that is neither raw data nor strictly typed", lacks a fixed
and rigid schema [Abi97]. Often their structure is irregular and implicit. Examples for semistructured data include HTML files, BibTEX files or genome data
stored in ASCII files. Recently, XML has emerged as a common syntactical representation for semistructured data. To us, the key problem of semistructured
data is to move from *content-based querying*, i.e., the UNIX `grep`-command or
simple WWW search engines, to *structure-based querying*, i.e., querying in an
SQL-like manner.

Before we present the idea of the paper we take a look at relational systems.
We identify three layers: the operational layer, the schema layer and the instance
layer. The tuples form the instance layer; and the tables form the schema layer.
On the operational layer we find queries, views, constraints etc. The items of
the operational layer are expressed using the items of the schema layer, i.e.,
queries are expressed using the tables. We would like to adapt this framework

---

[*] Contact author: André Bergholz, LFE Datenbanken und Informationssysteme, In-
stitut für Informatik, Humboldt-Universität zu Berlin, Unter den Linden 6, 10099
Berlin, Germany (phone: +49-30 2093 3024, fax: +49-30 2093 3010)

[**] This research was supported by the German Research Society, Berlin-Brandenburg
Graduate School in Distributed Information Systems (DFG grant no. GRK 316)

R. Connor and A. Mendelzon (Eds.): DBPL'99, LNCS 1949, pp. 168-183, 2000.

of querying for semistructured data. As we have learned, the serious problem of semistructured data is its lack of complete, known-in-advance structure. In this query framework for relational data every item on the instance layer (i.e., every tuple) belongs to exactly one item on the schema layer (i.e., to exactly one table). Certainly, this requirement has to be relaxed in the context of semistructured data.

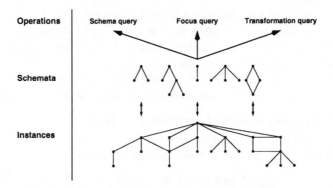

Fig. 1. A new query framework for semistructured data

The query framework, adapted to cover semistructured data, is shown in Figure 1. Because semistructured data is usually represented as a graph, we show example graphs for the two bottom layers. Partial schemata in the middle layer conform to some parts of the database in the bottom layer. There is no further restriction, i.e., a partial schema can have an arbitrary number of instances in the database, and instances can conform to an arbitrary number of schemata.

The crucial layer of this approach is the middle one, the layer of the schemata. There are a number of interesting questions: How do we get those schemata? What are they good for? How do we manage them? The simplest way to get them is from a database designer. Remember that the data is called semistructured rather than unstructured. So at least some parts of a database can potentially be modeled. A database designer may thus be able to provide some meaningful partial schemata. Another way to get partial schemata is the following. A query posed to the system uses both schema and operational layer. In other words, a query consists of a "What"-part (i.e., a partial schema) and a "How"-part (i.e., an operation). As an analogy, in the relational world we can consider a selection to correspond to the "What"-part and a projection correspond to the "How"-part of a query. Now, an obvious approach is to cache the "What" 's, i.e., to extract partial schemata out of queries. To make this possible we lift some concepts typically found in queries (such as selection conditions) to the layer of the schemata. Partial schemata are useful for two main purposes. First, they can give users hints on the content of a database. Second, they can be used for query optimization. Note, that schemata being good for the former are not necessarily good for the latter and vice versa.

What are the advantages of our approach? A system designed in this way reflects the degree of structure of a database on many levels. If a database is well structured there will be large schemata with many instances. Thus, users will get a lot of information about the data; and the performance of the system will be good as well. If, however, the database is not well structured there will be only some useful schemata. Thus, the user will not get full knowledge about the database; and the performance will suffer as well. The schema layer can serve as an indication on the degree of structure of the database. The existence of large schemata with many instances indicates that the database is rather well structured. Parts of the database, that are not covered by any schema, are probably not very interesting or have a rather obscure structure. We will conclude this section with three paradigms that shall guide our approach:

1. Answering a query *works without* schema information.
2. Answering a query *benefits from* schema information.
3. Answering a query *induces new* schema information.

This paper is organized as follows. Section 2 presents the syntactical data representation we are using. In Section 3 we define our semantically rich notion of schema that forms the base for the queries that are introduced in Section 4. The second part of the paper deals with query processing based on constraints. This is outlined in Section 5. We conclude with related work and a discussion.

2   Labeled graphs as data representation

In this section we describe the underlying data model of our proposal. It is a graph-based approach because graph models seem to be "the unifying idea in semi-structured data" [Bun97]. We try to be very general and do not require any specific restrictions to our graphs.

Definition 1 (Total directed graph). *A tuple $G = (V, A, s, t)$ is a total directed graph if V is a set of vertices, A a set of arcs and, furthermore, s and t are total functions from A to V assigning each arc its source and target vertex, respectively.*

We also use the term *node* instead of vertex. However, we use the term arc instead of edge to emphasize that we consider directed graphs. In our model two nodes can be linked by more than one arc. Cycles are allowed. The following definition introduces labels on vertices and arcs.

Definition 2 (Labeled directed graph). *Let $\mathcal{L}$ be an arbitrary set of labels. A tuple $G = (V, A, s, t, l)$ is a ($\mathcal{L}$-)labeled directed graph if (V, A, s, t) is a total directed graph and $l : V \cup A \longrightarrow \mathcal{L}$ is a total label function assigning each vertex and arc a label from $\mathcal{L}$.*

Now, an *object* is a labeled directed graph. We also use the term *database* instead of object when we talk about a "large" object that is to be queried. Note, that we usually denote objects with lower-case letters (i.e., $o_1, o_2, \dots$), but graphs with upper-case letters (i.e., $G_1, G_2, H, \dots$) in order to be consistent with both worlds.

Figure 2 presents an example that we shall use throughout the paper. It shows a semistructured database on persons having names, surnames, a year of birth, a profession etc. Additionally, a sibling relationship relates different people.

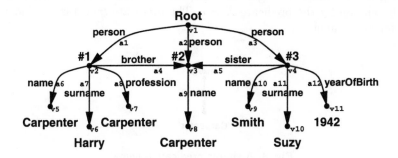

Fig. 2. A labeled directed graph

For specifying answers to queries we will need the notion of a subobject of a database. This assumes some basic knowledge of partial orders, for an introduction see [Tro92].

Definition 3 (Subobject). *An object* $o_2 = (V^{(o_2)}, A^{(o_2)}, s^{(o_2)}, t^{(o_2)}, l^{(o_2)})$ *is a subobject of* $o_1 = (V^{(o_1)}, A^{(o_1)}, s^{(o_1)}, t^{(o_1)}, l^{(o_1)})$ *if* $V^{(o_2)} \subseteq V^{(o_1)}$, $A^{(o_2)} \subseteq A^{(o_1)}$, $s^{(o_2)} = s^{(o_1)}|_{A^{(o_2)}}$, $t^{(o_2)} = t^{(o_1)}|_{A^{(o_2)}}$ *and* $l^{(o_2)} = l^{(o_1)}|_{V^{(o_2)} \cup A^{(o_2)}}$. *We denote this by* $o_2 \subseteq o_1$.

For a given object o we denote the set of all its subobjects by $\mathfrak{P}(o)$.

Lemma 1. *For a given object o the structure $[\mathfrak{P}(o), \subseteq]$ is a partially ordered set, i.e., $\subseteq$ is a reflexive, antisymmetric and transitive binary relation over $\mathfrak{P}(o)$.*

Lemma 2. *For a given object o the structure $[\mathfrak{P}(o), \subseteq]$ is a lattice, i.e., every nonempty subset of $\mathfrak{P}(o)$ has a least upper and a greatest lower bound.*

3   Schemata

This section introduces the notions of schema and conformity between schema and object. Informally, a schema is an object that describes a set of objects. In the simpler syntactic framework of the label world this schema concept certainly exists as well. One label might describe a set of other labels. This is frequently done – data types, predicates and regular expressions are examples.

As as first step towards schemata in the graph world we assign schemata from the label world to the elements of the graph. We choose predicates to be the label world schemata.

Definition 4 (Predicate schema). *Given a set of unary predicates* $\mathcal{P}$, *a predicate schema (over* $\mathcal{P}$*) is an object* $s = (V^{(s)}, A^{(s)}, s^{(s)}, t^{(s)}, l^{(s)})$ *where the elements are labeled with predicates* $(l : V^{(s)} \cup A^{(s)} \longrightarrow \mathcal{P})$.

We give an example in Figure 3. Note, that we treat a quoted constant c as an abbreviation for the predicate $X = c$. The predicate $true()$ is a wildcard; it holds for every label.

Fig. 3. A simple predicate schema

To establish a relationship between a schema and the objects described by it we must establish the notion of *conformity* between schemata and objects. Depending on the direction of the mapping we say that we *match* a schema into an object or we *interpret* an object by a schema.

Definition 5 (Naive conformity). *A* match *of a predicate schema* s *into an object* o *is an isomorphic embedding* m *of* s *into* o*, such that for all* $x \in V^{(s)} \cup A^{(s)}$ *the predicate* $l^{(s)}(x)$ *holds for* $l^{(o)}(m(x))$.

If there exists a match of the schema s into the object o we say that o *conforms* to s and we call o an *instance* (or also a *match*) of s.

Let o be a database, s be a schema and $o_1 \subseteq o$ a match of s. Then every object o_2 with $o_1 \subseteq o_2 \subseteq o$ is also a match of s. Let $\mathfrak{M}^{(s)}(o)$ denote the set of all matches of s in o. Because $\mathfrak{M}^{(s)}(o) \subseteq \mathfrak{P}(o)$ (in set semantics) $[\mathfrak{M}^{(s)}(o), \subseteq]$ is also a partially ordered set. We call a minimal element of this partially ordered set a *minimal match* (or a *minimal instance*) of s in o. We denote the set of minimal matches of s in o with $\mathfrak{M}^{(s)}_{min}(o)$. In Figure 4 we show the same schema as in Figure 3, but this time together with its minimal matches in the database in Figure 2.

We enrich the semantics of our schemata by adding concepts typically found in query languages. Variables can be used to link (or join) different parts of a database based on the equality of labels. We add variables to our schemata in the following manner: Let s be a schema, $\mathcal{V}$ be a set of variables and $v : V^{(s)} \cup A^{(s)} \longrightarrow \mathcal{V}$ be a partial mapping from the nodes and arcs in the schema into the variables.

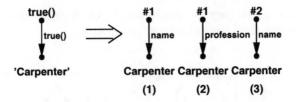

Fig. 4. The predicate schema and its minimal matches

For a mapping m to be a match of s into an object o we additionally require for all $x_1, x_2 \in V^{(s)} \cup A^{(s)}$ that if $v(x_1)$ and $v(x_2)$ exist and $v(x_1) = v(x_2)$ then $l^{(o)}(m(x_1)) = l^{(o)}(m(x_2))$, i.e., the labels of the corresponding elements in the match are the same. A predicate schema with variables together with its minimal match is shown in Figure 5. Due to the very nature of semistructured

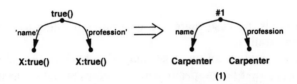

Fig. 5. Adding variables

data variables can be used to link data and structural parts of the database.

For adding paths to our notion of schema we have to take into account structural aspects of graphs. Let $G = (V, A, s, t)$ be a total directed graph. A *trail* is an arc sequence $(a_{i_1}, \ldots, a_{i_m})$ where all a_{i_j} are distinct and there exist nodes $v_{i_0}, \ldots, v_{i_m}$, such that for all a_{i_j} $s(a_{i_j}) = v_{i_{j-1}}$ and $t(a_{i_j}) = v_{i_j}$ hold. Note, that we do not require the $v_{i_0}, \ldots, v_{i_m}$ to be distinct. Thus, the notion of trail is more general than that of a path, yet the number of trails in an arbitrary graph is always finite, which makes it possible to handle cyclic structures. The number of arcs in a trail is called the *length* of the trail. Despite the fact that we are talking about trails we denote the set of all trails in a graph by P and the set of nonempty trails by P^+, because from the intuition point of view we are talking about paths. For a nonempty trail $p_i = (a_{i_1}, \ldots, a_{i_m}) \in P^+$ we introduce source and target function $s_P, t_P : P^+ \longrightarrow V$ being defined in a canonical manner as $s_P(p_i) = s(a_{i_1})$ and $t_P(p_i) = t(a_{i_m})$, respectively.

Definition 6 (Corresponding trail graph). *The* corresponding trail graph *to a graph* $G = (V^{(G)}, A^{(G)}, s^{(G)}, t^{(G)})$ *is defined as* $G_P = (V^{(G)}, P^{+(G)}, s_P^{(G)}, t_P^{(G)})$.

Intuitively, in the corresponding trail graph the trails are materialized as arcs. This notion is related to the notion of transitive closure of a graph. The only difference between the two notions is that in the transitive closure only one arc is included for every pair of reachable nodes, whereas we include an arc for every trail via which they are reachable. Figure 6 shows three examples of directed graphs and their corresponding trail graphs.

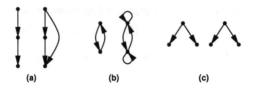

(a)   (b)   (c)

Fig. 6. Three directed graphs and their corresponding trail graphs

Lemma 3. *A directed graph is always a subgraph of its corresponding trail graph.*

The lemma holds, because there is a natural embedding $a_i \longrightarrow (a_i)$ of the arcs in A into the trails in P^+.

Now we can extend our notion of schema. We introduce two additional functions q_{min} and q_{max} that let us specify length constraints on paths in the matching objects. Furthermore, in order to incorporate the previously mentioned variables, we need a set of variables V and a variable mapping v.

Definition 7 (Schema). *Given a set of labels $\mathcal{L}$ and a set of variables V a schema s is a tuple $(V^{(s)}, A^{(s)}, s^{(s)}, t^{(s)}, l^{(s)}, v^{(s)}, q^{(s)}_{min}, q^{(s)}_{max})$ where*

1. *$V^{(s)}, A^{(s)}, s^{(s)}, t^{(s)}, l^{(s)}$ are defined as before,*
2. *$v : V^{(s)} \cup A^{(s)} \longrightarrow V$ is the variable mapping, a partial mapping from the nodes and arcs in the schema into the variables, and*
3. *$q^{(s)}_{min} : A^{(s)} \longrightarrow \mathbb{N}^+$ and $q^{(s)}_{max} : A^{(s)} \longrightarrow \mathbb{N}^+ \cup \{+\infty\}$ are length restrictions.*

Furthermore, if for an arbitrary arc $a_i \in A^{(s)}$ a variable binding $v^{(s)}(a_i)$ exists, then $q^{(s)}_{min}(a_i) = q^{(s)}_{max}(a_i) = 1$ holds.

Of course we have to redefine the notion of conformity between schema and object.

Definition 8 (Conformity). *A match of a schema s into an object o is an isomorphic embedding of s into o_P, i.e., an isomorphic embedding of $(V^{(s)}, A^{(s)}, s^{(s)}, t^{(s)})$ into $(V^{(o)}, P^{+(o)}, s^{(o)}_P, t^{(o)}_P)$, so that the following properties hold:*

1. *For all nodes $x \in V^{(s)}$ the predicate $l^{(s)}(x)$ is true for $l^{(o)}(m(x))$.*
2. *For all arcs $x \in A^{(s)}$ the predicate $l^{(s)}(x)$ is true for the labels $l^{(o)}(y_j)$ of all the arcs y_j in the trail $m(x)$.*
3. *For all elements $x_1, x_2 \in V^{(s)} \cup A^{(s)}$ for which $v^{(s)}(x_1)$ and $v^{(s)}(x_2)$ exist and $v^{(s)}(x_1) = v^{(s)}(x_2)$, the labels are the same $l^{(o)}(m(x_1)) = l^{(o)}(m(x_2))$.*

4. *For all arcs* $x \in A^{(s)}$ *the length of the trail* $m(x)$ *is at least* $q_{min}^{(s)}(x)$ *and no greater than* $q_{max}^{(s)}(x)$.

If a match between a schema s and an object o exists we say that o conforms to *s.*

If an object o conforms to a schema s we again call o an *instance* (or also a *match*) of s. To distinguish between functions that are matches and objects that are matches we also call the functions *match functions*.

The following theorem states that we indeed enhanced our initial notion of schema, i.e., our new notion of schema does not contradict the initial one. Due to space limitations we omit the prove of this theorem.

Theorem 1. *A predicate schema s conforms to an object o in the naive manner if and only if it conforms to o, assuming that* $v^{(s)}$ *is the empty mapping and* $q_{min}^{(s)}$ *and* $q_{max}^{(s)}$ *equal one for all arcs in s.*

Consider the example in Figure 7. There is a '+'-sign on the first arc in the schema. It indicates that the length of the paths it matches is bound by 1 and $+\infty$. So the schema matches everything that emanates from the root and leads to a 'name'-arc.

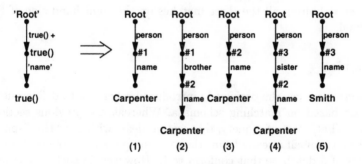

Fig. 7. Adding paths

There are some subtleties here. A match of s in o is supposed to be a subobject of o. However, the scope $m(s)$ of the match function m is a subobject of o_P. These subtleties become a serious problem when we want to adapt the definition of minimal match. The notion of minimal match is particularly important for the definition of queries as will be seen in the next section. Consider Figure 8. (We omitted the node labels there, because they are not relevant to this problem.)

The schema on the left is matched to the database next to it. All the three matches are potentially "interesting", but only the first one is minimal, because it is a subobject of the other two. Beside, if one of the matches was more interesting than the others, wouldn't it be the one with the longest path, i.e., the one on the right? But we observe that all the three matches result from different

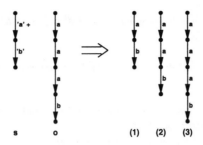

Fig. 8. A problem with the minimal matches of paths

match functions. The scopes of their respective match functions are incomparable subobjects of o_P. Thus, we define minimal matches with respect to the match function. To achieve this we need a *flatten*-function that takes a subobject of o_P and produces a subobject of o. Informally, *flatten* decomposes the trails into arcs and adds all their source and target nodes to the node set. Then we can define the set of *minimal matches* of s in o, denoted by $\mathfrak{M}^{(s)}_{min}(o)$, as $\{flatten(m(s))|m$ is a match of s into $o\}$. We observe that every $flatten(m(s))$ is indeed a match of s in o, because s can be embedded into $flatten(m(s))_P$ using m. Furthermore, for every match of s in o (i.e., every element of $\mathfrak{M}^{(s)}(o)$) there is a minimal match in $\mathfrak{M}^{(s)}_{min}(o)$ that is a subobject of the former match. With this revised definition all the three matches on the right hand side of Figure 8 are minimal.

4 Queries

In this section we use the previously introduced schemata to define queries. All queries are based on matching schemata. Whereas the previous section dealt with the "What"-part of a query, this section deals with the "How"-part.

A schema in itself already forms the most simple kind of query. It queries all subobjects of a database that conform to it. However, in such a case we would be interested only in the minimal matches.

Definition 9 (Schema query). *A schema query is a tuple $q = (s)$ where s is a schema. The answer to q with respect to a database o is the set of minimal matches of s in o $\mathfrak{M}^{(s)}_{min}(o)$.*

As an example you can imagine any of the schemata from the previous section. With a schema we can formulate conditions that any match must fulfill. This roughly corresponds to a selection in the relational world. However, we would like to have a concept that is comparable to a projection.

Definition 10 (Focus query). *A focus query is a tuple $q = (s_1, s_2)$ where s_1 is a schema and s_2, the focus, is a subobject of s_1. The answer to q with respect to a database o is the union of the minimal matches of s_2 over all minimal matches of s_1 in o, i.e., $\bigcup_{x \in \mathfrak{M}^{(s_1)}_{min}(o)} \mathfrak{M}^{(s_2)}_{min}(x)$.*

The example in Figure 9 queries for the surnames of all persons with the name 'Carpenter'. The subschema s_2 is indicated by the dashed box.

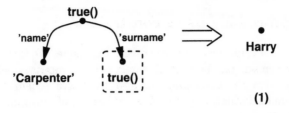

Fig. 9. A focus query

Sometimes we want to restructure the answer completely. Therefore we introduce the *transformation query* where we can specify a graph structure and compute new labels by using terms over the old ones.

Definition 11 (Transformation query). *A transformation query is a tuple $q = (s, t)$ where s is a schema and t is an object labeled with terms over the elements in s. The answer to q is built by creating for every match of s in o a new object isomorphic to t, labeled with the evaluated terms of t, instantiating the terms by using the match.*

The example in Figure 10 queries for the age of Suzy Smith. The age is computed from the year of birth.

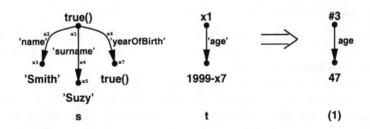

Fig. 10. A transformation query

Note, that schema and focus queries can be expressed as transformation queries.

An obvious limitation of our approach is that we always get one answer per schema match. Thus, we currently do not support aggregation. However, we were able to express the operations of the relational algebra using our approach and the encoding for relational databases into graph models presented in [BDHS96].

For querying semistructured data our appraoch has the property that no knowl-edge of a root node or specific paths going out from a root is necessary, because the approach is based on graph matching.

5   Query processing using constraints

In this section we outline our query processing technique. We focus on finding the matches for a given schema, because this part is the computationally challenging part. We start with the description of how to match schemata without any additional schema information given. A great benefit of our approach is that we can use previously matched schemata to speed up query processing. We outline this advantage at the end of the section.

We base our query processing on constraint satisfaction techniques. There are at least two good reasons for this approach. First, the area of constraint satisfaction is well-studied with many techniques and heuristics available. Sec-ond, constraint satisfaction problems form a reasonably general class of search problems. Thus, we use a well-established framework for specifying our needs, for adapting our algorithms for richer kinds of schemata and, most important, for formulating our query processing based on previously matched schemata.

Constraint satisfaction deals with solving problems by stating properties or constraints that any solution must fulfill. A *Constraint Satisfaction Problem (CSP)* is a tuple (X, D, C) where

- X is a set of *variables* $\{x_1, \ldots, x_m\}$,
- D is a set of finite *domains* D_i for each variable $x_i \in X$ and
- C is a set of *constraints* $\{C_{S_1}, \ldots, C_{S_n}\}$ restricting the values that the vari-ables can simultaneously take. The $S_i = (x_{S_{i_1}}, \ldots, x_{S_{i_k}})$ are arbitrary tuples of variables from X and each C_{S_i} is a relation over the crossproduct of the domains of these variables $(C_{S_i} \subseteq D_{S_{i_1}} \times \cdots \times D_{S_{i_k}})$.

Solving a CSP is finding assignments of values from the respective domains to the variables, so that all constraints are satisfied. In our context we are interested in finding all solutions of a CSP.

The basic idea is as follows and is summarized in Figure 11. The database graph is transformed into suitable domains; and variables are introduced for the elements in the schema. Furthermore, constraints representing the match semantics are introduced. They can be categorized into the ones that represent the label part and the ones that represent the structural part of the match semantics.

We depict the domains of the vertices and arcs from the database graph in Figure 2.

$$D_V = \{v_1, v_2, v_3, \ldots, v_{11}\}$$
$$D_A = \{a_1, a_2, a_3, \ldots, a_{12}\}$$

The example schema in Figure 12 (the same as in Figure 3) gives us the variables and the domain assignments.

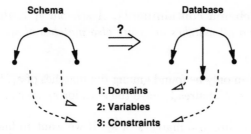

Fig. 11. Schema matching as a Constraint Satisfaction Problem

Fig. 12. A simple predicate schema

$$X = \{x_1, x_2, x_3\}$$
$$D_1 = D_3 = D_V$$
$$D_2 = D_A$$

Constraints are derived from the labels in the schema ...

$$C^{lab}_{(x_1)} = \{(v_1), (v_2), (v_3), \ldots, (v_{11})\}$$
$$C^{lab}_{(x_2)} = \{(a_1), (a_2), (a_3), \ldots, (a_{12})\}$$
$$C^{lab}_{(x_3)} = \{(v_5), (v_7), (v_8)\}$$

... and the structure of the schema.

$$C^{src}_{(x_2,x_1)} = \{(a_1, v_1), (a_2, v_1), (a_3, v_1), (a_4, v_2), (a_5, v_4), (a_6, v_2),$$
$$(a_7, v_2), (a_8, v_2), (a_9, v_3), (a_{10}, v_4), (a_{11}, v_4), (a_{12}, v_4)\}$$
$$C^{tar}_{(x_2,x_3)} = \{(a_1, v_2), (a_2, v_3), (a_3, v_4), (a_4, v_3), (a_5, v_3), (a_6, v_5),$$
$$(a_7, v_6), (a_8, v_7), (a_9, v_8), (a_{10}, v_9), (a_{11}, v_{10}), (a_{12}, v_{11})\}$$

Our sample CSP has the solutions (v_2, a_6, v_5), (v_2, a_8, v_7), and (v_3, a_9, v_8) for the variables (x_1, x_2, x_3). They correspond to the matches of the schema as shown in Figure 4. Note, that if injectivity of the match is to be ensured, additional constraints must be introduced.

More details about this part of the work (e.g., variables and paths) and about techniques for solving CSPs can be found in [BF99].

We conclude this section by discussing how to find the matches of a schema using previously matched schemata. The basic underlying notion for this approach is the notion of *schema containment*. It is related to the traditional notion of query containment.

Definition 12 (Schema containment). *A schema s_1 contains a schema s_2 if for all databases o all matches of s_2 are also matches of s_1.*

If s_1 contains s_2

1. matches of s_2 can only be found among the matches of s_1. If we want to find the matches of s_2 and already have the ones for s_1 we can *reduce the search space*.
2. all matches of s_2 are also matches of s_1. If we want to find the matches of s_1 and already have the ones for s_2 we can present the *first few matches immediately*. There may exist more matches for s_1, though.

Figure 13 shows three schemata. They contain one another left to right.

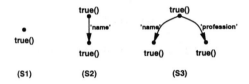

Fig. 13. Schema containment

Let us assume a notion of containment for predicates. p_1 contains p_2 if for all labels x the implication $p_2(x) \longrightarrow p_1(x)$ holds. Now, informally, a schema s_1 contains another schema s_2 if s_1 is a subgraph of s_2 and the predicates of s_1 contain the respective predicates of s_2 and the paths in s_1 are no longer than the respective ones in s_2. The other direction of this implication does not hold.

We reduce the testing of these sufficient conditions for schema containment again to the Constraint Satisfaction Problem. Once we find a schema s' that contains our current schema s we can reduce the search space for the problem of finding the matches of s.

In Figure 14 the schema s that is to be matched (the schema on top) is contained in the schema s' on the left. The variables x_1, x_2, and x_3, that are introduced when constructing the CSP for s, correspond to y_1, y_2, and y_3, respectively. In the matches for s' y_1 is matched to v_2, v_3, and v_4; y_2 is matched to a_6, a_9, and a_{10}; and y_3 is matched to v_5, v_8, and v_9. Thus, we can construct the reduced domains for x_1, x_2, and x_3.

$$D_1 = \{v_2, v_3, v_4\}$$
$$D_2 = \{a_6, a_9, a_{10}\}$$
$$D_3 = \{v_5, v_8, v_9\}$$

In order to fully capture the containment information we introduce an additional constraint.

$$C^{sol}_{(x_1, x_2, x_3)} = \{(v_2, a_6, v_5), (v_3, a_9, v_8), (v_4, a_{10}, v_9)\}$$

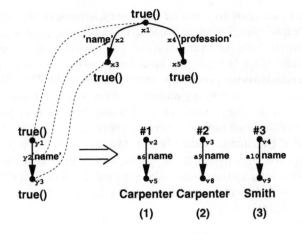

Fig. 14. Reducing the search space

6 Related work

Core issues and basic characterizations of semistructured data are discussed in [Abi97] and [Bun97]. Query languages include Lorel [MAG+97] and UnQL [BDHS96]. XML-QL is similar to our approach in that it uses so called element patterns as the "What"-part of a query [DFF+99]. Work on schema information for semistructured data concentrates on computing an ad hoc complete schema. One example are DataGuides [GW97,GW99]. Another notion of schema is introduced in [BDFS97]. Much related work arises also in the context of query languages suited for the Web and Web-site management systems ([AMM97], [FFK+98], [KS95], [LSS96], [MMM96]). A fundamental work on data stored in files is [ACM93]. Structured files are transformed to databases such that file querying and manipulating by using database technology becomes possible.

We were inspired in our query processing by the area of graph transformations. Graph transformations address the dynamic aspects of graphs. Systems are typically rule-based and can be used to model behavior. Thus, these systems must incorporate techniques for graph pattern matching. Rudolf uses constraint satisfaction techniques for simple graph pattern matching [Rud98]. A more database-like approach to this problem can be found in [Zue93].

An introduction to the field of constraint satisfaction is provided in [Bar98] and [Kum92]. They give various algorithms, heuristics, and useful background information to efficiently solve CSPs. A theoretical study of backtracking algorithms can be found in [KvB97].

7 Conclusion

In this paper we have presented a flexible approach to querying semistructured data. It is based on the intuition that a query consists of a "What"-part and a "How"-part. In contrast to more ad hoc query languages this split allows us to reuse the "what"-part for optimization. We have proposed a general graph model as the underlying data representation. The matching of a (partial) schema (representing the "What") forms the base for querying. We proposed a rather rich kind of schema covering predicates, variables and paths. Bringing the notion of schema closer to that of a query allows us to reuse query results more easily. The "How"-part of a query comes in by defining how to manipulate schema matches. We have outlined how to process a query based on posing constraints. In particular, it is possible to make use of previously matched schemata.

We have started to implement our ideas into a Prolog-based system and are currently switching to the commercial constraint solver ECLiPSe [Ecl]. Additional future work lies in assessing schemata in order to determine "good" schemata for optimization.

Acknowledgement

The authors wish to thank all members of the Berlin-Brandenburg Graduate School in Distributed Information Systems for providing an inspiring environment and for many interesting discussions. We are especially grateful to Felix Naumann for numerous useful comments and for reviewing our manuscript.

References

[Abi97]   S. Abiteboul. Querying semi-structured data. In *Proceedings of the International Conference on Database Theory (ICDT)*, pages 1–18, Delphi, Greece, January 1997.

[ACM93]   S. Abiteboul, S. Cluet, and T. Milo. Querying and updating the file. In *Proceedings of the International Conference on Very Large Databases (VLDB)*, pages 73–84, Dublin, Ireland, August 1993.

[AMM97] P. Atzeni, G. Mecca, and P. Merialdo. To weave the web. In *Proceedings of the International Conference on Very Large Databases (VLDB)*, pages 206–215, Athens, Greece, August 1997.

[Bar98]   R. Bartak. Guide to constraint programming, 1998. http://kti.ms.mff.cuni.cz/ bartak/constraints/.

[BDFS97] P. Buneman, S. Davidson, M. Fernandez, and D. Suciu. Adding structure to unstructured data. In *Proceedings of the International Conference on Database Theory (ICDT)*, pages 336–350, Delphi, Greece, January 1997.

[BDHS96] P. Buneman, S. Davidson, G. Hillebrand, and D. Suciu. A query language and optimization techniques for unstructured data. In *Proceedings of the ACM SIGMOD International Conference on Management of Data*, pages 505–516, Montreal, Canada, June 1996.

[BF99]   A. Bergholz and J. C. Freytag. Matching schemata by utilizing constraint satisfaction techniques. In *Proceedings of the Workshop on Query Processing for Semistructured Data and Non-Standard Data Formats (in conjunction with ICDT'99)*, Jerusalem, Israel, January 1999.

[Bun97]   P. Buneman. Semistructured data. In *Proceedings of the Symposium on Principles of Database Systems (PODS)*, pages 117–121, Tucson, AZ, USA, May 1997.

[DFF+99]   A. Deutsch, M. Fernandez, D. Florescu, A. Levy, and D. Suciu. A query language for XML. In *Proceedings of the International World Wide Web Conference*, pages 1155–1169, Toronto, Canada, May 1999.

[Ecl]   ECLiPSe - The ECRC Constraint Logic Parallel System, http://www.ecrc.de/eclipse/.

[FFK+98]   M. Fernandez, D. Florescu, J. Kang, A. Levy, and D. Suciu. Catching the boat with Strudel: Experiences with a web-site management system. In *Proceedings of the ACM SIGMOD International Conference on Management of Data*, pages 414–425, Seattle, WA, USA, June 1998.

[GW97]   R. Goldman and J. Widom. DataGuides: Enabling query formulation and optimization in semistructured databases. In *Proceedings of the International Conference on Very Large Databases (VLDB)*, pages 436–445, Athens, Greece, August 1997.

[GW99]   R. Goldman and J. Widom. Approximate DataGuides. In *Proceedings of the Workshop on Query Processing for Semistructured Data and Non-Standard Data Formats (in conjunction with ICDT'99)*, Jerusalem, Israel, January 1999.

[KS95]   D. Konopnicki and O. Shmueli. W3QS: A query system for the World-Wide Web. In *Proceedings of the International Conference on Very Large Databases (VLDB)*, pages 54–65, Zürich, Switzerland, September 1995.

[Kum92]   V. Kumar. Algorithms for constraint satisfaction problems: A survey. *AI Magazine*, 13(1):32–44, 1992.

[KvB97]   G. Kondrak and P. van Beek. A theoretical evaluation of selected backtracking algorithms. *Artificial Intelligence*, 89:365–387, 1997.

[LSS96]   L. V. S. Lakshmanan, F. Sadri, and I. N. Subramanian. A declarative language for querying and restructuring the web. In *Proceedings of the International Workshop on Research Issues in Data Engineering (RIDE)*, pages 12–21, New Orleans, LA, USA, February 1996.

[MAG+97] J. McHugh, S. Abiteboul, R. Goldman, D. Quass, and J. Widom. Lore: A database management system for semistructured data. *SIGMOD Record*, 26(3):54–66, 1997.

[MMM96]   A. O. Mendelzon, G. A. Mihaila, and T. Milo. Querying the World-Wide Web. In *Proceedings of the Conference on Parallel and Distributed Information Systems (PDIS)*, pages 80–91, Miami Beach, FL, USA, December 1996.

[Rud98]   M. Rudolf. Utilizing constraint satisfaction techniques for efficient graph pattern matching. In *Proceedings of the International Workshop on Theory and Application of Graph Transformations (TAGT)*, Paderborn, Germany, November 1998.

[Tro92]   W. T. Trotter. *Combinatorics and Partially Ordered Sets*. The John Hopkins University Press, Baltimore, MD, USA, 1992.

[Zue93]   A. Zuendorf. A heuristic for the subgraph isomorphism problem in executing PROGRES. Technical Report AIB 93-5, RWTH Aachen, Aachen, Germany, 1993.

Union Types for Semistructured Data

Peter Buneman and Benjamin Pierce

University of Pennsylvania, Dept. of Computer & Information Science
200 South 33rd Street, Philadelphia, PA 19104-6389, USA
{peter,bcpierce}@cis.upenn.edu

Abstract. Semistructured databases are treated as dynamically typed: they come equipped with no independent schema or type system to constrain the data. Query languages that are designed for semistructured data, even when used with structured data, typically ignore any type information that may be present. The consequences of this are what one would expect from using a dynamic type system with complex data: fewer guarantees on the correctness of applications. For example, a query that would cause a type error in a statically typed query language will return the empty set when applied to a semistructured representation of the same data.

Much semistructured data originates in structured data. A semistructured representation is useful when one wants to add data that does not conform to the original type or when one wants to combine sources of different types. However, the deviations from the prescribed types are often minor, and we believe that a better strategy than throwing away all type information is to preserve as much of it as possible. We describe a system of untagged *union types* that can accommodate variations in structure while still allowing a degree of static type checking.

A novelty of this system is that it involves non-trivial equivalences among types, arising from a law of distributivity for records and unions: a value may be introduced with one type (e.g., a record containing a union) and used at another type (a union of records). We describe programming and query language constructs for dealing with such types, prove the soundness of the type system, and develop algorithms for subtyping and typechecking.

1 Introduction

Although semistructured data has, by definition, no schema, there are many cases in which the data obviously possesses some basic structure, perhaps with mild deviations from that structure. Moreover it typically has this structure because it is derived from sources that have structure. In the process of annotating data or combining data from different sources one needs to accommodate the irregularities that are introduced by these processes. Because there is no way of describing "mildly irregular" structure, current approaches start by ignoring the structure completely, treating the data as some dynamically typed object such as a labelled graph and then, perhaps, attempting to recover some structure by

R. Connor and A. Mendelzon (Eds.): DBPL'99, LNCS 1949, pp. 184–207, 2000.
© Springer-Verlag Berlin Heidelberg 2000

a variety of pattern matching and data mining techniques [NAM97,Ali99]. The purpose of this structure recovery is typically to provide optimization techniques for query evaluation or efficient storage storage structures, and it is partial. It is not intended as a technique for preserving the integrity of data or for any kind of static type-checking of applications.

When data originates from some structured source, it is desirable to preserve that structure if at all possible. The typical cases in which one cannot require rigid conformance to a schema arise when one wants to annotate or modify the database with unanticipated structure or when one merges two databases with slight differences in structure. Rather than forgetting the original type and resorting to a completely dynamically type, we believe a more disciplined approach to maintaining type information is appropriate. We propose here a type system that can "degrade" gracefully if sources are added with variations in structure, while preserving the common structure of the sources where it exists.

The advantages of this approach include:

- The ability to check the correctness of programs and queries on semistructured data. Current semistructured query languages [BDHS96,AQM$^+$96,DFF$^+$] have no way of providing type errors – they typically return the empty answer on data whose type does not conform to the type assumed by the query.
- The ability to create data at one type and query it at another (equivalent) type. This is a natural consequence of using a flexible type system for semistructured data.
- New query language constructs that permit the efficient implementation of "case" expressions and increase the expressive power of a OQL-style query languages.

As an example, biological databases often have a structure that can be expressed naturally using a combination of tuples, records, and collection types. They are typically cast in special-purpose data formats, and there are groups of related databases, each expressed in some format that is a mild variation on some original format. These formats have an intended type, which could be expressed in a number of notations. For example a source ($source_1$) could have type

set[*id*: *Int*,
    description: *Str*,
    bibl: set[*title*: *Str*, *authors*: list[*name*: *Str*, *address*: *Str*], *year*: *Int*...],
    ...]

A second source ($source_2$) might yield a closely related structure:

set[*id*: *Int*,
    description: *Str*,
    bibl: set[*title*: *Str*, *authors*: list[*fn*: *Str*, *ln*: *Str*, *address*: *Str*], *year*: *Int* ...],
    ...]

This differs only in the way in which author names are represented. (This example is fictional, but not far removed from what happens in practice.)

The usual solution to this problem in conventional programming languages is to represent the union of the sources using some form of tagged union type:

$$\mathsf{set}(\langle\, tag_1 : [\, id\colon\, Int, \ldots\,], \; tag_2 : [\, id\colon\, Int, \ldots\,]\,\rangle).$$

The difficulty with this solution is that a program such as

$$\text{for each } x \text{ in } source_1 \text{ do } \mathsf{print}(x.description) \tag{1}$$

that worked on $source_1$ must now be modified to

```
foreach x in source₁ union source₂ do
   case x of
        ⟨ tag₁ = y₁ ⟩ ⇒ print(y₁.description)
      | ⟨ tag₂ = y₂ ⟩ ⇒ print(y₂.description)
```

in order to work on the union of the sources, even though the two branches of the case statement contain identical code! This is also true for the (few) database query languages that deal with tagged union types [BLS$^+$94].

Contrast this with a typical semi-structured query:

$$\mathsf{select}\ [\,description = d,\ title = t\,] \tag{2}$$
$$\mathsf{where}\ [\,description = d,\ bibl = [\,Title = t\,]\,] \leftarrow source_1$$

This query works by pattern matching based on the (dynamically determined) structure of the data. Thus the *same* query works equally well against either of the two sources, and hence also against their union[1]. The drawback of this approach, however, is that incorrect queries – for example, queries that use a field that does not exist in *either* source – yield the empty set rather than an error.

In this paper we define a system that combines the advantages of both approaches, based on a system of type-safe *untagged* union types. As a first example, consider the two forms of the *author* field in the types above. We may write the union of these types as:

$$[\,name\colon Str,\ address\colon Str\,] \vee [\,ln\colon Str,\ fn\colon Str,\ address\colon Str\,]$$

It is intuitively obvious that an *address* can always be extracted from a value of such a type. To express this formally, we begin by writing a multi-field record type $[l_1 : T_1, l_2 : T_2, \ldots]$ as a product of single-field record types: $[l_1 : T_1] \times [l_2 : T_2] \times \ldots$. In this more basic form, the union type above is:

$$([\,name\colon Str\,] \times [\,address\colon Str\,]) \vee ([\,ln\colon Str\,] \times [\,fn\colon Str\,] \times [\,address\colon Str\,])$$

---

[1] One could also achieve the same effect through the use of inheritance rather than union types in some object-oriented language. This would involve the introduction of named classes with explicit subclass assertions. As we shall shortly see, the number of possible classes is exponential in the size of the type.

We now invoke a *distributivity* law that allows us to treat

$$[a : T_a] \times ([b : T_b] \vee [c : T_c]) \quad \text{and} \quad ([a : T_a] \times [b : T_b]) \vee ([a : T_a] \times [c : T_c])$$

as equivalent types. Using this, the union type above rewrites to:

$$([\,name:\ Str\,] \vee [\,fn:\ Str \times ln:\ Str\,]) \times [\,address:\ Str\,]$$

In this form, it is evident that the the selection of the *address* field is an allowable operation.

Type-equivalences like this distributivity rule allow us to introduce a value at one type and operate on it another type. Under this system both the program (1) and the query (2) above will type-check when extended to the union of the two sources. On the other hand, queries that reference a field that is not in either source will fail to type check.

Some care is needed in designing the operations for manipulating values of union types. Usually, the interrogation operation for records is field selection and the corresponding operation for unions is a case expression. However it is not enough simply to use these two operations. Consider the type $([a_1 : T_1] \vee [b_1 : U_1]) \times \ldots \times ([a_n : T_n] \vee [b_n : U_n])$. The form of this type warrants neither selecting a field nor using a case expression. We can, if we want, use distributivity to rewrite it into a disjunct of products, but the size of this disjunct is exponential in n and so, presumably, would be the corresponding case expression. We propose, instead, an extended pattern matching syntax that allows us to operate on the type in its original, compact, form.

More sophisticated pattern matching operations may be useful additions even to existing semistructured query languages. Consider the problem of writing a query that produces a uniform output from a single source that contains two representations of names:

(select [*description* = d, *name* = n]
  where [*description* = d, *bibl* = [*author* = [*name* = n]]] ← *source*)
union
(select [*description* = d, *name* = *string-concat*(f, l)]
  where [*description* = d, *bibl* = [*author* = [*ln* = l, *fn* = f]]] ← *source*)

This is the only method known to the authors of expressing this query in current semistructured query languages. It suggests an inefficient execution model and may not have the intended semantics when, for example, the source is a list and one wants to preserve the order. Thus some enhancement to the syntax is desirable.

This paper develops a type system based on untagged union types along with operations to construct and deconstruct these types. In particular, we define a syntax of patterns that may be used both for an extended form of case expression and as an extension to existing query languages for semi-structured data. We should remark that we cannot capture all aspects of semistructured query languages. For example, we have nothing that corresponds to "regular path expressions" [BDHS96,AQM+96]. However, we believe that for most examples of "mildly" semistructured data – especially the forms that arise from the integration of typed data sources – a language such as proposed here will be adequate. Our main technical contribution is a proof of the decidabiliity of subtyping for this type system (which is complicated by the non-trivial equivalences involving union and record types).

To our knowledge, untagged union types never been formalized in the context of database programming languages. *Tagged* union types have been suggested in several papers on data models [AH87,CM94] but have had minimal impact on the design of query languages. CPL [BLS+94], for example, can match on only one tag of a tagged union, and this is one of the few languages that makes use of union types. Pattern matching has been recently exploited in languages for semi-structured data and XML [BDHS96,DFF+]. In the programming languages and type theory communities, on the other hand, untagged union types have been studied extensively from a theoretical perspective [Pie91,BDCd95,Hay91,Dam94,DCdP96, etc.], but the interactions of unions with higher-order function types have been shown to lead to significant complexities; the present system provides only a very limited form of function types (like most database query languages), and remains reasonably straightforward.

Section 2 develops our language for programming with record and union types, including pattern matching primitives that can be used in both case expressions and query languages. Section 3 describes the system formally and demonstrates the decidability of subtyping and type equivalence. Proofs will be provided in the full paper. Section 4 offers concluding remarks.

2   Programming with Union Types

In this section we shall develop a syntax for the new programming constructs that are needed to deal with union types. The presentation is informal for the moment – more precise definitions appear in Section 3. We start with operations on records and extend these to work with unions of records; we then deal with operations on sets. Taken in conjunction with operations on records, these operations are enough to define a simple query language. We also look at operations on more general union types and give examples of a "typecase" operation.

2.1   Record Formation

We have formulated record types $[l_1 : T_1, \ldots, l_n : T_n]$ as products $[l_1 : T_1] \times \ldots \times [l_n : T_n]$ of elementary or "singleton" record types. For record values, we use the standard presentation in terms of multi-field values $[l_1 = e_1, \ldots, l_n = e_n]$.

2.2   Case Expressions

Records are decomposed through the use of case expressions. These allow us to take alternative actions based on the structure of values. We shall also be able to use components of the syntax of case expressions in the development of matching constructs for query languages. The idea in developing a relatively complex syntax for the body of case expressions is that the structure of the body can be made to match the expected structure of the type of the value on which it is operating. There should be no need to "flatten" the type into disjunctive normal form and write a much larger case expression at that type.

We start with a simple example:

case e of $[\,fn = f{:}Str,\ ln = l{:}Str\,] \Rightarrow string\text{-}concat(f, l)$
| $[\,name = n{:}Str\,] \Rightarrow n$

This matches the result of evaluating e to one of two record types. If the result is a record with fn and ln fields, the variables f and l are bound and the right-hand side of the first clause is evaluated. If the first pattern does not match, the second clause is tried. This case expression will work provided e has type $[\,fn{:}\ Str, ln{:}\ Str\,] \vee [\,name{:}\ Str\,]$.

We should note that pattern matching introduces identifiers such as l, f, n in this example, and we shall make a short-sighted assumption that identifiers are introduced when they are associated with a type $(x : T)$. This ignores the possibility of type inference. See [BLS+94] for a more sophisticated syntax for introducing identifiers in patterns.

Field selection is given by a one-clause case expression: case e of $[\,l = x{:}T\,] \Rightarrow x$.

We shall also allow case expressions to dispatch on the run-time type of an argument:

case e of $x{:}Int \Rightarrow x$
| $y{:}set(Int) \Rightarrow sum(y)$

This will typecheck when $e : Int \vee set(Int)$

The clauses of a case expression have the form $p \Rightarrow e$, where p is a *pattern* that introduces (binds) identifiers which may occur free in the expression e. Thus each clause defines a *function*. Two or more functions can be combined by writing $p_1 \Rightarrow e_1 \mid p_2 \Rightarrow e_2 \mid \dots$ to form another function. The effect of the case expression case e of f is to apply this function to the result of evaluating e.

Now suppose we want to extract information from a value of type

$$([\,name{:}\ Str\,] \vee [\,ln{:}\ Str, fn{:}\ Str\,]) \times [\,age{:}\ Int\,] \tag{2}$$

The *age* field may be extracted using field selection using a one-clause case expression as described above. However information from the left-hand component cannot be extracted by extending this case expression. What we need is need something that will turn a multi-clause function back into a pattern that binds a new identifier. We propose the syntax x as f, in which f is a multi-clause function. In the evaluation of x as f, f is applied to the appropriate structure and x is bound to the result.

case   e of
    x as ([fn = f:Str, ln = l:Str] ⇒ string-concat(f, l) | [name = n:Str] ⇒ n)
    # [age = a:Int]
    ⇒ [name = x, age = a + 1]

could be applied to an expression e of type (2) above. Note the use of # to combine two patterns so that they match on a product type. This symbol is used to concatenate patterns in the same way that it is used to concatenate record types.

There are some useful extensions to case expressions and pattern matching that we shall briefly mention here but omit in the formal development (they are essentially syntactic sugar). The first is the addition of a "fall-through" or *else* branch of a case expression. The pattern else matches any value that has not been matched in a previous clause. Most programming languages have an analogous construct.

Such branches are particularly useful if we allow constants in patterns. For example

case   e of [name = n:Str, age = 21] ⇒ e
    | else ⇒ ...

Here only tuples with a specific value for *age* are matched. Tuples with a different value will be matched in the *else* clause. Note that patterns bind variables, and that if one allows constants in patterns, one wants to discriminate between those variables that are used as constants and those that are bound in the pattern. CPL [BLS+94] uses a special marker to flag bound variables. In that language [name = n, age = \a] is a pattern in which a is bound and n is treated as a constant – it is bound in some outer scope. This extended syntax of patterns is especially convenient when used in query languages for sets.

2.3   Sets

We shall follow the approach to collection types given in [BNTW95]. It is known that both relational and complex-object languages can be expressed using this formalism. The operations for forming sets are {e} (singleton set) and e union e (set union).[2] For "iterating" over a set we use the form

collect e where p ← e'.

Here, e and e' are both expressions of set type, and p is a pattern as described above. The meaning of this is (informally) $\bigcup\{\sigma(e) \mid \sigma(p) \in e'\}$, in which σ is a substitution that binds the variables of p to match an element of e'.

These operations, taken in conjunction with the record operations described above and an equality operation, may be used as the basis of practical query languages. Conditionals and booleans may be added, but they can also be simulated with case expressions and some appropriately chosen constants.

---

[2] The present system does not include {} (empty set). It can be added, at the cost of a slight extension to the type system; see Section 4.

Unlike typed systems with tagged unions, in our system there is no formation operation directly associated with the union type. However we may want to introduce operators such as "relaxed set-union," which takes two sets of type set(t_1) and set(t_2) and returns a set of type set($t1 \vee t2$).

2.4   Examples

We conclude this section with some remarks on high-level query languages. A typical form of a query that makes use of pattern matching is:

select e
where $p_1 \leftarrow e_1$,
      $p_2 \leftarrow e_2$,
      $\ldots$
      condition

Here the p_i are patterns and the expressions $e_1, \ldots, e_i$ have set types. Variables introduced in pattern p_i may be used in expression e_j and (as constants) in pattern p_j where $j > i$. They may also be used in the expression e and the *condition*, which is simply a boolean expression. This query form can be implemented using the operations described in the previous section.

As an example, here is a query based on the example types in the introduction. We make use of the syntax of patterns as developed for case expressions, but here we are using them to match on elements of one or more input sets.

select [*description* = d, authName = a, year = y]
where [*description* = d:Str, bibl = b:BT] $\leftarrow$ source$_1$ union source$_2$,
      [authors = aa:AT, year = y:Int] $\leftarrow$ b,
      a as ([fn = f:Str, ln = l:Str] $\Rightarrow$ string-concat(f, l) |
                                    [name = n:Str] $\Rightarrow$ n) $\leftarrow$ aa,
      y > 1991

Note that we have assumed a "relaxed" union to combine the two sources. In the interests of consistency with the formal development, we have also inserted all types for identifiers, so *AT* and *BT* are names for the appropriate fragments of the expected source type. In many cases such types can be inferred.

Here are two examples that show the use of paterns in matching on types rather than record structures. Examples of this kind are commomly used to illustrate the need for semistructured data.

select   x
where x as (s : set(*Num*) $\Rightarrow$ average(s) | r : Num $\Rightarrow$ r) $\leftarrow$ source

select   s
where s as (n : Str $\Rightarrow$ n | [fn = f:Str, ln = l:Str] $\Rightarrow$
                                    string-concat(f, l)) $\leftarrow$ source'

In the first case we have a set *source* that may contain both numbers and sets of numbers. In the second case we have a set that may contain both base types and record types. Both of these can be statically type-checked. If, for example, in the first query, *s* has type set(*Str*), the query would not type-check.

To demonstrate the proposed syntax for the use of functions in patterns, here is one last (slightly contrived) example. We want to calculate the mass of a solid object that is either rectangular or a sphere. Each measure of length can be either integer or real. The type is

[*density*: *Real*]
×
([*intRadius*: *Int*] ∨ [*realRadius*: *Real*]
  ∨
  (([*intHeight*: *Int*] ∨ [*realHeight*: *Real*])
    ×
    ([*intWidth*: *Int*] ∨ [*realWidth*: *Real*])
    ×
    ([*intDepth*: *Int*] ∨ [*realDepth*: *Real*])))

The following case expression makes use of matching based on both unions and products of record structures. Note that the structure of the expression follows that of the type. It would be possible to write an equivalent case expression for the disjunctive normal form for the type and avoid the use of the form *x* as*f*, but such an expression would be much larger than the one given here.

case *e* of
    [*density* = *d*:*Real*]
    #
    v as
      (*r* as ([*intRadius* = *ir*:*Int*] ⇒ *float*(*ir*) | [*realRadius* = *rr*:*Real*] ⇒ *rr*)
           ⇒ *r*∗∗3)
      |
      (*h* as ([*intHeight* = *ih*:*Int*] ⇒ *float*(*ih*) | [*realHeight* = *rh*:*Real*] ⇒ *rh*)
        #
        w as ([*intWidth* = *iw*:*Int*] ⇒ *float*(*iw*)|[*realWidth* = *rw*:*Real*] ⇒ *rw*)
        #
        d as ([*intDepth* = *id*:*Int*] ⇒ *float*(*id*) | [*realDepth* = *rd*:*Real*] ⇒ *rd*)
           ⇒ *h* ∗ *w* ∗ *d*)
     ⇒ *d* ∗ *v*

3 Formal Development

With the foregoing intuitions and examples in mind, we now proceed to the formal definition of our language, its type system, and its operational semantics. Along the way, we establish fundamental properties such as run-time safety and the decidability of subtyping and type-checking.

3.1 Types

We develop a type system that is based on conventional complex object types, those that are constructed from the base types with record (tuple) and set constructors. As described in the introduction, the record constructors are [ ], the empty record type, $[l\colon T]$, the singleton record type, and $R \times R$, the *disjoint* concatenation of two record types. (By disjoint we mean that the two record types have no field names in common.) Thus a conventional record type $[l_1 : T_1, \ldots, l_n : T_n]$ is shorthand for $[l_1 : T_1] \times \ldots \times [l_n : T_n]$. To this we add an untagged union type $T \vee T$. We also assume a single base type B and a set type $\mathsf{set}(T)$. Other collection types such as lists and multisets would behave similarly,

The syntax of types is described by the following grammar:

$$
\begin{array}{lll}
T ::= & \mathsf{B} & \text{base type} \\
& [\,] & \text{empty record type} \\
& [l : T] & \text{labeling (single-field record type)} \\
& T_1 \times T_2 & \text{record type concatenation} \\
& T_1 \vee T_2 & \text{union type} \\
& \mathsf{set}(T) & \text{set type}
\end{array}
$$

3.2 Kinding

We have already noted that certain operations on types are restricted. For example, we cannot form the product of two record types with a common field name. In order to control the formation of types we introduce a system of *kinds*, consisting of the kind of all types, Type, and a subkind $\mathsf{Rcd}(L)$, which is the kind of all record types whose labels are included in the label set L.

$$
\begin{array}{ll}
K ::= & \mathsf{Type} \quad \text{kind of all types} \\
& \mathsf{Rcd}(L) \ \text{kind of record types with (at most) labels L}
\end{array}
$$

The kinding relation is defined as follows:

$$\mathsf{B} \in \mathsf{Type} \tag{K-Base}$$

$$[\,] \in \mathsf{Rcd}(\{\}) \tag{K-Empty}$$

$$\frac{T \in \mathsf{Type}}{[l : T] \in \mathsf{Rcd}(\{l\})} \tag{K-Field}$$

$$\frac{S \in \mathsf{Rcd}(L_1) \quad T \in \mathsf{Rcd}(L_2) \quad L_1 \cap L_2 = \emptyset}{S \times T \in \mathsf{Rcd}(L_1 \cup L_2)} \tag{K-Rcd}$$

$$\frac{S \in K \quad T \in K}{S \vee T \in K} \tag{K-Union}$$

$$\frac{T \in \mathsf{Type}}{\mathsf{set}(T) \in \mathsf{Type}} \qquad \text{(K-SET)}$$

$$\frac{T \in \mathsf{Rcd}(L_1)}{T \in \mathsf{Rcd}(L_1 \cup L_2)} \qquad \text{(K-SUBSUMPTION-1)}$$

$$\frac{T \in \mathsf{Rcd}(L)}{T \in \mathsf{Type}} \qquad \text{(K-SUBSUMPTION-2)}$$

There are two important consequences of these rules. First, record kinds extend to the union type. For example, $([A : t] \times [B : t]) \times ([C : t] \vee [D : t])$ has kind $\mathsf{Rcd}(\{A, B, C, D\})$. Second, the kinding rules require the labels in a concatenation of two record types to be disjoint. (However the union type constructor is not limited in the same way; $Int \vee Str$ and $Int \vee [a : Str]$ are well-kinded types.)

In what follows, we will assume that all types under consideration are well kinded.

3.3   Subtyping

As usual, the subtype relation written $S <: T$ captures a principle of "safe substitutibility": any element of S may safely be used in a context expecting an element of T.

For sets and records, the subtyping rules are the standard ones: $\mathsf{set}(S) <: \mathsf{set}(T)$ if $S <: T$ (e.g., a set of employees can be used as a set of people), and a record type S is a subtype of a record type T if S has more fields than T and the types of the common fields in S are subtypes of the corresponding fields in T. This effect is actually achieved by the combination of several rules below. This "exploded presentation" of record subtyping corresponds to our presentation of record types in terms of separate empty set, singleton, and concatenation constructors.

For union types, the subtyping rules are a little more interesting. First, we axiomatize the fact that $S \vee T$ is the least upper bound of S and T – that is, $S \vee T$ is above both S and T, and everything that is above both S and T is also above their union (rules S-UNION-UB and S-UNION-L below). We then have two rules (S-DIST-RCD and S-DIST-FIELD) showing how union distributes over records.

Formally, the subtype relation is the least relation on well-kinded types closed under the following rules.

$$T <: T \qquad \text{(S-REFL)}$$

$$\frac{R <: S \qquad S <: T}{R <: T} \qquad \text{(S-TRANS)}$$

$$[l:T] <: [\,] \qquad\qquad \text{(S-Rcd-FE)}$$

$$S \times T <: S \qquad\qquad \text{(S-Rcd-RE)}$$

$$S \times T <: T \times S \qquad\qquad \text{(S-Rcd-Comm)}$$

$$S \times (T \times U) <: (S \times T) \times U \qquad\qquad \text{(S-Rcd-Assoc)}$$

$$S <: S \times [\,] \qquad\qquad \text{(S-Rcd-Ident)}$$

$$\frac{S <: T}{[l:S] <: [l:T]} \qquad\qquad \text{(S-Rcd-DF)}$$

$$\frac{S_1 <: T_1 \qquad S_2 <: T_2}{S_1 \times S_2 <: T_1 \times T_2} \qquad\qquad \text{(S-Rcd-DR)}$$

$$\frac{S <: T}{\mathsf{set}(S) <: \mathsf{set}(T)} \qquad\qquad \text{(S-Set)}$$

$$\frac{R <: T \qquad S <: T}{R \vee S <: T} \qquad\qquad \text{(S-Union-L)}$$

$$S_i <: S_1 \vee S_2 \qquad\qquad \text{(S-Union-UB)}$$

$$R \times (S \vee T) <: (R \times S) \vee (R \times T) \qquad\qquad \text{(S-Dist-Rcd)}$$

$$[l : S \vee T] <: [l:S] \vee [l:T] \qquad\qquad \text{(S-Dist-Field)}$$

Note that we restrict the subtype relation to *well-kinded* types: S is never a subtype of T if either S or T is ill-kinded. (The typing rules will be careful only to "call" the subtype relation on types that are already known to be well kinded.)

If both $S <: T$ and $T <: S$, we say that S and T are *equivalent* and write $S \sim T$. Note, for example, that the distributive laws S-Dist-Rcd and S-Dist-Field are actually equivalences: the other directions follow from the laws for union (plus transitivity). Also, note the absence of the "other" distributivity law for unions and records: $P \vee (Q \times R) \sim (P \vee Q) \times (P \vee R)$. This law doesn't make sense here, because it violates the kinding constraint that products of record types can only be formed if the two types have disjoint label sets.

The subtype relation includes explicit rules for associativity and commutativity of the operator $\times$. Also, it is easy to check that the associativity, commutativity and idempotence of $\vee$ follow directly from the rules given. We shall take advantage of this fluidity in the following by writing both records and unions in a compound, n-ary form:

$$[l_1 : T_1, \ldots, l_n : T_n] \stackrel{def}{=} [l_1 : T_1] \times \cdots \times [l_n : T_n]$$
$$\bigvee(T_1, \ldots, T_n) \stackrel{def}{=} T_1 \vee \cdots \vee T_n$$

(In the first line, n may be 0—we allow empty records—but in the second, it must be positive—for simplicity, we do not allow "empty unions" in the present system. See Section 4.)

We often write compound unions using a simple comprehension notation. For example,

$$\bigvee(A \times B \mid A \in A_1 \vee A_2 \vee \ldots \vee A_m \text{ and } B \in B_1 \vee B_2 \vee \ldots \vee B_n)$$

denotes

$$A_1 \times B_1 \vee A_1 \times B_2 \vee \ldots \vee A_1 \times B_n \vee A_2 \times B_1 \vee \ldots \vee A_m \times B_n.$$

3.4   Properties of Subtyping

For proving properties of the subtype relation, it is convenient to work with types in a more constrained syntactic form:

3.4.1 Definition: The sets of *normal* (N) and *simple* (A) types are defined as follows:

$$N ::= \bigvee(A_1, \ldots, A_n)$$

$$
\begin{aligned}
A ::= &\; \mathsf{B} \\
&\; [l_1 : A_1, \ldots, l_n : A_n] \\
&\; \mathsf{set}(N)
\end{aligned}
$$

Intuitively, a simple type is one in which unions only appear (immediately) inside of the set constructor; a normal type is a union of simple types. Note that every simple type is also normal. $\square$

The restricted form of normal and simple types can be exploited to give a much simpler subtyping relation, written $S \leq: T$, in terms of the following "macro rules":

$$\mathsf{B} \leq: \mathsf{B} \qquad\qquad\qquad\qquad \text{(SA-Base)}$$

$$\frac{N \leq: M}{\mathsf{set}(N) \leq: \mathsf{set}(M)} \qquad\qquad \text{(SA-Set)}$$

$$\frac{\{k_1, \ldots, k_m\} \subseteq \{l_1, \ldots, l_n\} \qquad \text{for all } k_i \in \{k_1, \ldots, k_m\}, \; A_{k_i} \leq: B_{k_i}}{[l_1 : A_{l_1}, \ldots l_m : A_{l_m}] \leq: [k_1 : B_{k_1}, \ldots, k_m : B_{k_m}]}$$
$$\text{(SA-Rcd)}$$

$$\frac{\forall i \leq m. \; \exists j \leq n. \; A_i \leq: B_j}{\bigvee(A_1, \ldots, A_m) \leq: \bigvee(B_1, \ldots, B_n)} \qquad\qquad \text{(SN-Union)}$$

3.4.2 Fact: $N \leq: M$ is decidable. $\square$

Proof: The macro rules can be read as a pair of algorithms, one for subtyping between simple types and one for subtyping between normal types. Both of these algorithms are syntax directed and obviously terminate on all inputs (all recursive calls reduce the size of the inputs).   □

3.4.3 Lemma: $N \leq: N$, for all N.   □

3.4.4 Lemma: If $N \leq: M$ and $M \leq: L$ then $N \leq: L$.   □

Proof: By induction on the total size of L, M, N. First suppose that all of L, M, N are simple. The induction hypothesis is immediately satisfied for SA-BASE and SA-SET. For SA-RCD use the transitivity of set inclusion and induction on the appropriate subterms.

If at least one of L, M, N is (non-trivially) normal, use the transitivity of the functional relationship expressed by the SN-Union rule and induction on the appropriate subterms.   □

To transfer the property of decidability from $\leq:$ to $<:$, we first show how any type may be converted to an equivalent type in *disjunctive normal form*.

3.4.5 Definition: The disjunctive normal form (dnf) of a type T is defined as follows:

$$
\begin{array}{lll}
\mathit{dnf}(\mathsf{B}) & = \mathsf{B} & \\
\mathit{dnf}([\,]) & = [\,] & \\
\mathit{dnf}(P \times Q) = \bigvee(A_i \times B_j \mid A_i \in \mathit{dnf}(P),\ B_j \in \mathit{dnf}(Q)) & & \text{(a)} \\
\mathit{dnf}([\,l : P\,]) = \bigvee([\,l : A_i\,] \mid A_i \in \mathit{dnf}(P)) & & \text{(b)} \\
\mathit{dnf}(P \vee Q) = \mathit{dnf}(P) \vee \mathit{dnf}(Q) & & \text{(c)} \\
\mathit{dnf}(\mathsf{set}(P)) = \mathsf{set}(\mathit{dnf}(P)) & & \text{(d)}
\end{array}
$$
    □

3.4.6 Fact: $\mathit{dnf}(P) \sim P$.   □

3.4.7 Fact: $\mathit{dnf}(P)$ is a normal type, for every type P.   □

3.4.8 Fact: $N \leq: M$ implies $N <: M$ □

3.4.9 Lemma: $S <: T$ iff $\mathit{dnf}(S) \leq: \mathit{dnf}(T)$ □

Proof: ($\Leftarrow$) By 3.4.6 we have derivations of $S <: \mathit{dnf}(S)$ and $\mathit{dnf}(T) <: T$, and by 3.4.8 we have a derivation of $\mathit{dnf}(S) <: \mathit{dnf}(T)$. Use transitivity to build a derivation of $S <: T$.

($\Rightarrow$) By induction on the height of the derivation of $S <: T$. We consider the final rule in the derivation. By induction we assume we can build a derivation of the normal forms for the antecedents, and now we consider all possible final rules.

We start with the axioms.

(S-REFL) By reflexivity of $\leq:$ (3.4.3).
(S-RCD-FE) $\mathit{dnf}([\,l : T\,]) = [\,l : \mathit{dnf}(T)\,]$, and $[\,l : \mathit{dnf}(T)\,] \leq: [\,]$ by SA-RCD.

(S-RCD-RE) $dnf(S \times T) = \bigvee(S_i \times T_j \mid S_i \in dnf(S),\ T_j \in dnf(T))$. Now $dnf(S_i) \times dnf(T_j) \mathrel{\underline{<}:} dnf(S_i)$ by SA-RCD, and the result follows from SN-UNION.

(S-RCD-COMM)

If $dnf(S)$ and $dnf(T)$ are simple then $dnf(S) \times dnf(T) \mathrel{\underline{<}:} dnf(T) \times dnf(S)$ by SA-RCD. If not, use SN-UNION first.

(S-RCD-ASSOC) As for S-RCD-COMM.

(S-RCD-IDENT) As for S-RCD-COMM.

(S-UNION-UB) By SN-UNION.

(S-DIST-RCD)
$$\begin{aligned} dnf(R \times (S \vee T)) &= \bigvee(R_i \times U_j \mid R_i \in dnf(R),\ U_j \in dnf(S \vee T)) \\ &= \bigvee(R_i \times S_j \mid R_i \in dnf(R),\ U_j \in dnf(S)) \vee \\ &\quad\ \bigvee(R_i \times T_k \mid R_i \in dnf(R),\ T_k \in dnf(T)) \\ &= dnf((R \times S) \vee (R \times T)) \end{aligned}$$

(S-DIST-FIELD)
$$\begin{aligned} dnf([\,l : S \vee T\,]) &= \bigvee([\,l : U_i\,] \mid U_i \in dnf(S \vee T)) \\ &= \bigvee([\,l : S_i\,] \mid S_i \in dnf(S)) \vee \bigvee([\,l : T_i\,] \mid T_i \in dnf(T)) \\ &= dnf([\,l : S\,]) \vee dnf([\,l : T\,]) \\ &= dnf([\,l : S\,] \vee [\,l : T\,]) \end{aligned}$$

Now for the inference rules. The premises for all the rules are of the form $S \mathrel{<}: T$ and our inductive hypothesis is that for the premises of the final rule we have obtained a derivation using SA-* and SN-UNION rules of the corresponding $dnf(S) \mathrel{\underline{<}:} dnf(T)$ Without loss of generality we may assume that the final rule in the derivation of each such premise is SN-UNION. We examine the remaining inference rules.

(S-TRANS) By Lemma 3.4.4.

(S-RCD-DF) Since $dnf(S) \mathrel{\underline{<}:} dnf(T)$ was derived by SN-UNION we know that for each $A_i \in dnf(S)$ there is a $B_j \in dnf(T)$ such that $A_i \mathrel{\underline{<}:} B_j$. Therefore, for each such A_i, we may use SA-RCD to derive $[\,l : A_i\,] \mathrel{\underline{<}:} [\,l : B_j\,]$. These derivations may be combined using SN-UNION to obtain a derivation of $dnf([\,l : S\,]) \mathrel{\underline{<}:} dnf([\,l : T\,])$.

(S-RCD-DR) For each $A_{i_1}^1 \in dnf(S_1)$ and each $A_{i_2}^2 \in dnf(S_2)$ there exist $B_{j_1}^1 \in dnf(T_1)$ and $B_{j_2}^2 \in dnf(T_2)$ such that we have a derivations of $A_{i_1}^1 \mathrel{\underline{<}:} B_{j_1}^1$ and $A_{i_2}^2 \mathrel{\underline{<}:} B_{j_2}^2$. For each such pair we can therefore use SA-RCD to derive $A_{i_1}^1 \times A_{i_2}^2 \mathrel{\underline{<}:} B_{j_1}^1 \times B_{j_2}^2$ and then use SN-UNION to derive $dnf(S_1 \times S_2) \mathrel{\underline{<}:} dnf(T_1 \times T_2)$.

(S-SET) Immediate, by SA-SET.

(S-UNION-L) For each $A_i \in dnf(R)$ there is a $C_j \in dnf(T)$ such that $A_i \mathrel{\underline{<}:} C_j$ and for each $B_k \in dnf(S)$ there is a $C_l \in dnf(T)$ such that $B_k \mathrel{\underline{<}:} C_l$. From these $dnf(R \vee S) \mathrel{\underline{<}:} dnf(T)$ can be derived directly using SN-UNION.   □

3.4.10 Theorem: The subtype relation is decidable.   □

Proof: Immediate from Lemmas 3.4.9 and 3.4.2.   □

We do not yet have any results on the *complexity* of checking subtyping (or equivalence). (The proof strategy we have adopted here leads to an algorithm with running time exponential in the size of its inputs.)

The structured form of the macro rules can be used to derive several *inversion properties*, which will be useful later in reasoning about the typing relation.

3.4.11 Corollary: If $S <: \mathsf{set}(T_1)$, then $S = \mathsf{set}(S_1)$, with $S_1 <: T_1$.   □

3.4.12 Corollary: If $W <: U$, with

$$W = [\, l_1 : W_1 \,] \times \ldots \times [\, l_m : W_m \,] \times \ldots \times [\, l_n : W_n \,]$$
$$U = [\, l_1 : U_1 \,] \times \ldots \times [\, l_m : U_m \,],$$

then $W_k <: U_k$ for each $k \leq m$.   □

Proof: From the definition of disjunctive normal forms, we know that $dnf(W) = \bigvee([\, l_1 : W_{i1} \,] \times \ldots \times [\, l_m : W_{im} \,] \times \ldots \times [\, l_n : W_{in} \,] \mid W_{i1} \ldots W_{im} \ldots W_{in} \in dnf(W_1) \ldots dnf(W_m) \ldots dnf(W_n))$ and $dnf(U) = \bigvee([\, l_1 : U_{j1} \,] \times \ldots \times [\, l_m : U_{jm} \,] \mid U_{j1} \ldots U_{jm} \in dnf(U_1) \ldots dnf(U_m))$. By SN-UNION,

for each $A_i = [\, l_1 : W_{i1} \,] \times \ldots \times [\, l_m : W_{im} \,] \times \ldots \times [\, l_n : W_{in} \,] \in dnf(W)$
there is some $B_j = [\, l_1 : U_{j1} \,] \times \ldots \times [\, l_m : U_{jm} \,] \in dnf(U)$
with $A_i \underline{<:} B_j$.

This derivation must be an instance of SA-RCD, with $W_{ik} \underline{<:} U_{jk}$. In other words, for each $W_{ik} \in dnf(W_k)$ there is some $Ujk \in dnf(U_k)$ with $W_{ik} \underline{<:} U_{jk}$. By SN-UNION, $dnf(W_k) \underline{<:} dnf(U_k)$. The desired result, $W_k <: U_k$ now follows by Lemma 3.4.9.   □

3.4.13 Corollary: If S is a simple type and $S <: T_1 \vee T_2$, then either $S <: T_1$ or else $S <: T_2$.   □

3.5   Terms

The sets of programs, functions, and patterns are described by the following grammar:

$e ::=$	b	base value
	x	variable
	$[\, l_1 = e_1, \ldots, l_n = e_n \,]$	record construction
	$\mathsf{case}\ e\ \mathsf{of}\ f$	pattern matching
	$\{\, e_1, \ldots, e_n \,\}$	set
	$e_1\ \mathsf{union}\ e_2$	union of sets
	$\mathsf{collect}\ e_1\ \mathsf{where}\ p \leftarrow e_2$	set comprehension
$p ::=$	$x : T$	variable pattern (typecase)
	$[\, l_1 = p_1, \ldots, l_n = p_n \,]$	record pattern
	$p_1 \,\#\, p_2$	pattern concatenation
	$x\ \mathsf{as}\ f$	function nested in pattern
$f ::=$	$p \Rightarrow e$	base function
	$f_1 \mid f_2$	compound function

3.6   Typing

The typing rules are quite standard.

Expressions $(\Gamma \vdash e \in T)$

$$\Gamma \vdash b \in B \qquad \text{(T-BASE)}$$

$$\Gamma \vdash x \in \Gamma(x) \qquad \text{(T-VAR)}$$

$$\frac{\Gamma \vdash e_i \in T_i \qquad \text{all the } l_i \text{ are distinct}}{\Gamma \vdash [\, l_1 = e_1, \ldots, l_n = e_n \,] \in [\, l_1 : T_1 \,] \times \cdots \times [\, l_n : T_n \,]} \qquad \text{(T-RCD)}$$

$$\frac{\Gamma \vdash f \in S{\to}T \qquad \Gamma \vdash e \in R \qquad R <: S}{\Gamma \vdash \text{case } e \text{ of } f \in T} \qquad \text{(T-CASE)}$$

$$\frac{\Gamma \vdash e_i \in T_i \quad \text{for each } i \qquad n \geq 1}{\Gamma \vdash \{\, e_1, \ldots, e_n \,\} \in \text{set}(T_1 \vee \cdots \vee T_n)} \qquad \text{(T-SET)}$$

$$\frac{\Gamma \vdash e_1 \in \text{set}(T_1) \qquad \Gamma \vdash e_2 \in \text{set}(T_2)}{\Gamma \vdash e_1 \text{ union } e_2 \in \text{set}(T_1 \vee T_2)} \qquad \text{(T-UNION)}$$

$$\frac{\Gamma \vdash e_2 \in \text{set}(S) \qquad \Gamma \vdash p \in U \Rightarrow \Gamma' \qquad S <: U}{\Gamma, \Gamma' \vdash e_1 \in \text{set}(T)} \qquad \text{(T-COLLECT)}$$
$$\frac{}{\Gamma \vdash \text{collect } e_1 \text{ where } p \leftarrow e_2 \in \text{set}(T)}$$

Functions $(\Gamma \vdash f \in S{\to}T)$

$$\frac{\Gamma \vdash p \in S \Rightarrow \Gamma' \qquad \Gamma, \Gamma' \vdash e \in T}{\Gamma \vdash p \Rightarrow e \in S{\to}T} \qquad \text{(TF-PAT)}$$

$$\frac{\Gamma \vdash f_1 \in S_1{\to}T_1 \qquad \Gamma \vdash f_2 \in S_2{\to}T_2}{\Gamma \vdash f_1 \mid f_2 \in S_1 \vee S_2 {\to} T_1 \vee T_2} \qquad \text{(TF-ALT)}$$

Patterns $(\Gamma \vdash p \in T \Rightarrow \Gamma')$

$$\frac{T \in K}{\Gamma \vdash x : T \in T \Rightarrow x : T} \qquad \text{(TP-VAR)}$$

$$\frac{\Gamma \vdash p_i \in T_i \Rightarrow \Gamma'_i \qquad \text{all the } l_i \text{ are distinct} \qquad \text{the } \Gamma'_i \text{ all have disjoint domains}}{\Gamma \vdash [\, l_1 = p_1, \ldots, l_n = p_n \,] \in [\, l_1 : T_1 \,] \times \cdots \times [\, l_n : T_n \,] \Rightarrow \Gamma'_1, \ldots, \Gamma'_n}$$
$$\text{(TP-RCD)}$$

$$\frac{\begin{array}{c} \Gamma \vdash p_1 \in [\,k_1 : S_1, \ldots, k_m : S_m\,] \Rightarrow \Gamma_1' \quad \Gamma \vdash p_2 \in [\,l_1 : T_1, \ldots, l_n : T_n\,] \Rightarrow \Gamma_2' \\ \{k_1, \ldots, k_m\} \cap \{l_1, \ldots, l_n\} = \emptyset \quad \Gamma_1' \text{ and } \Gamma_2' \text{ have disjoint domains} \end{array}}{\Gamma \vdash p_1 \,\#\, p_2 \in [\,k_1 : S_1, \ldots, k_m : S_m, l_1 : T_1, \ldots, l_n : T_n\,] \Rightarrow \Gamma_1', \Gamma_2'}$$

(TP-CONCAT)

$$\frac{\Gamma \vdash f \in S {\rightarrow} T}{\Gamma \vdash x \text{ as } f \in S \Rightarrow x : T}$$

(TP-AS)

3.7   Properties of Typing

3.7.1 Proposition: The typing relation is decidable.   □

Proof: Immediate from the decidability of subtyping and the syntax-directedness of the typing rules.   □

3.7.2 Definition: A substitution σ is a finite function from variables to terms. We say that a substitution σ *satisfies* a context Σ, written $\sigma \models \Sigma$, if they have the same domain and, for each x in their common domain, we have $\vdash \sigma(x) \in S_x$ for some S_x with $S_x <: \Sigma(x)$.   □

3.7.3 Definition: We say that a typing context Γ *refines* another context Γ', written $\Gamma <: \Gamma'$, if their domains are the same and, for each $x \in dom(\Gamma)$, we have $\Gamma(x) <: \Gamma'(x)$.   □

3.7.4 Fact [Narrowing]: If $\Gamma \vdash e \in T$ and $\Gamma <: \Gamma'$, then $\Gamma' \vdash e \in T$.   □

3.7.5 Lemma [Substitution preserves typing]:

1. If $\Sigma \models \sigma$ and $\Sigma, \Delta \vdash e \in Q$ then $\Delta \vdash \sigma(e) \in P$, for some $P <: Q$.
2. If $\Sigma \models \sigma$ and $\Sigma, \Delta \vdash f \in S \rightarrow Q$ then $\Delta \vdash \sigma(f) \in S \rightarrow P$, for some $P <: Q$.
3. If $\Sigma \models \sigma$ and $\Sigma, \Delta \vdash p \in U \Rightarrow \Delta'$ then $\Delta \vdash \sigma(p) \in U \Rightarrow \Delta''$, for some $\Delta'' <: \Delta$.   □

Proof: By simultaneous induction on derivations. The arguments are all straightforward, using previously established facts. (For the second property, note that substitution into a pattern only affects functions that may be embedded in the pattern, since all other variables mentioned in the pattern are binding occurrences. Moreover, by our conventions about names of bound variables, we must assume that the variables bound in an expression, function, or pattern are distinct from those defined by σ.)   □

3.8   Evaluation

The operational semantics of our language is again quite standard: we define a relation $e \Downarrow v$, read "(closed) expression e evaluates to result v," by a collection of syntax-directed rules embodying a simple abstract machine.

3.8.1 Definition: We will use the metavariables v and w to range over *values* – closed expressions not involving case, union, or collect.

$$v ::= \mathsf{b}$$
$$[\, l_1 = v_1, \ldots, l_n = v_n \,]$$
$$\{\, v_1, \ldots, v_n \,\}$$

We write $\bar{v}$ as shorthand for a set of values $v_1, \ldots, v_n$. ☐

3.8.2 Definition: A *substitution* σ is a finite function from variables to values. When σ_1 and σ_2 have disjoint domains, we write $\sigma_1 + \sigma_2$ for their combination. ☐

Reduction ($e \Downarrow v$, for closed terms e)

$$\mathsf{b} \Downarrow \mathsf{b} \qquad\qquad\qquad \text{(E-BASE)}$$

$$\frac{e_i \Downarrow v_i \quad \text{for each } i}{[\, l_1 = e_1, \ldots, l_n = e_n \,] \Downarrow [\, l_1 = v_1, \ldots, l_n = v_n \,]} \qquad \text{(E-RCD)}$$

$$\frac{e \Downarrow v \qquad match(v, f) \Rightarrow v'}{\mathsf{case}\ f\ \mathsf{of}\ e \Downarrow v'} \qquad \text{(E-CASE)}$$

$$\frac{e_i \Downarrow v_i \quad \text{for each } i}{\{\, e_1, \ldots, e_n \,\} \Downarrow \{\, v_1, \ldots, v_n \,\}} \qquad \text{(E-SET)}$$

$$\frac{e_1 \Downarrow \{\, \bar{v_1} \,\} \qquad e_2 \Downarrow \{\, \bar{v_2} \,\}}{e_1\ \mathsf{union}\ e_2 \Downarrow \{\, \bar{v_1} \cup \bar{v_2} \,\}} \qquad \text{(E-UNION)}$$

$$\frac{\begin{array}{c} e_2 \Downarrow \{\, v_1, \ldots, v_n \,\} \\ \text{for each } i, \quad match(v_i, p) \Rightarrow \sigma_i \text{ and } \sigma_i(e_1) \Downarrow \{\, \bar{w_i} \,\} \end{array}}{\mathsf{collect}\ e_1\ \mathsf{where}\ p \leftarrow e_2 \Downarrow \{\, \bar{w_1} \cup \cdots \cup \bar{w_n} \,\}} \qquad \text{(E-COLLECT)}$$

Function matching ($match(v, f) \Rightarrow v'$)

$$\frac{match(v, p) \Rightarrow \sigma \qquad \sigma(e) \Downarrow v'}{match(v, p \Rightarrow e) \Rightarrow v'} \qquad \text{(EF-PAT)}$$

$$\frac{match(v, f_1) \Rightarrow v'}{match(v, f_1 \mid f_2) \Rightarrow v'} \qquad \text{(EF-ALT1)}$$

$$\frac{\neg(match(v, f_1)) \qquad match(v, f_2) \Rightarrow v'}{match(v, f_1 \mid f_2) \Rightarrow v'} \qquad \text{(EF-ALT2)}$$

Matching ($match(v, p) \Rightarrow \Gamma$)

$$\frac{\vdash v \in S \qquad S <: T}{match(v, \, x : T) \Rightarrow x = v} \tag{EP-Var}$$

$$\frac{match(v_i, \, p_i) \Rightarrow \sigma_i \qquad \text{the } \sigma_i \text{ have disjoint domains}}{match([\, l_1 = v_1, \, \ldots, \, l_m = v_m, \, \ldots, \, l_n = v_n \,], \, [\, l_1 = p_1, \, \ldots, \, l_m = p_m \,])}{\Rightarrow \sigma_1 + \ldots + \sigma_m} \tag{EP-Rcd}$$

$$\frac{match(v, \, p_1) \Rightarrow \sigma_1 \qquad match(v, \, p_2) \Rightarrow \sigma_2 \qquad \sigma_1 \text{ and } \sigma_2 \text{ have disjoint domains}}{match(v, \, p_1 \, \# \, p_2) \Rightarrow \sigma_1 + \sigma_2} \tag{EP-Concat}$$

$$\frac{match(v, \, f) \Rightarrow v'}{match(v, \, x \text{ as } f) \Rightarrow x = v'} \tag{EP-As}$$

3.9 Properties of Evaluation

3.9.1 Fact: If v is a value and $\vdash v \in V$, then V is a simple type. $\qquad\square$

3.9.2 Theorem [Subject reduction]:

1. If $e \Downarrow v$
   $\vdash e \in Q$,
   then $\vdash v \in V$
   $V <: Q$.
2. If $match(v, \, f) \Rightarrow v'$
   $\vdash f \in U {\rightarrow} V$
   $\vdash v \in W$
   $W <: U$,
   then $\vdash v' \in X$
   $X <: V$.
3. If $match(v, \, p) \Rightarrow \sigma$
   $\vdash v \in W$
   $\vdash p \in U \Rightarrow \Sigma$
   $W <: U$,
   then $\Sigma \models \sigma$. $\qquad\square$

Proof: By simultaneous induction on evaluation derivations.

1. Straightforward, using part (2) of the induction hypothesis for the E-Case case and part (3) for E-Collect.
2. Consider the final rule in the given derivation.
   Case EF-Pat: $f = p \Rightarrow e$
   $match(v, \, p) \Rightarrow \sigma$
   $\sigma(e) \Downarrow v'$

   From $\vdash f \in U {\rightarrow} V$, we know $\vdash p \in U \Rightarrow \Sigma$ and $\Sigma \vdash e \in V$. By part (3) of the induction hypothesis, $\Sigma \models \sigma$. By Lemma 3.7.5, $\vdash \sigma(e) \in V$. Now, by the induction hypothesis, $\vdash v' \in X$ and $X <: V$, as required.

Case EF-ALT1: $f = f_1 \mid f_2$
$match(v, f_1) \Rightarrow v'$

From rule TF-ALT, we see that $\vdash f_1 \in U_1{\rightarrow}V_1$ and $\vdash f_2 \in U_2{\rightarrow}V_2$, with $U = U_1 \vee U_2$ and $V = V_1 \vee V_2$. The induction hypothesis yields $\vdash v' \in X$ with $X <: V_1$, from which the result follows immediately by S-UNION.

Case EF-ALT2: $f = f_1 \mid f_2$
$\neg(match(v, f_1))$
$match(v, f_2) \Rightarrow v'$

Similar.

3. Consider the final rule in the given derivation.

Case EP-VAR: $p = (x : T)$
$\vdash v \in S$
$S <: T$
$\sigma = (x = v)$
$\Sigma = (x : T)$

Immediate.

Case EP-RCD: $v = [l_1 = v_1, \ldots, l_m = v_m, \ldots, l_n = v_n]$
$p = [l_1 = p_1, \ldots, l_m = p_m]$
$match(v_i, p_i) \Rightarrow \sigma_i$
$\sigma = \sigma_1 + \ldots + \sigma + m$

From T-RCD, we have $W = [l_1 : W_1] \times \ldots \times [l_n : W_n]$ and $\vdash v_i \in W_i$ for each i. Similarly, by TP-RCD, we have $U = [l_1 : U_1] \times \ldots \times [l_m : W_m]$ with $\vdash p_i \in U_i \Rightarrow \Sigma_i$. Finally, by Corollary 3.4.12, we see that $W_i <: U_i$. Now, by the induction hypothesis, $\Sigma_i \models \sigma_i$ for each i. But this means that $\Sigma \models \sigma$, as required.

Case EP-CONCAT: $p = p_1 \mathbin{\#} p_2$
$match(v, p_1) \Rightarrow \sigma_1$ $match(v, p_2) \Rightarrow \sigma_2$
σ_1 and σ_2 have disjoint domains
$\sigma = \sigma_1 + \sigma + 2$

By TP-CONCAT, we have $U = [k_1 : S_1, \ldots, k_m : S_m, l_1 : T_1, \ldots, l_n : T_n]$ with $\vdash p_1 \in [k_1 : S_1, \ldots, k_m : S_m] \Rightarrow \Sigma_1$ and $\vdash p_2 \in [l_1 : T_1, \ldots, l_n : T_n] \Rightarrow \Sigma_2$. Since $U <: [k_1 : S_1, \ldots, k_m : S_m]$ and $U <: [l_1 : T_1, \ldots, l_n : T_n]$ by the subtyping laws, transitivity of subtyping gives us $W <: [k_1 : S_1, \ldots, k_m : S_m]$ and $W <: [l_1 : T_1, \ldots, l_n : T_n]$. Now, by the induction hypothesis, $\Sigma_1 \models \sigma_1$ and $\Sigma_2 \models \sigma_2$. But this means that $\Sigma \models \sigma$, as required.

Case EP-AS: $p = x \Rightarrow f$
$match(v, f) \Rightarrow v'$
$\sigma = (x = v')$

By TP-AS, $\vdash f \in U{\rightarrow}V$ and $\Sigma = (x : V)$. By part (2) of the induction hypothesis, $\vdash v' \in X$ for some $X <: V$. So $(x = v') \models (x : V)$ by the definition of satisfaction. $\square$

3.9.3 Theorem [Safety]:

1. If $\vdash e \in T$, then $e \Downarrow v$ for some v. (That is, the evaluation of a closed, well-typed expression cannot lead to a match-failure or otherwise "get stuck.")
2. If $\vdash f \in S \rightarrow T$ and $\vdash v \in R <: S$, then $match(v, f) \Rightarrow v'$ with $\vdash v' \in T' <: T$.
3. If $\vdash p \in U \Rightarrow \Gamma'$ and $\vdash v \in S <: U$, then $match(v, p) \Rightarrow \sigma$ with $\Gamma' \models \sigma$. $\square$

Proof: Straightforward induction on derivations. $\square$

4 Conclusions

We have described a type system that may be of use in checking programs or queries that apply to semistructured data. Unlike other approaches to the problem, it is a "relaxed" version of a conventional system that can handle the kinds of irregular types that occur in semistructurd data.

Although we have established the basic properties of the type system, a good deal of work remains to be done. First, there are some extensions that we do not see as problematic. These include:

– Both strict and relaxed set-union operations. (In the former case the two types are constrained to be equivalent.) Similarly, one can imagine strict and relaxed case expressions.
– Equality. Both "absolute" equality and "equality at type T" fit with this scheme.
– A $\perp$ ("bottom") type – the null-ary case of union types. An immediate application is in the typing rule T-SET for set formation, where we can remove the side condition $n \geq 1$ to allow formation of the empty set: $\{\emptyset\} \in \perp$.
– Additional base types such as booleans and operations such as set filtering.
– A $\top$ ("top") type. Such a type would be completely dynamic and would be analyzed by typecase expressions. One could also add type inspection primitives along the lines described for Amber [Carrk]
– An "otherwise" or "fall-through" branch in case expressions.

A number of more significant problems also remain to be addressed.

– **Complexity**. The obvious method of checking whether two types are equivalent or whether one is a subtype of the other involves first reducing both to disjunctive normal form. As we have observed, this process may be exponential in the size of the two type expressions. We conjecture that equivalence (and subtyping) can be checked faster, but we have not been able to show this.

Even if these problems turn out to be intractable in general, it does not necessarily mean that this approach to typing semistructured data is pointless. Type inference in ML, for example, is known to be exponential [KTU94], yet the forms of ML programs that are the cause of this complexity never occur in practice. Here, it may be the case that types that types that only have "small" differences will not give rise to expensive transformations.

- **Recursive types.** The proof of the decidability of subtyping (3.4.10) works by induction on the derivation tree of a type, which is closely related to the structure of the type. We do not know whether the same result holds in the presence of recursive types.
- **Relationship with other typing schemes.** There may be some relationship between the typing scheme proposed here and those mentioned earlier [NAM97,Ali99] that work by inferring structure from semi-structured data. Simulation, for example, gives rise to something like a subtyping relationship [BDFS97]; but it is not clear what would give rise to union types.
- **Applications.** Finally, we would like to think that a system like this could be of practical benefit. We mentioned that there is a group of biological data formats that are all derived from a common basic format. We should also mention that the pattern matching constructs introduced in section 2.2, independently of any typing issues, might be used to augment other query languages such as XML-QL [DFF+] that exploit pattern matching.

Acknowledgements

The idea of using untagged unions to type semistructured data started when Peter Buneman was on a visiting research fellowship provided by the Japanese Society for the Promotion of Science. He is grateful to Atsushi Ohori for stimulating discussions. Benjamin Pierce is supported by the National Science Foundation under CAREER grant CCR-9701826.

An implementation project and meticulous reading by Davor Obradovic helped us correct several flaws in an earlier version of this paper. Follow-on work with Haruo Hosoya, Philip Wadler, and Jérôme Vouillon on the XDuce language design has deepened our appreciation of numerous issues. We are also grateful to Luca Cardelli, who caught a serious bug in a late version of the paper.

References

AH87.   Serge Abiteboul and Richard Hull. IFO: A formal semantic database model. *ACM Transactions on Database Systems*, 12(4):525–565, December 1987.

Ali99.   Alin Deutsch and Mary Fernandez and Dan Suciu. Storing semistructured data with STORED. In *Proceedings of ACM SIGMOD International Conference on Management of Data*, June 1999.

AQM+96. S. Abiteboul, D. Quass, J. McHugh, J. Widom, and J. Wiener. The lorel query language for semistructured data. *Journal on Digital Libraries*, 1(1), 1996.

BDCd95.   Franco Barbanera, Mariangiola Dezani-Ciancaglini, and Ugo de'Liguoro. Intersection and union types: Syntax and semantics. *Information and Computation*, 119(2):202–230, June 1995.

BDFS97.   P. Buneman, S. Davidson, M. Fernandez, and D. Suciu. Adding structure to unstructured data. In *Proc. ICDT*, 1997.

BDHS96.   P. Buneman, S. Davidson, G. Hillebrand, and D. Suciu. A query language and optimization techniques for unstructured data. In *ACM-SIGMOD*, pages 505–516, 1996.

BLS⁺94.   P. Buneman, L. Libkin, D. Suciu, V. Tannen, and L. Wong. Comprehension syntax. *SIGMOD Record*, 23(1):87–96, March 1994.

BNTW95. Peter Buneman, Shamim Naqvi, Val Tannen, and Limsoon Wong. Principles of programming with complex objects and collection types. *Theoretical Computer Science*, 149(1):3–48, September 1995.

Carrk.   L. Cardelli. Amber. In B. Robinet G. Cousineau, P.L. Curien, editor, *Combinators and Functional programming languages*, page 1986. Springer-Verlag, New-York.

CM94.   M. Consens and T. Milo. Optimizing queries on files. In *Proc. ACM Sigmod, Minneapolis*, 1994.

Dam94.   Flemming M. Damm. Subtyping with union types, intersection types and recursive types. In Masami Hagiya and John C. Mitchell, editors, *Theoretical Aspects of Computer Software*, volume 789 of *Lecture Notes in Computer Science*, pages 687–706. Springer-Verlag, April 1994.

DCdP96. M. Dezani-Ciancaglini, U. de'Liguoro, and A. Piperno. Filter models for conjunctive-disjunctive λ-calculi. *Theoretical Computer Science*, 170(1-2):83–128, December 1996.

DFF⁺.   A. Deutsch, M. Fernandez, D. Florescu, A. Levy, and D. Suciu. Xml-ql: A query language for xml. `http://www.w3.org/TR/NOTE-xml-ql`.

Hay91.   Susumu Hayashi. Singleton, union and intersection types for program extraction. In T. Ito and A. R. Meyer, editors, *Theoretical Aspects of Computer Software (Sendai, Japan)*, number 526 in Lecture Notes in Computer Science, pages 701–730. Springer-Verlag, September 1991. Full version in *Information and Computation*, 109(1/2):174-210, 1994.

KTU94.   A. J. Kfoury, J. Tiuryn, and P. Urzyczyn. An analysis of ML typability. *Journal of the ACM*, 41(2):368–398, March 1994.

NAM97.   S. Nestorov, S. Abiteboul, and R. Motwani. Inferring structure in semistructured data. In *Proceedings of the Workshop on Management of Semi-structured Data*, 1997. Available from `http://www.research.att.com/~suciu/workshop-papers.html`.

Pie91.   Benjamin C. Pierce. Programming with intersection types, union types, and polymorphism. Technical Report CMU-CS-91-106, Carnegie Mellon University, February 1991.

Query Optimization for Semistructured Data Using Path Constraints in a Deterministic Data Model

Peter Buneman[1]*, Wenfei Fan[2]**, and Scott Weinstein[1]***

[1] University of Pennsylvania, Philadelphia, PA 19104, U.S.A.
{peter, weinstein}@central.cis.upenn.edu
[2] Temple University, Philadelphia, PA 19122, U.S.A.
fan@joda.cis.temple.edu

Abstract. Path constraints have been studied for semistructured data modeled as a rooted edge-labeled directed graph [4, 11–13]. In this model, the implication problems associated with many natural path constraints are undecidable [11, 13]. A variant of the graph model, called *the deterministic data model*, was recently proposed in [10]. In this model, data is represented as a graph with deterministic edge relations, i.e., the edges emanating from any node in the graph have distinct labels. This model is more appropriate for representing, e.g., ACeDB [27] databases and Web sites. This paper investigates path constraints for the deterministic data model. It demonstrates the application of path constraints to, among others, query optimization. Three classes of path constraints are considered: the language P_c introduced in [11], an extension of P_c, denoted by P_c^w, by including wildcards in path expressions, and a generalization of P_c^w, denoted by P_c^*, by representing paths as regular expressions. The implication problems for these constraint languages are studied in the context of the deterministic data model. It is shown that in contrast to the undecidability result of [11], the implication and finite implication problems for P_c are decidable in cubic-time and are finitely axiomatizable. Moreover, the implication problems are decidable for P_c^w. However, the implication problems for P_c^* are undecidable.

1 Introduction

Semistructured data is usually modeled as an edge-labeled rooted directed graph [1, 8]. Let us refer to this graph model as the *semistructured data model (SM)*. For data found in many applications, the graph is *deterministic*, i.e., the edges emanating from each node in the graph have distinct labels. For example, when modeling Web pages as a graph, a node stands for an HTML document and an edge represents a link with an HTML label from one document (source) to another (target). It is reasonable to assume that the HTML label uniquely identifies the target document. Even if this is not literally the case, one can achieve this

---

* Partly supported by NSF Grant CCR92-16122.
** Supported in part by Temple University. Contact author.
*** Supported by NSF Grant CCR-9820899.

by including the URL (Universal Resource Locator) of the target document in the edge label. This yields a deterministic graph. As another example, consider ACeDB [27], which is a database management system popular with biologists. A graph representing an ACeDB database is also deterministic. In general, any database with "exportable" data identities can be modeled as a deterministic graph by including the identities in the edge labels. Here by exportable identities we mean directly observable identities such as keys. Some relational and object-oriented database management systems support exportable identities. In the OEM model (see, e.g., [3]), there are also exportable object identities. To capture this, we consider a variant of SM, referred to as *the deterministic data model* (DM). In DM, data is represented as a deterministic, rooted, edge-labeled, directed graph. An important feature of DM is that in this model, each component of a database can be uniquely identified by a path.

A number of query languages (e.g., [3, 9, 24]) have been developed for semistructured data. The study of semistructured data has also generated the design of query languages (e.g., [17]) for XML (eXtensible Markup Language [7]) data. In these languages, queries are described in terms of navigation paths. To optimize path queries, it often appears necessary to use structural information about the data described by path constraints. Path constraints are capable of expressing natural integrity constraints that are a fundamental part of the semantics of the data, such as inclusion dependencies and inverse relationships. In traditional structured databases such as object-oriented databases, this semantic information is described in schemas. Unlike structured databases, semistructured data does not have a schema, and path constraints are used to convey the semantics of the data. The approach to querying semistructured data with path constraints was proposed in [4] and later studied in [11–13]. Several proposals (e.g., [6, 19, 21, 22]) for adding structure or type systems to XML data also advocate the need for integrity constraints that can be expressed as path constraints.

To use path constraints in query optimization, it is important to be able to reason about them. That is, we need to settle the question of constraint implication: given that certain constraints are known to hold, does it follow that some other constraint is necessarily satisfied? In the database context, only finite instances (graphs) are considered, and implication is referred to as *finite implication*. In the traditional logic framework, both infinite and finite instances (graphs) are permitted, and constraint implication is called *(unrestricted) implication*. For the model SM, it has been shown that the implication and finite implication problems associated with many natural constraints are undecidable. For example, these problems are undecidable for the simple constraint language P_c introduced in [11–13]. In addition, we have already studied the connection between object-oriented databases and semistructured databases in SM with P_c constraints [12]. The results of [12] show that the connection is not simple.

In this paper, we investigate path constraints for DM. We demonstrate applications of path constraints to semantic specification and query optimization, and study the implication problems associated with path constraints. We show that in contrast to the undecidability result of [11, 13], the implication and finite implication problems for P_c are decidable in cubic-time and are finitely axiomatizable in the context of DM. That is, there is a finite set of inference rules that is sound and complete for implication and finite implication of P_c constraints, and in addition, there is an algorithm for testing P_c constraint implication in time $O(n^3)$, where n is the length of constraints. This demonstrates that the determinism condition of DM simplifies the analysis of path constraint implication. We also introduce and investigate two generalizations of P_c. One generalization, denoted by P_c^w, is defined by including wildcards in path expressions. The other, denoted by P_c^*, represents paths by regular expressions. We show that in the context of DM, the implication and finite implication problems for P_c^w are also decidable. However, these problems are undecidable for P_c^* in the context of DM. This undecidability result shows that the determinism condition of DM does not reduce the analysis of path constraint implication to a trivial problem.

The rest of the paper is organized as follows. Section 2 uses an example to illustrate how path constraints can be used in query optimization. Section 3 reviews the definition of P_c constraints proposed in [11], and introduces two extensions of P_c, namely, P_c^w and P_c^*. Section 4 studies the implication and finite implication problems for P_c, P_c^w and P_c^* for the deterministic data model. Finally, Section 5 identifies open problems and directions for further work.

2 An example

To demonstrate applications of path constraints, let us consider Fig. 1, which collects information on employees and departments. It is an example of semistructured data represented in the deterministic data model DM. In Fig. 1, there are two edges emanating from root r, labeled emp and dept and connected to nodes Emp and Dept, respectively. Edges emanating from Emp are labeled employee ID's and connected to nodes representing employees. An employee node may have three edges emanating from it: an edge labeled manager and connected to his/her manager, an edge labeled supervising that connects to a node from which there are outgoing edges to employees under his/her supervision, and an edge labeled name. Similarly, there are vertices representing departments that may have edges connected to employees. Observe that Fig. 1 is deterministic.

Path constraints. Typical path constraints on Fig. 1 include:

$$\forall x\,(emp \cdot {\_} \cdot manager(r, x) \to emp \cdot {\_}\,(r, x)) \tag{ϕ_1}$$
$$\forall x\,(emp \cdot {\_} \cdot supervising \cdot {\_}\,(r, x) \to emp \cdot {\_}\,(r, x)) \tag{ϕ_2}$$
$$\forall x\,(emp \cdot {\_}\,(r, x) \to \forall y\,(manager(x, y) \to supervising \cdot {\_}\,(y, x))) \tag{ϕ_3}$$

Here r denotes the root of the graph, variables x and y range over vertices, and "$\_$" is a "wildcard" symbol, which matches any edge label. A path in the graph is a sequence of edge labels, including wildcards. Path constraints describe inclusion relationships. For example, ϕ_1 states that if a node is reached from the root r by following emp $\cdot\_\cdot$ manager, then it is also reachable from r by following emp $\cdot\_$. It asserts that the manager of any employee is also an employee that occurs in the database. The constraints given above are in the language P_c^w.

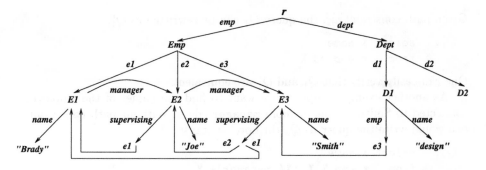

Fig. 1. An example semistructured database in DM

We generalize P_c^w by representing paths as regular expressions. This generalization is denoted by P_c^*. For example, the following are constraints of P_c^*:

$$\forall x \, (emp \cdot \_ \, (r, x) \rightarrow \forall y \, (manager \cdot manager^*(x, y)$$
$$\rightarrow supervising \cdot \_ \, (y, x))) \qquad (\psi_1)$$
$$\forall x \, (emp \cdot \_ \, (r, x) \rightarrow \forall y \, (supervising \cdot \_ \, (x, y)$$
$$\rightarrow manager \cdot manager^*(y, x))) \qquad (\psi_2)$$

Here $*$ is the Kleene star. These constraints describe an inverse relationship between manager·manager* and supervising·_. For example, ψ_1 asserts that for any employee x and for any y, if y is reachable from x by following one or more manager edges, then x is reachable from y by following path supervising·_.

A subclass of P_c^*, P_c, has been investigated in [11–13] for the graph model SM for semistructured data. As opposed to P_c^* constraints, path constraints of P_c contain neither wildcards nor the Kleene star. In DM, P_c constraints express path equalities. For example, the following can be described by P_c constraints:

$$emp \cdot e1 \cdot manager \quad = \quad emp \cdot e2 \qquad (\varphi_1)$$
$$dept \cdot d1 \cdot emp \cdot e3 \quad = \quad emp \cdot e3 \qquad (\varphi_2)$$

Semantic specification with path constraints. The path constraints above describe certain typing information about the data. For example, abusing object-oriented database terms, ϕ_1 asserts that a manager of an employee has an "employee type", and in addition, is in the "extent" of "class" employee. By using ϕ_1, it can be shown that for any employee x and any y, if y is reachable from x by following zero or more manager edges, then y also has an "employee type" and is in the "extent" of employee. A preliminary type system was proposed in [10] for the deterministic data model, in which the types of paths are defined by means of path constraints. This is a step towards unifying the (programming language) notion of a type with the (database) notion of a schema.

Query optimization with path constraints. To illustrate how path constraints can be used in query optimization, consider again the database shown in Fig. 1. Suppose, for example, we want to find the name of the employee with ID $e3$ in department $d1$. One may write the query as Q_1 (in Lorel syntax [3]):

Q_1:   select X.name
       from   r.dept.d1.emp.e3 X

Given path constraint φ_2, the query Q_1 can be rewritten as Q_1':

Q_1':   `select X.name`
            `from   r.emp.e3 X`

One can easily verify that Q_1 and Q_1' are equivalent.

As another example, suppose we want to find the names of the employees connected to Smith by one or more `manager` edges. Without path constraints, one would write the query as Q_2 (in Lorel syntax):

Q_2:   `select X.name`
           `from   r.emp.% X, X(.manager)+ Y`
           `where  Y.name = "Smith"`

In Lorel, % denotes wildcard and (`.manager`)+ means one or more occurrences of `manager` edges. Given constraints ψ_1, ψ_2, ϕ_1 and ϕ_2, we can rewrite Q_2 as Q_2', which finds the names of the employees under the supervision of Smith:

Q_2':   `select X.name`
            `from   r.emp.% Y, Y.supervising.% X`
            `where  Y.name = "Smith"`

It can be verified that given those path constraints, Q_2 and Q_2' are equivalent. In addition, Q_2' is more efficient than Q_2 because it does not require the traversal of sequences of `manager` edges. It should be mentioned that to show Q_2 and Q_2' are equivalent, we need to verify that certain constraints necessarily hold given that ψ_1, ψ_2, ϕ_1 and ϕ_2 hold. That is, they are implied by ψ_1, ψ_2, ϕ_1 and ϕ_2. In particular, we need to show that ψ_3 below is implied by ψ_1, ψ_2, ϕ_1 and ϕ_2:

$$\forall x \, (emp \cdot \_ \cdot manager^*(r, x) \rightarrow emp \cdot \_ (r, x)) \qquad (\psi_3)$$

Related work. Path constraints have been studied in [4, 11–13] for the model SM. The constraints of [4] have either the form $p \subseteq q$ or $p = q$, where p and q are regular expressions representing paths. The decidability of the implication problems for this form of constraints was established in [4] for SM. Another path constraint language, P_c, was introduced in [11]. It was shown there that despite the simple syntax of P_c, its associated implication and finite implication problems are undecidable in the context of SM. Detailed proofs of these undecidability results can be found in [13]. However, these papers have considered neither the deterministic data model DM nor the path constraint languages P_c^w and P_c^*.

Recently, the application of integrity constraints to query optimization was also studied in [25]. Among other things, [25] developed an equational theory for query rewriting by using a certain form of constraints.

The connection between object-oriented (OO) databases and semistructured databases in SM with P_c constraints has been studied in [12]. OO databases are constrained by types, e.g., class types with single-valued and set-valued attributes, whereas databases in SM are in general free of these type constraints. These types cannot be expressed as path constraints and *vice versa*. As an example, it has been shown in [12] that there is a P_c constraint implication problem that is decidable in PTIME in the context of SM, but that becomes undecidable when an OO type system is added. On the other hand, there is a P_c constraint implication problem that is undecidable in the context of SM, but becomes decidable in PTIME when an OO type system is imposed.

There is a natural analogy between the work on path constraints and inclusion dependency theory developed for relational databases. Path constraints specify inclusions among certain sets of objects, and can be viewed as a generalization of inclusion dependencies. They are important in a variety of database contexts beyond relational databases, ranging from semistructured data to OO databases. It should be mentioned that the path constraints considered in this paper are not expressible in any class of dependencies studied for relational databases, including inclusion and tuple-generating dependencies [5].

The results established on path constraint implication in this paper may find applications to other fields. Indeed, if we view vertices in a graph as states and labeled edges as actions, then the deterministic graphs considered here are in fact Kripke models studied in deterministic propositional dynamic logic (DPDL. See, e.g., [20, 28]), which is a powerful language for reasoning about programs. These deterministic graphs may also be viewed as feature structures studied in feature logics [26]. It should be mentioned that DPDL and feature logics are modal logics, in which our path constraints are not expressible.

Description logics (see, e.g., [16]) reason about concept subsumption, which can express inclusion assertions similar to path constraints. There has been work on specifying constraints on semistructured data by means of description logics [15]. One of the most expressive description logics used in the database context is $\mathcal{ALCQI}_{reg}$ [16]. It is known that $\mathcal{ALCQI}_{reg}$ corresponds to propositional dynamic logic (PDL) with converse and graded modalities [16, 20]. We should remark here that our path constraints are not expressible in $\mathcal{ALCQI}_{reg}$.

3 Deterministic graphs and path constraints

In this section, we first give an abstraction of semistructured databases in DM, and then present three path constraint languages: P_c, P_c^w and P_c^*.

3.1 The deterministic data model

In the graph model SM, a database is represented as an edge-labeled rooted directed graph [1, 8]. An abstraction of databases in SM has been given in [11] as (finite) first-order logic structures of a relational signature

$$\sigma = (r, \ E),$$

where r is a constant denoting the root and E is a set of binary relation symbols denoting the edge labels.

In the deterministic data model DM, a database is represented as an edge-labeled rooted directed graph satisfying the *determinism condition*. That is, for any edge label K and node a in the graph, there is at most one edge labeled K going out of a. Along the same lines of the abstraction of databases in SM, we model a database in DM as a (finite) σ-structure satisfying the determinism condition. Such structures are called *deterministic structures*. A deterministic structure G is specified by $(|G|, r^G, E^G)$, where $|G|$ is the set of nodes in G, r^G is the root node, and E^G is the set of binary relations on $|G|$.

3.2   Path constraint language P_c

Next, we review the definition of P_c constraints introduced in [11]. To do this, we first present the notion of paths.

A path is a sequence of edge labels. Formally, paths are defined by the syntax:

$$\rho ::= \epsilon \mid K \mid K \cdot \rho$$

Here ϵ is the empty path, $K \in E$, and $\cdot$ denotes path concatenation. For example, $emp \cdot e1 \cdot manager$ and $dept \cdot d1 \cdot emp \cdot e3$ are paths given in Sect. 2.

A path can be expressed as a first-order logic formula $\rho(x, y)$ with two free variables x and y, which denote the tail and head nodes of the path, respectively. For example, the paths given above can be described by:

$$\exists z \, (emp(x, z) \wedge \exists w \, (e1(z, w) \wedge manager(w, y)))$$
$$\exists z \, (dept(x, z) \wedge \exists w \, (d1(z, w) \wedge \exists u \, (emp(w, u) \wedge e3(u, y))))$$

We write $\rho(x, y)$ as ρ when the parameters x and y are clear from the context.

By treating paths as logic formulas, we are able to borrow the standard notion of models from first-order logic [18]. Let G be a deterministic structure, $\rho(x, y)$ be a path formula and a, b be nodes in $|G|$. We use $G \models \rho(a, b)$ to denote that $\rho(a, b)$ holds in G, i.e., there is a path ρ from a to b in G.

A path ρ is said to be a *prefix* of ϱ if there exists γ, such that $\varrho = \rho \cdot \gamma$.

The *length* of path ρ, $|\rho|$, is defined as follows: $|\rho| = 0$ if $\rho = \epsilon$; $|\rho| = 1 + |\varrho|$ if ρ can be written as $K \cdot \varrho$, where $K \in E$. For example, $|emp \cdot e1 \cdot manager| = 3$.

By a straightforward induction on the lengths of paths, it can be verified that in DM, any component of a database can be uniquely identified by a path.

Lemma 3.1: Let G be a deterministic structure. Then for any path ρ and node $a \in |G|$, there is at most one node b such that $G \models \rho(a, b)$.   ∎

The path constraint language P_c introduced in [11] is defined in terms of path formulas. A *path constraint* φ of P_c is an expression of either

- the *forward* form: $\forall x \, (\alpha(r, x) \rightarrow \forall y \, (\beta(x, y) \rightarrow \gamma(x, y)))$, or
- the *backward* form: $\forall x \, (\alpha(r, x) \rightarrow \forall y \, (\beta(x, y) \rightarrow \gamma(y, x)))$.

Here α, β, γ are path formulas. Path α is called the *prefix* of φ, denoted by $pf(\varphi)$. Paths β and γ are denoted by $lt(\varphi)$ and $rt(\varphi)$, respectively.

For example, φ_1 and φ_2 given in Sect. 2 can be described by P_c constraints.

A proper subclass of P_c was introduced and studied in [4]. A *word constraint* has the form $\forall x \, (\beta(r, x) \rightarrow \gamma(r, x))$, where β and γ are path formulas. In other words, a word constraint is a forward P_c constraint with its prefix being the empty path. It has been shown in [11] that many P_c constraints cannot be expressed as word constraints or even by the more general constraints of [4].

Next, we describe implication and finite implication of P_c constraints in the context of the deterministic data model. We assume the standard notion of models from first-order logic [18]. Let $\Sigma \cup \{\varphi\}$ be a finite subset of P_c. We use $\Sigma \models \varphi$ to denote that Σ *implies* φ in the context of DM. That is, for any deterministic structure G, if $G \models \Sigma$, then $G \models \varphi$. Similarly, we use $\Sigma \models_f \varphi$ to denote that Σ *finitely implies* φ. That is, for any finite deterministic structure G, if $G \models \Sigma$, then $G \models \varphi$.

In the context of DM, the *implication problem for P_c* is the problem to determine, given any finite subset $\Sigma \cup \{\varphi\}$ of P_c, whether $\Sigma \models \varphi$. Similarly, the *finite implication problem for P_c* is the problem of determining whether $\Sigma \models_f \varphi$.

In the context of SM, the structures considered in the implication problems are not necessarily deterministic. For SM, the following was shown in [11, 13].

Theorem 3.2 [11, 13]: In the context of SM, the implication problem for P_c is r.e. complete, and the finite implication problem for P_c is co-r.e. complete. ∎

We shall show that this undecidability no longer holds in the context of DM.

3.3 Path constraint language P_c^w

Let us generalize path expressions by including the union operator $+$ as follows:

$$w ::= \epsilon \mid K \mid w \cdot w \mid w + w$$

That is, we define path expressions to be regular expressions which do not contain the Kleene closure. Let us refer to such expressions as *union regular expressions*.

Let p be a union regular expression and ρ be a path. We use $\rho \in p$ to denote that ρ is in the regular language defined by p.

We also treat a union regular expression p as a logic formula $p(x, y)$, where x and y are free variables. We say that a deterministic structure G *satisfies* $p(x, y)$, denoted by $G \models p(x, y)$, if there is $\rho \in p$ and $a, b \in |G|$ such that $G \models \rho(a, b)$.

The following should be noted about union regular expressions.

- The regular language defined by a union regular expression is finite.
- Recall that the wildcard symbol "$\_$" matches any edge label. When E, the set of relation symbols in signature σ, is finite, we can express "$\_$" as a union regular expression. More specifically, let E be enumerated as K_1, K_2, ..., K_n. Then "$\_$" can be defined as union regular expression: $K_1 + K_2 + \dots + K_n$.

For example, $emp \cdot \_ \cdot manager$ and $emp \cdot \_ \cdot supervising \cdot \_$ can be represented as union regular expressions.

We define P_c^w using the same syntax of P_c. But in P_c^w we use union regular expressions instead of simple paths to represent path expressions.

For example, path constraints ϕ_1, ϕ_2 and ϕ_3 given in Sect. 2 are P_c^w constraints, but they are not in P_c.

A deterministic structure G *satisfies* a constraint ϕ of P_c^w, denoted by $G \models \phi$, if the following condition is satisfied:

- when ϕ is a forward constraint $\forall x\, (p(r, x) \rightarrow \forall y\, (q(x, y) \rightarrow s(x, y)))$: for all vertices $a, b \in |G|$, if there exist paths $\alpha \in p$ and $\beta \in q$ such that $G \models \alpha(r^G, a) \land \beta(a, b)$, then there exists a path $\gamma \in s$ such that $G \models \gamma(a, b)$;

– when ϕ is a backward constraint $\forall x\,(p(r,x) \rightarrow \forall y\,(q(x,y) \rightarrow s(y,x)))$: for all vertices $a,b \in |G|$, if there exist paths $\alpha \in p$ and $\beta \in q$ such that $G \models \alpha(r^G, a) \wedge \beta(a, b)$, then there exists $\gamma \in s$ such that $G \models \gamma(b, a)$.

The implication and finite implication problems for P_c^w are formalized in the same way as for P_c, as described in Sect. 3.2. Obviously, P_c is properly contained in P_c^w. Thus the corollary below follows immediately from Theorem 3.2.

Corollary 3.3: In the context of SM, the implication and finite implication problems for P_c^w are undecidable. ∎

We shall show that this undecidability result also breaks down in DM.

3.4   Path constraint language P_c^*

We next further generalize the syntax of path expressions by including the Kleene closure $*$ as follows:
$$e ::= \epsilon \mid K \mid e \cdot e \mid e + e \mid e^*$$
That is, we define path expressions to be general regular expressions. Recall that the wildcard symbol can be expressed as a (union) regular expression if E is finite. In Sect. 2, we have seen the following path expressions that can be expressed as regular expressions: $manager \cdot manager^*$, $emp \cdot \_ \cdot manager^*$, etc.

Let p be a regular expression and ρ be a path. As in Sect. 3.3, we use $\rho \in p$ to denote that ρ is in the regular language defined by p. We also treat p as a logic formula $p(x, y)$, and define $G \models p(x, y)$ for deterministic structure G.

The syntax of P_c^* constraints is the same as that of P_c^w. But path expressions are represented by general regular expressions in P_c^* constraints, rather than by union regular expressions.

For example, ψ_1, ψ_2 and ψ_3 given in Sect. 2 are P_c^* constraints, but they are in neither P_c nor P_c^w.

As in Sect. 3.3, for a deterministic structure G and a P_c^* constraint ψ, we can define the notion of $G \models \psi$. Similarly, we can formalize the implication and finite implication problems for P_c^*.

For example, recall constraints ψ_1, ψ_2, ϕ_1, ϕ_2 and ψ_3 given in Sect. 2 and let Σ be $\{\psi_1, \psi_2, \phi_1, \phi_2\}$. Then the question whether $\Sigma \models \psi_3$ ($\Sigma \models_f \psi_3$) is an instance of the (finite) implication problem for P_c^*. In Sect. 2, this implication is used in the proof of the equivalence of the queries Q_2 and Q_2'.

Clearly, P_c^w is a proper subset of P_c^*. Therefore, by Corollary 3.3, we have:

Corollary 3.4: In the context of SM, the implication and finite implication problems for P_c^* are undecidable. ∎

We shall show that this undecidability still holds in the context of DM.

4   Path constraint implication

In this section, we study the implication problems associated with P_c, P_c^w and P_c^* for the deterministic data model DM. More specifically, we show the following.

Theorem 4.1: In the context of DM, the implication and finite implication problems for P_c are finitely axiomatizable and are decidable in cubic-time.   ∎

Proposition 4.2: In the context of DM, the implication and finite implication problems for P_c^w are decidable.   ∎

Theorem 4.3: In the context of DM, the implication and finite implication problems for P_c^* are undecidable.   ∎

In contrast to Theorem 3.2 and Corollary 3.3, Theorem 4.1 and Proposition 4.2 show that for DM, the implication problems for P_c and P_c^w are decidable. These demonstrate that the determinism condition of DM may simplify reasoning about path constraints. However, Theorem 4.3 shows that this determinism condition does not trivialize the problem of path constraint implication.

4.1   Decidability of P_c

We prove Theorem 4.1 in two steps. We first present a finite axiomatization for P_c in the context of DM. That is, a finite set of inference rules that is sound and complete for implication and finite implication of P_c constraints. We then show that there is a cubic-time algorithm for testing P_c constraint implication.

A finite axiomatization. Before we present a finite axiomatization for P_c, we first study basic properties of P_c constraints in the context of DM. While Lemma 4.6 given below holds in both SM and DM, Lemmas 4.4 and 4.5 hold in the context of DM but not in SM. Their proofs require Lemma 3.1. We omit the proofs due to the lack of space, but we encourage the reader to consult [14].

Lemma 4.4: For any $\varphi = \forall x \, (\alpha(r, x) \rightarrow \forall y \, (\beta(x, y) \rightarrow \gamma(x, y)))$, i.e., forward constraint of P_c, there is a word constraint: $\psi = \forall x \, (\alpha \cdot \beta(r, x) \rightarrow \alpha \cdot \gamma(r, x))$ such that for any deterministic structure G, $G \models \varphi$ iff $G \models \psi$.   ∎

Lemma 4.5: For any $\varphi = \forall x \, (\alpha(r, x) \rightarrow \forall y \, (\beta(x, y) \rightarrow \gamma(y, x)))$, i.e., backward constraint of P_c, there is a word constraint: $\psi = \forall x \, (\alpha(r, x) \rightarrow \alpha \cdot \beta \cdot \gamma(r, x))$ such that for any deterministic structure G, if $G \models \psi$ then $G \models \varphi$. In addition, if $G \models \exists x \, (\alpha \cdot \beta(r, x)) \wedge \varphi$, then $G \models \psi$.   ∎

Lemma 4.6: For any finite subset $\Sigma \cup \{\varphi\}$ of P_c,

$$\Sigma \models \varphi \quad \text{iff} \quad \Sigma \cup \{\exists x \, (pf(\varphi) \cdot lt(\varphi)(r, x))\} \models \varphi,$$

$$\Sigma \models_f \varphi \quad \text{iff} \quad \Sigma \cup \{\exists x \, (pf(\varphi) \cdot lt(\varphi)(r, x))\} \models_f \varphi,$$

where $pf(\varphi)$ and $lt(\varphi)$ are described in Sect. 3.2.   ∎

Based on Lemma 4.6, we extend P_c by including constraints of the *existential form* as follows:

$$P_c^e = P_c \cup \{\exists x \, \rho(r, x) \mid \rho \text{ is a path}\}.$$

Constraints of the existential form enable us to assert the existence of paths. As pointed out by [23], they are important for specifying Web link characteristics.

For P_c^e, we consider a set of inference rules, $\mathcal{I}_c$, given below. Note that the last four inference rules in $\mathcal{I}_c$ are sound in DM because of Lemmas 4.4 and 4.5.

- Reflexivity:

$$\frac{}{\forall x \, (\alpha(r, x) \rightarrow \alpha(r, x))}$$

- Transitivity:
$$\frac{\forall x\ (\alpha(r,x) \to \beta(r,x)) \qquad \forall x\ (\beta(r,x) \to \gamma(r,x))}{\forall x\ (\alpha(r,x) \to \gamma(r,x))}$$

- Right-congruence:
$$\frac{\forall x\ (\alpha(r,x) \to \beta(r,x))}{\forall x\ (\alpha \cdot \gamma(r,x) \to \beta \cdot \gamma(r,x))}$$

- Empty-path:
$$\frac{}{\exists x\ \epsilon(r,x)}$$

- Prefix:
$$\frac{\exists x\ (\alpha \cdot \beta(r,x))}{\exists x\ \alpha(r,x)}$$

- Entail:
$$\frac{\exists x\ \alpha(r,x) \qquad \forall x\ (\alpha(r,x) \to \beta(r,x))}{\exists x\ \beta(r,x)}$$

- Symmetry:
$$\frac{\exists x\ \alpha(r,x) \qquad \forall x\ (\alpha(r,x) \to \beta(r,x))}{\forall x\ (\beta(r,x) \to \alpha(r,x))}$$

- Forward-to-word:
$$\frac{\forall x\ (\alpha(r,x) \to \forall y\ (\beta(x,y) \to \gamma(x,y)))}{\forall x\ (\alpha \cdot \beta(r,x) \to \alpha \cdot \gamma(r,x))}$$

- Word-to-forward:
$$\frac{\forall x\ (\alpha \cdot \beta(r,x) \to \alpha \cdot \gamma(r,x))}{\forall x\ (\alpha(r,x) \to \forall y\ (\beta(x,y) \to \gamma(x,y)))}$$

- Backward-to-word:
$$\frac{\exists x\ (\alpha \cdot \beta(r,x)) \qquad \forall x\ (\alpha(r,x) \to \forall y\ (\beta(x,y) \to \gamma(y,x)))}{\forall x\ (\alpha(r,x) \to \alpha \cdot \beta \cdot \gamma(r,x))}$$

- Word-to-backward:
$$\frac{\forall x\ (\alpha(r,x) \to \alpha \cdot \beta \cdot \gamma(r,x))}{\forall x\ (\alpha(r,x) \to \forall y\ (\beta(x,y) \to \gamma(y,x)))}$$

Let $\Sigma \cup \{\varphi\}$ be a finite subset of P_c^e. We use $\Sigma \vdash_{\mathcal{I}_c} \varphi$ to denote that φ is provable from Σ using $\mathcal{I}_c$. That is, there is an $\mathcal{I}_c$-proof of φ from Σ.

The following theorem shows that $\mathcal{I}_c$ is indeed a finite axiomatization of P_c.

Theorem 4.7: In the context of DM, for each finite subset $\Sigma \cup \{\varphi\}$ of P_c,

$$\Sigma \models \varphi \text{ iff } \Sigma \cup \{\exists x\ (pf(\varphi) \cdot lt(\varphi)(r,\ x))\} \vdash_{\mathcal{I}_c} \varphi,$$
$$\Sigma \models_f \varphi \text{ iff } \Sigma \cup \{\exists x\ (pf(\varphi) \cdot lt(\varphi)(r,\ x))\} \vdash_{\mathcal{I}_c} \varphi. \qquad \blacksquare$$

Proof sketch: It suffices to show that $\Sigma \cup \{\exists x\ (pf(\varphi) \cdot lt(\varphi)(r,\ x))\} \models \varphi$ if and only if $\Sigma \cup \{\exists x\ (pf(\varphi) \cdot lt(\varphi)(r,\ x))\} \vdash_{\mathcal{I}_c} \varphi$, because of Lemma 4.6.

Soundness of $\mathcal{I}_c$ can be verified by induction on the lengths of $\mathcal{I}_c$-proofs. For the proof of completeness, it suffices to show the following *claim*: There is a finite deterministic structure G such that $G \models \Sigma \cup \{\exists x\ (pf(\varphi) \cdot lt(\varphi)(r^G,\ x))\}$. In addition, if $G \models \varphi$, then $\Sigma \cup \{\exists x\ (pf(\varphi) \cdot lt(\varphi)(r,\ x)))\} \vdash_{\mathcal{I}_c} \varphi$.

To see this, suppose that $\Sigma \cup \{\exists x\ (pf(\varphi) \cdot lt(\varphi)(r,\ x)))\} \models \varphi$. By the claim, $G \models \Sigma \cup \{\exists x\ (pf(\varphi) \cdot lt(\varphi)(r,\ x)))\}$. Thus we have $G \models \varphi$. In addition, since G is finite, if $\Sigma \cup \{\exists x\ (pf(\varphi) \cdot lt(\varphi)(r,\ x))\} \models_f \varphi$, then $G \models \varphi$. Thus again by the claim, $\Sigma \cup \{\exists x\ (pf(\varphi) \cdot lt(\varphi)(r,\ x))\} \vdash_{\mathcal{I}_c} \varphi$. Space limitations do not allow us to include the lengthy definition of G. The interested reader should consult [14]. $\blacksquare$

As an immediate corollary of Theorem 4.7, in the context of DM, the implication and finite implication problems for P_c coincide and are decidable.

In addition, it can be shown that $\mathcal{I}_c$ is also a finite axiomatization of P_c^e, by using a proof similar to that of Theorem 4.7.

Theorem 4.8: In the context of DM, for any finite subset $\Sigma \cup \{\varphi\}$ of P_c^e, if φ is in P_c, then $\Sigma \models \varphi$ iff $\Sigma \cup \{\exists x \, (pf(\varphi) \cdot lt(\varphi)(r, x))\} \vdash_{\mathcal{I}_c} \varphi$ iff $\Sigma \models_f \varphi$. Otherwise, i.e., when φ is an existential constraints, $\Sigma \models \varphi$ iff $\Sigma \vdash_{\mathcal{I}_c} \varphi$ iff $\Sigma \models_f \varphi$. ∎

For SM, [4] has shown that the first three rules of $\mathcal{I}_c$, i.e., Reflexivity, Transitivity and Right-congruence, are sound and complete for word constraints. In the context of DM, however, these rules are no longer complete. To illustrate this, let α be a path and consider the word constraints: $\varphi = \forall x \, (\epsilon(r, x) \to \alpha(r, x))$ and $\phi = \forall x \, (\alpha(r, x) \to \epsilon(r, x))$. By Lemma 3.1, it can be verified that $\varphi \models \phi$. However, this implication cannot be derived by using these three rules.

In the context of DM, the first seven rules of $\mathcal{I}_c$ are sound and complete for word constraint implication. Let $\mathcal{I}_w$ be the set consisting of these seven rules. With slight modification, the proof of Theorem 4.7 can show the following.

Theorem 4.9: In the context of DM, for each finite set $\Sigma \cup \{\varphi\}$ of word constraints, $\Sigma \models \varphi$ iff $\Sigma \cup \{\exists x \, (lt(\varphi)(r, x))\} \vdash_{\mathcal{I}_w} \varphi$ iff $\models_f \varphi$. ∎

A cubic-time algorithm. Based on Theorem 4.7, we can show the following:

Proposition 4.10: There is an algorithm that, given a finite subset Σ of P_c and paths α, β, computes a finite deterministic structure G in time $O(n^3)$, where n is the length of Σ and $\alpha \cdot \beta$. The structure G has the following property: there are $a, b \in |G|$ such that $G \models \alpha(r^G, a) \wedge \beta(a, b)$, and moreover, for any path γ,
$G \models \gamma(a, b)$ iff $\Sigma \cup \{\exists x \, (\alpha \cdot \beta(r, x))\} \vdash_{\mathcal{I}_c} \forall x \, (\alpha(r, x) \to \forall y \, (\beta(x, y) \to \gamma(x, y)))$,
$G \models \gamma(b, a)$ iff $\Sigma \cup \{\exists x \, (\alpha \cdot \beta(r, x))\} \vdash_{\mathcal{I}_c} \forall x \, (\alpha(r, x) \to \forall y \, (\beta(x, y) \to \gamma(y, x)))$. ∎

The algorithm takes advantage of Lemma 3.1 and has low complexity. It constructs the structure described in the proposition. Each step of the construction corresponds to an application of some inference rule in $\mathcal{I}_c$. By Theorem 4.7, it can be used for testing P_c constraint implication in the context of DM. We do not include the proof of the proposition due to the lack of space. The interested reader should see [14] for a detailed proof and the algorithm.

4.2 Decidability of P_c^w

We next prove Proposition 4.2. To establish the decidability of the implication and finite implication problems for P_c^w, it suffices to give a small model argument:

Claim: Given any finite subset $\Sigma \cup \{\varphi\}$ of P_c^w, we can effectively compute a bound k such that if $\Sigma \cup \varphi$ has a deterministic model then it has a finite deterministic model of size at most k.

For if the claim holds, then the implication and finite implication problems for P_c^w coincide and are decidable.

To show the claim, let $\phi = \bigwedge \Sigma \wedge \neg \varphi$ and assume that there is a deterministic structure G satisfying ϕ. Let

$PEs(\phi) = \{pf(\psi) \cdot lt(\psi),\ pf(\psi) \cdot rt(\psi) \mid \psi \in \Sigma \cup \{\varphi\},\ \psi \text{ has the forward form}\}$
$\qquad\qquad \cup\ \{pf(\psi) \cdot lt(\psi) \cdot rt(\psi) \mid \psi \in \Sigma \cup \{\varphi\},\ \psi \text{ has the backward form}\},$
$Pts(\phi)\ = \{\varrho \mid \varrho \text{ is a path},\ p \in PEs(\phi),\ \varrho \in p\},$
$CloPts(\phi) = \{\rho \mid \varrho \in Pts(\phi),\ \rho \preceq \varrho\}.$

Here $pf(\psi)$, $lt(\psi)$ and $rt(\psi)$ are union regular expressions, $\varrho \in p$ means that path ϱ is in the regular language defined by regular expression p, and $\rho \preceq \varrho$ denotes that path ρ is a prefix of path ϱ. Let E_ϕ be the set of edge labels appearing in some path in $Pts(\phi)$. Then we define structure H to be $(|H|, r^H, E^H)$ such that $|H| = \{a \mid a \in |G|,\ \rho \in CloPts(\phi),\ G \models \rho(r^G, a)\}$, $r^H = r^G$, and for all $a, b \in |H|$ and $K \in E$, $H \models K(a, b)$ iff $K \in E_\phi$ and $G \models K(a, b)$. It is easy to verify that $H \models \phi$ and H is deterministic, since G has these properties. By Lemma 3.1, the size of $|H|$ is at most the cardinality of $CloPts(\phi)$, which is finite because the regular language defined by a union regular expression is finite.

It should be noted that E_ϕ and $CloPts(\phi)$ are determined by ϕ only. Thus Proposition 4.2 holds even if E, the set of relation symbols in signature σ, is infinite. However, when wildcards are considered, we require E to be finite so that the wildcard can be expressed as a union regular expression. Note that the proof above is uniform in the size of E. More specifically, the proof gives an effective way of going from the number of labels n to a decision procedure D_n.

4.3   Undecidability of P_c^*

Next, we show Theorem 4.3. We establish the undecidability of the (finite) implication problem for P_c^* by reduction from the word problem for (finite) monoids. Before we give the proof, we first review the word problem for (finite) monoids.

The word problem for (finite) monoids. Let Γ be a finite alphabet and $(\Gamma^*, \cdot, \epsilon)$ be the free monoid generated by Γ. An *equation* over Γ is a pair (α, β) of strings in Γ^*.

Let $\Theta = \{(\alpha_i, \beta_i) \mid \alpha_i, \beta_i \in \Gamma^*,\ i \in [1, n]\}$ and a *test equation* θ be (α, β). We use $\Theta \models \theta$ $(\Theta \models_f \theta)$ to denote that for any (finite) monoid $(M, \circ, id)$ and any homomorphism $h : \Gamma^* \to M$, if $h(\alpha_i) = h(\beta_i)$ for $i \in [1, n]$, then $h(\alpha) = h(\beta)$.

The *word problem for (finite) monoids* is the problem to determine, given any Θ and θ, whether $\Theta \models \theta$ $(\Theta \models_f \theta)$.

The following result is well-known (see, e.g., [2]).

Theorem 4.11: Both the word problem for monoids and the word problem for finite monoids are undecidable.   ∎

Reduction from the word problem. We next present an encoding of the word problem for (finite) monoids. Let Γ_0 be a finite alphabet and Θ_0 be a finite set of equations over Γ_0. Without loss of generality, assume $\Gamma_0 \subseteq E$, where E is the set of binary relation symbols in signature σ described in Sect. 3.1. Assume

$$\Gamma_0 = \{K_j \mid j \in [1, m],\ K_i \neq K_j \text{ if } i \neq j\},$$
$$\Theta_0 = \{(\alpha_i, \beta_i) \mid \alpha_i, \beta_i \in \Gamma_0^*,\ i \in [1, n]\}.$$

Note here that each symbol in Γ_0 is a binary relation symbol in E. Therefore, each string α in Γ_0^* can be represented as a path, also denoted by α.

Let e_0 be the regular expression defined by $e_0 = (K_1 + K_2 + \ldots + K_m)^*$. We encode Θ_0 with a subset Σ of P_c^*, which includes the following: for $i \in [1, n]$,

$$\forall x \, (e_0(r, x) \to \forall y \, (\alpha_i(x, y) \to \beta_i(x, y))),$$
$$\forall x \, (e_0(r, x) \to \forall y \, (\beta_i(x, y) \to \alpha_i(x, y))).$$

We encode test equation (α, β), where α and β are arbitrary strings in Γ_0^*, with

$$\varphi = \forall x \, (e_0(r, x) \to \forall y \, (\alpha(x, y) \to \beta(x, y))).$$

The lemma below shows that the encoding given above is indeed a reduction from the word problem for (finite) monoids. From this lemma and Theorem 4.11, Theorem 4.3 follows immediately.

Lemma 4.12: In the context of DM,

$$\Theta_0 \models (\alpha, \beta) \quad \text{iff} \quad \Sigma \models \varphi, \tag{a}$$
$$\Theta_0 \models_f (\alpha, \beta) \quad \text{iff} \quad \Sigma \models_f \varphi. \tag{b}$$
∎

Proof sketch: We give a proof sketch of (b). The proof of (a) is similar and simpler. Owing to the space limit, we omit the details of the lengthy proof, but we encourage the interested reader to consult [14].

(*if*) Suppose $\Theta_0 \not\models_f (\alpha, \beta)$. Then there is a finite monoid M and a homomorphism $h : \Gamma_0^* \to M$ such that $h(\alpha_i) = h(\beta_i)$ for $i \in [1, n]$, but $h(\alpha) \neq h(\beta)$. We show that there is a finite deterministic structure G, such that $G \models \Sigma$ and $G \not\models \varphi$. To do this, we define an equivalence relation on Γ_0^*:

$$\rho \approx \varrho \quad \text{iff} \quad h(\rho) = h(\varrho).$$

For each string $\rho \in \Gamma_0^*$, let $\hat{\rho}$ be the equivalence class of ρ with respect to $\approx$, and let $o(\hat{\rho})$ be a distinct node. Then we define a structure $G = (|G|, r^G, E^G)$, such that $|G| = \{o(\hat{\rho}) \mid \rho \in \Gamma_0^*\}$ and the root $r^G = o(\hat{\epsilon})$. The binary relations are populated in G such that for any $K \in E$ and $o(\hat{\rho}), o(\hat{\varrho}) \in |G|$, $G \models K(o(\hat{\rho}), o(\hat{\varrho}))$ iff $\rho \cdot K \in \hat{\varrho}$. It can be verified that G is indeed a finite deterministic structure. In addition, $G \models \Sigma$ and $G \not\models \varphi$. A property of e_0 used in the proof is $\epsilon \in e_0$. That is, the empty path is in the language defined by the regular expression e_0.

(*only if*) Suppose that there is a finite deterministic structure G such that $G \models \Sigma$ and $G \models \neg\varphi$. Then we define a finite monoid $(M, \circ, id)$ and a homomorphism $h : \Gamma_0^* \to M$ such that for each $i \in [1, n]$, $h(\alpha_i) = h(\beta_i)$, but $h(\alpha) \neq h(\beta)$. To do this, we define another equivalence relation $\sim$ on Γ_0^* as follows:

$$\rho \sim \varrho \quad \text{iff} \quad G \models \forall x(e_0(r, x) \to \forall y \, (\rho(x, y) \to \varrho(x, y))) \wedge$$
$$\forall x \, (e_0(r, x) \to \forall y \, (\varrho(x, y) \to \rho(x, y))).$$

For each $\rho \in \Gamma_0^*$, let $[\rho]$ denote the equivalence class of ρ with respect to $\sim$. We define $M = \{[\rho] \mid \rho \in \Gamma_0^*\}$, operator $\circ$ by $[\rho] \circ [\varrho] = [\rho \cdot \varrho]$, identity $id = [\epsilon]$, and $h : \Gamma_0^* \to M$ by $h : \rho \mapsto [\rho]$. It can be verified that $(M, \circ, [\epsilon])$ is a finite monoid, h is a homomorphism, and moreover, $h(\alpha_i) = h(\beta_i)$ for $i \in [1, n]$, but $h(\alpha) \neq h(\beta)$. The proof uses a property of e_0: for any $\rho \in \Gamma_0^*$, $e_0 \cdot \rho \subseteq e_0$. That is, the language defined by the regular expression $e_0 \cdot \rho$ is contained in the language defined by e_0. ∎

5   Conclusion

We have investigated path constraints for the deterministic data model DM. Three path constraint languages have been considered: P_c, P_c^w and P_c^*. We have demonstrated how constraints of these languages might be used for, among others, query optimization. We have also studied implication problems for these constraint languages in the context of DM. More specifically, we have shown that in contrast to the undecidability result of [11, 13], the implication and finite implication problems for P_c and P_c^w are decidable in the context of DM. In particular, the implication problems for P_c are decidable in cubic-time and are finitely axiomatizable. These results show that the determinism condition of DM may simplify the analysis of path constraint implication. However, we have also shown that the implication and finite implication problems for P_c^* remain undecidable in the context of DM. This shows that the determinism condition does not trivialize the problem of path constraint implication.

A number of questions are open. First, a more general deterministic data model, DDM, was proposed in [10], in which edge labels may also have structure. A type system for DDM is currently under development, in which certain path constraints are embedded. A natural question here is: do the complexity results established here hold in DDM? This question becomes more intriguing when types are considered. As shown in [12], adding a type to the data in some cases simplifies reasoning about path constraints, and in other cases makes it harder. Second, to define a richer data model for semistructured data, one may want to label edges with logic formulas. In this setting, do the decidability results of this paper still hold? Third, can path constraints help in reasoning about the equivalence of data representations? Finally, how should path constraints be used in reasoning about the containment and equivalence of path queries?

Acknowledgements. We thank Victor Vianu for valuable suggestions.

References

1. S. Abiteboul. "Querying semi-structured data". In *Proc. 6th Int'l. Conf. on Database Theory (ICDT'97)*, 1997.
2. S. Abiteboul, R. Hull, and V. Vianu. *Foundations of Databases*. Addison-Wesly, 1995.
3. S. Abiteboul, D. Quass, J. McHugh, J. Widom, and J. Weiner. "The lorel query language for semistructured data". *J. Digital Libraries*, 1(1), 1997.
4. S. Abiteboul and V. Vianu. "Regular path queries with constraints". In *Proc. 16th ACM Symp. on Principles of Database Systems (PODS'97)*, 1997.
5. C. Beeri and M. Y. Vardi. "Formal systems for tuple and equality generating dependencies". *SIAM J. Comput.*, 13(1): 76 - 98, 1984.
6. T. Bray, C. Frankston, and A. Malhotra. "Document Content Description for XML". W3C Note, 1998. http://www.w3.org/TR/NOTE-dcd.
7. T. Bray, J. Paoli, and C. M. Sperberg-McQueen. "Extensible Markup Language (XML) 1.0". W3C Recommendation, 1998. http://www.w3.org/TR/REC-xml.
8. P. Buneman. "Semistructured data". Tutorial in *Proc. 16th ACM Symp. on Principles of Database Systems (PODS'97)*, 1997.

9. P. Buneman, S. Davidson, G. Hillebrand, and D. Suciu. "A query language and optimization techniques for unstructured data". In *Proc. ACM SIGMOD Int'l. Conf. on Management of Data*, 1996.
10. P. Buneman, A. Deutsch, and W. Tan. "A deterministic model for semi-structured data". In *Proc. Workshop on Query Processing for Semistructured Data and Non-Standard Data Formats*, 1999.
11. P. Buneman, W. Fan, and S. Weinstein. "Path constraints on semistructured and structured data". In *Proc. 17th ACM Symp. on Principles of Database Systems (PODS'98)*, 1998.
12. P. Buneman, W. Fan, and S. Weinstein. "Interaction between path and type constraints". In *Proc. 18th ACM Symp. on Principles of Database Systems (PODS'99)*, 1999.
13. P. Buneman, W. Fan, and S. Weinstein. "Path constraints in semistructured databases". To appear in *J. Comput. System Sci. (JCSS)*.
14. P. Buneman, W. Fan, and S. Weinstein. "Path constraints on deterministic graphs". Technical report MS-CIS-98-33, CIS, University of Pennsylvania, 1998. ftp://ftp.cis.upenn.edu/pub/papers/db-research/tr9833.ps.gz.
15. D. Calvanese, G. De Giacomo, and M. Lenzerini. "What can knowledge representation do for semi-structured data?" In *Proc. 15th National Conf. on Artificial Intelligence (AAAI/IAAI'98)*, 1998.
16. D. Calvanese, G. De Giacomo, M. Lenzerini, and D. Nardi. "Reasoning in expressive description logics". In A. Robinson and A. Voronkov, editors, *Handbook of Automated Reasoning*. Elsevier, 1999.
17. A. Deutsch, M. Fernandez, D. Florescu, A. Levy, and D. Suciu. "XML-QL: a query language for XML". W3C Note, 1998. http://www.w3.org/TR/NOTE-xml-ql.
18. H. B. Enderton. *A mathematical introduction to logic*. Academic Press, 1972.
19. M. Fuchs, M. Maloney, and A. Milowski. "Schema for object-oriented XML". W3C Note, 1998. http://www.w3.org/TR/NOTE-SOX.
20. D. Harel. "Dynamic logic". In D. M. Gabbay and F. Guenthner, editors, *Handbook of Philosophical Logic. II: Extensions of Classical Logic*. D. Reidel Publ. Co., 1984.
21. O. Lassila and R. R. Swick. "Resource Description Framework (RDF) model and syntax specification". W3C Working Draft, 1998. http://www.w3.org/TR/WD-rdf-syntax.
22. A. Layman, E. Jung, E. Maler, H. S. Thompson, J. Paoli, J. Tigue, N. H. Mikula, and S. De Rose. "XML-Data". W3C Note, 1998. http://www.w3.org/TR/1998/NOTE-XML-data.
23. E. Maler and S. De Rose. "XML Linking language (XLink)". W3C Working Draft, 1998. http://www.w3.org/TR/WD-xlink.
24. A. O. Mendelzon, G. A. Mihaila, and T. Milo. "Querying the World Wide Web". *J. Digital Libraries*, 1(1), 1997.
25. L. Popa and V. Tannen. "An equational chase for path-conjunctive queries, constraints, and views". In *Proc. of 7th Int.'l Conf. on Database Theory (ICDT'99)*, 1999.
26. W. C. Rounds. "Feature logics". In J. van Benthem and A. ter Meulen, editors, *Handbook of Logic and Language*. Elsevier, 1997.
27. J. Thierry-Mieg and R. Durbin. "Syntactic definitions for the ACEDB data base manager". Technical Report MRC-LMB xx.92, MRC Laboratory for Molecular Biology, Cambridge, CB2 2QH, UK, 1992.
28. M. Y. Vardi and P. Wolper. "Automata-theoretic techniques for modal logic of programs". *J. Comput. System Sci. (JCSS)*, 32(2), 1986.

Expressing Topological Connectivity
of Spatial Databases

Floris Geerts and Bart Kuijpers*

University of Limburg (LUC)
Department WNI
B-3590 Diepenbeek, Belgium
{floris.geerts, bart.kuijpers}@luc.ac.be

Abstract. We consider two-dimensional spatial databases defined in terms of polynomial inequalities and focus on the potential of programming languages for such databases to express queries related to *topological connectivity*. It is known that the topological connectivity test is *not* first-order expressible. One approach to obtain a language in which connectivity queries can be expressed would be to extend FO+POLY with a generalized (or Lindström) quantifier expressing that two points belong to the same connected component of a given database. For the expression of topological connectivity, extensions of first-order languages with recursion have been studied (in analogy with the classical relational model). Two such languages are *spatial Datalog* and FO+POLY+WHILE. Although both languages allow the expression of non-terminating programs, their (proven for FO+POLY+WHILE and conjectured for spatial Datalog) computational completeness makes them interesting objects of study.

Previously, spatial Datalog programs have been studied for more restrictive forms of connectivity (e.g., piece-wise linear connectivity) and these programs were proved to correctly test connectivity on restricted classes of spatial databases (e.g., linear databases) only.

In this paper, we present a spatial Datalog program that correctly tests topological connectivity of arbitrary compact (i.e., closed and bounded) spatial databases. In particular, it is guaranteed to terminate on this class of databases. This program is based on a first-order description of a known topological property of spatial databases, namely that locally they are conical.

We also give a very natural implementation of topological connectivity in FO+POLY+WHILE, that is based on a first-order implementation of the *curve selection lemma*, and that works correctly on arbitrary spatial databases inputs. Finally, we raise the question whether topological connectivity of arbitrary spatial databases can also be expressed in spatial Datalog.

* Research done while this author was at the Department of Mathematics and Computer Science of the University of Antwerp (UIA) as post-doctoral research fellow of the Fund for Scientific Research of Flanders (FWO-Vlaanderen).

R. Connor and A. Mendelzon (Eds.): DBPL'99, LNCS 1949, pp. 224-238, 2000.

1   Introduction

The framework of *constraint databases*, introduced by Kanellakis, Kuper and Revesz [10] (an overview of the area of constraint databases can be found in [14]), provides a rather general model for spatial databases [16]. In this context, a spatial database, which conceptually can be viewed as an infinite set of points in the real space, is finitely represented as a union of systems of polynomial equations and inequalities (in mathematical terminology, such figures are called *semi-algebraic sets* [3]). The set of points in the real plane that are situated between two touching circles together with a segment of a parabola, depicted in Figure 1, is an example of such a spatial database and it could be represented by the polynomial constraint formula

$$(x^2 + (y-1)^2 \leq 1 \wedge 25x^2 + (5y-4)^2 > 16) \vee (y^2 - x = 0 \wedge (0 \leq y \wedge x \leq 1)).$$

In this paper, we will restrict our attention to two-dimensional spatial databases, a class of figures that supports important spatial database applications such as geographic information systems (GIS).

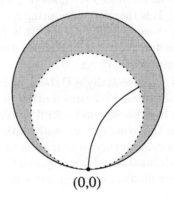

(0,0)

Fig. 1. An example of a spatial database.

In the past ten years, several languages to query spatial databases have been proposed and studied. A very natural query language, commonly known as FO+POLY, is obtained by extending the relational calculus with polynomial inequalities [16]. The query that returns the topological interior of a database S is expressed by the FO+POLY-formula

$$(\exists \varepsilon > 0)(\forall x')(\forall y')((x - x')^2 + (y - y')^2 < \varepsilon^2 \rightarrow S(x', y')),$$

with free variables x and y that represent the co-ordinates of the points in the result of the query. Although variables in such expressions range over the real numbers, FO+POLY queries can still be effectively computed [5, 18].

A combination of results by Benedikt, Dong, Libkin and Wong [2] and results of Grumbach and Su [6] implies that one cannot express in FO+POLY that a database is *topologically connected*. The topological connectivity test and the computation of connected components of databases are decidable queries [8, 17] and are of great importance in many spatial database applications, however.

One approach to obtain a language in which connectivity queries can be expressed would be to extend FO+POLY with a generalized (or Lindström) quantifier expressing that two points belong to the same connected component of a given database. In analogy with the classical graph connectivity query, which cannot be expressed in the standard relational calculus but which can be expressed in languages that typically contain a recursion mechanism (such as Datalog), we study extensions of FO+POLY with recursion for expressing topological connectivity, however. Two such languages are *spatial Datalog* and FO+POLY+WHILE.

Both languages suffer from the well-known defect that their recursion, that involves arithmetic over an unbounded domain (namely polynomial inequalities over the real numbers), is no longer guaranteed to terminate. Therefore, these languages are *not* closed. FO+POLY+WHILE is known to be a computationally complete language for spatial databases [7], however. Spatial Datalog is believed to be complete too [11, 13]. It is therefore interesting to establish the termination of particular programs in these languages (even be it by ad hoc arguments) as it is interesting to do this for programs in computationally complete general-purpose programming languages.

Spatial Datalog [10, 11, 13] essentially is Datalog augmented with polynomial inequalities in the bodies of rules. Programs written in spatial Datalog are not guaranteed to terminate. It is known that useful restrictions on the databases under consideration or on the syntax of allowed spatial Datalog programs are unlikely to exist [11]. As a consequence, termination of particular spatial recursive queries has to be established by ad-hoc arguments. On the other hand, if a spatial Datalog program terminates, a finite representation of its output can be effectively computed.

A first attempt [11] to express the topological connectivity test in this language consisted in computing a relation *Path* which contains all pairs of points of the spatial database which can be connected by a straight line segment that is completely contained in the database and by then computing the transitive closure of the relation *Path* and testing whether the result contains all pairs of points of the input database. In fact, this program tests for *piece-wise linear connectivity*, which is a stronger condition than connectivity. The program, however, cannot be guaranteed to work correctly on non-linear databases [11]: it experiences both problems with termination and with the correctness of testing connectivity (as an illustration: the origin of the database of Figure 1 (a) is a cusp point and cannot be connected to any interior point of the database by means of a finite number of straight line segments).

In this paper, we follow a different approach that will lead to a correct implementation of topological connectivity queries in spatial Datalog for compact database inputs. In our approach we make use of the fact that locally around each of its points a spatial database is conical [3]. Our implementation first determines (in FO+POLY) for each point a radius within which the database is conical. Then all pairs of points within that radius are added to the relation *Path* and, finally we use the recursion of spatial Datalog to compute the transitive closure of the relation *Path*.[1]

We raise the question whether topological connectivity of arbitrary (not necessarily compact) spatial databases can be implemented in spatial Datalog. It can be implemented in FO+POLY+WHILE, the extension of FO+POLY with a while-loop. FO+POLY+WHILE is a computationally complete language for spatial databases [7], and therefore the known algorithms to test connectivity (One of the oldest methods uses homotopy groups computed from a CAD [17]. A more recent and more efficient method uses Morse functions [9]) can be implemented in this language. Our implementation is a very natural one, however. It is based on a constructive version of the *curve selection lemma* of semi-algebraic sets [3, Theorem 2.5.5]. We show that this curve selection can be performed in FO+POLY. Also in this implementation the transitive closure of a relation *Path* (this time initialized using an iteration) is computed. Once this transitive closure is computed, a number of connectivity queries, such as "Is the spatial database connected?", "Return the connected component of the point p in the database", "Are the points p and q in the same connected component of the database?" can be formulated. Grumbach and Su give examples of other interesting queries that can be reduced to connectivity [6].

Both of the spatial Datalog and of the FO+POLY+WHILE implementation we prove they are guaranteed to terminate and to give correct results.

This paper is organized as follows. In the next section we define spatial databases and the mentioned query languages and recall the property that spatial databases are locally conical. In Section 3, we will describe our spatial Datalog and FO+POLY+WHILE implementations. In Section 4, we will prove their correctness and termination.

2   Preliminaries

In this section, we define spatial databases and three query languages for spatial databases. Let $\mathbf{R}$ denote the set of the real numbers, and $\mathbf{R}^2$ the real plane.

2.1   Definitions

Definition 1. A *spatial database* is a geometrical figure in $\mathbf{R}^2$ that can be defined as a Boolean combination (union, intersection and complement) of sets of the form $\{(x,y) \mid p(x,y) > 0\}$, where $p(x,y)$ is a polynomial with integer coefficients in the real variables x and y.

---

[1] In fact, for our purposes it would suffice to consider the extension of FO+POLY with an operator for transitive closure, rather than the full recursive power of spatial Datalog.

Note that $p(x, y) = 0$ is used to abbreviate $\neg(p(x, y) > 0) \wedge \neg(-p(x, y) > 0)$.

In this paper, we will use the relational calculus augmented with polynomial inequalities, FO+POLY for short, as a query language.

Definition 2. A formula in FO+POLY is a first-order logic formula built using the logical connectives and quantifiers from two kinds of atomic formula: $S(x, y)$ and $p(x_1, \ldots, x_k) > 0$, where S is a binary relation name representing the spatial database and $p(x_1, \ldots, x_k)$ is a polynomial in the variables $x_1, \ldots, x_k$ with integer coefficients.

Variables in such formulas are assumed to range over $\mathbf{R}$. A second query language we will use is FO+POLY+WHILE.

Definition 3. A program in FO+POLY+WHILE is a finite sequence of *statements* and *while-loops*. Each statement has the form $R := \{(x_1, \ldots, x_k) \mid \varphi(x_1, \ldots, x_k)\}$, where φ is an FO+POLY formula that uses the binary relation name S (of the input database) and previously introduced relation names. Each while-loop has the form **while** φ **do** P **od**, where P is a program and φ an FO+POLY formula that uses the binary relation name S and previously introduced relation names.

The semantics of a program applied to a spatial databases is the operational, step by step execution. Over the real numbers it is true that for every computable constraint query, such as connectivity, there is an equivalent FO+POLY+WHILE program.

A restricted class of FO+POLY+WHILE programs consists of programs in spatial Datalog.

Definition 4. *Spatial Datalog* is Datalog where,

1. The underlying domain is $\mathbf{R}$;
2. The only EDB predicate is S, which is interpreted as the set of points in the spatial database (or equivalently, as a binary relation);
3. Relations can be infinite;
4. Polynomial inequalities are allowed in rule bodies.

We interpret these programs under the the bottom-up semantics. To conclude this section, we remark that a well-known argument can be used to show that FO+POLY can be expressed in (recursion-free) spatial Datalog with stratified negation [1]. In this paper we also admit stratified negation in our Datalog program.

2.2 Spatial databases are locally conical

Property 1 ([3], Theorem 9.3.5). For a spatial database A and a point p in the plane there exists a radius ε_p such that for each $0 < \varepsilon < \varepsilon_p$ holds that $B^2(p, \varepsilon) \cap A$ is isotopic to the cone with top p and base $S^1(p, \varepsilon) \cap A$.[2]

---

[2] With $B^2(p, \varepsilon)$ we denote the closed disk with center p and radius ε and with $S^1(p, \varepsilon)$ its bordering circle. A homeomorphism $h : \mathbf{R}^2 \to \mathbf{R}^2$ is continuous bijective function

We remark that a spatial database is also conical towards infinity. In the next section, we will show that such a radius ε_p, can be uniformly defined in FO+POLY.

The database of Figure 1 is locally around the origin isotopic to the cone that is shown in Figure 2. It is a basic property of semi-algebraic sets that the base $S^1(p, \varepsilon) \cap A$ is the finite union of points and open arc segments on $S^1(p, \varepsilon)$ [3]. We will refer to the parts of $B^2(p, \varepsilon) \cap A$ defined by these open intervals and points as the *sectors of p in A*. In the example of Figure 2, we see that the origin has five sectors: two arc segments of the larger circle, a segment of the parabolic curve and two areas between the two circles. Sectors are *curves* or *fully two-dimensional*.

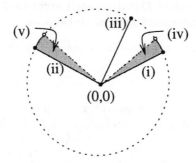

Fig. 2. The cone of $(0, 0)$ of the spatial database in Figure 1.

In the next sections, we will use the following property. It can be proven similarly as was done for closed spatial databases [12].

Property 2. Let A be a spatial database. Then the following holds:

1. Only a finite number of cone types appear in A;
2. A can only have infinitely many points of five cone types (interior points, points on a smooth border of the interior that (don't) belong to the database, points on a curve, points on a curve of the complement);
3. The number of cone types appearing in A is finite and hence the number of points in A with a cone different from these five is finite.

The points with a cone of the five types mentioned in (2) of Property 2 are called *regular* points of the database. Non-regular points are called *singular*. We remark that the regularity of a point is expressible in FO+POLY [12].

---

whose inverse is also continuous. An isotopy of the plane is an orientation-preserving homeomorphism. Two sets are said to be *isotopic* if there is an isotopy that maps one to the other.

3 Connectivity queries in spatial Datalog

In general, a set S of points in the plane is defined to be *topologically connected* if it cannot be partitioned by two disjoint open subsets. This second-order definition seems to be unsuitable for implementation in spatial Datalog. Fortunately, for spatial databases S, we have the property that S is topologically connected if and only if S is *path connected* [3, Section 2.4] (i.e., if and only if any pair of points of S can be connected by a semi-algebraic curve that is entirely contained in S). In this section, we will show that for compact spatial databases path connectivity *can* be implemented in spatial Datalog and that for arbitrary databases it can be implemented in FO+POLY+WHILE.

3.1 A program in spatial Datalog with stratified negation for connectivity of compact spatial databases

The spatial Datalog program for testing connectivity that we describe in this section is given in Figure 3.

$$
\begin{aligned}
Path(x,y,x',y') &\longleftarrow \varphi_{\text{cone}}(S,x,y,x',y') \\
Obstructed(x,y,x',y') &\longleftarrow \neg S(\bar{x},\bar{y}),\ \bar{x} = a_1 t + b_1,\ \bar{y} = a_2 t + b_2, \\
&\qquad 0 \le t, t \le 1, b_1 = x, b_2 = y, \\
&\qquad a_1 + b_1 = x', a_2 + b_2 = y' \\
Path(x,y,x',y') &\longleftarrow \neg Obstructed(x,y,x',y') \\
Path(x,y,x',y') &\longleftarrow Path(x,y,x'',y''),\ Path(x'',y'',x',y') \\
Disconnected &\longleftarrow S(x,y),\ S(x',y'),\ \neg Path(x,y,x',y') \\
Connected &\longleftarrow \neg Disconnected.
\end{aligned}
$$

Fig. 3. A program in spatial Datalog with stratified negation for topological connectivity of compact databases.

The first rule is actually an abbreviation of a spatial Datalog program that computes an FO+POLY formula $\varphi_{\text{cone}}(S,x,y,x',y')$ that adds to the relation *Path* all pairs of points $((x,y),(x',y')) \in S \times S$ such that (x',y') is within distance $\varepsilon_{(x,y)}$ of (x,y), where $\varepsilon_{(x,y)}$ is such that S is conical (in the sense of Property 1) in $B^2((x,y),\varepsilon_{(x,y)})$. We will make the description of $\varphi_{\text{cone}}(S,x,y,x',y')$ more precise below. Then all pairs of points of the spatial database are added in the relation *Path* which can be connected by a straight line segment that is completely contained in the database. Next, the transitive closure of the relation *Path* is computed and in the final two rules of the program of Figure 3 it is tested whether the relation *Path* contains all pairs of points of the input database.

Variations of the last two rules in the program of Figure 3 can then be used to formulate several connectivity queries (e.g., the connectivity test or the computation of the connected component of a given point p in the input database).

The description of $\varphi_{\text{cone}}(S,x,y,x',y')$ in FO+POLY will be clear from the proof of the following theorem.

Theorem 1. *There exists an* FO+POLY *formula that returns for a given spatial database A and a given point p a radius ε_p such that the database A is conical within $B^2(p, \varepsilon_p)$ (in the sense of Property 1).*

Proof. (Sketch) Let A be a spatial database and p be a point. If p is an interior point of A, this is trivial. Assume that p is not an interior point of A. We compute within the disk $B^2(p, 1)$ the set $\gamma_{A,p}$ in FO+POLY. For each $\varepsilon \leq 1$, $S^1(p, \varepsilon) \cap A$ is the disjoint union of a finite number of intervals and points. We then define $\gamma_{A,p} \cap S^1(p, \varepsilon)$ to consists of these points and the midpoints of these intervals. For the database A of Figure 4 (a), $\gamma_{A,p}$ is shown in (b) of that figure in full lines and $\gamma_{A^c,p}$ is shown in dotted lines. These sets can be defined in FO+POLY using the predicate $Between_{p,\varepsilon}(x', y', x_1, y_1, x_2, y_2)$. $Between_{p,\varepsilon}(x', y', x_1, y_1, x_2, y_2)$ expresses for points (x', y'), (x_1, y_1) and (x_2, y_2) on $S^1(p, \varepsilon)$ that (x', y') is equal to (x_1, y_1) or (x_2, y_2) or is located between the clockwise ordered pair of points $((x_1, y_1), (x_2, y_2))$ of $S^1(p, \varepsilon)$ (for a detailed description of the expression of this relation in FO+POLY we refer to [12]).

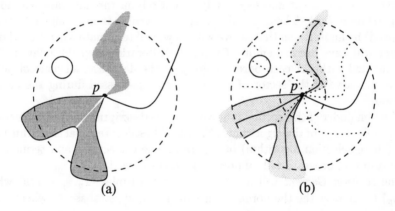

(a)   (b)

Fig. 4. The 1-environment of a database around p (a) and the construction to determine an ε_p-environment (smaller dashed circle) in which the database is conical (b). In (b), $\gamma_{A,p}$ is given in full lines and $\gamma_{A^c,p}$ in dotted lines.

Next, the singular points of $\gamma_{A,p} \cup \gamma_{A^c,p}$ can be found in FO+POLY. Let d be the minimal distance between p and these singular points. Any radius strictly smaller than d, e.g., $\varepsilon_p = d/2$, will satisfy the condition of the statement of this Theorem.

Then $B^2(p, \varepsilon_p) \cap (\gamma_{A,p} \cup \gamma_{A^c,p})$ consists of a finite number of non-intersecting (simple Jordan) curves starting in points $S^1(p, \varepsilon_p) \cap (\gamma_{A,p} \cup \gamma_{A^c,p})$ and ending in p and that for every $\varepsilon \leq \varepsilon_p$ each have a single intersection point with $S^1(p, \varepsilon)$. It is easy (but tedious) to show that there is an isotopy that brings $B^2(p, \varepsilon_p) \cap (\gamma_{A,p} \cup \gamma_{A^c,p})$ to the cone with top p and base $S^1(p, \varepsilon_p) \cap (\gamma_{A,p} \cup \gamma_{A^c,p})$. This is the isotopy we are looking for.   □

3.2   An FO+POLY+WHILE program for connectivity of arbitrary spatial databases

For compact spatial databases, all sectors of a boundary point p are all in the same connected component of the database (because a boundary point is always part of the database). Therefore all pairs of points in an ε_p-environment of p, can be added to the relation *Path*, even if they are in different sectors of p. For arbitrary databases, the sectors of a point $p \in \partial S \setminus S^3$ are *not necessarily* in the same connected component of the database.[4] This means that in general only pairs of points can be added to the relation *Path* if they are in the same sector of a point. We can achieve this by iteratively processing all sectors of the border points and adding only pairs of points that are in the same sector of a border point to the relation *Path*. For this iterative process we use the language FO+POLY+WHILE. The resulting program is shown in Figure 5.

As in the compact case, we first initialize a relation *Path* and end with computing the transitive closure of this relation.

In the initialization part of the program, first all pairs of points which can be connected by a straight line segment lying entirely in the database, are added to the relation *Path*. Then, a 5-airy relation *Current* is maintained (actually destroyed) by an iteration that, as we will show, will terminate when the relation *Current* will have become empty. During each iteration step the relation *Path* is augmented with, for each border point p of the database, all pairs of points on the midcurve of the sector of p that is being processed during the current iteration.

The remainder of this section is devoted to the description of the implementations in FO+POLY of the algorithms *INIT*, *SeRA* (sector removal algorithm) and *CSA* (curve selection algorithm) of Figure 5. The correctness and termination of the resulting program will be proved in the next section.

The relation *Current* will at all times contain tuples $(x_p, y_p, \varepsilon, x, y)$ where (x_p, y_p) range over the the border points of the input database A, where ε is a radius and where (x, y) belong to a set containing the part of the ε-environment of (x_p, y_p) that still has to be processed. Initially, $INIT(S, x_p, y_p, \varepsilon_p, x, y)$ sets the relation *Current* to the set of five-tuples

$$\{(x_p, y_p, \varepsilon_p, x, y) \mid (x_p, y_p) \in \partial S, \varepsilon_p = 1, (x, y) \in B^2((x_p, y_p), \varepsilon_p) \cap S\}.$$

It is clear that *INIT* can be defined in FO+POLY.

Next, for all border points $p = (x_p, y_p)$ of the database, both in *SeRA* and *CSA* the "first sector" of p in the relation $Current(x_p, y_p, \varepsilon_p, x, y)$ will be determined. This is implemented as follows. We distinguish between a sector that is a curve and a fully two-dimensional one. We look at the latter case (the former is similar).

---

[3] We denote the topological border of S by ∂S.

[4] The same is true for the point at infinity, which can be considered as a boundary point of the database that does not belong to the database. To improve readability, we only consider *bounded* inputs in this section.

$Path := \{(x, y, x', y') \mid S(x, y) \wedge S(x', y') \wedge \overline{(x, y)(x', y')} \subseteq S\}$
$Current := INIT(S, x_p, y_p, \varepsilon, x, y)$
while $Current \neq \emptyset$ **do**
    $Current := SeRA(Current(x_p, y_p, \varepsilon, u, v), \varepsilon^{new}, x, y)$
    $Path := CSA(Current(x_p, y_p, \varepsilon, u, v), x, y, x', y')$
od
$Y := \emptyset$
while $Y \neq Path$ **do**
    $Y := Path;$
    $Path := Path \cup \{(x, y, x', y') \mid (\exists x'')(\exists y'')(Path(x, y, x'', y'') \wedge$
                                              $Path(x'', y'', x', y'))\}$
od.

Fig. 5. An FO+POLY+WHILE program for topological connectivity of arbitrary databases. The notation $\overline{(x, y)(x', y')}$ stands for the line segment between the points (x, y) and (x', y').

We define an order on the circle $S^1(p, \varepsilon)$ with $0 < \varepsilon < \varepsilon_p$, by using the relation $Between_{p,\varepsilon}(x', y', x_1, y_1, x_2, y_2)$, and by taking the point $p + (0, \varepsilon)$ as a starting point (see proof of Theorem 1). For each $0 < \varepsilon < \varepsilon_p$, the intersection of the "first fully two-dimensional sector" with $S^1(p, \varepsilon)$ is defined as the first (using the just defined order) open interval on this circle. This is clearly dependent on the radius ε. For the database of Figure 6 (a) this dependency is illustrated in (b) of that figure. The "first sector" falls apart into four parts (shaded dark), depending on the radius ε. Furthermore, as in Theorem 1, the first midcurve, i.e. the midcurve of the "first sector", within radius ε_p is computed in FO+POLY (the thick curve segments in Figure 6 (b)). By our definition of the "first sector", this first midcurve needs not to be connected. Hence, we obviously do not want to add all pairs (q, q') of points in this set to the relation $Path$.

We can, however, compute a new (and smaller) ε_p^{new} such that the curve of midpoints has no longer singular points within $B^2(p, \varepsilon_p^{new})$. In Figure 6 (b), the small dashed circle around p has radius ε_p^{new}. Within the radius ε_p^{new} the midcurve is connected and the point p belongs to its closure.

$SeRA$ now updates ε_p in the relation $Current$ to ε_p^{new} and removes the first sector from the relation $Current$. This means that the set of points (x, y) that are in the relation $Current$ with the point $p = (x_p, y_p)$ will initially be $B^2(p, \varepsilon_p) \cap A$, then $B^2(p, \varepsilon_p^{new}) \cap A$ minus the first sector of p (after the first iteration), then $B^2(p, \varepsilon_p^{new'}) \cap A$ minus the first two sectors of p (after the second iteration), etc.

CSA will add to the relation $Path$, all pairs (q, q') of midpoints at different distances $\varepsilon, \varepsilon' < \varepsilon_p^{new}$ from p (ε can be taken 0, if p belongs to the database) of the sector that has just been removed by $SeRA$.

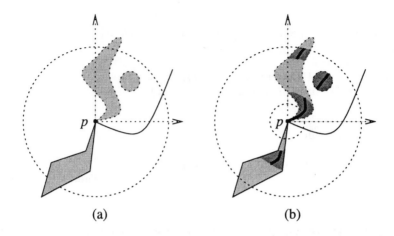

(a)   (b)

Fig. 6. The ε_p-environment of the point p in (a) and the "first sector" of p, the midcurve of the "first sector" and $\varepsilon_p^{\mathrm{new}}$ in (b).

4   Correctness and termination of the programs

In this section, we prove the correctness and termination of both programs of the previous section.

Theorem 2. *The spatial Datalog program of the previous section correctly tests connectivity of compact spatial databases and the* FO+POLY+WHILE *program of the previous section correctly tests connectivity of arbitrary spatial databases. In particular, the spatial Datalog program is guaranteed to terminate on compact input databases and* FO+POLY+WHILE *program terminates on all input databases.*

Proof. (Sketch) To prove *correctness,* we first have to verify that for every input database S our programs are *sound* (i.e., two points in S are in the same connected component of S if and only if they are in the relation *Path*). Secondly, we have to determine the *termination* of our programs (i.e., we have to show that the first while-loop in Figure 5 that initializes the relation *Path* ends after a finite number of steps and that for both programs the computation of the transitive closure of the relation *Path* ends). To prove the latter it is sufficient that we show that there exists a bound $\alpha(S)$ such that any two points in the same connected component of S end up in the relation *Path* after at most $\alpha(S)$ iterations of the computation of the transitive closure. To improve readability, we only consider *bounded* inputs of the FO+POLY+WHILE program in this proof.

Soundness. The if-implication of soundness (cf. supra) is trivial. So, we concentrate on the only-if implication. We use Collins's Cylindrical Algebraic Decomposition (CAD) [5] to establish the only-if direction. This decomposition returns for a polynomial constraint description of S, a decomposition $c(S)$ of the plane in a finite number of cells. Each cell is either a *point*, a 1-dimensional *curve* (without endpoints), or a two-dimensional open *region*. Moreover, every cell is either part of S or of the complement of S. In order to prove that any two points in the same connected component of S are in the transitive closure of the relation *Path*, it is sufficient to prove this for

1. any two points of S that are in one cell of $c(S)$, in particular,
   a. two points of S that are in the same region,
   b. two points of S that are on the same curve, and
2. any two points of S that are in adjacent cells of $c(S)$, in particular,
   a. a point that is in a region and a point that is on an adjacent curve,
   b. a point that is in a region and an adjacent point,
   c. a point that is on a curve and an adjacent point.

1.a. In this case the two points p and q are part of a region in the interior of S, they can be connected by a semi-algebraic curve γ lying entirely in the interior of S [3]. Since uniformly continuous curves (such as semi-algebraic ones) can be arbitrarily closely approximated by a piece-wise linear curve with the same endpoints [15], p and q can be connected by a piece-wise linear curve lying entirely in the interior of S, we are done.

1.b. The curves in the decomposition are either part of the boundary of S or vertical lines belonging to S. In the latter case, the vertical line itself connects the two points. For the former case, let p and q be points on a curve γ in the cell decomposition. We prove for the case of the FO+POLY+WHILE program that p and q are in the transitive closure of the relation *Path*. For the spatial Datalog program the proof is analogous. Let γ_{pq} be the curve segment of γ between p and q. Since all points r on γ_{pq} belong to the border of S, the algorithm *SeRA* processes the curve γ twice as sectors of r. We cover γ_{pq} with disks $B^2(r, \varepsilon_r)$, where ε_r is the radius constructed by *SeRA* when processing γ as a sector of r. Since γ_{pq} is a compact curve this covering has a finite sub-covering of, say, m closed balls. Then, the points p and q are in the relation *Path* after m iterations in the computation of the transitive closure.

2.a. A point on a vertical border line of a region can be connected by one single horizontal line with a point in the adjacent region. Hence, this case reduces to Case 1.a. If the point is on a non-vertical boundary curve of S, the sector around that point, intersecting the adjacent region contains a midcurve, connecting the point to the interior of the adjacent region (in the case of the spatial Datalog program even more pairs are added). Again this case reduces to Case 1.a.

2.b. In this case there is a midcurve from p in to the two-dimensional sector intersecting the region cell in $c(S)$. We distinguish between two cases. These two cases are depicted in Figure 7. In (a) the midcurve intersects the cell, while in (b) this is not the case. In Case (a), point p is connected by this midcurve to the cell, hence this case reduces to Case 1.a. For Case (b), we let r be a midpoint of a curve computed by *SeRA* belonging to the connected component of the interior of S that contains q. Hence, after using a similar argument as in Case 1.a, p and q belong to the transitive closure of the relation *Path* via a curve that passes

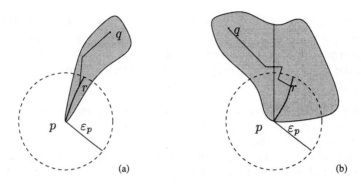

Fig. 7. The two cases in 2.b.

through r. the vertical line through p adjacent to the region.

2.c. There are various cases to be distinguished here. A vertical curve can be dealt with as before. A non-vertical curve is either a curve belonging to the border of S or a curve belonging to the interior of S. The latter case can be dealt with like in Case 2.b. For the former case, the algorithm *SeRA* will add p and a point of the border curve to the relation *Path*. The desired path to the border point can be found as in Case 1.b.

Termination. The first while-loop of the program in Figure 5 terminates since every border point of a spatial database has only a finite number of sectors in its cone and furthermore this number is bounded (this follows immediately from Property 2). After a finite number of runs of *SeRA*, the relation *Current* will therefore become empty.

To prove the termination of the computation of the transitive closure of the relation *Path* in both programs, we return to Collins's CAD. From the soundness-proof it is clear that it is sufficient to show that there exists an upper bound $\alpha(c)$ on the number of iterations of the transitive closure to connect two points in a cell c of $c(S)$.

We now show that for each region (i.e., two-dimensional cell) c in the CAD, there is a transversal $\gamma(c)$ in the relation *Path* from the bottom left corner of c to the upper right corner of c of finite length $\beta(c)$. Any two points of c can then be connected by at most $\alpha(c) = \beta(c) + 2$ iterations of the transitive closure of the relation *Path* (namely by vertically connecting to the transversal and following it). For this we remark that the bottom left corner point of the cell c can be connected by a finite and fixed number of steps (see proof of soundness) with a point p in the interior of c. Similarly, the upper right corner point of c can be connected to some interior point q of c. The points p and q can be connected by a piece-wise linear curve, consisting of $\beta(c)$ line segments. This gives the desired transversal $\gamma(c)$. For cells c which are vertical line segments or single points the upper bound is 1. Remark that points on a one-dimensional cell c can also be connected by a finite number $\alpha(c)$ of line segments. This follows from the compactness of the curves (see Case 1.b of the soundness proof).   □

5 Discussion

It is not clear whether the first while-loop of the FO+POLY+WHILE program of Figure 5, which initializes the *Path* relation, can be expressed in spatial Datalog with stratified negation. More generally, we can wonder about the following.

Question: Can spatial Datalog with stratified negation express all computable spatial database queries?

References

1. S. Abiteboul, R. Hull, and V. Vianu. *Foundations of Databases*. Addison-Wesley, 1995.
2. M. Benedikt, G. Dong, L. Libkin, and L. Wong. Relational expressive power of constraint query languages. *Journal of the ACM*, 45(1):1–34, 1998.
3. J. Bochnak, M. Coste, and M.-F. Roy. *Géométrie Algébrique Réelle*. Springer-Verlag, Berlin, 1987 (also *Real Algebraic Geometry*. Springer-Verlag, Berlin, 1998).
4. B.F. Caviness and J.R. Johnson (eds.) *Quantifier Elimination and Cylindrical Algebraic Decomposition* Springer-Verlag, Wien New York, 1998.
5. G.E. Collins. Quantifier elimination for real closed fields by cylindrical algebraic decomposition. In H. Brakhage, editor, *Automata Theory and Formal Languages*, volume 33 of *Lecture Notes in Computer Science*, pages 134–183, Berlin, 1975. Springer-Verlag.
6. S. Grumbach and J. Su. Finitely representable databases. *Journal of Computer and System Sciences*, 55(2):273–298, 1997.
7. M. Gyssens, J. Van den Bussche, and D. Van Gucht. Complete geometrical query languages. in *Proceedings of the 16th ACM Symposium on Principles of Database Systems*, pages 62–67, ACM Press, New York, 1997.
8. J. Heintz, T. Reico, and M.-F. Roy. Algorithms in Real Algebraic Geometry and Applications to Computational Geometry. *Discrete and Computational Geometry: Selected Papers from the DIMACS Special Year*, Eds. J.E. Goodman, R. Pollack and W. Steiger, AMS and ACM, 6:137–164, 1991.
9. J. Heintz, M.-F. Roy, and P. Solernò. Description of the Connected Components of a Semi-Algebraic Set in Single Exponential Time. *Discrete and Computational Geometry*, 11: 121–140, 1994.
10. P.C. Kanellakis, G.M. Kuper, and P.Z. Revesz. Constraint query languages. *Journal of Computer and System Sciences*, 51(1):26–52, 1995 (Originally in *Proceedings of the 9th ACM Symposium on Principles of Database Systems*, pages 299–313, ACM Press, New York, 1990).
11. B. Kuijpers, J. Paredaens, M. Smits, and J. Van den Bussche. Termination properties of spatial Datalog programs. In D. Pedreschi and C. Zaniolo, editors, *Proceedings of "Logic in Databases"*, number 1154 in Lecture Notes in Computer Science, pages 101–116, Berlin, 1996. Springer-Verlag.
12. B. Kuijpers, J. Paredaens, and J. Van den Bussche. Topological elementary equivalence of closed semi-algebraic sets in the real plane. *The Journal of Symbolic Logic*, to appear, 1999.
13. B. Kuijpers and M. Smits. On expressing topological connectivity in spatial Datalog. In V. Gaede, A. Brodsky, O. Gunter, D. Srivastava, V. Vianu, and M. Wallace,

editors, *Proceedings of Workshop on Constraint Databases and their Applications*, number 1191 in Lecture Notes in Computer Science, pages 116–133, Berlin, 1997. Springer-Verlag.

14. G. Kuper, L. Libkin, and J. Paredaens. *Constraint databases*. Springer-Verlag, 2000.

15. E.E. Moise. *Geometric topology in dimensions 2 and 3*, volume 47 of *Graduate Texts in Mathematics*. Springer, 1977.

16. J. Paredaens, J. Van den Bussche, and D. Van Gucht. Towards a theory of spatial database queries. In *Proceedings of the 13th ACM Symposium on Principles of Database Systems*, pages 279–288, ACM Press, New York, 1994.

17. J.T. Schwartz and M. Sharir. On the piano movers' problem II. In J.T. Schwartz, M. Sharir, and J. Hopcroft, editors, *Planning, Geometry, and Complexity of Robot Motion*, pages 51–96. Ablex Publishing Corporation, Norwood, New Jersey, 1987.

18. A. Tarski. *A Decision Method for Elementary Algebra and Geometry*. University of California Press, Berkeley, 1951.

A Representation Independent Language for Planar Spatial Databases with Euclidean Distance

Gabriel M. Kuper[1] and Jianwen Su[2]

[1] Bell Labs, 600 Mountain Ave., Murray Hill, NJ 07974.
kuper@research.bell-labs.com
[2] Department of Computer Science, University of California, Santa Barbara, CA
93106. su@cs.ucsb.edu

Abstract. Linear constraint databases and query languages are appropriate for spatial database applications. Not only the data model is natural to represent a large portion of spatial data such as in GIS systems, but also there exist efficient algorithms for the core operations in the query languages. However, an important limitation of the linear constraint data model is that it cannot model constructs such as "Euclidean distance." A previous attempt to expend linear constraint languages with the ability to express Euclidean distance, by Kuijpers, Kuper, Paredaens, and Vandeurzen is to adapt two fundamental Euclidean constructions with ruler and compass in a first order logic over points. The language, however, requires the input database to be encoded in an ad hoc LPC representation so that the logic operations can apply. This causes a problem that sometimes queries in their language may depend on the encoding and thus do not have any natural meaning. In this paper, we propose an alternative approach and develop an algebraic language in which the traditional operators and Euclidean constructions work directly on the data represented by "semi-circular" constraints. By avoiding the encoding step, our language do not suffer from this problem. We show that the language is closed under these operations.

1 Introduction

First-order logic with linear constraints (FO+lin) has turned out to be an appropriate language for expressing queries over spatial data, as in GIS systems, for example. There are, however, certain limitations on the expressive power of FO+lin. Some of these limitations are inherent to first-order languages in general, including the fact that connectivity cannot be expressed, and the tradeoffs between expressive power and efficiency in such cases have been well studied [BDLW98,PVV98,GS97]. There are, however, additional limitations that are a result not of the language itself, but rather of the class of linear constraints. The most significant of these restrictions is the inability to express the notion of Euclidean distance.

If we were to consider a query language with polynomial constraints (FO+poly), we would clearly be able to express such queries, but such a lan-

R. Connor and A. Mendelzon (Eds.): DBPL'99, LNCS 1949, pp. 239–251, 2000.
© Springer-Verlag Berlin Heidelberg 2000

guage would be far too powerful for our purposes and would be more difficult to implement. Although such a language is theoretically feasible, practical algorithms for efficient implementation of database systems with FO+poly are still a research issue. A natural question is to ask whether there is a language between FO+lin and FO+poly with additional expressive power, but without the full power of FO+poly. The naive approach, restricting our attention to quadratic constraints, does not work—the requirement that the language be closed enables one to write queries whose results require higher-order polynomials. In addition, adding some geometric primitives, such as collinearity, to a first-order language, again yields the full power of FO+poly. A more successful approach is the PFOL language of [VGV98]. This language enables one to express queries on finite databases that use Euclidean distance. However, as long as one restricts the attention to databases in FO+lin, one will still not be able to deal with queries such as "return all the points within a given distance," over finitely representable databases.

In DBPL '97, a first attempt was made at a different approach to this problem [KKPV97]. The key observation used there is that the two relevant concepts, linear constraints and Euclidean distance, correspond to the two basic operations of Euclidean geometry: constructions with ruler and compass. [KKPV97] defines a query language Φ_{circ} that is situated strictly between FO+lin and FO+poly and that expresses those queries that can be described as ruler-and-compass constructions on the input database.

The original idea in the work of Kuijpers et al [KKPV97] had been to use lines and circles as primitive objects, and define operations on them. This did not work, as Euclidean geometry provided a clear intuition for what to do with these lines and circles, but not about interiors of regions – in other words, there was no natural way to define the operations on interiors of a region that were naturally derived from operations on their boundaries. For this reason, Φ_{circ} applied to an encoding of objects as tuples of points. Using this encoding, Φ_{circ} had the desired properties.

Since objects in constraint databases are not encoded, a Φ_{circ} query consists of three parts: an encoding step, that maps a flat relation to its encoding, the "real" query, that works on this encoding, and a decoding step. The semantics of the query language depends on a specific, but arbitrary, encoding and this causes certain problems in Φ_{circ}. Indeed the query language allows queries with no natural meaning ("return the object whose representative is closest to the origin") to be expressed.

In this paper we propose a different approach in which the data is represented directly as spatial objects. The model is reminiscent of nested extension [GS95] of the standard constraint model. The purpose is to avoid the need to use an encoding to refer to distinct geometrical objects. Our main contribution is to provide a natural extension of standard Euclidean operations to *interiors* of regions. We generalize the notion of drawing a line (or circle) between 2 points to that of drawing a line between 2 objects. The idea is that, given two objects, we take the union of all the lines that go through pairs of points from the two given objects. (A similar idea, drawing lines through the origin, was used in [VGV98], but only for linear databases). This may appear to give no additional power: as we shall see, the result can always be described by taking the boundary of the objects, drawing the appropriate lines between boundary points, and taking the interior of the result. Our direct approach, however, has the advantage of establishing a *direct*, natural connection between the original objects and the result of the operation, thus eliminating the need for auxiliary information to specify which interiors are in the database.

In the next section we give basic definitions, and the following section defines the Euclidean operations on regions and the EuAlg languages based on them. We then prove that the language is closed, and conclude with related work and directions for future research.

2 Basic Notions

We consider spatial databases in the plane. In order to accommodate Euclidean operations, these must be over a subfield $\mathbb{D}$ of $\mathbb{R}$ that is closed under square roots. Most of our results apply to any such field. The minimal such field is known as the field of *constructible numbers*. As in [KKPV97], we consider sets of points that can be described by lines and circles. These are called *semi-circular sets*.

Definition. A subset of $\mathbb{D}^2$ is called a *semi-circular set* iff it can be defined as a Boolean combination of sets of the form

$$\{(x,y) \mid ax + by + c \ \theta \ 0\}$$

or

$$\{(x,y) \mid (x-a)^2 + (y-b)^2 \ \theta \ c^2\},$$

where a, b, and c are in the domain $\mathbb{D}$ and θ in $\{\leq, <, =, \geq, >\}$. Let P be the set of all semi-circular sets over $\mathbb{D}^2$.

Definition. A *Euclidean constraint* is an equation in one of the following two forms:

$$ax + by + c = 0$$

or

$$(x-a)^2 + (y-b)^2 = c^2,$$

with a, b, and c in the domain $\mathbb{D}$.

A semi-circular set is called *rectangular* if it can be represented by a formula of the form $a < x < b \wedge c < y < d$, with a, b, c, $d \in \mathbb{D}$.

Definition. Let r be a semi-circular set.

1. The *boundary* of r is the set of all points p in in $\mathbb{D}^2$, such that every non-empty rectangular set that contains p contains both points in r and points not in r.
2. A *side* of r is a maximal set of all those boundary points that satisfy a single Euclidean constraint.
3. A point p in r is an *isolated point* of r if there is a non-empty rectangular set that contains p, but contains no other point of r.
4. A point p in $\mathbb{D}^2$ is a *corner* of a region r if p is either (1) an isolated point of r, or (2) a boundary point of r that is a member of at least two sides of r.

Note that the notions of sides and corners are defined in such a way to generalize the intuitive notion of a "side" of a semi-linear set to include segments of circles as well as straight lines. It is straightforward to show (1) that any semi-circular set has a finite number of sides, (2) that each side of a semi-circular set is itself semi-circular set, and (3) that the boundary of a semi-circular set is also a semi-circular set. Note that the definitions apply to unbounded sets as well; in particular, $\mathbb{D}^2$ has no sides and has empty boundary.

3   The EuAlg Language

We first define the data model. The basic types are 2-dimensional semi-circular sets. We shall use the term *semi-circular relation* for relations over these types (our terminology here is different from that used in [KKPV97], which uses a flat model, where relations are simply semi-circular sets).

Definition. A *semi-circular n-tuple* is a tuple $t = (t_1, \ldots, t_n)$, where each t_i is a semi-circular set. Two tuples t and t' are *equivalent* if the semi-circular sets represented by $t_1, \ldots, t_n$ are equal to the semi-circular sets represented by $t'_1, \ldots, t'_n$, respectively. A *semi-circular relation R of arity n* is a finite set of semi-circular n-tuples.

Equivalence and containment of semi-circular relations can now be defined in a natural way; these are decidable, which follows from the decidability of the theory of real closed fields. Note that equivalence of relations differs from equivalence in the sense of [KKR95], as the current model is a nested one. In the current paper, we ignore non-spatial (thematic attributes), though these can be easily added to the model.

EuAlg is a nested algebraic query language, but with only one level of nesting (this is just to provide names for spatial objects). The nested model itself similar to the ones used in [BBC97], as well as the Dedale [GRS98] and Cosmos [KRSS98] prototypes.

We now turn to the spatial primitives. The novel ones are extensions of the Euclidean primitives for drawing lines and circles to handle regions. We start with lines. The intuition is that the generalization of the notion of drawing a line between two points, to that of drawing lines between two regions, is to take the union of all lines that go through any point in the first region and any point in the second. For technical reasons, we actually use rays, rather than lines, a ray from p_1 to p_2 being a "half-line," starting at p_1, and going through p_2 (a line is then easily definable as the union of two rays).

How do we handle circles? A circle in [KKPV97] is represented by a triple (p_1, p_2, p_3), where p_1 is the center, and $d(p_2, p_3)$ is the radius. We generalize this directly to semi-circular sets, by taking the union of all circles with center in the first set, and radius equal to the distance between a point in the second and one in the third. (Alternative approaches are discussed in Section 5).

Definition. Let p_1, p_2, and p_3 be points in $\mathbb{D}^2$.

1. $ray(p_1, p_2)$ is the half line that starts at p_1 (including p_1 itself)and goes through the point p_2.
2. $circ(p_1, p_2, p_3)$ is the circle with center p_1, and radius equal to $d(p_2, p_3)$.

Definition. Let r_1, r_2, and r_3 be semi-circular sets.

1. $\text{RAY}(r_1, r_2) = \bigcup_{p_1 \in r_1, p_2 \in r_2} ray(p_1, p_2)$.
2. $\text{CIRC}(r_1, r_2, r_3) = \bigcup_{p_1 \in r_1, p_2 \in r_2, p_3 \in r_3} circ(p_1, p_2, p_3)$.
3. $\text{BDR}(r_1) = \{p \mid p \text{ is a boundary point of } r_1\}$.
4. $\text{SIDES}(r_1) = \{r' \mid r' \text{ is a side of } r_1\}$.
5. $\text{CORNERS}(r_1) = \{p \mid p \text{ is a corner of } r_1\}$.

Example 1. *Consider the two regions r_1 and r_2, where*

$$r_1 = 1 \leq x \leq 2 \wedge 1 \leq y \leq 2$$

and

$$r_2 = 3 \leq x \leq 4 \wedge 2 \leq y \leq 3 \, ,$$

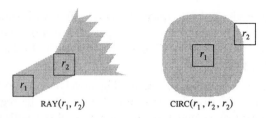

Fig. 1. Ray and circle drawing on two rectangles

Then

$$\begin{aligned}
\text{RAY}(r_1, r_2) \quad &= s_1 = (0 \le 2y - x \le 3 \wedge x \ge 1 \wedge y \ge 1) \\
&\quad \vee (y - 2x \le 3 \wedge y \ge 2) \\
\text{RAY}(r_1, r_1) \quad &= s_2 = \mathbb{D}^2 \\
\text{CIRC}(r_1, r_2, r_2) &= s_3 = (1 - \sqrt{2} \le x \le 2 + \sqrt{2} \wedge 1 \le y \le 2) \\
&\quad \vee (1 \le x \le 2 \wedge 1 - \sqrt{2} \le y \le 2 + \sqrt{2}) \\
&\quad \vee ((x-1)^2 + (y-1)^2 \le 2) \\
&\quad \vee ((x-1)^2 + (y-2)^2 \le 2) \\
&\quad \vee ((x-2)^2 + (y-1)^2 \le 2) \\
&\quad \vee ((x-2)^2 + (y-2)^2 \le 2) \\
\text{CIRC}(r_1, r_1, r_2) &= s_4 = (1 - \sqrt{13} \le x \le 2 + \sqrt{13} \wedge 1 \le y \le 2) \\
&\quad \vee (1 \le x \le 2 \wedge 1 - \sqrt{13} \le y \le 2 + \sqrt{13}) \\
&\quad \vee ((x-1)^2 + (y-1)^2 \le 13) \\
&\quad \vee ((x-1)^2 + (y-2)^2 \le 13) \\
&\quad \vee ((x-2)^2 + (y-1)^2 \le 13) \\
&\quad \vee ((x-2)^2 + (y-2)^2 \le 13) \\
\text{SIDES}(r_1) \quad &= \{r_{1,1}, r_{1,2}, r_{1,3}, r_{1,4}\}, \\
&\quad where \quad r_{1,1} = x = 1 \wedge 1 \le y \le 2 \\
&\qquad\qquad\quad r_{1,2} = x = 2 \wedge 1 \le y \le 2 \\
&\qquad\qquad\quad r_{1,3} = 1 \le x \le 2 \wedge y = 1 \\
&\qquad\qquad\quad r_{1,4} = 1 \le x \le 2 \wedge y = 2 \\
\text{BDR}(r_1) \quad &= r_{1,1} \vee r_{1,2} \vee r_{1,3} \vee r_{1,4} \\
\text{CORNERS}(r_1) &= \{(1,1), (2,1), (1,2), (2,2)\}
\end{aligned}$$

Figure 1 shows the result of $\text{RAY}(r_1, r_2)$ *and* $\text{CIRC}(r_1, r_2, r_2)$. ∎

The EuAlg algebra is standard relational algebra, together with special Euclidean operators. We start with the standard part:

Definition.

1. $r \cup s$ is the union of the relations r and s, i.e., the union of the sets of tuples in both relations with duplicates (i.e., equivalent tuples) eliminated.
2. $r \cap s$ is the set of those tuples in r that are equivalent to some tuple in s.
3. $r - s$ is the set of those tuples in r that are not equivalent to any tuple in s.

4. $r \times s$ is the Cartesian product of r and s.
5. $\sigma_F(r)$ where F is one of $i = j$, $i \subseteq j$, $i \cap j = \emptyset$ (where r has arity n, and $i, j \leq n$) is the set of those tuples in r for which the sets in columns i and j satisfy F.
6. $\pi_X r$ is the set of all tuples of the for $\pi_X(t)$ for $t \in r$.

We now turn to the Euclidean operators. These operators have a certain resemblance to aggregate operators or functions in the relational model, in that each operators adds an additional column to the relation, whose value depends on the values of the other columns of each tuple. In the following definition, r will be a relation of arity n, and i, j and $k \leq n$. The result of $\mathcal{E}_{\mathrm{OP}}(r)$ will be a relation of arity $n + 1$, defined as follows:

Definition.

1. Set operators on the spatial extent:
   - Union: $\mathcal{E}_{i \cup j}(r) = \{(t, t.i \cup t.j) \mid t \in r\}$.
   - Intersection: $\mathcal{E}_{i \cap j}(r) = \{(t, t.i \cap t.j) \mid t \in r\}$.
   - Difference: $\mathcal{E}_{i-j}(r) = \{(t, t.i - t.j) \mid t \in r\}$.
2. $\mathcal{E}_{\mathrm{RAY}(i,j)}(r) = \{(t, \mathrm{RAY}(t.i, t.j)) \mid t \in r\}$.
3. $\mathcal{E}_{\mathrm{CIRC}(i,j,k)}(r) = \{(t, \mathrm{CIRC}(t.i, t.j, t.k)) \mid t \in r\}$.
4. $\mathcal{E}_{\mathrm{BDR}(i)}(r) = \{(t, \mathrm{BDR}(t.i)) \mid t \in r\}$.
5. $\mathcal{E}_{\mathrm{SIDES}(i)}(r) = \{(t, s) \mid t \in r, s \in \mathrm{SIDES}(t.i)\}$.
6. $\mathcal{E}_{\mathrm{CORNERS}(i)}(r) = \{(t, s) \mid t \in r, s \in \mathrm{CORNERS}(t.i)\}$.

Finally, the EuAlg language also has two constant relations e_o and e_u (for "origin" and "unit), that contain the tuples $\{(0,0)\}$ and $\{(0,1)\}$ respectively. The need for 2 fixed points was discussed in [KKPV97]: These points can be used to simulate choice constructs ("select an arbitrary point on a line"), that are used in many geometric constructions.

Example 2. *Consider the relations*

$$r = \{(r_1, r_2), (r_1, r_3)\}$$

and

$$s = \{(r_1, r_2, r_2), (r_1, r_1, r_2)\} ,$$

where

$$r_1 = 1 \leq x \leq 2 \wedge 1 \leq y \leq 2$$
$$r_2 = 3 \leq x \leq 4 \wedge 2 \leq y \leq 3$$
$$r_3 = y = x + 4$$

Then

1. $\mathcal{E}_{\text{RAY}(1,2)}(r) = \{(r_1, r_2, s_1), (r_1, r_3, s_5)\}$, where $s_1 = \text{RAY}(r_1, r_2)$ was described in Example 1 and $s_5 = y > x - 1$.

2. $\mathcal{E}_{\text{CIRC}(1,2,3)}(s) = \{(r_1, r_2, r_2, s_3), (r_1, r_1, r_2, s_4)\}$ where $s_3 = \text{CIRC}(r_1, r_2, r_2)$ and $s_4 = \text{CIRC}(r_1, r_1, r_2)$ were also described in Example 1.

Example 3. *We now illustrate how Euclidean constructions can be expressed in* EuAlg. *Let r be a binary relation that represents a set of pairs of lines. More formally, if (l_1, l_2) in a tuple in r, then each l_i represents a line. Suppose that we want to bisect the angles defined by these pairs of lines, i.e., to compute a relations s such that (l_1, l_2, l) is in s iff (l_1, l_2) is in r and l is the line that bisecting the angle from l_1 to l_2. We can express this as follows:*

1. *Compute the intersection of each pair of lines:*

   $$r_1 = \mathcal{E}_{1 \cap 2}(r) \, .$$

2. *Draw all circles with centers at these intersection points, and with radius equal to unity. Then take the intersections of these circles with the original lines:*

   $$r_2 = \mathcal{E}_{2 \cap 6} \mathcal{E}_{1 \cap 6} \mathcal{E}_{\text{CIRC}(3,4,5)} r_1 \times e_o \times e_u \, .$$

3. *Draw the two circles with centers at these intersections, and with radii equal to the distance between them:*

   $$r_3 = \mathcal{E}_{\text{CIRC}(7,7,8)} \mathcal{E}_{\text{CIRC}(8,7,8)} r_2 \, .$$

4. *Take the intersections of these circles, and then draw the rays through these points and through the vertex of the angle (the entire line is thus computed (note that each line is computed twice, but that duplicates are automatically eliminated). Finally the intermediate results are projected out:*

   $$r_4 = \pi_{(1,2,12)} \mathcal{E}_{\text{RAY}(3,11)} \mathcal{E}_{9 \cap 10} r_3 \, .$$

4 Closure

Our main result is that the EuAlg is closed:

Theorem 1. *Let Q be a* EuAlg *expression, and r a semi-circular relation. The $Q(r)$ is also a semi-circular relation.*

Proof Sketch:

Note first that closure under the standard, non-Euclidean, operators is immediate, as is closure under the Euclidean operators $\mathcal{E}_{\text{BDR}}$, $\mathcal{E}_{\text{SIDES}}$, $\mathcal{E}_{\text{CORNERS}}$, $\mathcal{E}_{i \cup j}$, $\mathcal{E}_{i \cap j}$, and $\mathcal{E}_{i-j}$. The proof will focus therefore on the remaining operators, $\mathcal{E}_{\text{RAY}}$ and $\mathcal{E}_{\text{CIRC}}$. We can show:

Lemma 2. *If the boundary of a set r is semi-circular, so is r.*   ∎

We now observe that RAY and CIRC are monotone, i.e., for example, $\text{RAY}(r_1, r_2 \cup r_3) = \text{RAY}(r_1, r_2) \cup \text{RAY}(r_1, r_3)$. We shall make frequent use of this fact: to start with, we may therefore assume that all input regions are connected, using an an induction argument together with monotonicity.

Lemma 2 shows that we need only show that the boundary of the *output* of an operation is semi-circular. We would like to be able to consider only the boundary of the *input* as well, using an identity such as $\text{BDR}(\text{RAY}(r, s)) = \text{RAY}(\text{BDR}(r), \text{BDR}(s))$. Unfortunately, this does not hold in general (since the RAY operation will likely produce regions), but we can show:

Lemma 3. *Let r and s be connected, non-empty, semi-circular sets. Then*

$$\text{BDR}(\text{RAY}(r, s)) = \text{BDR}(r \cup s \cup \text{RAY}(\text{BDR}(r), \text{BDR}(s))) .$$

This is sufficient to show that if r, s and $\text{RAY}(\text{BDR}(r), \text{BDR}(s))$ are semi-circular sets, so is $\text{RAY}(r, s)$. To prove that $\text{RAY}(r, s)$ is always semi-circular, whenever r and s are, it therefore suffices to use a case analysis on r and s and then use the monotonicity of RAY. Several cases are illustrated in the following figures.

1. r: point; s: line segment without endpoints. $\text{RAY}(r, s)$ is the (open) region in the left side of Figure 2.
2. r: point; s: ray without endpoint. See the right side of Figure 2.

Fig. 2. Cases 1 and 2

3. r: point; s: circle. If r is inside s, $\text{RAY}(r, s)$ is $\mathbb{D}^2$; otherwise, $\text{RAY}(r, s)$ is similar to the left side of Figure 3.
4. s: line segment. See the left side of Figure 4.
5. For r: circle segment, and s: point. See the right side of Figure 4.

This completes the proof that $\text{RAY}(r, s)$ is semi-circular. We now sketch the proof for CIRC. Let r, s and t be semi-circular sets. We show that

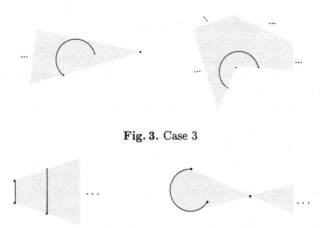

Fig. 3. Case 3

Fig. 4. Cases 4 and 5

CIRC(r, s, t) is semi-circular. By monotonicity, we can assume that r, s, and t, are all connected. For the same reason, we consider the interior of r and $r \cap$ BDR(r) separately; in fact we consider each side of the latter separately. One further assumption that we make is that the BDR(r) is connected. Let

$$\mathcal{R} = \{d(q_s, q_t) \mid q_s \in s, q_t \in t\}$$

Then CIRC(r, s, t) is the union of all circles with center in r and radius equal to a number in $\mathcal{R} \subseteq \mathbb{D}^+$.[1] We claim that $\mathcal{R}$ is actually an interval. Assume that n, $n' \in \mathcal{R}$ and $n < n'' < n'$. Then there are points p_s, q_s in s, and p_t, q_t in t, such that $d(p_s, p_t) = n$ and $d(q_s, q_t) = n'$. Since s and t are connected, there are paths connecting p_s to q_s, and p_t to q_t, that are contained in s and t, respectively. It immediately follows that there are points p and q on these paths with $d(p, q) = n''$.

By monotonicity, the following cases for $\mathcal{R}$ have to be considered: $[a]$, (a, a'), (a, ∞). Most of these are proven by induction from base cases similar to rays. The main exception is the case $\mathcal{R} = (a, \infty)$. Here we need the set of points that are of distance more than $> a$ from *some* point in r. The idea here is to construct the complement instead, i.e., the set of all points p that are of distance $\leq a$ from *every* point of r.

First observe that if r is unbounded the result must be empty. We then proceed in two steps: (1) show that circular sides can be replaced by straight edges, without changing the result, and then (2) showing that the result is semi-circular, when r is bounded semi-*linear* set.

For the first step there are two cases, depending on whether the arc is "convex" or "concave." We show here the proof works in the case of concave

---

[1] $\mathbb{D}^+$ is the set of numbers in $\mathbb{D}$ that are greater or equal to 0.

arc. Let r' be result of replacing a concave arc in r by a straight edge, and let q_1 and q_2 be the endpoints of this arc. Assume that the arc is at most half a circle (one can add an extra vertex to assure this). Since r' contains r, it follows that if p is at distance $\leq a$ from every point in r', that it is at distance $\leq a$ from every point of r. For the converse, assume that p is of distance $> a$ from some point q in $r' - r$. If the line from p to q, when extended, intersects r, then there must be a point in r of distance $> a$ from p. Otherwise, it follows, using standard geometric techniques, that either $d(p, q_1)$ or $d(p, q_2)$ is greater or equal to $d(p, q)$, which is greater than a, by assumption.

For (2), let r be semi-linear and bounded. Then it can be shown that a point p is at distance $\leq a$ from every point in r iff it is at distance $\leq a$ from every vertex of r. The latter set is the intersection of the circles with centers at the vertices of r and radii a, hence semi-circular.   ∎

5   Discussion and Future Work

In this paper, we have proposed a language for spatial databases defined by line segments and circles, motivated by Euclidean geometry. One natural question is how does this language relate to that of [KKPV97]? In [KS98], we show that this language in fact captures a natural fragment of Φ_{circ}, and that this fragment captures all of FO+lin; it would be interesting to know more about the relationship of EuAlg to traditional constraint languages, as well studying its complexity. As the Euclidean query languages can be seen as a safe restriction of other constraint languages, it would be of interest to see how they relate to the safe languages of [BL98].

Another interesting question concerns the choice of an encoding for circles. While other representations (by 3 points, or center and point on circle) may also seem reasonable approaches, and are in fact equivalent in the framework of [KKPV97], in our approach the representation seems to be critical. If we were to define $\mathcal{E}_{\text{CIRC}(i,j)}$ to be the union of all circles that have a center in region i and go through a point in region j, the resulting language is not closed: if column 1 contains a circle, and column 2 a point, column 3 will contain a limaçon, which is known not to be semi-circular (see [Due25] for the original definition and [Loc61] for a reduction of the construction of this curve to trisection of an angle). An alternative definition, using 3 points to define a circle, appears on the the other hand to be too weak.

In spite of providing distance functions with the Euclidean construction based query languages, developing appropriate query languages for fixpoint queries remain as an interesting issue. It is unclear how EuAlg can be extended to capture fixpoint queries, as it was done for FO+lin [GK97] and for topological queries [SV98].

Finally, while the restriction to Euclidean geometry is motivated by the importance of the distance function in many spatial applications, it remains a natural question to ask whether the current approach can be adapted to more general objects. The most obvious such extension would be to allow ellipses as well as circles, and to use as a generalization of the circle-drawing primitive the construction ellipses with radii from a given set of intervals, and foci taken from 2 given objects. Unfortunately, this breaks down even when we consider a single radius and foci on a single circle: as shown in [KS98], the language we get is not closed. It is an open question whether other approaches would be more successful.

Acknowledgments

The authors wish to thank Jan van den Bussche and Leonid Libkin for their comments. Work by Jianwen Su is supported in part by NSF grants IRI-9411330, IRI-9700370, and IIS-9817432, and part of his work was done while visiting Bell Labs.

References

[AB95]   S. Abiteboul and C. Beeri. The power of languages for the manipulation of complex values. *VLDB Journal*, 4(4):727–794, October 1995.

[AHV95] S. Abiteboul, R. Hull, and V. Vianu. *Foundations of Databases*. Addison-Wesley, 1995.

[BDLW98] M. Benedikt, G. Dong, L. Libkin, and L. Wong. Relational expressive power of constraint query languages. *Journal of the ACM*, 45:1–34, 1998.

[BL98]   M. Benedikt and L. Libkin. Safe constraint queries. *Proc. ACM Symp. on PODS, 1998*

[BBC97] A. Belussi, E. Bertino, and B. Catania. Manipulating spatial data in constraint databases. In M. J. Egenhofer and J. R. Herring, editors, *Intl. Conf. on Advances in Spatial Databases (SSD'97)*, pages 115–141. Springer Verlag, LNCS 1262, 1997.

[Col75] G. E. Collins. Quantifier elimination for real closed fields by cylindric decompositions. In *Proc. 2nd GI Conf. Automata Theory and Formal Languages*, volume 35 of *Lecture Notes in Computer Science*, pages 134–83. Springer-Verlag, 1975.

[Due25] A. Dürer. Underweysung der Messung. Nürnberg, 1525

[GK97]   S. Grumbach and G. Kuper. Tractable recursion over geometric data. In *International Conference on Constraint Programming*, 1997.

[GRS98] S. Grumbach, P. Rigaux, and L. Segoufin. The DEDALE system for complex spatial queries. In *Proc. ACM SIGMOD*, 1998.

[GS95]   S. Grumbach and J. Su. Dense order constraint databases. In *Proc. ACM PODS*, 1995.

[GS97]   S. Grumbach and J. Su. Finitely representable databases. *Journal of Computer and System Sciences*, 55(2):273–298, 1997.

[KKPV97] B. Kuijpers, G. Kuper, J. Paredaens and L. Vandeurzen. First Order Languages Expressing Constructible Spatial Database Queries *Journal of Computer and System Sciences*, to appear. Preliminary version appeared as J. Paredaens, B. Kuijpers, G. Kuper and L. Vandeurzen. Euclid, Tarski, and Engeler Encompassed. *Proceedings of DBPL'97*, LNCS 1369.

[KKR95] P. Kanellakis, G. Kuper, and P. Revesz. Constraint query languages. *Journal of Computer and System Sciences*, 51(1):26–52, 1995.

[KRSS98] G. Kuper, S. Ramaswamy, K. Shim, and J. Su. A constraint-based spatial extension to SQL. In *Proc. of ACM Symp. on GIS*, 1998.

[KS98] G. Kuper and J. Su Representation Independence and Effective Syntax of Euclidean based Constraint Query Languages. Bell Labs Technical Report 981116-13, 1998.

[Loc61] E. H. Lockwood. A Book of Curves. *Cambridge University Press*, 1961.

[PVV98] J. Paredaens, J. Van den Bussche, and D. Van Gucht. First-order queries on finite structures over the reals. *SIAM Journal on Computing*, 27(6):1747–1763, 1998.

[SV98] L. Segoufin and V. Vianu Querying Spatial Databases via Topological Invariants *Proc. ACM Symp. on PODS*, 89–98, 1998.

[Tra50] B. A. Trakhtenbrot. The impossibility of an algorithm for the decision problem for finite models. *Doklady Akademii Nauk SSR*, 70:569–572, 1950.

[Vau60] R. L. Vaught. Sentences true in all constructive models. *Journal of Symbolic Logic*, 25(1):39–53, March 1960.

[VGV98] L. Vandeurzen, M. Gyssens, and D. Van Gucht. An expressive language for linear spatial database queries. *Proc. ACM Symp. on PODS*, 109–118, 1998.

An Abstract Interpretation Framework for Termination Analysis of Active Rules

James Bailey and Alexandra Poulovassilis

Dept. of Computer Science, Birkbeck College, University of London,
Malet Street, London WC1E 7HX.
{james,ap}@dcs.bbk.ac.uk

Abstract. A crucial requirement for active databases is the ability to analyse the behaviour of the active rules. A particularly important type of analysis is termination analysis. We define a framework for modelling the execution of active rules, based on abstract interpretation. Specific methods for termination analysis are modelled as specific approximations within the framework. The correctness of a method can be established by proving two generic requirements provided by the framework. This affords the opportunity to compare and verify existing methods for termination analysis of active rules, and also to develop new ones.

1 Introduction

Active databases are capable of reacting automatically to state changes without user intervention by supporting *active rules* of the form "on *event* if *condition* do *action*". An important behavioural property of active rules is that of *termination* and many methods for analysing termination have been proposed. However, in many cases it is not clear whether a method developed for one active database system would be correct if applied to another. It may also not be clear whether there is a general strategy for proving the correctness of a method and understanding the trade-offs made in its design.

Abstract interpretation has proven a useful tool in the analysis of imperative, functional and logic programs [1,10,16]. In this paper we apply it to developing, and proving the correctness of, techniques for termination analysis of active rules. We develop a general framework for relating real and abstract rule execution. Specific termination analysis techniques are modelled in this framework by defining specific approximations. The correctness of a technique is established by proving two generic requirements provided by the framework. These requirements relate only to individual rules, *not* to recursive firings of rules. The class of active database systems which the framework can model is broad and does not assume a particular rule definition language. The formal nature of the framework allows a smooth adoption of previous work in query satisfiability, incremental evaluation techniques, and approximation techniques. We illustrate the use of the framework by developing two abstractions for static termination analysis of active rules and a third for dynamic termination analysis.

R. Connor and A. Mendelzon (Eds.): DBPL'99, LNCS 1949, pp. 252–270, 2000.

Section 2 presents the framework. This involves defining the concrete execution semantics and their abstract counterpart. Section 3 describes how the framework can be applied to a particular rule language, rule scheduling semantics, and approximation. Sections 4, 5 and 6 give three example applications of the framework. Section 7 discusses and compares these three techniques. Section 8 compares our approach to rule termination analysis with related work. We give our conclusions and directions for future research in Section 9.

2   The Framework

We use a typed functional metalanguage to specify both the actual execution semantics and their abstract counterpart. In this language, the type $List(t)$ consists of lists of values of type t, $P(t)$ of sets of values of type t, $(t_1, \ldots, t_n)$ is the n-product of types $t_1, \ldots, t_n$ and $t_1 \rightarrow t_2$ is the function space from t_1 to t_2. The operator $\rightarrow$ is right-associative. Function application is left-associative and has higher precedence than any operator. $[]$ denotes the empty list and $(x : y)$ a list with head x and tail y. The function $map : (a \rightarrow b) \rightarrow P(a) \rightarrow P(b)$ applies its first argument to each element of its second argument. We also require the following function which "folds" a binary function f into a list:

```
fold : (a->b->a) -> a -> List(b) -> a
fold f x []       = x
fold f x (y:ys) = fold f (f x y) ys
```

Our specifications are reminiscent of a denotational approach [23] in that we represent the database state as a function from a set of identifiers to a semantic domain, and define how this state is transformed during rule execution. However, our specifications are executable. As we will see, this means that the abstract semantics can form the basis for developing practical tests for rule termination.

2.1   The Execution Semantics

Each active rule is modelled as a four-tuple consisting of an *event query*, a *condition query*, a list of *actions*, and an *execution mode*. The type *Rule* is thus:

```
Rule = (Query,Query,List(Action),Mode)
```

A rule's execution mode encodes information about where on the current schedule the rule's actions should be placed if the rule fires (e.g. Immediate or Deferred scheduling) and to what database state these actions should be bound (e.g. the state in which the condition was evaluated, or the state in which the action will be executed) — see [17] for a description of the scheduling and binding possibilities for active rules. We assume that the currently defined rules are held in a global list $RULES : List(Rule)$ in order of their priority [1]. We also assume

---

[1] Thus rules are totally ordered and rule firing is deterministic. Handling non-deterministic firings of rules of the same priority is an area of future work.

that it is possible to derive a *delta query* from each rule action which encodes the change that the action would make to the database state.

Schedules are lists of actions, and database states are modelled as functions from a set of database object identifiers, Id, to a semantic domain, D:

```
Schedule = List(Action)
DBState  = Id -> D
```

We assume that there is a distinguished value $\emptyset \in D$. A rule *fires* if its event query and condition query both evaluate to a value other than $\emptyset$.

The Id, D, *Query*, *Action* and *Mode* types referred to above may clearly be different for different active database systems. In Section 3 we define them for a relational database system, but they can be defined for other types of system, such as object-oriented ones.

There are three kinds of database object identifiers: the set of *data identifiers*, $DataId$, the set of *view identifiers*, $ViewId$, and the set of *binding identifiers*, $BindId$ (so that $Id = DataId \cup ViewId \cup BindId$).

Data identifiers: These are objects over which users can specify queries and actions e.g. the names of base relations and the names of delta relations in a relational database system.

View identifiers: Suppose that $RULES$ contains n rules, so that there are n event queries $eq_1, \ldots eq_n$, n condition queries $cq_1, \ldots, cq_n$ and $m \geq n$ delta queries $dq_1, \ldots dq_m$. Then, the domain of the database state will contain a set of corresponding view identifiers, $e_1, \ldots e_n, c_1, \ldots, c_n, d_1, \ldots d_m$, which are mapped to the current values of their corresponding queries.

Binding identifiers: These record a history of the values that the view identifiers take throughout the rule execution. As we will see below, this history is needed in order to support a variety of rule binding modes.

We specify the rule execution semantics by a function *execSched*, listed below. This takes a database state and a schedule, and repeatedly executes the first action on the schedule, updating the schedule with the actions of rules that fire along the way. If *execSched* terminates, it outputs the final database state and the final, empty, schedule. If it fails to terminate, it produces no output.

The function *exec* (see below) executes the first action, a, on the schedule and returns a new database state. This new state, db' say, is then passed to a function `createSnapshot:DBState->DBState` whose definition is straight-forward and not listed here. *createSnapshot* extends the domain of db' with a new binding identifier for each view identifier $i \in dom(db')$, setting the value of this new binding identifier to be $db'(i)$. These binding identifiers thus create a "snapshot" of the current values of the view objects. The event, condition, and delta queries of rules that fire as a result of the execution of the action a can be bound to this snapshot by *updateSched* (see below). This snapshot is never updated[2].

---

[2] Clearly in a practical implementation the entire view state does not need to be copied each time, only the changes to it. Moreover, snapshots that are no longer referenced on the schedule can be discarded from the database state.

The function *schedRules* applies the function *schedRule* to each rule, in order of the rules' priority. *schedRule* determines whether a given rule (eq, cq, as, m) should fire. If the rule's event query eq or its condition query cq evaluate to $\emptyset$ in the current database state, then the rule does not fire and the database state and schedule remain unchanged. Otherwise, *updateSched* (see below) is called to update the database state and schedule.

```
execSched : (DBState,Schedule) -> (DBState,Schedule)
execSched (db,s) =
   if s = []
   then (db,s)
   else execSched (schedRules (execUpdate (db,s)))

execUpdate : (DBState,Schedule) -> (DBState,Schedule)
execUpdate (db,a:s) = (createSnapshot (exec (a,db)),s)

schedRules : (DBState,Schedule) -> (DBState,Schedule)
schedRules (db,s) = fold schedRule (db,s) RULES

schedRule : Rule -> (DBState,Schedule) -> (DBState,Schedule)
schedRule (eq,cq,as,m) (db,s) =
    if (empty eq db) or (empty cq db)
    then (db,s)
    else updateSched (as,m,db,s)
```

Three functions therefore remain to be defined for any specific rule language and execution semantics, *empty*, *exec* and *updateSched*.

`empty:Query -> DBState -> Bool` determines whether a query evaluates to $\emptyset$ with respect to the current database state.

`exec:(Action,DBState) -> DBState` takes an action, a, and a database state, db, and updates the values of the data objects and view objects in db to reflect the effect of a. We assume that if a rule's event query or condition query evaluates to $\emptyset$ then, were they to be scheduled, the rule's actions would have no effect i.e. that $exec\ (a, db) = db$ for any such action a and any database state db. We call such actions *null actions*. Null actions aren't actually scheduled by *execSched* but do need to be considered by the abstract execution semantics in order to reflect all possible concrete executions (see outline proof of Theorem 1 in Section 2.3). An easy way to guarantee that all rule actions satisfy this property is to encode the rule's event and condition queries within each of the rule's actions — note this has no effect on the semantics of a rule. Thus, each rule action has the notional form *if* $eq \wedge cq$ *then* $update(dq)$ where eq is the event query, cq the condition query, dq the delta query, and *update* is some expression. The precise syntax of rule actions will vary from system to system.

`updateSched:(List(Action),Mode,DBState,Schedule)->(DBState,Schedule)` takes a rule's list of actions as, its execution mode m, the current database state db, and the current schedule s, and does the following:

(i) Replaces the event and condition query encoded within each action $a \in as$ by its corresponding snapshot view identifier. This binds the encoded event and condition queries to the current database state.

(ii) If the execution mode m states that the rule's action must also be bound to the current state, then the delta query appearing within each $a \in as$ is also replaced by its corresponding snapshot view identifier.

(iii) The resulting reaction transaction is inserted into the appropriate part of the schedule, as indicated by m.

We assume that this processing is independent of the values that database identifiers are mapped to, so that *updateSched* in fact has a more general signature (`List(Action),Mode,Id->a,Schedule)->(Id->a,Schedule)` where `a` is a type variable. In other words, *updateSched* is polymorphic over the semantic domain D. This means that *updateSched* can also be used in the abstract execution semantics. We assume that *createSnapshot* is similarly polymorphic over D, and it too is also used in the abstract execution semantics.

2.2   The Abstract Execution Semantics

We are now ready to define the abstract counterpart, *execSched**, to *execSched*. The definition of *execSched** is listed below. We distinguish abstract types and functions by suffixing their names with a '*'. The abstract database state type is defined by $DBState^* = Id \rightarrow D^*$, where D^* is the abstract counterpart to the semantic domain D. In general, D^* will be different for each particular abstraction. There needs to be a distinguished constant $\emptyset^* \in D^*$ which is the abstract counterpart to $\emptyset \in D$. Rules and schedules are syntactic objects which are common to both the concrete and the abstract semantics.

We see that *execSched** is identical to *execSched* except that it operates on an abstract database state type and that at the "leaves" of the computation the functions *empty* and *exec* are replaced by abstract counterparts *empty** and *exec**. `empty*:Query->DBState*->Bool` determines whether a query evaluates to $\emptyset^*$ with respect to an abstract database state. `exec*:(Action,DBState*) ->DBState*` executes an action on the data objects and view objects in an abstract database state. As we discuss further in Section 3, these two functions need to be defined for each specific abstraction.

```
execSched* : (DBState*,Schedule) -> (DBState*,Schedule)
execSched* (db*,s) =
    if s = []
    then (db*,s)
    else  execSched* (schedRules* (execUpdate* (db*,s)))

execUpdate* : (DBState*,Schedule) -> (DBState*,Schedule)
execUpdate* (db*,a:s) = (createSnapshot (exec* (a,db*)),s)

schedRules* : (DBState*,Schedule) -> (DBState*,Schedule)
```

```
schedRules* (db*,s) = fold schedRule* (db*,s) RULES

schedRule* : Rule -> (DBState*,Schedule) -> (DBState*,Schedule)
schedRule* (eq,cq,as,m) (db*,s) =
    if (empty* eq db*) or (empty* cq db*)
    then (db*,s)
    else updateSched (as,m,db*,s)
```

2.3   Correctness of the Abstract Semantics

An abstract database approximates a number of real databases. These possible concretisations are obtained by applying a *concretisation function* (see Section 2.4) to the abstract database.

Termination is an undecidable property even for simple active rule languages [5]. *execSched** is a *safe* approximation if the equivalence below holds for all $db^* \in DBState^*$ and $s \in Schedule$, where *conc* is the chosen concretisation function and $\sqsubseteq$ the information ordering on $P(DBState, Schedule)$ (see Section 2.5):

$$conc \; (execSched^* \; (db^*, s)) \quad \sqsubseteq \quad map \; execSched \; (conc \; (db^*, s))$$

The LHS of this equivalence corresponds to the set of possible concrete databases and schedules obtained by first running the abstract execution on (db^*, s) and then deriving all possible concretisations of the resulting abstract database and schedule (note that if *execSched** terminates then all the concretised final schedules will be empty). The RHS corresponds to first deriving all possible concretisations of (db^*, s) and then applying the real execution to each concrete database and schedule pair.

Thus a safe approximation yields no more information than the real execution would. The following theorem states sufficient conditions for this property to hold:

Theorem 1. *execSched** is a safe approximation if
(i) for all actions a and all $db^* \in DBState^*$,
$conc \; (exec^* \; (a, db^*)) \sqsubseteq map \; exec \; (conc \; (a, db^*))$, and
(ii) for all event or condition queries q and all $db^* \in DBState^*$,
$empty^* \; q \; db^* = True \Rightarrow (\forall db \in conc \; db^* . empty \; q \; db = True)$

Proof (outline). Since we a using a functional metalanguage, fixpoint induction [23] can be employed. The values of *execSched** and *execSched* are given by $\sqcup\{F^i(\bot) \mid i \geq 0\}$ and $\sqcup\{G^i(\bot) \mid i \geq 0\}$ respectively, where

$$F = \lambda f.\lambda(db^*, s).if \; (s = [\,]) \; then \; (db^*, s) \; else \; f \; (schedRules^* \; (execUpdate^* \; (db^*, s)))$$
$$G = \lambda g.\lambda(db, s).if \; (s = [\,]) \; then \; (db, s) \; else \; g \; (schedRules \; (execUpdate \; (db, s)))$$

It is thus sufficient to show that $conc \circ F^i(\bot) \sqsubseteq (map \; G^i(\bot)) \circ conc$ for all $i \geq 0$. The base case of $i = 0$ is straightforward. For the inductive case, we can show by provisos (i) and (ii) of the theorem that

$$conc \circ schedRules^* \circ execUpdate^* \sqsubseteq (map \ (schedRules \circ execUpdate)) \circ conc$$

It is here that null actions may arise since the concretisation of the abstract database and schedule on the LHS may generate database, schedule pairs in which the schedule contains null actions whereas the corresponding database, schedule pair in the RHS will not include such actions. Using the above equivalence and the induction hypothesis, the inductive case of the theorem follows. □

2.4   Defining the *conc* Functions

A concretisation function is needed for the argument type of each of the functions called by $execSched^*$. We observe from the definition of $execSched^*$ that there are four different argument types: $DBState^*$, $(DBState^*, Schedule)$, $(Action, DBState^*)$, and $(List(Action), Mode, DBState^*, Schedule)$. We use the concretisation function over $DBState^*$ to define the concretisation functions over the other three argument types. *These definitions are independent of the particular abstraction adopted.* We give them here and they can be reused for each specific abstraction considered later in the paper. In particular, given a definition for $conc : DBState^* \rightarrow P(DBState)$, the concretisation functions over $(DBState^*, Schedule)$, $(Action, DBState^*)$ and $(List(Action), Mode, DBState^*, Schedule)$ are respectively defined as follows (we overload the identifier $conc$ since its type can always be inferred from context):

$$
\begin{aligned}
conc \ (db^*, s) &= \{(db, s) \mid db \leftarrow conc \ db^*\} \\
conc \ (a, db^*) &= \{(a, db) \mid db \leftarrow conc \ db^*\} \\
conc \ (as, m, db^*, s) &= \{(as, m, db, s) \mid db \leftarrow conc \ db^*\}
\end{aligned}
$$

2.5   Defining $\sqsubseteq$

The concrete domain D, together with the information ordering on it $\sqsubseteq_D$, need to be defined for a given active database system. For example, in Section 3 we define D for a relational database system. The domain $DBState$ is derived from D. The orderings on $DBState$, $Schedule$, $P(DBState)$ and $P(DBState, Schedule)$ are derived in a standard fashion, *independent of the particular choice of D.* We define these orderings here, and they can be reused for all the abstractions considered later in the paper.

The ordering on $DBState$, $\sqsubseteq_{DBState}$, is the usual ordering on a function space and is defined in terms of $\sqsubseteq_D$ as follows, where $db_1, db_2 \in DBState$:

$$db_1 \sqsubseteq_{DBState} db_2 \ \ if \ \ \forall i \in Id \, . \, db_1 \ i \ \sqsubseteq_D \ db_2 \ i$$

The ordering on $P(DBState)$ is as follows for $DB_1, DB_2 \in P(DBState)$:

$$DB_1 \sqsubseteq_{P(DBState)} DB_2 \ \ if \ \ \forall db_2 \in DB_2 \, . \, \exists db_1 \in DB_1 \, . \, db_1 \sqsubseteq_{DBState} db_2$$

Note that this is the Smyth powerdomain ordering [23]. Since the sets of database states that we consider in our abstract interpretation framework are generated by concretising a particular abstract database state, this reflects the intuition that more precise abstractions give rise to smaller sets of database states.

To define the ordering on $Schedule$ $(= List(Action))$ we require an operator $reduce : Schedule \rightarrow Schedule$ which removes all null actions from a schedule. Then $\sqsubseteq_{Schedule}$ is as follows for $s_1, s_2 \in Schedule$:

$$s_1 \sqsubseteq_{Schedule} s_2 \quad if \quad (reduce(s_1) = reduce(s_2)) \quad \wedge \quad (length(s_1) \geq length(s_2))$$

Thus s_1, s_2 are identical apart from any null actions they may contain, except that s_2 is no longer, and hence has no worse termination properties, than s_1.

Finally, the ordering on $P(DBstate, Schedule)$ is as follows for $DBS_1, DBS_2 \in P(DBState, Schedule)$: $DBS_1 \sqsubseteq_{P(DBState, Schedule)} DBS_2$ if

$$\forall(db_2, s_2) \in DBS_2 \,.\, \exists(db_1, s_1) \in DBS_1 \,.\, db_1 \sqsubseteq_{DBState} db_2 \wedge s_1 \sqsubseteq_{Schedule} s_2$$

Generally, we do not subscript the $\sqsubseteq$ symbol since which of the above orderings is meant can be inferred from context.

3   Applying the Framework

To summarise, in order to use the framework just described, one needs to define:

  (i)   the concrete domain D,
 (ii)   the *empty* and *exec* functions,
(iii)   the *updateSched* function,
 (iv)   the abstract domain D^*,
  (v)   the concretisation function $conc : DBState^* \rightarrow DBState$, and
 (vi)   the *empty** and *exec** functions.

Parts (i) and (ii) are specific to the particular query/update language, part (iii) to the particular rule scheduling semantics and parts (iv)-(vi) to the particular abstraction. Once an abstraction has been defined, one needs to show that the two requirements for Theorem 1 hold.

For the remainder of the paper we assume a relational database system, with the relational algebra as the query/update language. Referring to point (i) of the framework, in this case the concrete domain is

$$D = P(Const) + P(Const, Const) + P(Const, Const, Const) + \ldots$$

where $Const$ is a possibly infinite set of constants and $+$ is the disjoint union domain constructor [23]. Thus, each member of D is a set of n-tuples, for some $n > 0$. The distinguished constant $\emptyset$ is the empty set, $\{\}$.

Referring to point (ii) of the framework, in order to define *exec* and *empty* we first need some auxiliary sets. Let $Expr$ be the set of relational algebra expressions over D. Let $BaseRel$ be the set of base relation names and $DeltaRel$

the set of delta relation names, so that $DataId = BaseRel \cup DeltaRel$. The syntax of $e \in Expr$, $q \in Query$, $a \in Action$ and $dr \in DeltaId$ is then as follows, where $d \in D$, $i \in Id$ and $r \in BaseRel$:

$$e ::= d \mid e_1 \cup e_2 \mid e_1 \times e_2 \mid e_1 - e_2 \mid e_1 \cap e_2 \mid \sigma_\theta e \mid \pi_A e$$
$$q ::= i \mid q_1 \cup q_2 \mid q_1 \times q_2 \mid q_1 - q_2 \mid q_1 \cap q_2 \mid \sigma_\theta q \mid \pi_A q$$
$$a ::= insert \ r \ q \mid delete \ r \ q$$
$$dr ::= +\Delta r \mid -\Delta r$$

For ease of exposition, we assume that event queries have the form $+\Delta R$ or $-\Delta R$, although in principle they could be arbitrarily complex. An example active rule is thus: on $+\Delta R_1$ if $R_2 \cap R_3$ do $delete \ R_2 +\Delta R_1$.

With respect to point (iii) of the framework, we do not define a specific rule scheduling semantics for our archetypal relational database system as this is in fact immaterial to the termination analysis techniques that we will explore (hence, we have omitted the *mode* part from the above example active rule). For each abstraction that we consider in subsequent sections of the paper, it thus only remains to address points (iv)-(vi) of the framework.

We recall from Section 2.1 our requirement that if a rule's event query or condition query evaluates to $\emptyset$ then, were they to be scheduled, the rule's actions would have no effect. For any user-specified rule action of the form $insert \ r \ q$, the corresponding delta query is $q - r$ and the rule action can be rewritten to $insert \ r \ \pi_{atts(r)}(eq \times cq \times (q - r))$ where eq and cq are the rule's event query and condition query, respectively. This has the effect of encoding the rule's event and condition queries within the action, without changing the semantics of the action. Similarly, for any user-specified rule action of the form $delete \ r \ q$, the corresponding delta query is $q \cap r$ and the rule action can be rewritten to $delete \ r \ \pi_{atts(r)}(eq \times cq \times (q \cap r))$.

In order to define *exec* and *empty* we assume two auxiliary functions, *eval* and *bind*. The function $eval : Expr \rightarrow D$ is a relational algebra evaluator i.e. it evaluates an expression to the set of tuples in D that it denotes. The function $bind : Query \rightarrow DBState \rightarrow Expr$ substitutes occurrences of identifiers $i \in Id$ in a query by their values in the given database state and returns the resulting expression. *empty* and *exec* are then defined as follows [3]:

$$empty \ q \ db \qquad = (eval \ (bind \ q \ db) \ = \ \{\})$$
$$exec \ (insert \ r \ q, db) = let \ db_1 = db[r \mapsto eval \ (bind \ (r \cup q) \ db),$$
$$+\Delta r \mapsto eval \ (bind \ (q - r) \ db), -\Delta r \mapsto \{\},$$
$$\forall s \in BaseRel, s \neq r.(+\Delta s \mapsto \{\}, -\Delta s \mapsto \{\})]$$
$$in \ db_1[\forall i \in ViewId.(i \mapsto eval \ (bind \ iq \ db_1))]$$

---

[3] We assume that the queries q in the arguments to *exec* have been rewritten to encode the event and condition queries as described earlier. We use maplets, $a \mapsto b$, to denote members of functions. Given a function f, $f[a_1 \mapsto v_1, \ldots, a_n \mapsto v_n]$ is short-hand for the function $(f - \{a_1 \mapsto f \ a_1, \ldots, a_n \mapsto f \ a_n\}) \cup \{a_1 \mapsto v_1, \ldots, a_n \mapsto v_n\}$.

$$exec \ (delete \ r \ q, db) = let \ db_1 = db[r \mapsto eval \ (bind \ (r - q) \ db),$$
$$+\Delta r \mapsto \{\}, -\Delta r \mapsto eval \ (bind \ (q \cap r) \ db),$$
$$\forall s \in BaseRel, s \neq r.(+\Delta s \mapsto \{\}, -\Delta s \mapsto \{\})]$$
$$in \ db_1[\forall i \in ViewId.(i \mapsto eval \ (bind \ iq \ db_1))]$$

Thus, $empty \ q \ db$ binds the query q to the database state db and then calls $eval$ to evaluate the resulting expression. $exec \ (insert \ r \ q, db)$ replaces the current value of r in db by the result of evaluating $r \cup q$ w.r.t. db, updates the values of all the delta relations, and updates the values of all the view identifiers, where iq is the query corresponding to a view identifier i. $exec \ (delete \ r \ q, db)$ is similar.

4 Abstraction 1: An Abstraction for Static Termination Analysis

In this section we define an abstraction for statically inferring the termination of a set of rules and show that it is a safe approximation. We first address points (iv)-(vi) of the framework. The abstract domain D^* consists of the set of relational algebra queries $q \in Query$ as defined in the previous section, together with the value $\emptyset^* = \{\}$. $exec^*$ replaces the abstract value of each data identifier by a new abstract value, obtained by binding to the current abstract database state the query that would have been evaluated by $exec$ in the concrete semantics:

$$exec^* \ (insert \ r \ q, db^*) = let \ db_1^* = db^*[r \mapsto bind \ (r \cup q) \ db^*,$$
$$+\Delta r \mapsto bind \ (q - r) \ db^*, -\Delta r \mapsto \{\},$$
$$\forall s \in BaseRel, s \neq r.(+\Delta s \mapsto \{\}, -\Delta s \mapsto \{\})]$$
$$in \ db_1^*[\forall i \in ViewId.(i \mapsto bind \ iq \ db_1^*)]$$
$$exec^* \ (delete \ r \ q, db^*) = let \ db_1^* = db^*[r \mapsto bind \ (r - q) \ db^*,$$
$$+\Delta r \mapsto \{\}, -\Delta r \mapsto bind \ (q \cap r) \ db^*,$$
$$\forall s \in BaseRel, s \neq r.(+\Delta s \mapsto \{\}, -\Delta s \mapsto \{\})]$$
$$in \ db_1^*[\forall i \in ViewId.(i \mapsto bind \ iq \ db_1^*)]$$

The concretisation function $conc : DBState^* \rightarrow DBState$ when applied to an abstract database state db^* returns a set of concrete database states db; each db is obtained by first choosing a function $\rho_{db} : Id \rightarrow D$ which defines an initial value for each database identifier, and then setting $db \ i = eval \ (bind \ (db^* \ i) \ \rho_{db})$ for all $i \in Id$. The remaining $conc$ functions are derived as in Section 2.4.

Defining $empty^*$ amounts to selecting a method for analysing the satisfiability of queries. Satisfiability is undecidable for the general relational algebra, so we must ensure that the queries being tested are expressed in some decidable fragment. One decidable fragment consists of queries where the argument to projection operations does not contain any occurrence of set-difference [22]. To guarantee that the queries passed to $empty^*$ have this form, we use a function $normalise$ that safely rewrites a query into an approximating interval of two queries. This function applies bottom-up the following rules except that the rule for $e_1 - e_2$ becomes $[\{\}, b]$ for any sub-expression $e_1 - e_2$ occurring within the scope of a projection operation. In these rules, a, b, c, d are relational algebra expressions, $a \subseteq b$, $c \subseteq d$, $e_1 = [a, b]$ and $e_2 = [c, d]$:

$$
\begin{aligned}
e_1 \cup e_2 &= [a \cup c, b \cup d] & e_1 - e_2 &= [a - d, b - c] \\
e_1 \cap e_2 &= [a \cap c, b \cap d] & \sigma_\theta(e_1) &= [\sigma_\theta(a), \sigma_\theta(b)] \\
\pi_A(e_1) &= [\pi_A(a), \pi_A(b)] & e_1 \times e_2 &= [a \times c, b \times d] \\
[[a, b], [c, d]] &= [a, d]
\end{aligned}
$$

e.g. $normalise(\pi_x((R_1 \times R_2) - R_3) \times (R_2 - R_1)) = [\emptyset, \pi_x(R_1 \times R_2) \times (R_2 - R_1)]$. The definition of $empty^*$ is thus:

$$
empty^* \ q \ db^* \ = \ satisfiable \ (normalise \ (bind \ q \ db^*))
$$

where $satisfiable$ applies the satisfiability test of [22] to the upper query of the interval output by $normalise$.

The following theorem is then straight-forwardly shown:

Theorem 2. $execSched^*$ is a safe approximation of $execSched$, given the above definitions of D^*, $conc$, $exec^*$ and $empty^*$.

Example 1. Consider the following two rules:
Rule 1: on $+\Delta R$ if $(R \cap S) \times (R \cap T)$ do $delete \ R \ T$
Rule 2: on $-\Delta R$ if $true$ do $insert \ R \ (S - T)$

If rule 1 is the first rule triggered, then a trace of the abstract execution on each successive call to $execSched^*$ is as follows, where 'Iter' denotes the current iteration, $action(i)$ the action of the ith rule and I is an arbitrary unused identifier denoting that $+\Delta R$ is satisfiable at the first iteration:

Iter	Database State					Schedule
	R	S	T	$+\Delta R$	$-\Delta R$	
1	R_0	S_0	T_0	I	$\{\}$	$[action(1)]$
2	$R_0 - T_0$	S_0	T_0	$\{\}$	$R_0 \cap T_0$	$[action(2)]$
3	$(R_0 - T_0) \cup (S_0 - T_0)$	S_0	T_0	$(S_0 - T_0) - (R_0 - T_0)$	$\{\}$	$[action(1)]$

Note that in this example the execution mode of the rules is immaterial since at most one rule is ever triggered. At iteration 3, the condition of rule 1 expands to the expression $(((R_0 - T_0) \cup (S_0 - T_0)) \cap S_0) \times (((R_0 - T_0) \cup (S_0 - T_0)) \cap T_0)$, which is unsatisfiable. Hence $execSched^*$ terminates after three iterations and definite rule termination can be concluded if rule 1 is the first rule triggered. $\square$

Of course in general there is no guarantee that $execSched^*$ itself will terminate and so we need a criterion for halting it (concluding in such a case that the concrete rule execution may fail to terminate). A simple way is to choose *a priori* a bound on the number of iterations of $execSched^*$. Increasing this bound allows more precision but must be balanced against the time and space resources available. Another strategy for halting $execSched^*$ is to choose a more limited abstract domain D^* that makes $DBState^*$ finite. $execSched^*$ can then be halted if a repeating argument (db^*, s) is detected since in such a case $execSched^*$ would not terminate. We demonstrate such an abstraction in the next section.

5   Abstraction 2: A Coarser Abstraction for Static Termination Analysis

We now set D^* to be the two-valued domain $\{Unknown, False\}$, where $\emptyset^* = False$. $conc(db^*)$ returns the set of databases db such that

- the values assigned to the data identifiers and view identifiers are consistent,
- $db(i) = \emptyset$ if $db^*(i) = False$

$empty^*\ q\ db^*$ returns $True$ if $db^*(q)$ is $False$. Otherwise it returns $False$.

To define $exec^*$ we need to distinguish between view identifiers corresponding to event queries, condition queries and delta queries, so we assume that $ViewId = EqId \cup CqId \cup DqId$. $exec^*$ uses a function $infer(condition, update)$ to infer the new value of a condition query. The $infer$ function returns either (a) $Unknown$ if the condition *may* be true after the update executes, or (b) $False$ if the condition can *never* be true after the update executes. This kind of inference corresponds to the determination of arcs in an activation graph [7] and so a method such as the propagation algorithm described in [8] can be used to determine the effect of updates on conditions (with exponential complexity in the worst case). This, of course, is a non-effective method, and so $infer$ will in general sometimes return $Unknown$ when it could have returned $False$ (but if not, we term it a *perfect* inference function).

$exec^*$ $(insert\ r\ q, db^*)$ sets the values of r and $+\Delta r$ to $Unknown$ and the values of all other delta relations to $False$. It then updates the values of the view identifiers by setting to $Unknown$ the values of all event queries of the form $+\Delta r$ and to $False$ the values of all other event queries, using $infer$ to infer the new values of all the condition queries, and setting to $Unknown$ the values of all the delta queries:

$$
\begin{aligned}
exec^*\ (&insert\ r\ q, db^*)\ = \\
&let\ db_1^* = db^*[r \mapsto Unknown, +\Delta r \mapsto Unknown, -\Delta r \mapsto False, \\
&\qquad\qquad \forall s \in BaseRel, s \neq r.(+\Delta s \mapsto False, -\Delta s \mapsto False]\ \ in \\
&db_1^*[\forall e_i \in EqId, eq_i = +\Delta r.e_i \mapsto Unknown, \\
&\qquad \forall e_i \in EqId, eq_i \neq +\Delta r.e_i \mapsto False, \\
&\qquad \forall c_i \in CqId.c_i \mapsto infer(cq_i, insert\ r\ q), \\
&\qquad \forall d_i \in DqId.d_i \mapsto Unknown]
\end{aligned}
$$

Actions of the form $delete\ r\ q$ are handled similarly.

Theorem 3. $execSched^*$ is a safe approximation of $execSched$, given the above definitions of D^*, $conc$, $exec^*$ and $empty^*$,

The initial abstract database state now maps all identifiers to $Unknown$, apart from event queries that could not have triggered the initial rule and their corresponding delta relations, all of which are mapped to $False$.

Example 2. Consider again the rules defined in Example 1. The following is a trace of the abstract execution when rule 1 is triggered, assuming a perfect inference function ($cond(i)$ denotes the condition query of the ith rule):

Iter	Database state		Schedule
	$cond(1)$	$cond(2)$	
1	$Unknown$	$Unknown$	$[action(1)]$
2	$False$	$Unknown$	$[action(2)]$
3	$Unknown$	$Unknown$	$[action(1)]$

At iteration 2, rule 1's condition becomes $False$, since its action will always falsify $R \cap T$. At iteration 3 the execution of rule 2's action makes rule 1's condition $Unknown$ again (because only the overall truth values of conditions are recorded, so $infer$ cannot make use of the fact that $R \cap T$ was previously $False$). The third state is thus a repetition of the first, so $execSched^*$ is halted and possible rule non-termination is concluded if rule 1 is the first rule triggered.

Example 3. Suppose now we change the condition of rule 1 to be just $R \cap T$. The following trace is then obtained when rule 1 is the first rule triggered, again assuming a perfect inference function:

Iter	Database state		Schedule
	cond(1)	cond(2)	
1	$Unknown$	$Unknown$	$[action(1)]$
2	$False$	$Unknown$	$[action(2)]$
3	$False$	$Unknown$	$[action(1)]$

Changing rule 1's condition means that rule 2's action can no longer alter the truth value of this condition. Thus, $execSched^*$ terminates at iteration 3, since rule 1's condition is $False$, and definite rule termination is concluded if rule 1 is the first rule triggered.   □

The above $infer$ function uses only the syntax of conditions and actions to deduce new values for the event and condition queries. This motivates the development of our third abstraction which uses a more refined inferencing method and also more precise information about the initial abstract database state derived from the current concrete database state i.e. our third abstraction is useful for *dynamic* termination analysis.

6   Abstraction 3: An Abstraction for Dynamic Termination Analysis

As a third example application of our framework, we now show how to use the abstract execution semantics for dynamic, as opposed to static, termination analysis. This can give more precision because in a dynamic setting the initial database state can be described more accurately rather than just consisting of unknown information. This is reflected by the inclusion of the value $True$ in the abstract domain.

D^* is now the three-valued domain $\{True, Unknown, False\}$, where $\emptyset^* = False$. $conc(db^*)$ now returns the set of databases db such that

- the values assigned to the data identifiers and view identifiers are consistent,
- $db(i) = \emptyset$ if $db^*(i) = False$,
- $db(i) \neq \emptyset$ if $db^*(i) = True$.

$empty^*$ q db^* returns $True$ if $db^*(q)$ is $False$. Otherwise it returns $False$.

$exec^*$ calls an inference function $infer\_delt$ to compute the new truth value of the delta queries. This either (a) returns $True$ if a delta query was previously $True$ and the update to r can never cause deletions from it, or (b) returns $False$ if the delta query was previously $False$ and the update can never cause insertions to it, or (c) returns $Unknown$ otherwise. Such logic is implementable by incremental propagation techniques such as [20,11] which perform query rewriting to determine if insertions or deletions can have an effect on an expression, and has polynomial complexity. Once again, this is in general a non-effective method and the $infer\_delt$ function will sometimes have to return $Unknown$ instead of $True$ or $False$ in order to be safe.

The new value of the condition queries is similarly given by a function $infer\_con$. If the new value of the delta query for the update is $False$, then the value of the condition is unchanged. Otherwise, $infer\_con$ either (a) returns $True$ if the condition was previously $True$ and the update to r can never cause deletions from it, or (b) returns $False$ if the condition was previously $False$ and the update can never cause insertions to it, or (c) returns $Unknown$ otherwise. The new value of the event queries is given by a function $infer\_ev$ which sets the value of an event query to the value of its corresponding delta relation.

$exec^*$ $(insert$ r $q, db^*)$ infers new values for all the delta queries, sets the value of $+\Delta r$ to that of the delta query corresponding to the action $insert$ r q (this query is denoted by dq below), sets the value of $-\Delta r$ to $False$, sets the value of all other delta relations to $Unknown$, and infers new values for the view identifiers corresponding to event queries and condition queries:

$$exec^* \ (insert \ r \ q, db^*) \ =$$
$$let \ db_1^* = db^*[\forall d_i \in DqId.d_i \mapsto infer\_delt(db^* \ d_i, insert \ r)] \ in$$
$$let \ db_2^* = db_1^*[+\Delta r \mapsto db_1^* \ dq, -\Delta r \mapsto False,$$
$$\forall s \in BaseRel, s \neq r.(-\Delta s \mapsto Unknown, +\Delta s \mapsto Unknown)] \ in$$
$$db_2^*[\forall e_i \in EqId.e_i \mapsto infer\_ev(db_2^*),$$
$$\forall c_i \in CqId.c_i \mapsto infer\_con(db_2^* \ c_i, db_2^* \ dq, insert \ r)]$$

Actions of the form $delete$ r q are handled similarly.

Theorem 4. $execSched^*$ is a safe approximation of $execSched$, given the above definitions of D^*, $conc$, $exec^*$ and $empty^*$.

The initial abstract database state is the same as for Abstraction 2, except that (a) event queries that could have triggered the initial rule, and their associated delta relations, are now $True$ instead of $Unknown$, and (b) the values of the condition and delta queries will be one of $\{True, False, Unknown\}$ depending on the concrete run-time state when abstract execution is invoked.

Example 4. Consider again the rules 1 and 2 as originally defined in Example 1. For an initial database state in which rule 1's condition is known to be $True$ and rule 2's to be $False$, we obtain the following trace, assuming a perfect inference function:

Iter	Database state		Schedule
	$cond(1)$	$cond(2)$	
1	$True$	$False$	$[action(1)]$
2	$Unknown$	$False$	$[action(2)]$

Thus $execSched^*$ terminates at iteration 2 because of the falsity of rule 2's condition. If, however, this was initially $True$, the trace would be as shown below. The last state is now a repetition of the second and so possible rule non-termination is concluded:

Iter	Database state		Schedule
	$cond(1)$	$cond(2)$	
1	$True$	$True$	$[action(1)]$
2	$Unknown$	$True$	$[action(2)]$
3	$Unknown$	$True$	$[action(1)]$
4	$Unknown$	$True$	$[action(2)]$

7   Discussion and Comparison of Abstractions 1–3

The termination analysis directly provided by $execSched^*$ is for a given set of rules and a given initial schedule. For example, in Examples 1–4 the initial schedule consisted of the action of one of the rules. A broader question is, will a given set of rules terminate for *any* finite initial schedule? For reasons of space we cannot give an in-depth treatment of this issue here and will do so in a forthcoming paper. However, briefly, if all rules have Immediate coupling mode then it is sufficient to run $execSched^*$ on each possible singleton schedule i.e. on two schedules $[insert\ R\ I]$ and $[delete\ R\ I]$ for each base relation R in the database; $execSched^*$ terminates on all finite schedules if and only if it terminates on all singleton schedules. If some rules may have Deferred coupling mode, let $execSched^{*m}$ be $execSched^*$ modified so as to reinitialise the abstract database state at the start of each deferred sub-transaction; then, $execSched^*$ terminates on all finite schedules if $execSched^{*m}$ terminates on all singleton schedules. Unlike with Immediate-only coupling mode, this test is safe but may not be precise. Indeed, the general undecidability of termination of queue schedules [4] means that a precise test cannot be devised.

We now draw some comparisons between Abstractions 1–3. In general, none of them subsumes any of the others in the sense that all three can detect cases of definite termination that the other two cannot. Abst 3 is not directly comparable to Absts 1 and 2 since it will have available information about the initial database state. Abst 1 and 2 are distinct in that they use different satisfiability tests and so the resulting behaviour of $empty^*$ is different for each. With Abst 1, $exec_*$ maintains a precise record of the execution history (thus requirement (i) of Theorem 1 is actually an equality) and all the approximation is carried out by the $empty^*$ function. Limiting the abstract domain in order to be able to detect repeating states, as was done for Absts 2 and 3, moves the approximation functionality from $empty^*$ to $exec^*$.

We note that our framework provides a useful basis for determining the relative costs of different analysis methods, as these will only differ in their $exec^*$ and $empty^*$ functions. The table below summarises the worst case costs for Absts 1–3. The costs of $empty^*$ for Abst 1 and $exec^*$ for Abst 2 are both exponential in the size of the expressions input to them. However, the size of expressions input to the latter is constant, whereas for the former the expression size grows at each iteration. Thus, Abst 1 is likely to become more expensive in practice. We thus envisage Abst 2 being applied in scenarios where the rule set is very large (and hence a cheap analysis technique is required) whereas Abst 1 is more suitable for a deeper analysis of a small rule set. Its low computational cost makes Abst 3 suitable for run-time termination analysis.

Cost of Execution for N Rules		
Time		
Abst $empty^*$	$exec^*$	Space
1 Exponential	$\mathcal{O}(1)$	Unbounded
2 $\mathcal{O}(1)$	Exponential	$\mathcal{O}(2^N)$
3 $\mathcal{O}(1)$	Polynomial	$\mathcal{O}(3^N)$

8   Related Work

Previous methods of active rule analysis have often been closely linked to specific rule languages. In contrast, the framework that we have presented here does not assume any particular rule definition language. Our rule execution semantics can simulate most standard features of active database systems and prototypes. A detailed comparison is beyond the scope of this paper, but features such as SQL3's statement-level and row-level AFTER triggers [13], and variations of event consumption and rule coupling modes are either directly available or can be simulated within the framework. An alternative to the functional specification approach we have adopted would be to use $while$ or $while_N$ programs [18] for the concrete execution semantics, and derive abstract versions of these. The advantage of a functional approach is that parameters such as rule language and scheduling strategy are explicit. The advantage of $while$ programs would be easier identification of rule cycles and monotonicity of relations.

In [14], some general ideas regarding approximation in databases are discussed, motivated by the classification of methods for incompleteness of information. Other related work [9] looks at approximate query evaluation in the context of what precision is theoretically possible when approximating Datalog by conjunctive or first-order queries. Our work is complementary to [14,9] in that we have developed a framework designed specifically for active rule analysis and we have developed three example abstractions for a first-order language. These abstractions serve to illustrate the application and usefulness of our framework, as well as being useful heuristics for rule termination analysis in their own right.

Regarding other work in rule termination analysis, [12] proposed using satisfiability tests between pairs of rules to refine triggering graphs. This can be interpreted as a less sophisticated version of the *empty** function of our Abst 1 which does satisfiability testing for sequences of rule conditions and actions. Thus, in Example 1, if we only considered the relationship between pairs of rules, we would derive the information that rules 1 and 2 can mutually trigger each other. By itself, this information does not allow us to make any conclusions about termination behaviour. However, Example 1 demonstrated that by doing satisfiability testing on an accumulated "history" expression, it can be concluded that rule execution must terminate if rule 1 is the initially triggered rule.

Abst 2 does focus on pairwise relationships between rules and so is similar to graph-based analysis techniques based on the notions of triggering and activating rules [2,8,7,12]. Abst 2 is not identical to these, however, since in their pure form graph-based techniques do not "execute" the rule set and so have no notion of control flow. This can cause loss of precision for rule sets where the order of execution prohibits certain activation states of conditions. Extensions to these techniques are certainly possible to recognise such situations, but do not arise naturally from the specifications of the techniques themselves.

Using abstract interpretation for termination analysis of active rules was first considered in [3], for a theoretical rule language manipulating variables rather than relations and for a less expressive execution semantics. In [6] we refined that work to a full relational language and explored Abst 1 for the PFL active database system [21,19] i.e. assuming a specific `updateSched` function.

Of course an alternative to developing techniques for rule termination analysis is to design rule languages which *a priori* cannot give rise to non-terminating computations e.g [25,15,24]. However,the current SQL3 proposal [13] allows non-terminating rule sets to be defined. Thus we believe that developing techniques for rule termination analysis is both necessary and relevant to current practice.

9   Summary and Further Work

We have defined a framework for the abstract execution of active rules, and have illustrated its application by developing and showing the correctness of three techniques for rule termination analysis. Applying the framework is a matter of addressing points (i)-(vi) in Section 3 and proving that the two requirements of Theorem 1 hold. We envisage the framework as a useful general tool for the development, comparison and verification of abstraction-based analysis and optimisation methods for active databases. Of the three abstractions that we have presented here, the first provides a detailed static analysis, the second a cheaper static analysis and the third a cheap dynamic analysis.

We are currently implementing a rule analysis tool that supports our framework. Avenues for further work include: classifying other active rule analysis methods using our framework, and thereby verifying their correctness and domain of applicability; extending the framework to allow abstraction at different granularities of database objects, abstraction over schedules, and nondeterministic firings of rules with the same priority.

References

1. S. Abramsky and C. Hankin, editors. *Abstract Interpretation of Declarative Languages*. Ellis Horwood, 1987.
2. A. Aiken, J. Widom, and J. M. Hellerstein. Static analysis techniques for predicting the behavior of active database rules. *ACM TODS*, 20(1):3–41, 1995.
3. J. Bailey, L. Crnogorac, K. Ramamohanarao, and H. Søndergaard. Abstract interpretation of active rules and its use in termination analysis. In *Proc. ICDT'97, LNCS 1186*, pages 188–202, 1997.
4. J. Bailey, G. Dong, and K. Ramamohanarao. Structural issues in active rule systems. In *Proc. ICDT'97, LNCS 1186*, pages 203–214, 1997.
5. J. Bailey, G. Dong, and K. Ramamohanarao. Decidability and undecidability results for the termination problem of active database rules. In *Proc. PODS'98*, pages 264–273, 1998.
6. J. Bailey and A. Poulovassilis. Abstract interpretation for termination analysis in functional active databases. *Journal of Intelligent Information Systems*, 12(2/3):243–273, 1999.
7. E. Baralis, Ceri. S., and S. Paraboschi. Compile-time and runtime analysis of active behaviors. *IEEE Trans. on Knowledge and Data Engineering*, 10(3):353–370, 1998.
8. E. Baralis and J. Widom. An algebraic approach to rule analysis in expert database systems. In *Proc. VLDB'94*, pages 475–486, Santiago, Chile, 1994.
9. S. Chaudhuri and P. Kolaitis. Can datalog be approximated ? *Journal of Computer and System Sciences*, 55, 1997.
10. P. Cousot and R. Cousot. Abstract interpretation frameworks. *Journal of Logic Programming*, 13(2&3):103–179, 1992.
11. T. Griffin, L. Libkin, and H. Trickey. A correction to "Incremental recomputation of active relational expressions" by Qian and Wiederhold. *IEEE Trans. on Knowledge and Data Engineering*, 9(3):508–511, 1997.
12. A. Karadimce and S. Urban. Refined triggering graphs: A logic based approach to termination analysis in an active object-oriented database. In *Proc. 12th ICDE*, pages 384–391, 1996.
13. K. Kulkarni, N. Mattos, and R. Cochrane. Active database features in SQL3. In [17].
14. L. Libkin. Approximation in databases. In *Proc. ICDT'95*, pages 411–424, 1995.
15. B. Ludäscher, U. Hamann, and G. Lausen. A logical framework for active rules. In *Proc. 7th International Conference on Management of Data*, Pune, India, 1995.
16. K. Marriott, H. Søndergaard, and N. D. Jones. Denotational abstract interpretation of logic programs. *ACM TOPLAS*, 16(3):607–648, 1994.

17. N. Paton, editor. *Active Rules in Database Systems*. Springer-Verlag, 1999.
18. P. Picouet and V. Vianu. Semantics and expressiveness issues in active databases. In *Proc. PODS'95*, pages 126–138, 1995.
19. A. Poulovassilis, S. Reddi, and C. Small. A formal semantics for an active functional DBPL. *Journal of Intelligent Information Systems (special issue on Active Database Systems)*, 7(2):151–172, 1996.
20. X. Qian and G. Wiederhold. Incremental recomputation of active relational expressions. *IEEE Trans. on Knowledge and Data Engineering*, 3(3):337–341, 1991.
21. S. Reddi, A. Poulovassilis, and C. Small. Extending a functional DBPL with ECA-rules. In *Proc. RIDS'95*, pages 101–115, 1995.
22. Y. Sagiv and M. Yannakakis. Equivalences among relational expressions with the union and difference operators. *Journal of the ACM*, 27(4):633–655, 1980.
23. D. A. Schmidt. *Denotational Semantics*. Allyn and Bacon, 1986.
24. C. Zaniolo. Active database rules with transaction-conscious stable-model semantics. In *Proc. DOOD'95*, pages 55–72, 1995.
25. Y. Zhou and M. Hsu. A theory for rule triggering systems. In *Proc. EDBT'90, LNCS 416* pages 407–422, 1990.

On the Difference between Navigating Semi-structured Data and Querying It

Gösta Grahne[1] and Laks V. S. Lakshmanan[1,2]

[1] Department of Computer Science, Concordia University
Montreal, Canada, H3G 1M8
grahne,laks@cs.concordia.ca
[2] Computer Science and Engineering Department
I.I.T. Powai, Mumbai 400076

1 Introduction

Currently, there is tremendous interest in semi-structured (SS) data management. This is spurred by data sources, such as the ACeDB [29], that are inherently less rigidly structured than traditional DBMS, by WWW documents where no hard rules or constraints are imposed and "anything goes," and by integration of information coming from disparate sources exhibiting considerable differences in the way they structure information. Significant strides have been made in the development of data models and query languages [2,11,17,6,7], and to some extent, the theory of queries on semi-structured data [1,23,3,13,9]. The OEM model of the Stanford TSIMMIS project [2] (equivalently, its variant, independently developed at U. Penn. [11]) has emerged as the de facto standard model for semi-structured data. OEM is a light-weight object model, which unlike the ODMG model that it extends, does not impose the latter's rigid type constraints. Both OEM and the Penn model essentially correspond to labeled digraphs. A main theme emerging from the popular query languages such as Lorel [2], UnQL [11], StruQL [17], WebOQL [6], and the Ulixes/Penelope pair of the ADM model [7], is that *navigation* is considered an integral and essential part of querying. Indeed, given the lack of rigid schema of semi-structured data, navigation brings many benefits, including the ability to retrieve data regardless of the depth at which it resides in a tree (e.g., see [4]). This is achieved with programming primitives such as regular path expressions and wildcards. A second, somewhat subtle, aspect of the emerging trend is that query expressions are often dependent on the particular *instance* they are applied to. This is not surprising, given the lack of rigid structure and the absence of the notion of a predefined schema for semi-structured data. In fact, it has been argued [4] that it is unreasonable to impose a predefined schema.

There are two problems with the current state of affairs. First, while classical database theory tells us that queries are computable and generic functions from database instances over a predefined schema to (say) relations over another schema, the state-of-the-art theory of semi-structured databases (SSDB) does not exactly pin down the input/output type of queries. Indeed, it is unclear what it *means* to query SSDBs in a formal sense. Second, the notion of

R. Connor and A. Mendelzon (Eds.): DBPL'99, LNCS 1949, pp. 271–296, 2000.

genericity [16] plays a pivotal role in the theory of queries. We contend that this notion has not been satisfactorily addressed for semi-structured data. Genericity says that the order of columns or rows in a relation is irrelevant for purposes of querying. In its purest form, it also says that the domain values are uninterpreted. One may argue that the structure present in a SSDB, in the form of parent-child relationships and/or left-right ordering, carries inherent information, that should be regarded on a par with the data for purposes of querying. However, drawing lessons from the analogy to the classical notion of genericity, it stands to reason to say that if the same underlying data in one SSDB is modeled differently using different structure in a second SSDB, the two SSDBs should be insensitive to the difference in representation between the two SSDBs. We call this property *representation independence*. These notions are made precise in Section 3. Here we give some examples to illustrate the underlying intuition. We use the OEM model as a representative SS data model and the fragment of the StruQL language presented in [18] as a representative query language for convenience and conciseness. Our observations hold for any of the prominent models/query languages mentioned above.

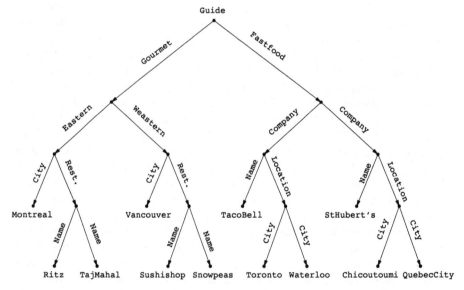

Fig. 1. A Semi-structured Restaurant Guide

Consider the OEM SSDB in Figure 1, showing (partial) details about restaurants in Canada. It shows information about gourmet and fastfood restaurants and has some heterogeneity in the way the information is represented. This could be the result of integration of information from different sources. Now, consider the query "find pairs of cities and restaurant names in them." One way to express this query in the StruQL fragment is to use two rules:

$r_1: q(X, Y) \longleftarrow$ Guide (Gourmet.*) Z, Z (City) X, Z (*.Name) Y.
$r_2: q(X, Y) \longleftarrow$ Guide (Fastfood.*) Z, Z (Name) Y, Z (*.City) X.

Here, X, Y, Z are node variables, and Guide is the entry point (for the root). To write this query expression, one needs to *know* that gourmet restaurants are organized with a different structure than the fastfood ones. If all information had been organized following the gourmet structure, we would have written the query using just rule r_1. If this rule were applied to an "equivalent" database storing the same information using the fastfood structure (for which r_2 would be the right rule) would *not* yield the expected answer. Thus, intuitively, none of these expressions is representation independent. One way out of this might be to write the one-rule expression

$r_3: q(X, Y) \longleftarrow$ Guide (*) Z, Z (*.City) X, Z (*.Name) Y.

Since the wildcard * can be mapped to the empty label, this seems to be able to find all city/restaurant pairs in a uniform way, independent of the structural differences. Unfortunately, this does not work (when r_3 is applied to the database of Figure 1: one of the valid substitutions would map Z to the left child of the root, which allows the last two path expressions in the body of r_3 to be mapped to the paths corresponding to the city Montreal and the restaurant Sushishop. This produces the pair (Montreal, Sushishop), an obviously incorrect answer. It is not clear whether one can write a fixed query expression in this language (or, for that matter, in any of the languages mentioned above) that can correctly find all city/restaurant pairs in a representation independent way.[1]

A possible objection against representation independence would be the following. Consider two nested relational databases $\mathcal{I}$ and $\mathcal{J}$ containing "equivalent" information on restaurants and cities, where $\mathcal{I}$ groups the information by city, whereas $\mathcal{J}$ groups by restaurant names. A query such as "find all city/restaurant pairs in flat form" would require two different expressions against $\mathcal{I}$ and $\mathcal{J}$ in nested relational algebra. If this is acceptable, isn't it unreasonable to impose the requirement of representation independence on SSDB query languages? The difference is that the nested relational model, like all traditional data models, has a well-defined notion of a predefined schema. Thus, the user can be reasonably expected to know the schema in full, which includes, among other things, structural information such as nesting order. Thus, we can live with representation dependence. By contrast, as argued by Abiteboul [4], it is unreasonable to assume a predefined schema or a complete structural/representational knowledge on the part of the user, for SSDBs. *In this context, we believe that representation independence is not only reasonable, but is an extremely important requirement for a SSDB query language to be practical.* We can trace the representation dependent nature of most prominent languages to their heavy reliance on navigation (e.g., via path expressions). Following Ullman [30], we contend that a high-level query language should enable the user to write queries without having to worry about navigational details.

---

[1] It is even less obvious whether representation independent expressions exist in these languages for *all* queries, since the issue is not addressed in those papers.

Another source of bewilderment in writing SSDB queries is that the propositions that are supposed to be expressed by a database are not clearly captured by existing SS data models, as these models are largely syntactic. In a traditional model like the relational model, the facts are the tuples in the various relations. Similarly, the fact structure for other traditional models is precisely captured by the data model. In the case of SSDBs, we note from the literature that the facts can sometimes be in the paths [28,6] and sometimes in certain subtrees (as in the example above; also see [17,11]). The consequence of the model not capturing the fact structure is that the burden of finding it is shifted to the query expressions the user has to write. Of course, here a possible objection would claim that there *is* no fact structure – that is why the database is "semi-structured." Since there is no fact structure, navigation-based querying is as good as any method. But if the user is able to navigate, he/she has to know the "schema" and since the "schema" is unknown a *priori*, the user must have seen the data in order to have seen the "schema." In this case, a navigational query seems to offer little additional advantage over further browsing by the user. And if the "schema", however primitive, is known a *priori*, then the database *does* express some propositions after all.

Our work was motivated by the following questions. Can we make a self-describing light-weight model such as OEM also capture the fact structure in a SSDB? What is an appropriate notion of genericity, and what is an appropriate definition of a query for SSDBs, in a formal sense? Can we design SSDB query languages that are representation independent and are "generic?" These are crucial questions that need to be answered before useful query languages can be designed and implemented, before the goal of *repository independence* [21] can be achieved, and before advances in areas such as expressive power and completeness can be made. Our main contributions can be summarized as follows:

1. We formalize the notion of *representation independence* and show that it is an important property for a SSDB query language. We also introduce a notion of *representation preservation* which intuitively says that queries should perturb existing structure as little as possible[2].
2. We take the core intuitions behind the OEM model and extend the model with a few minor amendments, while preserving its light-weight nature. We make precise the fact structure of a SSDB and give a formal definition of the *contents* of a SSDB.
3. We define the concept of *genericity* for SSDB's. Roughly speaking, genericity means that queries should be representation independent and should not interpret domain values. We give two possible notions of schema – a *conservative* predefined schema similar in spirit to that of traditional data models, and a *liberal* schema, which is essentially a finite set of attributes, not known in advance. We also extend the classical notion of BP-completeness [27,8] to the SSDB setting.

---

[2] This is not an argument against restructuring. On the contrary, we contend that restructuring should happen by design; not "accidentally" as a result of querying.

4. We define a calculus called *component calculus* (CC) and an algebra called *component algebra* (CA) and show that:
   (a) CC and CA are equivalent in expressive power.
   (b) CC is representation independent but not representation preserving, while CA is both.
   (c) CC and CA are BP-complete in our extended sense.
   (d) In comparison of CC with TRC$^\perp$, an extension of classical tuple relational calculus (TRC) to accommodate inapplicable nulls, it turns out that there are queries expressible in CC for which there is no equivalent expression in TRC$^\perp$ whose size is polynomially bounded in the size of the conservative schema. When the schema is liberal, there are queries expressible in CC which have no equivalent expressions in TRC$^\perp$.

2 Semi-structured Databases

2.1 Schema and Instance

Let $\mathcal{N}$, $\mathcal{A}$, and $\mathcal{V}$ be countable pairwise disjoint sets of *nodes* $\{v, u, w, u_i, v_j, \ldots\}$, *attribute names* $\{A_1, \ldots A_n, \ldots\}$, and *values* $\{a, b, c, \ldots\}$. In general, we may know the "schema" of a semi-structured database either completely, partially, or not at all. However, in practice, when dealing with such databases, based on the application domain, it is sometimes reasonable to assume we at least know what kind of attributes to expect, if not how/where to find them. To reflect this, we use two alternative notions of schema in this paper. In the most general scenario, the *schema* of a semi-structured database can be completely instance dependent, and thus can potentially be any finite subset of $\mathcal{A}$, which is *not* known a priori. This is called the *liberal schema*, and is perhaps the most realistic notion. A second, restrictive notion is that of a *conservative schema*, which is a predetermined finite subset $\mathbf{A} \subset \mathcal{A}$ of attributes. This notion may be appropriate when dealing with highly regular databases such as, e.g., bibtex databases (possibly in a fixed source such as [25]), set of machine generated homepages of employees in an organization, etc.

A *database tree* is a 5-tuple $T = \langle V, E, attr, val, label \rangle$, such that:

- $V \subset \mathcal{N}$ is a finite set of *nodes*.
- $E \subseteq V \times V$, is a set of edges such that the graph (V, E) is a rooted tree.
- $attr : V \rightarrow \mathcal{A}$ is a partial function that maps each node $v \in V$ to its attribute $attr(v)$. When $attr(v)$ is undefined, we write $attr(v) = \perp$. We refer to a node u such that $attr(u) = \perp$ as a *null node*.
- $val : V \rightarrow \mathcal{V}$ is a partial function that maps each node $v \in V$ to its value $val(v)$. When $val(v)$ is undefined, we write $val(v) = \perp$. We assume that if $attr(v) = \perp$, then necessarily $val(v) = \perp$.
- $label : V \rightarrow 2^{\{\oplus, \ominus\}}$ maps each node to a subset of labels from $\{\oplus, \ominus\}$.

Sometimes we will assume that the trees are ordered. For this we use a function ω that associates with each node in V a total order on its outgoing edges (see e.g. Beeri and Milo [9]). In essence then, a database tree is an ordered rooted tree whose nodes come with an attribute-value pair $(A : a)$, together with optional labels $\oplus, \ominus$. Either the value a, or both the attribute A and the value a could be null. The labels $\ominus, \oplus$ are called blockers, and they enable the query processor in not mixing up associations between different attribute-value pairs, thus capturing the inherent fact structure. Conceptually, this corresponds to transferring the navigational knowledge imposed on the user by navigational languages, to the data model and the source that implements it. Figure 2 shows three database trees.

Informally, a *fact* of a database tree T is any set $\{(A_1 : a_1), \ldots, (A_n : a_n)\}$ of attribute-value pairs from nodes in a subtree of T, such that no attribute is repeated and the subtree does not cross any of the blockers $\ominus$, or $\oplus$. Some of the values a_i might be the null $\perp$. Intuitively, fact $\{(A_1 : a_1), \ldots, (A_n : a_n)\}$ represents the tuple $[A_1 : a_1, \ldots, A_n : a_n]$. For instance, in Figure 2, the tree T_1 contains the facts $\{(A : a), (B : b), (C : \perp), (D : \perp)\}$ and $\{(A : a'), (B : b'), (D : \perp)\}$, while T_2 contains the facts $\{(A : a), (B : b), (E : \perp)\}$ and $\{(A : a'), (B : b'), (C : \perp)\}$. Note that the fact $\{(A : a), (B : b), (C : \perp), (D : \perp)\}$ in T_1 is "subsumed" by the fact $\{(A : a), (B : b)\}$. Tree T_3 in Figure 2 contains the facts $\{(A' : b), (B' : a), (F : \perp)\}$ and $\{(A' : b'), (B' : a'), (F : \perp)\}$. Intuitively, all three trees are "equivalent" in terms of the set of facts they represent. This intuition is captured in Definition 1, where "content equivalence" captures equivalence w.r.t. the underlying set of facts, and the other notions of equivalence there capture the various dissimilarities among the tree of Figure 2.

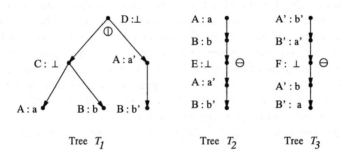

Tree T_1 Tree T_2 Tree T_3

Fig. 2. Three Database Trees

We can see from the example that $\oplus$ may be regarded as a kind of "light-weight" set node.[3] The role of $\ominus$ is to act as a scoping boundary for attribute names. For instance, if Name denotes the name of an employee, and the children's names of the employee are encoded in a subtree, we can use the blocker $\ominus$ at the root of the subtree to bound the scope of the two different occurences of the attribute Name. A tree encoding the facts that Joe is an employee with address

---

[3] Notice that the model permits heterogeneous sets in that different tuples can have different sets of attributes.

Westmount, and that he has two children, Sam and Brigitte, aged 5 and 3 resp. is shown in Figure 3. The nodes with ⊥ as values can be thought of as encoding objects. Thus EMP is an object, and Children is a subobject of Emp. Thus, intuitively, use of the blocker ⊖ can be viewed as declaring a new object (corresponding to the subtree) and a reference to the subobject in the parent object.

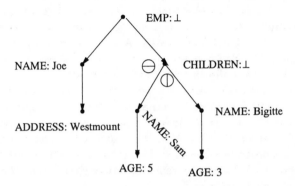

Fig. 3. The use of Blockers

A semi-structured *database instance* (SSDB) is a finite sequence of database trees $\mathcal{I} = \langle T_1, \ldots, T_n \rangle$. An example database appears in Figure 4 in Section 3.3. When we consider instances of a predefined schema **A**, we will assume that the range of the function *attr* is included in **A**. The *active domain* of a SSDB $\mathcal{I}$, denoted $adom(\mathcal{I})$, is the set of all values associated with nodes in $\mathcal{I}$'s trees.

2.2   Contents of Databases

It is clear that the same information can be represented as a semi-structured database in several "equivalent" ways. In this section, we formalize four notions of equivalence between SSDBs. Below, we informally explain these notions, first between trees.

- *Content equivalence*: Although two trees might have different "looks" they nevertheless represent the same "generic" information, where attribute names and constants are not interpreted.
- *Subsumption equivalence* (special case of content equivalence): The two trees, in addition, use the same constant and attribute names in the same contexts.
- *Partial isomorphism equivalence*: Full isomrphism would mean that the trees are isomorphic as labeled ordered trees and have the same generic information represented in structurally similar ways. However, since we will choose to disregard nodes with null values ⊥ in the isomorphism, we work with *partial isomorphism*.

– *Partial identity* (special case of partial isomorphism equivalence): The trees are identical, except for nodes with null values $\perp$.

We next formalize these notions.

A *path* in a database tree T, is a sequence $v_1, v_2, \ldots, v_k$ of nodes related through $E \cup E^{-1}$, subject to the following restrictions: (i) whenever v_i, v_j, v_m are three consecutive nodes on the path, and $(v_i, v_j) \in E^{-1}$ and $(v_j, v_m) \in E$, then $\oplus \notin label(v_j)$, and (ii) if v_i, v_j, v_m are three consecutive nodes on the path, and $(v_i, v_j), (v_j, v_m) \in E$, then $\ominus \notin label(v_j)$. In tree T_1, Figure 2, the sequences of nodes corresponding to $(A : a), (C : \perp), (B : b)$ and that corresponding to $(D : \perp), (C : \perp), (A : a)$ are both paths. A path is *simple* provided no node repeats along the path. Nodes v and w are *connected* if there is a simple path between them. A set of nodes is connected if every pair of nodes in the set is connected (by a simple path). A *connected component* (*component*, for short) of a tree T is a subtree of T induced by a maximal connected subset of nodes of T. Note that unlike in classical graph theory, two components can overlap. The set of attribute-value pairs associated with the nodes of any component of T, such that no attribute repeats, is a *fact* in T. More than one fact may thus come from the same component (if it contains repeated attributes). Thus, the information content of T is the set of facts in T.

Let $T = \langle V, E, attr, val, label \rangle$ and $T' = \langle V', E', attr', val', label' \rangle$ be database trees. and let $U = \{v \in V : val(v) \neq \perp\}$. A mapping $h : U \to V'$ is called a *tree morphism* if for all nodes v_i and v_j in U, the following holds: (i) if $attr(v_i) = attr(v_j)$ then $attr'(h(v_i)) = attr'(h(v_j))$; (ii) if $val(v_i) = val(v_j)$ then $val'(h(v_i)) = val'(h(v_j))$. We sometimes denote a tree morphism as $h : T \to T'$. Basically, tree morphisms are consistent w.r.t. the attributes and values associated with nodes.

Let $\mathcal{A}(T)$ (resp., $\mathcal{V}(T)$) denote the set of attribute names (resp., values) of the nodes in T. Then a tree morphism $h : T \to T'$ induces the (partial) attribute mapping $h_{attr} : \mathcal{A}(T) \to \mathcal{A}(T')$, defined as $h_{attr}(A) = attr'(h(v))$, where v is any node in V for which $attr(v) = A$. Similarly, it induces a value mapping $h_{val} : \mathcal{V}(T) \to \mathcal{V}(T')$, defined as $h_{val}(a) = val'(h(v))$, where v is any node in V for which $val(v) = a$. Clearly, these mappings are well defined.

Definition 1. A tree morphism $h : T \to T'$ is called a *content embedding* if the following conditions hold: (i) the attribute mapping h_{attr} induced by h is injective; (ii) the value mapping h_{val} induced by h is injective; (iii) whenever v_i and v_j are connected in T, then $h(v_i)$ and $h(v_j)$ are connected in T'. □

If there is a content embedding from T to T', we say that T is *content-homomorphic* to T' and write $T \leq_{\text{cont}} T'$. If T and T' are content-homomorphic to each other, we say they are *content equivalent*, i.e. $T \equiv_{\text{cont}} T'$ iff $T \leq_{\text{cont}} T'$ and $T' \leq_{\text{cont}} T$. We will also be interested in *special* content embeddings h, which are content embeddings for which the induced mappings h_{attr} and h_{val} are identity mappings. In case there is a content embedding from T to T' via a special mapping $h : T \to T'$, we say that T is *subsumed* by T' and write $T \leq_{\text{sub}} T'$. If T

and T' are subsumed by each other, we say they are *subsumption equivalent*, i.e. $T \equiv_{\text{sub}} T'$ iff $T \leq_{\text{sub}} T'$ and $T' \leq_{\text{sub}} T$.

For nodes u, v in a tree T, u *preorder precedes* v provided u comes before v in the preorder enumeration of T's nodes. It is extended to a SSDB instance $\mathcal{I}$ in the obvious way: u preorder precedes v whenever both come from the same tree and the above condition holds, or u (v) comes from T_i (T_j) and T_i comes before T_j in the standard enumeration of the trees in $\mathcal{I}$.

The next notion we introduce is partial isomorphism equivalence. Thereto, we say that a tree morphism $h : T \rightarrow T'$ is a *tree embedding*, if it is a content embedding and further, whenever both u and v have non-null values, if $(u, v) \in E$, then $(h(u), h(v)) \in E'$, and if u preorder preserves v in T, then $h(u)$ preorder precedes $h(v)$ in T'. If there is a tree embedding from T to T' we write $T \leq_{\text{piso}} T'$, since, loosely speaking, a subtree of T is isomorphic to a subtree of T'. If both $T \leq_{\text{piso}} T'$ and $T' \leq_{\text{piso}} T$, then T and T' are *partial isomorphism equivalent*, denoted $T \equiv_{\text{piso}} T'$. The final notion is partial identity. Suppose there is a tree embedding h from T to T', such that h is special. Then, informally speaking, the non-null portion of T is identical to a subtree of T', so we write $T \leq_{\text{pid}} T'$. If both $T \leq_{\text{pid}} T'$ and $T' \leq_{\text{pid}} T$, then T and T' are *partially identical*, denoted $T \equiv_{\text{pid}} T'$. The various notions of homomorphism are related as follows.

Lemma 1. (1) If $T \leq_{\text{sub}} T'$ then $T \leq_{\text{cont}} T'$. (2) If $T \leq_{\text{pid}} T'$ then $T \leq_{\text{piso}} T'$. (3) If $T \leq_{\text{piso}} T'$ then $T \leq_{\text{cont}} T'$. (4) None of the reverse implications holds.

These notions of equivalence are illustrated in Figure 2 from Section 2.1. For the trees in the figure, we have $T_1 \equiv_{\text{sub}} T_2$ and $T_1 \equiv_{\text{cont}} T_3$. We also have $T_2 \equiv_{\text{piso}} T_3$. Clearly $T_1 \not\equiv_{\text{piso}} T_3$.

Finally, let $\leq_*$ denote any of the notions of embedding above. For two database instances $\mathcal{I}, \mathcal{J}$, we define $\mathcal{I} \leq_* \mathcal{J}$ provided for all trees $T \in \mathcal{I}$, there is a tree $T' \in \mathcal{J}$ such that $T \leq_* T'$. $\mathcal{I} \equiv_* \mathcal{J}$ iff $\mathcal{I} \leq_* \mathcal{J}$ and $\mathcal{J} \leq_* \mathcal{I}$.

In Section 3.2, in defining operators of our algebra, we will often need to create identical copies of trees or components. An *identical copy* of a database tree T is another database tree T' such that there is a special embedding $h : T \rightarrow T'$ which is 1-1 and onto on the nodes of T, and preserves node labels. The following theorem characterizes the complexity of checking the different notions of embedding.

Theorem 1. Deciding whether $T \leq_{\text{cont}} T'$ is NP-complete. Deciding whether $\mathcal{I} \equiv_* \mathcal{J}$ can be done in PTIME for $\equiv_* \in \{\equiv_{\text{piso}}, \equiv_{\text{sub}}, \equiv_{\text{pid}}\}$.

3   Querying Semi-structured Databases

In the classical setting of relational databases, queries are defined as computable functions from database instances of a given schema to relations over another given schema, that are generic, in the sense of commuting with database isomorphisms. For SSDBs, a complication arises because instances do not come with a predefined schema in general. The "right" *definition* of queries depends

on what one perceives as the information content of a SSDB. E.g., consider
Figure 4 (Section 3.3), which shows two database trees T_1 and T_2 representing
the resources and industries in various Canadian provinces and cities. In T_1,
one can argue that the fact that provinces come below regions is significant. A
problem with this position, however is that a different presentation of the information in Figure 4 might simply list the information for each province in the
form of a set of tuples over region, province, capital, population, and resource.
In a SSDB context, it is unreasonable to assume complete user knowledge of the
exact structural organization of information. We postulate that the right level
of abstraction of information content in a SSDB is the set of associations between various attribute values as captured by the paths connecting them in the
SSDB. In keeping with this, queries should not distinguish between two SSDBs
that are considered equivalent w.r.t. their contents. Let $\mathcal{I}$ be any SSDB, and π
any permutation on its active domain $adom(\mathcal{I})$. Then we extend π to $\mathcal{I}$ in the
obvious manner: $\pi(\mathcal{I})$ is the database forest obtained by replacing all non-null
attribute values a by $\pi(a)$. Then we have

Definition 2. A *query* is a computable function Q from the set of SSDBs to the
set of database trees such that: (i) Q is invariant under permutations of the active
domain, i.e. for any instance $\mathcal{I}$ and any permutation π on its active domain,
$Q(\pi(\mathcal{I})) \equiv_{\mathrm{pid}} \pi(Q(\mathcal{I}))$; and (ii) whenever $\mathcal{I} \equiv_{\mathrm{cont}} \mathcal{J}$, then $Q(\mathcal{I}) \equiv_{\mathrm{cont}} Q(\mathcal{J})$.   □

As illustrated in Section 1, one of the desirable properties for a query language
for SSDBs is the "robustness" with which it can accommodate modifications
to the structural presentation of data while the contents are left intact. More
formally, we have

Definition 3. A query language $\mathcal{L}$ for SSDBs is *representation independent* (RI)
provided for every expression E in $\mathcal{L}$, and for any two SSDBs $\mathcal{I}$ and $\mathcal{J}$, $\mathcal{I} \equiv_{\mathrm{cont}} \mathcal{J}$
implies $E(\mathcal{I}) \equiv_{\mathrm{cont}} E(\mathcal{J})$.[4]   □

A user of a representation independent query language can remain oblivious
to differences in the actual representation of a given piece of information. None
of the langauges surveyed in Section 1 is representation independent.

A second desirable property of query languages is representation preservation. Intuitively, it means the expressions in the language should perturb the
original structure present among elements of the output, *as little as possible*.
We believe queries expressed in a representation preserving language, requiring
minimal structural alterations, will lead to efficient implementation. We distinguish between querying and restructuring in the sense of [20] and postulate that
the spirit of pure querying is captured by representation preservation.

Definition 4. A query language $\mathcal{L}$ is *representation preserving* (RP) provided
for every expression E in $\mathcal{L}$, and for every instance $\mathcal{I}$, there is a partial isomorphic
embedding of $E(\mathcal{I})$ into $\mathcal{I}$, that is, $E(\mathcal{I}) \leq_{\mathrm{piso}} \mathcal{I}$.   □

---

[4] Note that this is stronger than saying that for every query Q expressible in $\mathcal{L}$, there
is an expression E in $\mathcal{L}$ that computes Q and returns equivalent answers on content
equivalent databases.

3.1   Component Calculus

In our model for semi-structured data, we regard the connected components of the database forest as the basic information carrying units which define the fact structure of the database. In the component calculus, we give primacy to these components, by letting the variables range over them. Let $\mathbf{V}$ be a countable set $\{s, t, \ldots\}$ of *component variables*, or variables for short. To accommodate inapplicable nulls which are natural in SSDBs, following Manna [22], we use two kinds of equalities, namely $=$ and $\doteq$. An *atom* of component calculus is an expression of the form[5] $t.A = a$, $t.A \doteq a$, $t.A = \bot$, $t.A = s.B$, $t.A \doteq s.B$, $t \sqsubseteq s$, $t \sqsubseteq_{\bar{A}} s$, $t[a]$, or $T(t)$, where T is a tree, t and s are variables, A and B are attribute names, and a is a domain value. The set of all *well-formed formulas* of component calculus is formed by closing the atoms under $\wedge$, $\neg$, and $\exists$ in the usual way. We will use the shorthands: $t.A \neq a$ for $\neg(t.A = a)$, $t.A \not\doteq a$ for $\neg(t.A \doteq a)$, etc. We will use the special abbreviation $t[A]$ for $t.A \neq \bot$, which in turn abbreviates $\neg(t.A \doteq \bot)$.

Throughout the paper, when we construct new trees, by a "new" node, we mean a node that appears nowhere else before. A tree is said to be *multiple-free* w.r.t. a set of attributes X if no attribute in X occurs more than once in T. It is multiple-free if no attribute occurs more than once. Let T be a tree. By the *universe of* T we mean the set of all multiple-free line trees, constructed in such a way that each attribute-value pair in it is equal to some attribute-value pair in T, and the line trees do not contain null nodes. The notion of universe is extended in the obvious way to a database instance $\mathcal{I}$. Furhtermore, let φ be a formula in component calculus, and $\mathcal{I}$ and instance. Then the universe of $(\mathcal{I}, \varphi)$ is defined as the universe of $\mathcal{I}$ except that it additionally has components obtained as folllows: for each line tree τ in the universe of $\mathcal{I}$, rename any subset of attributes of τ with distinct attributes appearing in φ.

Let θ be a valuation into $\mathcal{I}$, i.e. a mapping from the variable set $\mathbf{V}$ to the universe of $\mathcal{I}$. We now define *satisfaction* of a component calculus formula φ by a database $\mathcal{I}$ under a valuation θ, in symbols $\mathcal{I} \models \varphi\theta$.

$\mathcal{I} \models (t.A = a)\theta$, if $attr(v) = A$ and $val(v) = a$, for some node v in $\theta(t)$.

$\mathcal{I} \models (t.A = s.B)\theta$, if $attr(u) = A$, $attr(v) = B$, $val(u)$ and $val(v)$ are defined, and $val(u) = val(v)$, for some nodes u in $\theta(t)$ and v in $\theta(s)$.

$\mathcal{I} \models (t.A \doteq \alpha)\theta$, if $attr(v) = A$, and either $val(v)$ is defined, α is a domain value, and $val(v) = \alpha$, or $val(v)$ is undefined and α is $\bot$, for some node v in $\theta(t)$.

$\mathcal{I} \models (t.A \doteq s.B)\theta$, if $attr(u) = A$, $attr(v) = B$, and either $val(u)$ and $val(v)$ are defined, and $val(u) = val(v)$, or $val(u)$ and $val(v)$ are both undefined, for some nodes u in $\theta(t)$ and v in $\theta(s)$.

$\mathcal{I} \models (t[a])\theta$, if $val(v) = a$, for some node v in $\theta(t)$.

$\mathcal{I} \models (t \sqsubseteq s)\theta$, if $\theta(t) \leq_{\text{sub}} \theta(s)$.

---

[5] For expressive power issues, following standard practice, we focus attention on the fragment of CC without the atoms $t.A = a$ and $t.A \doteq a$.

$\mathcal{I} \models (t \sqsubseteq_{\bar{A}} s)\theta$, if $\tau \leq_{\mathrm{sub}} \theta(s)$, where τ is a $\leq_{\mathrm{sub}}$-maximal component without any occurences of attribute A, such that $\tau \leq_{\mathrm{sub}} \theta(t)$.

$\mathcal{I} \models (T(t))\theta$, if $\theta(t) \equiv_{\mathrm{sub}} C$ for some component C of T.

The semantics of $\wedge$ and $\neg$ is as usual, and for quantification we need to say that $\theta(t/\tau)$ is the valuation θ except that it maps the variable t to the line tree τ in the universe of $(\mathcal{I}, \varphi)$. Then

$$\mathcal{I} \models (\exists t\varphi)\theta, \text{ if } \mathcal{I} \models \varphi\theta(t/\tau), \text{ for some } \tau \text{ in the universe of } (\mathcal{I}, \varphi).$$

It will be convenient to work with finite subuniverses of a pair $(T, varphi)$. Let k be a natural number. Then the *k-universe* of (T, φ) is the subuniverse of (T, φ) consisting of line trees with at most k nodes. The definition of the k-universe of the pair $(\mathcal{I}, \varphi)$ for an instance $\mathcal{I}$ is similar.

A *component calculus query expression* E is an expression of the form $(t|\varphi(t))$, where $\varphi(t)$ is a component calculus formula with t as its only free variable. Let the length (in number of symbols) of E be k. When applied to an instance $\mathcal{I}$, E defines a tree $E(\mathcal{I})$ with a "new" node v as its root, where $attr(v) = \bot$ $val(v) = \bot$, and $label(v) = \textcircled{1}$. The subtrees of the root are determined as follows: Let $\theta_1, \ldots, \theta_q$ be all assignments into the k-universe of $\mathcal{I}$ such that for $i \in [1, q]$, $\mathcal{I} \models \varphi(t)\theta_i$. Now take the forest $\{\theta_i(t)\}_{i=1}^q$ and reduce this forest under $\leq_{\mathrm{sub}}$. If there are several equivalent $\leq_{\mathrm{sub}}$-minimal line trees, choose one representative of each equivalence class, say the line tree that has the smaller attributes (in some standard enumeration of the attributes) higher up. This will yield a subsumption equivalent forest $\{T_1, \ldots, T_p\}, p \leq q$. The root then has subtrees $T_1, \ldots T_p$. Sample queries can be found in Section 3.3.

3.2   The Component Algebra

In this section, we define an algebra called the *component algebra* (CA), whose expressions map SSDBs to database trees. This is achieved by extending the classical relational operators to the SSDB setting. We shall find it convenient to have the notion of a canonical form an instance. First we recall that a *null node* is a node u where both $attr(u)$ and $val(u)$ equal $\bot$. A database instance $\mathcal{I}$ is in *canonical form* if every node in $\mathcal{I}$ that has a blocker is a null node. It turns out that every instance $\mathcal{I}$ can be easily converted into an "equivalent" instance that is in canonical form, as follows. (1) For every non-null node u with attribute-value pair $A : a$ [6] and a horisontal blocker, replace u with three nodes x, y, z such that: (i) x and z both have the attribute-value pair $A : a$ associated with them, while y is a null node; (ii) the parent of u becomes the parent of x, while every child of u becomes a child of z; (iii) y gets a horisontal blocker, is the only child of x, and is the parent of z; and (iv) if u *additionally* had a vertical blocker, then z gets a vertical blocker. (2) For every non-null node u with attribute-value pair $A : a$ and a vertical blocker, let $v_1, \ldots, v_n$ be the children of u. Then replace u with $n + 1$ nodes $r, x_1, \ldots, x_n$ such that: (i) x_i is a child of r, has

---

[6] a can be $\bot$.

attribute-value pair $A : a$, and is the parent of v_i, $i = 1, ..., n$; (ii) r is a null node, has a vertical blocker, and is a child of u's parent. It is straightforward to verify that the instance so constructed is partially isomorphic to $\mathcal{I}$. *In the sequel, we shall assume without loss of generality that the instances we consider are in canonical form.*

We begin with the simplest operator, union. Let T_1 and T_2 be any database trees (which may be the result of applying CA expressions to a database). Let T_i' denote a copy of T_i, $i = 1, 2$. Then $T_1 \cup T_2$ is the tree T with a new null node u as its root, with $label(u) = \{\oplus\}$, which has the roots of T_1' and T_2' as its children, in that order. Note that the operands are not required to be union-compatible, as such an assumption would be inappropriate for the SSDB setting.

Each of our remaining operators can be conceptually regarded as involving two steps.[7] First, one marks a set of nodes and erases the attribute/value pairs associated with them. Second, one makes the resulting tree compact by contracting "redundant" nodes. For conceptual clarity, we thus define these auxiliary "operations" first. Let $T = \langle V, E, label, attr, val \rangle$ be a database tree and N a subset of T's nodes. Then $\text{ERASE}(N, T)$ is obtained by taking an identical copy of T and erasing for each node $u \in N$, the attribute/value pair associated with u. More precisely, let $T' = \langle V', E', label', attr', val' \rangle$ be an identical copy of T, $h : T \rightarrow T'$ be an 1-1 onto special tree embedding from T to T', and let $h(N) = \{h(u) \mid u \in N\}$. Then $\text{ERASE}(N, T)$ is the database tree $T'' = \langle V', E', attr'', val'', label' \rangle$, such that $\forall u \in h(N)$, $attr''(u) = val''(u) = \bot$, and $\forall u \in V' - h(N)$, $attr''(u) = attr'(u)$, and $val''(u) = val'(u)$. In the sequel, we will abuse terminology and say erase a node to mean erase the attribute/value pair associated with it.

The second auxiliary operator is REDUCE. Applying it to a database tree results in a tree which has no more nodes than T, but which is content equivalent to it. Intuitively, whenever T contains a parent node u and a null child node v, both belonging to a common component, then u and v can identified (i.e. merged). This will leave the contents unchanged as long as the child (null) node does not have any associated horisontal blocker.[8] Formally, $\text{REDUCE}(T)$ is obtained by repeatedly applying the following step to an identical copy T' of T, until there is no change: whenever T' has a null node u whose parent is v, and u, v belong to a common component, and u does not have a horisontal blocker, identify (i.e. merge) u and v. Note that this step only applies to null nodes different from the root, and also that the result of applying REDUCE to T is always unique.

Renaming is defined in a straightforward manner. Given a tree T, the operator $\rho_{B \leftarrow A}(T)$ replaces every occurrence of an attribute A (at any node of T) by attribute B. When there is no occurrence, this is a nop.

---

[7] Join also involves something more, of course.

[8] Identifying two adjacent nodes is similar to the edge contraction operation in the theory of graph minors.

The allowable selection conditions in CA are of one of the following forms:[9] (i) $A\theta a$, (ii) $A\theta B$, (iii) $A \doteq \perp$, $A \not\doteq \perp$, and (iv) $\_ = a$, where A, B are attributes, a is a value, and θ is one of $=, \neq, \doteq, \not\doteq$, and their boolean combinations. We include conditions of form (iv) since in a SSDB where a predefined schema may not exist, it is often convenient to search for occurrence of values without knowing a *priori* their associated attributes.[10] Let T be a database tree and $\mathcal{C}$ any allowable selection condition of the form, say $A\theta B$. Then a component C of T satisfies this selection condition exactly when C contains two nodes u, v such that $attr(u) = A$, $attr(v) = B$, and $val(u)$ and $val(v)$ stand in the relationship indicated, as per the definition of satisfaction given for CC. Satisfaction of other conditions is similar. In particular, C satisfies $\_ = a$, provided C contains some node with associated value a. Our definition of selection follows. Recall that we assume database trees are in canonical form.

Definition 5. Let T be a database tree, $\mathcal{C}$ and any allowable selection condition. Then

$$\sigma_{\mathcal{C}}(T) = \text{REDUCE}(\text{ERASE}(\{u \in T \mid u \text{ belongs to component } C \text{ of } T \ \& \ C \text{ does not satisfy } \mathcal{C}\}, T)).$$

Intuitively, selection erases the attribute/value information on all nodes belonging to those components of T which do not satisfy $\mathcal{C}$ and reduces the resulting tree.

Definition 6. Let T be a database tree, X any set of attributes. Then

$$\pi_X(T) = \text{REDUCE}(\text{ERASE}(\{u \in T \mid attr(u) \notin X\}, T)).$$

Projection on a set of attributes X erases all nodes whose attribute is not in X, and reduces the resulting tree. When we work with liberal schema, we will find it convenient to use dual projection, which amounts to dropping attributes.

Definition 7. Let T be a database tree, A any attribute. Then

$$\overline{\pi}_A(T) = \text{REDUCE}(\text{ERASE}(\{u \in T \mid attr(u) = A\}, T)).$$

This operator erases all nodes with associated attribute A (if any) and reduces the resulting tree.

The minus operator is based on the notion of subsumption. A component C of a tree T is subsumed by a component C' of a tree T' exactly when C as a tree is subsumed by C' (cf. Section 2.2).

Definition 8. Let T_1, T_2 be any database trees. Then

$$T_1 - T_2 = \text{REDUCE}(\text{ERASE}(\{u \in C \mid C \text{ is a component of } T \ \& \ \exists \text{ a component } C' \text{ of } T_2 : C \leq_{\text{sub}} C'\}, T_1)).$$

---

[9] As mentioned for CC, when considering expressive power issues, we will drop form (i).
[10] This feature is exhibited by previous SSDB languages.

Basically, $T_1 - T_2$ is obtained by erasing (the nodes in) those components of T_1 which are subsumed by some component of T_2 and then reducing the resulting tree. The last operator is join. Since we are operating in a model where we use attribute names (as opposed to position numbers as in classical relational model), it is more appropriate to define join as a primitive operator. Thereto, we need the following notions.

The preorder precedes relation Section 2 is extended to components of trees: a component C of T preorder precedes another component C' of T provided for every non-null node v in C', there is a non-null node u in C such that u preorder precedes v. Recall that components of trees in canonical form never share non-null nodes. Consequently, on such trees, the preorder precedes relation is a total order on components.

Let T and T' be any trees. Then we can form a new tree $T \odot T'$ by taking a new node v as root, with $attr(v) = \bot$, $val(v) = \bot$, and $label(v) = \{\}$, and by making copies of T and T' subtrees of v, in that order.

For an enumeration of trees $T_1, \ldots, T_n$, we abuse notation and let $\oplus(T_1, \ldots, T_n)$ denote the tree with a new null node u as its root with label $\oplus$, and the roots of copies of $T_1, \ldots, T_n$ as its children, in that order.

Let C be a component of a tree T and let X be a set of attributes appearing in C. Suppose C has one or more nodes corresponding to each of the attributes in X. A *cutset* of C w.r.t. X is any set of nodes V_X in C such that there is exactly one node in V_X corresponding to each attribute in X. Clearly, a cutset need not be unique. Each cutset V_X leads to a component which is multiple-free w.r.t. X, as follows. Let $V_X^2 = \{u \mid u \in \text{nodes}(C) - V_X \ \& \ attr(u) \in X\}$, i.e. V_X^2 consists of precisely those nodes in C not in V_X, which contain an attribute in X. Then REDUCE(ERASE(V_X^2, C)) denotes the component obtained from C by erasing all nodes outside V_X which contain an attribute in X, and then reducing the resulting component. Finally, the decomposition of C w.r.t. X is defined as DECOMP(C, X) = {REDUCE(ERASE(V_X^2, C)) | V_X is a cutset of C w.r.t. X}. Clearly, when C is multiple-free w.r.t. X, DECOMP(C, X) = C.

Let C, C' be any components of trees T_1, T_2. Suppose C (resp., C') is multiple-free w.r.t. A (resp., B). Then the pair (C, C') satisfies the condition $A = B$ provided there is a pair of nodes $u \in C$ and $v \in C'$ whose associated attributes are A and B respectively, associated values are defined, and are equal. Satisfaction for $A \neq B, A \doteq B, A \not\doteq B$ is similarly defined. In particular, the pair (C, C') satisfies $A \doteq B$ provided there is a pair of nodes $u \in C$ and $v \in C'$ whose associated attributes are A and B respectively, and either both their associated values are undefined, or both are defined and equal. Whenever (C, C') satisfies $A\theta B$, we say (C, C') is *(theta-)joinable*. When C and/or C' is not multiple-free w.r.t the appropriate attribute, we work with the components in their decomposition. Let DECOMP(C, A) = $\{C_1, \ldots, C_k\}$, where C_i preorder precedes $C_{i+1}, 1 \leq i < k$, and DECOMP(C', B) = $\{C'_1, \ldots, C'_m\}$, where and C'_j preorder precedes $C'_{j+1}, 1 \leq j < m$. Then define $C \star_{A\theta B} C' = \oplus(C_i \odot C'_j \mid C_i$ and C'_j are joinable$)$. Here, the pairs of components are enumerated in a manner that respects the preorder sequence.

Let C be a component of T_1 and let T_2 be any tree. Then $C \star_{A\theta B} T_2 = \textcircled{1}(C \star_{A\theta B} D_1, \ldots, C \star_{A\theta B} D_n)$ where $D_1, \ldots D_n$ are all the components of T_2 and D_i preorder precedes $D_{i+1}, 1 \leq i < n$. For a tree T and a binary relation $r = \{(C, D) \mid C \text{ is a component of } T, D \text{ is any tree}\}$, let REPL$(T, r)$ denote the result of replacing, in a copy of T, (the corresponding copy of) each component C of T, by the tree D, whenever $r(C, D)$ holds.

Definition 9. Let T_1 and T_2 be any database trees, and $A \in \mathcal{A}(T_1), B \in \mathcal{A}(T_2)$ be any attributes appearing in them. Then $T_1 \bowtie_{A\theta B} T_2$, where θ is one of $=, \neq, \doteq, \not\doteq$, is defined as $T_1 \bowtie_{A\theta B} T_2 = \text{REPL}(T_1, \{(C, C \star_{A\theta B} T_2) \mid C \text{ is a component of } T_1\})$.

In words, join works as follows. Create a copy T_1' of T_1. For each component C of T_1' do the following: (i) concatenate (in the sense of $\odot$) C with each component C' of T_2 with which it is joinable; (ii) then "merge" the resulting set of trees using the $\textcircled{1}$ operator above; this gives rise to the tree $C \star_{A\theta B} T_2$ above; (iii) next, replace C by the tree $C \star_{A\theta B} T_2$ in T_1'. A technicality arises due to the fact that C (resp., C') may not be multiple-free w.r.t. attribute A (resp., B), which is handled by decomposing C (C') w.r.t. A (B) and "processing" the resulting pieces w.r.t. their preorder enumeration.

We note that the definition of natural join is analogous. The main issue, however, is when we can consider a pair of components natural joinable. There are several ways to define this, depending on which notion of equality is adopted. We argue that when no notion of predefined schema is applicable (as is common with most SSDB applications), practically the most likely useful definition is one that says whenever both components have defined values for any common attribute, then they must agree. We note that this definition of natural join is in the spirit of the polymorphic join defined by Buneman and Ohori [12]. Formally, we say that a pair (C, C') of components of T_1, T_2 respectively, is *natural joinable*, provided for every attribute A, *if* there are nodes $u \in C$ and $v \in C'$ such that their associated attribute is A and their associated values are both defined, *then* they are equal. Define the notions $C \star C'$, $C \star T_2$ analogously to $C \star_{A\theta B} C'$ and $C \star_{A\theta B} T_2$, but incorporating the condition for natural joinability instead of theta-joinability. Necessary decompositions must be done w.r.t. the set of common defined attributes for the pair of components being joined. We have the following definition of natural join.

Definition 10. Let T_1 and T_2 be any database trees. Then

$$T_1 \bowtie T_2 = \text{REPL}(T_1, \{(C, C \star T_2) \mid C \text{ is a component of } T_1\}).$$

Samples of algebraic queries can be found below in the next section.

3.3   Examples

Here we illustrate the query languages. Consider the following database forest representing information on Canadian provinces (Figure 4). In tree T_1, the

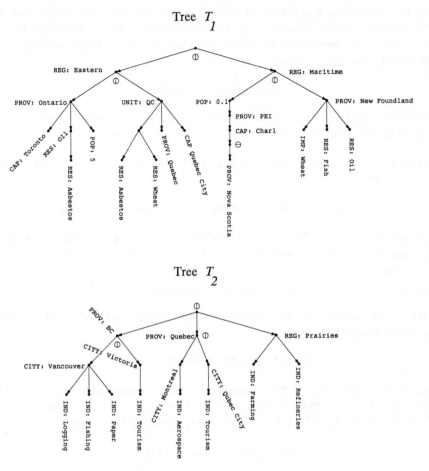

Fig. 4. A Canadiana Forest

provinces are grouped into two subtrees: the Eastern provinces and the Maritimes. For each province, the database records its name. PEI stands for Prince Edward Island. For some provinces the main resources (RES) are recorded, and likewise for the capital (CAP), and population (POP). Only for New Foundland is the main import goods (IMP) recorded. The tree T_2 shows major cities and industries in each province.

Consider now the following queries.

Query 1 Suppose we want the name and capital of all recorded provinces in tree T_1. Note that the user does not necessarily have any knowledge about the structure of the database. This query is expressed by

$$(t \mid \exists s : T_1(s) \ \wedge \ t.\mathtt{PROV} = s.\mathtt{PROV} \ \wedge \ t.\mathtt{CAP} \doteq u.\mathtt{CAP}).$$

This CC expression will return (a tree with) the following set of components (as branches): $\{$(PROV : Ontario, CAP : Toronto), (PROV : Quebec, CAP : QuebecCity), (PROV : PEI, CAP : Charlottetown), (PROV : NovaScotia), (PROV : NewFoundland)$\}$. In component algebra this query is formulated as

$$\pi_{\text{PROV,CAP}}(\sigma_{\text{PROV} \neq \perp}(T_1)).$$

Note that the Component Algebra query would return a "substructure" of T_1, induced by the PROV and CAP nodes (if any), as the answer.

Query 2 List those provinces in T_1 that are in any way associated with wheat, and their capitals.

$$(t \mid \exists s : T_1(s) \wedge t.\text{PROV} = s.\text{PROV} \wedge t.\text{CAP} \doteq s.\text{CAP} \wedge s[\text{wheat}]).$$

The answer will include the following components $\{$(PROV : Quebec, CAP : QuebecCity), (PROV : NewFoundland)$\}$. In component algebra, this query can be expressed as

$$\pi_{\text{PROV,CAP}}(\sigma_{\text{PROV} \neq \perp \wedge \_=\text{wheat}}(T_1)).$$

Query 3 List all information about those provinces in T_1 for which the capital and population is recorded

$$(t \mid T_1(t) \wedge t[\text{PROV}] \wedge t[\text{CAP}] \wedge t[\text{POP}]).$$

The answer will be $\{$(PROV : Ontario, CAP : Toronto, RES : Oil, POP : 5), $\{$(PROV : Ontario, CAP : Toronto, RES : Asbestos, POP : 5), (PROV : PEI, CAP : Charlottetown, POP : 0.1)$\}$ In algebra this would be written as

$$\sigma_{\text{PROV} \neq \perp \wedge \text{CAP} \neq \perp \wedge \text{POP} \neq \perp}(T_1).$$

Query 4 Join the information in T_1 and T_2.

$$(t \mid \exists u, v : T_1(u) \wedge T_2(v) \wedge u \sqsubseteq t \wedge v \sqsubseteq t).$$

The answer will contain the components $\{$(UNIT : QC, PROV : Quebec, CAP : QuebecCity, RES : Asbestos, CITY : Montreal, IND : Aerospace), (UNIT : QC, PROV : Quebec, CAP : QuebecCity, RES : Wheat, CITY : Montreal, IND : Aerospace), (UNIT : QC, PROV : Quebec, CAP : QuebecCity, RES : Asbestos, CITY : QuebecCity, IND : Tourism)$\}$ (UNIT : QC, PROV : Quebec, CAP : QuebecCity, RES : Wheat, CITY : QuebecCity, IND : Tourism)$\}$ In Component Algebra we would simply write

$$T_1 \bowtie T_2.$$

The result of the algebraic join is shown in Figure 5

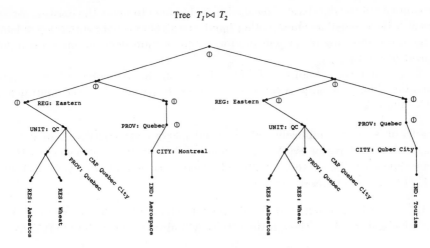

Fig. 5. The result of a natural join

4   On the Expressive Power of Component Calculus and Algebra

4.1   Calculus vs. Algebra

In this section, we study the expressive power of Component Calculus/Algebra. First, we establish that while CC is representation independent but not representation preserving, CA is both. Next we show that CC is *instance complete*. Instance completeness is a notion that generalizes the BP-completeness of Bancilhon and Paredaens to semi-structured databases. The natural next question is whether Component Calculus collapses to Relational Calculus when inputs and outputs are relational. We show that when we consider instances of a predefined (i.e. conservative) schema **A**, then CC and Tuple Relational Calculus (TRC) indeed have the same expressive power. However, there are queries expressible in CC, such that no equivalent TRC expression has size polynomial in the size of **A**. In the case where instances can have arbitrary (i.e. liberal) schemas, we show that there are queries expressible in CC that are not expressible in TRC.

Theorem 2. (1) The component calculus is representation independent, but not representation preserving. (2) The component algebra is both representation independent and representation preserving.

This phenomenon is due to the declarative/procedural dichotomy between calculus and algebra. The Component Calculus "talks" about (connected) components of the input databases. It does not distinghuish between content equivalent representations of the same components. Therefore the calculus is representation independent. On the other hand, the calculus always returns components in a canonical form (the minimal line tree). The calculus is thus not representation preserving. The component algebra operates directly on the tree underlying the contents of the database. The algebra is designed to upset the existing structure as little as possible. On the other hand, the algebra is not syntax-dependent, in the sence that any query will produce content equivalent ouputs on content equivalent inputs.

Notice that the semantics of CC is based on the extended active domain semantics. Thus, the issue of safety does not arise. We can show the equivalence of CC and CA.

Theorem 3. The component calculus and algebra are equivalent in expressive power. That is, for every expression E_c of the component calculus, there is an expression E_a in the component algebra, such that for every instance $\mathcal{I}$, $E_c(\mathcal{I}) \equiv_{\text{cont}} E_a(\mathcal{I})$, and vice versa.

It is important to notice that calculus and algebra expressions will not produce identical results, although the results will always be content equivalent.

4.2   Instance Completeness

In this section, we extend the classical notion of BP-completeness due to [8,27] to SSDBs. Recall that in the classical case, a language $\mathcal{L}$ is BP-complete provided for every instance $\mathcal{I}$, for every query Q (that is computable and is invariant under automorphisms), there is an expression E in $\mathcal{L}$ such that $E(\mathcal{I}) = Q(\mathcal{I})$. In the case of SSDBs, because of structural variations among equivalent representations of the same information, we modify this notion as follows. In order to avoid confusion, we term the extended notion instance completeness, rather than BP-completeness. A query language $\mathcal{L}$ for SSDBs is *instance complete* provided for every instance $\mathcal{I}$, for every query Q, there is an expression E in $\mathcal{L}$ such that $E(\mathcal{I}) \equiv_{\text{cont}} Q(\mathcal{I})$. We have the following results.

Theorem 4. The component calculus and component algebra both compute only queries.

Theorem 5. The component calculus is instance complete.

Corollary 1. The component algebra is instance complete.

Our proof is based on an extension of the technique developed by Paredaens. One of the novelties is finding a tree representation for the auto-embedding group of an instance [19].

4.3   Component vs. Relational Calculus

A semi-structured database has its schema implicitly defined in the extension. Thus the schema is not known before processing the instance. The Component Calculus is designed so that it can deal with the situation in an instance independent manner. All we know is that the attribute names come from a countable set $\mathcal{A}$. Thus, the relevant notion of schema in this case is that of a liberal schema.

On the other hand, if we have a predetermined collection of semi-structured databases, the set of all attributes occurring in the collection is finite, and one can apply the notion of the so-called conservative schema.

To understand how CC compares with tuple relational calculus (TRC) in terms of expressive power, we need to extend the latter to handle inapplicable nulls [24]. This we do by introducing the equality $\doteq$ and adding the symbol $\perp$ to TRC's vocabulary. Specifically, the extended language, $\text{TRC}^\perp$, consists of all atoms of TRC, together with $t.A \doteq s.B$, and $t.A \doteq \perp$, where t, s are tuple variables and A, B are attributes. Their semantics is exactly that in CC.

Consider a set of attributes $\mathbf{A} = \{A_1, \ldots, A_n\}$, and relations over $\mathbf{A}$, possibly containing inapplicable nulls. Define a query $Q_{\text{rel}}^{\mathbf{A}}$ over such relations r as follows.

$$
Q_{\text{rel}}^{\mathbf{A}}(r) = \begin{cases} \{()\} \text{ if} & (\exists t \in r : t.A_1 \not\doteq \perp \ \& \ t.A_n \not\doteq \perp) \\ & \text{or } \exists t_1, t_2 \in r : t_1[A_1] \ \& \ t_2[A_n] \ \& \\ & \forall A \in \mathbf{A} : [t_1.A \not\doteq \perp \ \& \ t_2.A \not\doteq \ \Rightarrow \ t_1.A = t_2.A]. \\ \{\} \quad \text{otherwise.} \end{cases}
$$

$$
Q_{\text{rel}}^{\mathbf{A}}(r) = \begin{cases} \{()\} \text{ if} & \exists t \in r : t.A_1 \not\doteq \perp \ \& \ t.A_n \not\doteq \perp \\ & \text{or} \\ & \exists t_1, t_2 \in r : t_1[A_1] \ \& \ t_2[A_n] \ \& \\ & \forall A \in \mathbf{A} : t_1.A \not\doteq \perp \ \& \ t_2.A \not\doteq \ \Rightarrow \ t_1.A = t_2.A. \\ \{\} \quad \text{otherwise.} \end{cases}
$$

By adopting the technique for simulating relational databases as SSDBs (e.g., see [11]) with a $\oplus$ placed at the root node, we can see that $Q_{\text{rel}}^{\mathbf{A}}$ is a query over SSDBs in the sense of Definition 2. For simplicity, below we blur the distinction between a relational database and its SSDB simulation. We have the following results.

Theorem 6. There is an expression in the component calculus, with size linear in the number of attributes in $\mathbf{A}$, that computes $Q_{\text{rel}}^{\mathbf{A}}$.

Theorem 7. (1) There is an expression in $\text{TRC}^\perp$ that computes $Q_{\text{rel}}^{\mathbf{A}}$. (2) However, there is no expression E in $\text{TRC}^\perp$, with size polynomial in the number of attributes in $\mathbf{A}$, such that E computes $Q_{\text{rel}}^{\mathbf{A}}$.

Recall that $\mathcal{A}$ denotes the countable set of all possible attributes. In most "real-life" SS applications, the schema of the potential input databases is not known, just as the number of tuples in a relation in the classical model is not known in advance. In this case, the notion of liberal schema, i.e. an arbitrary finite subset of $\mathcal{A}$, not known a priori, applies. We extend the above query $Q_{\text{rel}}^{\mathbf{A}}$ to this situation as follows. Let T be a relation over an arbitrary finite subset $\mathbf{A} \subset \mathcal{A}$, which is not known a priori. The definition of $Q_{\text{rel}}^{\mathcal{A}}$ is exactly the same as that of $Q_{\text{rel}}^{\mathbf{A}}$ for the conservative schema.

The CC query expression

$$
(t \mid (\exists t : T(t) \wedge t[A_1] \wedge t[A_n]) \vee
$$
$$
(\exists t, s_1, s_2 : T(s_1) \wedge T(s_2) \wedge s_1[A_1] \wedge s_2[A_n] \wedge s_1 \sqsubseteq t \wedge s_2 \sqsubseteq t))
$$

clearly computes $Q_{\text{rel}}^{\mathcal{A}}$. Indeed, the same formula computes $Q_{\text{rel}}^{\mathbf{A}}$ when the schema is conservative. We have

Theorem 8. The query $Q_{\text{rel}}^{\mathcal{A}}$ is expressible in the component calculus. However, there is no expression in $\text{TRC}^{\perp}$ which can compute this query.

A restricted version of this result has been independently discovered recently by van den Busche and Waller [15].

5   Where Do the Labels Come From?

Our data model assumes that the trees are approprately labeled with blockers. How does the system obtain these blockers? There are two answers to this question. First, the data may be "raw data" obtained from the web. In this case, schema mining techniques similar to [26] can be used. We do not explore this approach further in this context. Second, the trees might be the result of exporting structured or semi-structured data into a common exchange format. We contend that our enhanced OEM model is well suited for this purpose. To substantiate this claim, we briefly sketch how relations, nested relations, and XML data can represented in our enhanced OEM model in a manner that makes the fact structure explicit.

Relational data. A tuple $[A : a, B : b, C : c]$ can be modelled as any connected component with three nodes, having atttribute-value pairs $(A : a)$, $(B : b)$, and $(C : c)$, respectiveley. A relation $R = \{t_1, \ldots, t_n\}$ is modelled as a tree with root with attribute-value pair $(R : \perp)$ and label ①, and subtrees corresponding to the components for the tuples $t_1, \ldots, t_n$.

Nested Relational data.
Relational tuples and relations are modelled as above. A possibly nested tuple $[A_1 : v_1, \ldots, A_n : v_n]$ is represented as a tree with a null node as root. The root has children representing each pair $(A_i : v_i)$ If v_i is an atomic value, then the pair is modelled as above. Otherwise we create node with value $(A_i : \perp)$, and a horisontal blocker If v_i is a tuple, then the created node has one child, which is the root of the component representing the tuple v_i. If v_i is a set, then the created node also has a vertical blocker, and children representing the elements.

XML data. The structure of XML documents are described through Data Type Definitions (DTD's) [10]. In Figure 6 we see a simple example of a DTD specification for a course calendar. The specification states that a calendar consists of graduate and undergraduate courses. A course entry gives a title and a schedule for a course, or just the title.

Using the DTD in Figure 6, an XML instance can be parsed into a labeled tree in the obvious way. All we need to add is the placement of the blockers ①, ⊖ in the parsed instance. For this we use the following (informal) rules: (1) A node labeled with an element name that appears in a list specification (e. g. `Gradcourse`) is labeled with ⊖. (2) The parent of a node labeled with an element name that appears in a star specification (e. g. `Gradcourse`) is labeled with ①. (3) Leaves are not labeled with blockers.

```
<DOCTYPE Calendar
    <!ELEMENT Calendar (Gradcourse, Ugradcourse)>
    <!ELEMENT Gradcourse (Entry*)>
    <!ELEMENT Ugradcourse (Entry*)>
    <!ELEMENT Entry (Title, Schedule) | Title>
    <!ELEMENT Title CharData>
    <!ELEMENT Title Chardata>
]>
```

Fig. 6. A DTD Specification

Following the method sketched above, the XML instance in Figure 7 would result in the database tree in Figure 8. Note that the method is informal. We are currently investigating automated wrapping of XML data into our enhanced OEM-model.

```
<CALENDAR> <GRADCOURSE> <ENTRY> Databases, Mo-We-5-9 <\ENTRY>
                        <ENTRY> OLAP<\ENTRY>

            <\GRADCOURSE>
            <UGRADCOURSE> <ENTRY> Datastructures <\ENTRY>

            <\UGRADCOURSE>
<\CALENDAR>
```

Fig. 7. An XML instance

6   Related Work

In a recent paper, Abiteboul and Vianu [1] study generic computations over the world wide web. They model the web as a simple relational database with links as relations, and equipped with certain functional and inclusion dependencies. Their notion of genericity is based on the classical database isomorphisms on the simple relational database. Abiteboul and Vianu study the expressive power of existing languages, such as FO and Datalog. In a related paper, Mendelzon and Milo [23] propose essentially an object-based version of the model of Abiteboul and Vianu. The notion of genericity is still confined to the classical domain permutations. Mendelzon and Milo propose a web-calculus that operates on web-objects. Both aforementioned works [1,23] deal only with world wide web computations, and their analyses do not spell out the fact structure of SSDBs. As far as we know, the notions of representation independence and preservation have not been addressed before.

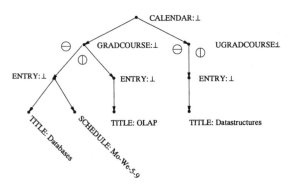

Fig. 8. The Labeled Tree

7   Summary and Future Work

BP-completeness, originally proposed in [8,27] was a breakthrough which led
to the subsequent development of the notions of genericity and complete query
languages by [16], which in turn plays a central role in the theory of classical database queries. BP-completeness essentially provides an instance dependent characterization of the expressive power of a query language. The analog
of BP-completeness for object creating languages was developed by [5] which
subsequently led to the development of an appropriate extension of the notion
of genericity as well as a complete query language for the graph-based object-
oriented GOOD data model [14].

In this paper, we have extended BP-completeness for SSDBs. In this connection, we have introduced the notion of representation independence for SSDB
query languages, which can be regarded as a first important step toward achieving the repository independence envisioned by Hull [21]. We have also introduced
a notion of genericity and representation preservation for SSDB query languages.
The latter captures the spirit of pure querying as opposed to restructuring. We
have defined a calculus and an equivalent algebra for SSDBs, and shown that
both languages are generic and representation independent, and that the algebra
is also representation preserving, thus lending itself to efficient implementation.
Both languages are instance complete. Finally, the component calculus can express queries much more concisely than $TRC^{\perp}$, an extension to classical TRC for
handling inapplicable nulls. Moreover, when the schema is not predefined, CC
can express queries that $TRC^{\perp}$ cannot.

It is our hope that work presented in this paper will be useful in the development of a comprehensive theory of queries for SSDBs. Clearly, much work
remains to be done. In this paper we have concentrated on SSDBs which are
forests. Handling more general SSDBs is an important problem. In this vein, a
particularly promising direction is to explore a model in the spirit of the hy-
pertrees of [6] with cross-links between trees, possibly with cycles, rather than
a completely arbitrary digraph. Another interesting direction is to extend the

theory to include restructuring, a feature already exhibited by many of the languages surveyed in Section 1.

References

1. Abiteboul, S., and V. Vianu. Queries and computation on the Web. *ICDT '97*.
2. Abiteboul, S. et al. The Lorel query language for semistructured data. *Intl. J. on Digital Libraries*, 1:68–88, 1997.
3. Abiteboul, S., and V Vianu. Regular path queries with constraints. *PODS '97*.
4. Abiteboul, S. Querying Semi-Structured Data. *ICDT '97*.
5. Andries, M., and Paredaens, J.. On instance-completeness for database query languages involving object creation. *J. Comp. Syst. Sci.*, 52(2):357–373, 1996.
6. Arocena, G., and A. O. Mendelzon. WebOQL: Restructuring documents, databases and webs. *ICDE '98*.
7. Atzeni, P., G. Mecca, and P. Merialdo. To weave the web. *VLDB '97*.
8. Bancilhon, F.. On the Completeness of Query Languages for Relational Data Bases. *MFOCS '78*.
9. Beeri, C., and T. Milo. Schemas for Integration and Translation of Structured and Semi-Structured data. *ICDT '99*.
10. Brey, T., J. Paoli, and S. Sperberg-McQuenn. Extensible Markup Language (XML) 1.0. http://www.w3.org/TR/REC-xml
11. Buneman,P. et al. A query language and optimization techniques for unstructured data. *SIGMOD '96*.
12. Buneman, P., and A. Ohori. Polymorphism and Type Inference in Database Programming. *ACM TODS*, 21:30–76, 1996.
13. Buneman,P. et al. Adding structure too unstructured data. *ICDT '97*.
14. Bussche, J. Van den et al. On the Completeness of Object-Creating Database Transformation Languages. *JACM*, 44(2):272–319.
15. Bussche, J. Van den, and E. Waller. Type inference in the polymorphic relational algebra. *PODS 99*.
16. Chandra A. K. and D. Harel. Computable queries for relational data bases. *J. Comp. Syst. Sci.*, 21:156–178, 1980.
17. Fernandez, M., D. Florescu, A. Levy, and D. Suciu. A query language for a web-site management system. *SIGMOD Record*, 26(3):4–11, September 1997.
18. Florescu, D., A. Levy, and D. Suciu. Query containment for conjunctive queries with regular expressions. *PODS '98*.
19. Grahne, G., and L. V. S. Lakshmanan. On the Difference between Navigating Semi-structured Data and Querying It. Technical report, Concordia University, Montreal, Canada, August 1999. in preparation.
20. Gyssens, M., L. V. S. Lakshmanan, and I. N. Subramanian Tables as a paradigm for querying and restructuring. *PODS '96*.
21. Hull, R.. Managing Semantic Heterogeneity in Databases: A Theoretical Perspective. *PODS '97*.
22. Manna, Z., *Mathematical Theory of Computation*. McGraw-Hill, New York, Montreal, 1974.
23. Mendelzon, A. O., and T. Milo. Formal models of web queries. *PODS '97*.
24. Lerat, N., and W. Lipski. Nonapplicable nulls. *TCS*, 46:67–82, 1986.
25. Ley, M.. Database Systems and Logic Programming Bibliography Server. http://www.informatik.uni-trier.de/ ley/db/.

26. Nestorov, S., S. Abiteboul, and R. Motwani. Extracting Schema from Semistructured Data. *SIGMOD '98*.
27. Paredaens, J. On the expressive power of the relational algebra. *IPL*, 7:107–110, 1978.
28. Rajaraman, A., and J. D. Ullman. Integrating Information by Outerjoins and Full Disjunctions. *PODS '96*.
29. Thierry-Mieg, J., and R. Durbin. A C.elegans database: syntactic definitions for the ACEDB data base manager, 1992.
30. Ullman, J. D. Database Theory - Past and Future. *PODS '87*.

Ozone: Integrating Structured and Semistructured Data*

Tirthankar Lahiri[1], Serge Abiteboul[2], Jennifer Widom[1]

[1] Stanford University, {tlahiri,widom}@db.stanford.edu
[2] INRIA Rocquencourt, serge.abiteboul@inria.fr

Abstract. Applications have an increasing need to manage *semistructured* data (such as data encoded in XML) along with conventional *structured* data. We extend the structured object database model ODMG and its query language OQL with the ability to handle semistructured data based on the OEM model and Lorel language, and we implement our extensions in a system called *Ozone*. In our approach, structured data may contain entry points to semistructured data, and vice-versa. The unified representation and querying of such "hybrid" data is the main contribution of our work. We retain strong typing and access to all properties of structured portions of the data while allowing flexible navigation of semistructured data without requiring full knowledge of structure. Ozone also enhances both ODMG/OQL and OEM/Lorel by virtue of their combination. For instance, Ozone allows OEM semantics to be applied to ODMG data, thus supporting semistructured-style navigation of structured data. Ozone also enables ODMG views of OEM data, allowing standard ODMG applications to access semistructured data without losing the benefits of structure. Ozone is implemented on top of the ODMG-compliant O_2 database system, and it fully supports our extensions to the ODMG model and OQL.

1 Introduction

Database management systems traditionally have used data models based on regular structures, such as the relational model [Cod70] or the object model [Cat94]. Meanwhile, the growth of the internet and the recent emergence of *XML* [LB97] have motivated research in the area of *semistructured* data models, e.g., [BDS95, FFLS97, PGMW95]. Semistructured data models are convenient for representing irregular, incomplete, or rapidly changing data. In this paper, we extend the

---

* This work was supported by the Air Force Rome Laboratories under DARPA Contract F30602-95-C-0119.

R. Connor and A. Mendelzon (Eds.): DBPL'99, LNCS 1949, pp. 297–323, 2000.

standard well-structured model for object databases, the *ODMG* model [Cat94], and its query language, *OQL*, to integrate semistructured data with structured data. We present our implementation of the extended ODMG model and query language in a system called *Ozone*.

We will see that Ozone is well suited to handling *hybrid* data—data that is partially structured and partially semistructured. We expect hybrid data to become more common as more applications import data from the Web, and the integration of semistructured data within ODMG greatly simplifies the design of such applications. The exclusive use of a structured data model for hybrid data would miss the many advantages of a semistructured data model [Abi97, Bun97]—structured encodings of irregular or evolving semistructured data are generally complex and difficult to manage and evolve. On the other hand, exclusive use of a semistructured data model precludes strong typing and efficient implementation mechanisms for structured portions of the data. Our approach based on a hybrid data model provides the advantages of both worlds.

Our extension to the ODMG data model uses the *Object Exchange Model* (*OEM*) [PGMW95] to represent semistructured portions of the data, and it allows structured and semistructured data to be mixed together freely in the same physical database. Our OQL^S query language for Ozone is nearly identical to OQL [Cat94] but extends the semantics of OQL for querying hybrid data. An interesting feature of our approach is that it also enables structured data to be treated as semistructured data, if so desired, to allow navigation of structured data without full structural knowledge. Conversely, it enables structured views on semistructured data, allowing standard ODMG applications access to semistructured data. We have implemented the full functionality of Ozone on top of the O_2 [BDK92] ODMG-compliant database management system (a product of ArdentSoftware Inc., http://www.ardentsoftware.com).

Related Work

Data models, query languages, and systems for semistructured data are areas of active research. Of particular interest and relevance, *eXtensible Markup Language* (*XML*) [LB97] is an emerging standard for Web data, and bears a close correspondence to semistructured data models introduced in research, e.g., [BDS95, FFLS97, PGMW95]. An example of a complete database management system for semistructured data is *Lore* [MAG+97], a repository for OEM data featuring the Lorel query language. Another system devoted to semistructured data is the *Strudel* Web site management system, which features the *StruQL* query language [FFLS97] and a data model similar to OEM. *UnQL* [BDHS96, BDS95] is a query language that allows queries on both the content and structure of a semistructured database and also uses a data model similar to Strudel and OEM. All of these data models, languages, and systems are dedicated to pure semistructured data. We know of no previous research that has explored the integration of structured and semistructured data as exhibited by Ozone. Note also that our query language OQL^S is supported by a complete implementation in the Ozone system.

There has been some work in extracting structural information and building structural summaries of semistructured databases. For example, [NAM98] shows how schema information can be extracted from OEM databases by typing semistructured data using Datalog. Structural properties of semistructured data can be described and enforced using *graph schemas* as shown in [BDFS97]. Structural summaries called *DataGuides* are used in the Lore system as described in [GW97]. These lines of research are dedicated to finding the structural properties of purely semistructured data and do not address the integration of structured and semistructured data as performed by Ozone.

The *OQL-doc* query language [ACC$^+$97] is an example of an OQL extension with a semistructured flavor: it extends OQL to navigate document data without precise knowledge of its structure. However, OQL-doc still requires some form of structural specification (such as an XML or SGML *Document Type Definition (DTD)* [LB97]), so OQL-doc does not support the querying of arbitrary semistructured data.

2   Background and Motivating Example

2.1   The structured ODMG model and OQL

The ODMG data model is the accepted standard for object databases [Cat94]. ODMG has all the necessary features of object-orientation: classes with attributes and methods, subtyping, and inheritance. The basic primitives of the model are *objects* (values with unique identifiers) and *literals* (values without identifiers). All values in an ODMG database must have a valid *type* defined in the schema, and all values of an object type or *class* are members of a collection known as the *extent* for that class. Literal types include *atomic* types (e.g., integer, real, string, nil, etc.), *structured* types with labeled components (e.g. tuple(a:integer, b:real)), and *collection* types (set, bag, list, and array).

A *class* type encapsulates some ODMG type, and may define *methods* that specify the legal set of operations on objects belonging to the class. A class may also define *relationships* with other classes. Classes most commonly encapsulate structured types, and the different fields in the encapsulated structure (along with methods without arguments) denote the *attributes* of the class. ODMG defines the class Object to be the root of the class hierarchy. An attribute of a class in the ODMG model may have a literal type and therefore not have identity. *Named* objects and literals form entry points into an ODMG database.

The *Object Query Language*, or *OQL*, is a declarative query language for ODMG data. It is an *expression-oriented* query language: an OQL query is composed of one or more expressions or subqueries whose types can be inferred statically. Complex queries can be formed by composing expressions as long as the compositions respect the type system of ODMG. Details of the ODMG model and the OQL query language can be found in [Cat94], but are not essential for understanding this paper.

2.2   The semistructured OEM model and Lorel

The *Object Exchange Model*, or *OEM*, is a self-describing semistructured data model, useful for representing irregular or dynamically evolving data [PGMW95]. OEM objects may either be *atomic*, containing atomic literal values (of type integer, real, string, binary, etc.), or *complex*, containing a set of labeled OEM subobjects. A complex OEM object may have any number of children (subobjects), including multiple children with the same label. Note that all OEM subobjects have identity, unlike ODMG class attributes. An OEM database may be viewed as a labeled directed graph, with complex OEM objects as internal nodes and atomic OEM objects as leaf nodes. Named OEM objects form entry points into an OEM database.

Lorel is a declarative query language for OEM data and is based on OQL. Some important features of Lorel are listed below. Details of OEM and Lorel can be found in [AQM+97], but again are not crucial to understanding this paper.

- *Path expressions:* Lorel queries navigate OEM databases using *path expressions*, which are sequences of labels that may also contain wildcards and regular expression operators. For instance, the query "Select D From A(.b | .c%)*.d D" selects all objects reachable from entry-point A by following zero or more edges each having either label b or a label beginning with the character c, followed by a single edge labeled d.
- *Automatic coercion:* Lorel attempts to coerce operands to compatible types whenever it performs a comparison or other operation on them. For instance,

if X is an atomic OEM object with the string value "4", then for the evaluation of $X < 10$, Lorel coerces X to the integer value 4. If no such coercion is
possible (for instance, if X were an image or a complex object) the predicate
returns false. Lorel also coerces between sets and singleton values whenever
appropriate.

– *No type errors:* To allow flexible navigation of semistructured data, Lorel
never raises type errors. For instance, an attempted navigation from an OEM
object using a nonexistent label simply produces an empty result, and a
comparison between non-comparable values evaluates to false. Thus, any
Lorel query can be executed on an OEM database with unknown or partially
known structure, without the risk of run-time errors.

2.3   Example of hybrid data and queries

Our motivating example, used throughout the paper, considers a database behind a simplified on-line broker that sells products on behalf of different companies. There are three ODMG classes in this database: Catalog, Company, and
Product. Class Catalog has one object, which represents the on-line catalog maintained by the broker. The object has two attributes: a vendors attribute of type
set(Company), denoting the companies whose products are sold in the catalog,
and a products attribute of type set(Product), denoting the products sold in the
catalog. The Company class defines a one-to-many produces relationship with the
class Product of type list(Product). This relationship specifies the list of products manufactured by the company, ordered by product number. Likewise, the
Product class defines the inverse many-to-one madeby relationship with the class
Company, denoting the product's manufacturer. The Company class contains
other attributes such as name and address, and an inventory() method that takes
a product name argument and returns the number of stocked units of the product of that name. The Product class contains other attributes such as name and
prodnum (product number). The named object Broker of type Catalog provides
an entry point to this database. Figure 1 depicts this schema without atomic
attributes.

In addition to this structured data, let us suppose that we have product-
specific XML information available for some products, e.g., drawn from Web
sites of companies and analyst firms. This data might include manufacturer
specifications (power ratings, weight, etc.), compatibility information if it applies (for instance, the strobes compatible with a particular camera), a listing of
competing companies and products, etc. To integrate this XML data within our

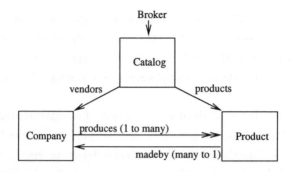

Fig. 1. Structured ODMG classes in the retail-broker database

database, we enhance the Product class with a prodinfo attribute for this product-specific data. Since this data is likely to vary widely in format, we cannot easily use a fixed ODMG type for its representation, and it is much more convenient to use the semistructured OEM data model. Therefore, we let the prodinfo attribute be a "crossover point" (described below) from ODMG to OEM data.

There is also a need for referencing structured data from semistructured data. If a competing product (or company) or a compatible product appears in the broker's catalog, then it should be represented by a direct reference to the ODMG object representing that product or company. If the competing product or company is not part of the catalog, only then is a complex OEM object created to encode the XML data for that product or company.

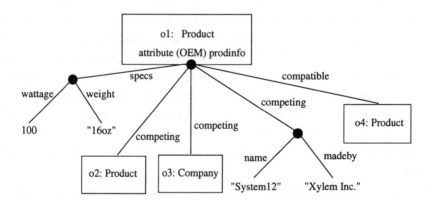

Fig. 2. Example OEM graph for the prodinfo attribute of a Product object

An example OEM database graph for the prodinfo attribute of a product is shown in Figure 2. Note that in Figure 2, the competing product named "System12" is not part of the catalog database and therefore is represented by a (complex) OEM object; the other competing product and company are part of the catalog and are represented by references to Product and Company objects.

To continue with the example, let us also suppose that we have some review data available in XML for products and companies. The information is available from Web pages of different review agencies and varies in structure. We enhance our example database with a second entry point: the named object Reviews integrates all the XML review data from different agencies. Once again, the diverse and dynamic nature of this data means that it is better represented by the OEM data model than by any fixed ODMG type. Thus, Reviews is a complex OEM object integrating available reviews of companies and products. Here too we may reference structured data from semistructured data, since reviewed companies and products that are part of the catalog should be denoted by references to the ODMG objects representing them.

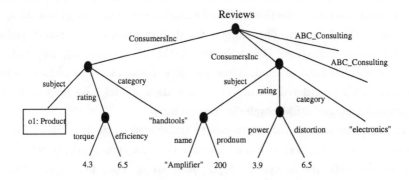

Fig. 3. Semistructured Reviews data for the broker catalog

Figure 3 is a simplified example of this semistructured Reviews data. We assume that the reviews by a given agency reside under distinct subobjects of Reviews, and the names of the review agencies (ConsumersInc, ABC_Consulting, etc.) form the labels for these subobjects. For subsequent examples, we restrict ourselves to reviews by ConsumersInc. Reviews by this agency have a subject subobject denoting the subject of the review (either a product or a company), which may be a reference to the ODMG object representing the company or product, or may be a complex OEM object. Both cases are depicted in Figure 3.

Our overall example scenario consists of *hybrid* data. Some of the data is structured, such as the Product class without the prodinfo attribute, while some of the data is semistructured, such as the data reachable via a prodinfo attribute or via the Reviews entry point.

3 The Extended ODMG Data Model

Our basic extension to the ODMG data model to accommodate semistructured data is therefore relatively straightforward. We extend the ODMG model with a new built-in class type OEM. Using this OEM type, we can construct ODMG types that include semistructured data. For instance, we can define a partially semistructured Product class (as described above) with a prodinfo attribute of type OEM. There is no restriction on the use of the type OEM—it can be used freely in any ODMG type constructor, e.g., tuple(x:OEM, y:integer) and list(OEM) are both valid types.

Objects in the class OEM are of two categories: OEMcomplex and OEMatomic, representing complex and atomic OEM objects respectively.[3] An OEMcomplex object encapsulates a collection of (*label,value*) pairs, where *label* is a string and *value* is an OEM object. The original OEM data model specification included only unordered collections of subobjects [AQM+97, PGMW95], but XML, for example, is inherently ordered. Thus we allow complex OEM objects with either unordered or ordered subobjects in our data model, and refer to them as OEMcomplexset and OEMcomplexlist respectively.

To allow semistructured references to structured data, the value of an OEMatomic object may have any valid ODMG type (including OEM). Thus, apart from the ODMG atomic types integer, real, string, etc., the value of an OEMatomic object may for example be of type Product, tuple(a:integer, b:OEM), etc. When the content of an OEMatomic object is of type T, we will say that its type is OEM(T). Since OEM objects are actually untyped, OEM(T) denotes a "dynamic type" that does not impose any typing constraint. For example, an object of type OEM(integer) may be compared with an object of type OEM(string) or OEM(set(Product)) without raising a type error; further discussion of such operations is provided in Section 5.3. Intuitively, atomic OEM objects can be thought of as *untyped containers* for typed values. Note that an OEMatomic object of type OEM(OEM) can be used to store a reference to another OEM object (possibly external to the database). Also note that OEM(nil) is a valid type for an OEMatomic object, and we assume that there is a single named object OEMNil of this type in the OEM class.

---

[3] These categories do not represent subclasses since, as we will see, OEM objects are untyped.

4   Benefits of a Hybrid Approach

We now reinforce the benefits of a hybrid approach. An important advantage of our approach over a purely structured approach is that we can formulate queries on semistructured portions of the data without requiring full structural knowledge. With a purely structured approach, representation of XML data, for example, would require a different set of ODMG classes for each distinct XML DTD, possibly leading to complex schemas that the user would be required to have full knowledge of in order to formulate valid queries. Furthermore, modifications to the XML data might require expensive schema evolution operations. In contrast, the OEM model does not rely on a known schema, and the semantics of Lorel permits formulating queries without full knowledge of structure.

At the same time, an important benefit of our approach over a purely semistructured approach such as *Lore* [MAG+97] is that we are capable of exploiting structure when it is available. In particular, we can more easily take advantage of known query optimization techniques for structured data, and we can take advantage of strong typing when portions of the data are typed.

Finally, we can optionally apply the semantics of one data model to the other, so that the benefits of both models are available to us whether the data is structured or semistructured. For instance, treating ODMG data as OEM allows queries to be written without complete knowledge of the schema, while still retaining access to all ODMG properties (such as methods, indexes, etc.). On the other hand, we will show in Section 5.2 how our approach enables typed ODMG views of untyped OEM data, so that standard ODMG applications can access semistructured data using standard API's and structural optimizations.

5   The OQL^S Query Language

The query language for the Ozone system is OQL^S. OQL^S is not a new query language—except for some built-in functions and syntactic conveniences derived from Lorel, it is syntactically identical to OQL. The semantics of OQL^S on structured data is identical to OQL on standard ODMG data. OQL^S extends OQL with additional semantics that allow it to access semistructured data. The semistructured capabilities of OQL^S are mostly derived from Lorel, which is based on OQL but was designed specifically for querying pure semistructured data. Like Lorel, OQL^S allows querying of semistructured data without the possibility of run-time errors. OQL^S also provides new features necessary for the navigation of hybrid data: since OQL^S expressions can contain both structured and semistructured operands, OQL^S defines new semantics that allow such queries to be interpreted appropriately.

Space limitations preclude a complete specification for OQL^S in this paper. Since its syntax combines OQL and Lorel, interested readers are referred to [AQM+97, Cat94]. In the remainder of this section we describe some of the more interesting aspects of the semantics of OQL^S, using simple self-explanatory queries to illustrate the points. In Section 5.1 we describe path expression "crossovers" from structured to semistructured data and vice-versa. In Section 5.2 we describe how our approach enables structured ODMG views over semistructured data. Section 5.3 discusses the semantics of OQL^S constructs such as arithmetic and logical expressions involving hybrid operands.

5.1   Path expression crossovers

When we evaluate a *path expression* in an OQL^S query (recall Section 2.2), a corresponding database path may involve all structured data, all semistructured data, or there may be *crossover points* that navigate from structured to semistructured data or vice-versa. Crossing boundaries from structured to semistructured data is fairly straightforward, since we can always identify the crossover points statically. For example, the following query selects the names of all competing products and companies for all products in the broker catalog from Section 2.3:

```
Select N
From   Broker.products P, P.prodinfo.competing C, C.name N
```

P is statically known to be of type Product, but prodinfo is an OEM attribute, and C is therefore of type OEM; prodinfo is thus a crossover point from structured to semistructured data.

Semistructured to structured crossover is more complicated, and we focus on this case. It is not possible to identify such crossover points statically without detailed knowledge of the structure of a hybrid database. To define the semantics of queries with transparent crossover from semistructured to structured data, we introduce (below) the logical concept of *OEM proxy* for encapsulating structured data in OEM objects. We also discuss in Section 5.1 an explicit form of crossover for users who do have detailed knowledge of structure.

In the purely semistructured OEM data model, atomic OEM objects are leaf nodes in the database graph. The result of attempting to navigate an edge from an atomic OEM object is defined in Lorel to be the empty set, i.e., the result of evaluating $X.label$ is empty if X is not a complex OEM object. However, in our extended ODMG model, OEMatomic objects are containers for values with any ODMG type (recall Section 3), so in addition to containing atomic values, they may provide semistructured crossover to structured data.

Thus, OQL^S extends Lorel path expressions with the ability to navigate structured data encapsulated by OEMatomic objects, in addition to navigating semistructured data represented by OEMcomplex objects. In our running example, some of the objects in the Reviews graph labeled subject are OEMatomic objects of type OEM(Product) and OEM(Company). Thus, the following query has a semistructured to structured crossover since some of the bindings for C are OEM(Company) and OEM(Product) objects:

```
Select  A
From    Reviews.ConsumersInc R, R.subject C, C.address A
```

For C bindings of type OEM(Company), the evaluation of C.address generates the *OEM proxy* (defined below) of the address attribute in the Company class. For C bindings of type OEM(Product), the evaluation of C.address yields the empty set.

To allow flexible navigation of structured data from semistructured data, at the same time retaining access to all properties of the structured data, we define the logical notion of *OEM proxy* objects, as follows:

Definition 1. (OEM Proxy) An OEM proxy object is a temporary OEM object created (perhaps only logically) to encapsulate a value of any ODMG type. It is an OEMatomic object that serves as a *proxy* or a surrogate for the value it encapsulates.   □

Semistructured to structured crossover is accomplished by (logically) creating OEM proxy objects, perhaps recursively, to contain the result of navigating past an OEMatomic object. It is important to note that this concept of OEM proxy is a logical rather than a physical concept. It specifies how a query over hybrid data is to be interpreted, but does not specify anything about the actual implementation of the query processor. All we require is that the result of a query should be the same as the result that would be produced if proxy objects were actually created for every navigation past every OEMatomic object. For C bindings of type OEM(Company) in our example query, the corresponding A bindings are OEM proxy objects of type OEM(tuple(street:string, city:string, zip:integer)) encapsulating the address attribute of the corresponding Company objects.

The general algorithm for evaluating $X.l$ when X is an OEMatomic object of type $OEM(T)$ encapsulating the value Y follows. Consider the different cases for T:

1. *T is an atomic ODMG type* (i.e., one of integer, real, char, string, boolean, binary, or nil): For any label l, the result of evaluating $X.l$ is the empty set.

2. *T is a tuple type:* For all non-collection fields in the tuple whose labels match l (note that a label with wildcards can match more than one field) a proxy object is created encapsulating the value of the field. If the label of a collection-valued field matches l, proxies are created encapsulating each element of the collection. The result of evaluating $X.l$ is the set of all such proxies.

3. *T is a collection:* If T is a set or a bag type, $X.l$ returns a set. This set is empty unless the label l is the specific label item. For this built-in system label, the value of $X.l$ is a set of OEM proxies encapsulating the elements in the collection Y. If T is a list or an array type, $X.l$ is evaluated similarly, except that the ordering of the elements of Y is preserved by returning a list of proxies instead of a set. Note that navigation past such objects requires some knowledge of the type T, since the user needs to use label item (or a wildcard) to navigate below the encapsulated collection.

4. *T is a class*: Here, Y is an object encapsulating some value—let Z be an OEM proxy for that value. The result of evaluating $X.l$ is a set including the OEM proxies obtained by evaluating $Z.l$ (by recursively applying these rules), the OEM proxies encapsulating the values of any relationships with names matching l, and the OEM proxies encapsulating the results of invoking any methods with names matching l. If T is OEM, X is a reference to an OEM object Y, and the result of $X.l$ is the same as the result of evaluating $Y.l$, i.e., automatic dereferencing is performed.

To illustrate these rules, consider the following query, which selects the names of all products manufactured by all companies reviewed by ConsumersInc:

```
Select N
From   Reviews.ConsumersInc R, R.subject C,
       C.produces P, P.name N
```

Here, for those C bindings that are of type OEM(Company), the corresponding P bindings are proxies of type OEM(Product), encapsulating the elements of the relationship produces in the Company class. Finally, the N bindings encapsulate the name attributes of the Product objects encapsulated by the P bindings, and the type of these N bindings is OEM(string). Proxies thus allow "transparent navigation" to structured data from semistructured data.

Queries should be able to access all properties of structured data referenced by semistructured data, and OQL^S therefore allows queries to invoke methods with arguments on structured objects encapsulated by OEMatomic objects. The expression $X.m(arg_1, arg_2, \ldots, arg_n)$ applies the method $m()$ with the specified list of arguments to the object encapsulated by X. If X is of type $OEM(T)$, the result of this expression is a set containing the OEMatomic object encapsulating the return value of the method, provided T is a class that has a method of this name and with formal parameters whose types match the types of the actual parameters $arg_1, arg_2, \ldots arg_n$. If T is not a class, or if it is a class without a matching method, or if X is of type OEMcomplex, this expression returns the empty set. As an example, the following query selects the inventories of "camera1" for all companies in the catalog and reviewed by ConsumersInc:

```
Select C.inventory("camera1")
From   Reviews.ConsumersInc R, R.subject C,
```

For those C bindings that are not of type OEM(Company), the evaluation of C.inventory("camera1") yields the empty set. For those C bindings that are of type OEM(Company), the evaluation of C.inventory("camera1") returns a singleton set containing an OEM(integer) object encapsulating the result value.

OQL allows casts on objects, and as a ramification of our approach, OQL^S allows any object to be cast to the type OEM by creating the appropriate proxy for the object, allowing semistructured-style querying of structured data. For instance, an object C of type Company can be cast to an OEM proxy object of type OEM(Company) by the expression (OEM) C. Once this casting is performed, the proxy can be queried without full knowledge of its structure. This casting approach is useful when users have approximate knowledge of the structure of some (possibly very complex) structured ODMG data but prefer not to study its schema in detail. Queries with casts to OEM are also useful when the structure of the database changes frequently and users want the same query to run against the changing database without errors.

Semistructured to structured crossover by explicit coercion. OQL^S provides another mechanism for accessing structured data from semistructured data: a modified form of casting that extracts the structured value encapsulated by an OEMatomic object. Although OEM proxies allow all properties of structured data contained in OEMatomic objects to be accessed without casts, casts enable static type checking. Furthermore, casting a semistructured operand to its true structured type may also provide performance advantages, since it may allow the query processor to exploit the known structure of the data.

In OQL, a standard cast on a structured operand "$(T)X$" may produce a runtime error if the X binding is not a subtype of T. However, this approach is not suitable for casts on OEM objects, since it contradicts our philosophy of not mandating structural knowledge of semistructured data. Therefore, OQL^S provides a separate mechanism for performing casts on OEM objects without type error, through the built-in Coerce function defined as follows:

Definition 2. (The Coerce function) Let O be an OEM object. The value of Coerce(C, O) is the singleton set set((C) X) if O is an OEMatomic object encapsulating an object X in class C (or a subclass of C). Otherwise the value of Coerce(C, O) is the empty set.   □

As an example, the following query selects the products of all Company subjects of reviews by ConsumersInc. Since the type of the C bindings is known to be Company, the type of the result returned by the query can be determined statically to be set(list(Product)):

```
Select  P
From    Reviews.ConsumersInc R, R.subject S,
        Coerce(Company, S) C, C.produces P
```

In the future we may also consider a more powerful "case" construct that successively tries to coerce an OEM object into a structured object from a list of classes, returning the first non-empty result obtained.

5.2   Structured access to semistructured data

A powerful feature of OQL^S is its support for *structured views* of semistructured data. Intuitively, structured data can be synthesized from semistructured operands when the semistructured data is known to exhibit some regularity, e.g., based on an XML DTD or from an analysis of the data. Such structured views may provide faster access paths for queries (e.g., via standard indexes), and the structured results can be exported to standard ODMG applications that do not understand the OEM model, and that may use API's such as Java or C++ bindings to access the database.

The synthesis of structured data from semistructured data is accomplished in OQL^S (once again, without the possibility of type error) using the built-in Construct function defined as follows:

Definition 3. (The Construct function) Let O be an OEM object. The expression Construct(T, O) returns a value of type set(T) that is either a singleton set containing a value of type T constructed from the OEM object O, or the empty set if no such construction is possible.   □

The Construct function may be viewed as a rich coercion function from OEM to a given type. If O is an OEMatomic object, then Construct behaves similarly to Coerce in Definition 2 above. If O is an OEMcomplex object, then Construct creates a structured ODMG tuple. Construct(T, O) is defined recursively as follows:

1. If O is an OEMatomic object of type OEM(T'), and if T' is identical to or is coercible to a subtype of T, then a singleton set containing the value encapsulated by O is returned.

2. If T is a class encapsulating a type T', and if Construct(T', O) = $\{v\}$, then Construct(T, O) is a singleton set containing a new T object encapsulating the value v.

3. If T is a tuple type, then each field labeled l must be constructed:

   (a) If l is a collection of values of type T', then for each l-labeled subobject O' of O, we evaluate Construct(T', O'). The result v_l is a collection of the non-empty results of this evaluation. If O is an OEMcomplexlist object and l is an ordered collection, the ordering of the subobjects of O is preserved in the construction. Otherwise, an arbitrary order is used for the resulting collection v_l.

   (b) l has a non-collection type T': The construction is successful if there is exactly one l-child O' of O and if Construct(T', O') = $\{v_l\}$.

   Finally, Construct(T, O) is a singleton set containing the tuple with value v_l for each l-field in the tuple.

4. If T is a collection of values of type T', then for each subobject O' of O with the reserved label item, we evaluate Construct(T', O'). The result is a collection of the non-empty results of these evaluations. Once again, if T is an ordered collection, the ordering of the subobjects of O is preserved in the construction; otherwise an arbitrary order is produced.

5. In all other cases, Construct returns an empty set.

As an example, let us suppose (simplistically) that we know that the manufacturer specifications for electrical products in our broker catalog always includes an integer wattage value and a real weight value. We define a class Espec encapsulating the type tuple(wattage:integer, weight:real). The query below selects a structured set of specifications:

```
Select E
From    Broker.products P, P.prodinfo.specs S,
        Construct(Espec, S) E
```

The type of the S bindings is OEM, and the type of the E bindings is Espec. The result of the query is therefore of type set(Espec). Thus, the result is a set of structured objects that may be materialized for indexing purposes, and may easily be exported to a Java or C++ application. While this example is very simple (and in fact a similar effect could have been achieved by using a tuple constructor in the Select clause), it does illustrate the general principle, which is to create structured views over portions of the data that are semistructured but have known components.

5.3   Semantics of mixed expressions

In OQL, expressions (queries) can be composed to form more complex expressions as long as the expressions have types that can be composed legally. OQL provides numerous operators for compositions, such as arithmetic operators (e.g., $+$), comparison operators (e.g., $<$), boolean operators (e.g., AND), set operators (e.g., UNION), indexing operators (e.g., $\langle list\_name \rangle[\langle position \rangle]$), etc. (See [Cat94] for an exhaustive specification of all OQL compositions.) OQL^S extends the composition rules of OQL to allow semistructured and structured expressions to be mixed freely in such compositions. We refer to expressions that include a semistructured subexpression as *mixed expressions*. Space limitations preclude an exhaustive treatment of all possible OQL^S expressions in this paper, but several important aspects of the interpretation of mixed expressions are highlighted in the remainder of this section.

Run-time coercion is used in the evaluation of mixed expressions. Faithful to the Lorel philosophy, the OQL^S query processor evaluates mixed expressions by attempting to coerce their subexpressions to types that can be composed legally. As an example, we consider the interpretation of compositions involving the comparison operator "$<$".

In OQL, the expression $(X < Y)$ is legal provided X and Y both have types integer or real (interpreted as arithmetic comparison), string (interpreted as string comparison), boolean (interpreted as boolean comparison), or set(T) or bag(T) (interpreted as set inclusion). A type error is raised in OQL for all other cases. OQL^S additionally allows X, Y, or both to be of type OEM, and the type of the mixed boolean expression $(X < Y)$ in that case is also OEM: OEM(true),

OEM(false), or OEMNil (recall Section 3 for definitions of these types). For instance, the value of (OEM(4) < 5) and (OEM(4) < "5") are both OEM(true). The value of (OEM(4) < set(1, 3)) is OEMNil since the two operands cannot be coerced into comparable types.

OEMNil is used to implement three-valued logic for mixed boolean expressions. Mixed boolean expressions are evaluated in OQL^S according to the rules of three-valued logic, similar to Lorel and just as NULL values are treated in SQL [MS93]. There are two important aspects to the use of OEMNil for implementing three-valued logic: First, if the Where clause of a query is a mixed-boolean expression, a value of OEMNil for the Where clause is interpreted as false. Second, if a query returns a collection of OEM objects, any OEMNil values are filtered out from the result; however, OEMNil values may appear in OEM components of structured query results.

The latter point is illustrated by the following two queries, which have identical From clauses but differ in their Select clauses.

```
Select P.prodnum + 100              Select tuple(prod:P,
From    Reviews.ConsumersInc R,            newpnum:P.prodnum+100)
        R.subject P                 From    Reviews.ConsumersInc R,
                                            R.subject P
```

In both queries, since OEM entry point Reviews is used, variable P is of type OEM. If for a particular P binding passed to the Select clause, the value of P.prodnum + 100 is OEMNil (because P.prodnum cannot be coerced to an integer or a real, e..g, it has string value "123A"), then the value OEMNil is discarded from the query result. On the other hand, the query on the right has a (structured) Select clause of type tuple(prod:OEM, newpnum:OEM). For this query, a similar P binding would produce an OEMNil value for the newpnum component of the tuple. That OEMNil value is retained in the result, since it is part of a tuple in which the prod component has the non-nil value P.

OEM operands can be used in any expression without type error. Since an OEM object can be a container for any type, OQL^S allows OEM operands to be used in any expression without type error. An OEM expression may therefore be used in a query as an atomic value, a collection, a structure, or a class. For instance, in OQL, the index expression $X[Y]$ is a legitimate expression only when X is of type string, $list(T)$, or $array(T)$, and when Y is an integer. In OQL^S, $X[Y]$ is also a legitimate expression when X, Y, or both are of type

OEM. Consider when X is of type OEM. If Y is an integer or an OEMatomic object encapsulating an integer (or a string coercible to an integer), and if X is of type OEM(string), then $X[Y]$ is of type OEM(char) and encapsulates the Yth character in the string. If X is of type OEM(list(T)) or OEM(array(T)), then $X[Y]$ has type OEM(T) and encapsulates the Yth element in the ordered collection encapsulated by X. Finally, if X is of type OEMcomplexlist, then $X[Y]$ returns the Yth subobject of X. For all other types of X, the value of $X[Y]$ is OEMNil.

6   Implementation

The Ozone system is fully implemented on top of the ODMG-compliant O_2 object database system. An *Ozone database* is simply an O_2 database whose schema has been enhanced by a *schema manager* module that adds predefined classes for the storage and management of OEM objects. OQL^S queries are compiled by a *preprocessor* module into intermediate OQL queries on the Ozone database, and query results are presented to the user via a *postprocessor* module. Ozone also provides a *loader* module for bulk-loading semistructured data from files, and the semistructured data in the load files may include references to structured data. See Figure 4 for a depiction of the overall architecture. In this section, we first describe how OEM objects are represented in an Ozone database, and then describe the main aspects of the translation from OQL^S to OQL. Space limitations preclude a complete description of our implementation.

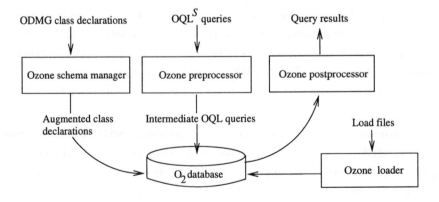

Fig. 4. Architecture of the Ozone system

6.1   Representation of OEM objects in O₂

Ozone defines a class OEM to represent OEM objects in O_2. This class is the base class for OEM objects, and the different kinds of OEM objects introduced in Section 3 are represented by subclasses of OEM, as follows.

Complex OEM objects. The class OEMcomplex represents complex OEM objects. This class has two subclasses for representing ordered and unordered complex OEM objects: OEMcomplexset and OEMcomplexlist. Since complex OEM objects are collections of (*label, value*) pairs, the types encapsulated by these classes are set(tuple(label:string, value:OEM)) and list(tuple(label:string, value:OEM)) respectively.

Atomic OEM objects encapsulating atomic values. Atomic OEM objects encapsulating atomic values also are represented by subclasses of OEM. For example, the class OEM_integer (encapsulating the type integer) represents OEM(integer) objects. The class OEM_Object (encapsulating the class Object) represents the type OEM(Object). (Recall that Object is a supertype of all classes in ODMG.) The remaining atomic classes are OEM_real, OEM_boolean, OEM_char, OEM_string, OEM_binary, and OEM_OEM (encapsulating the class OEM and representing the type OEM(OEM)). The class OEM itself encapsulates the type nil, and the extent for this class consists of the single named object OEMNil. The classes described here and in the previous section are the *fixed classes* of Ozone—they are present in every Ozone schema.

Atomic OEM objects encapsulating ODMG objects. Recall from Section 3 that an atomic OEM object can encapsulate a value of any ODMG type. We distinguish between two cases for non-atomic types: classes (this section), and non-atomic literal types such as tuples or collections (next section).

When C is a class, atomic OEM objects of type OEM(C) could be represented as instances of the class OEM_Object (previous section): since Object is the root of the ODMG class hierarchy, the class OEM_Object can store references to objects in any class. However, the use of a single class has performance limitations, since the exact types of encapsulated objects would have to be determined at run-time through potentially expensive schema lookups. Therefore, for performance reasons, Ozone defines a *proxy class* OEM_C for representing atomic OEM objects of type OEM(C) for each user-defined class C. Operations on an object belonging to a proxy class need not consult the schema and can exploit the structural properties of the encapsulated structured object (whose exact type is known from the proxy class). The Field() method, described later in Section 6.2, is example of an operation that can exploit structure through this approach. In our running example, the Ozone schema manager defines proxy classes OEM_Catalog (encapsulating the class Catalog), OEM_Product (encapsulating the class Product), and OEM_Company (encapsulating the class Company). These classes represent the types OEM(Catalog), OEM(Product), and OEM(Company).

Atomic OEM objects encapsulating non-atomic literals. Atomic OEM objects encapsulating non-atomic literal values (tuple, set, list, etc.) could be represented by equivalent complex OEM objects. For instance, an atomic OEM object encapsulating the value tuple(name:"foo", oid:4) could be represented in Ozone by an equivalent OEMcomplexset object with two children:("name", OEM_string("foo")) and ("oid", OEM_Integer(3)).

For performance reasons once again, Ozone defines additional OEM subclasses encapsulating the types of non-atomic class properties (attributes, relationships, and methods) since these are the non-atomic literal types that are most commonly encountered in queries. For each such $\langle property \rangle$ of type P in each class C, Ozone creates a new *auxiliary class* OEM_C_$\langle property \rangle$ to represent atomic OEM objects of type OEM(P). As with proxy classes, a query on an auxiliary class object is faster than a query over an equivalent OEMcomplex object representing the same data. Of course, it is not possible to define auxiliary classes encapsulating all possible non-atomic types, since the space of temporary literal types that can be synthesized by queries and subqueries is infinite. For values of such types, Ozone must create equivalent OEM objects.

Referring again to our running example, the produces relationship of Company has the non-atomic literal type list(Product), and the Ozone schema manager creates the auxiliary class OEM_Company_produces encapsulating the type list(Product). This auxiliary class represents the type OEM(list(Product)). The class Company also has the non-atomic address attribute, and the schema manager creates the auxiliary class OEM_Company_address. Similarly, the schema manager creates the classes OEM_Catalog_vendors and OEM_Catalog_products for the vendors attribute and the products attribute in the Catalog class.

The complete set of fixed, proxy, and auxiliary classes added by the Ozone schema manager to the schema of Section 2.3 is depicted in Figure 5. Note that this class hierarchy is invisible to the user; the type OEM is the only user-visible type added by Ozone.

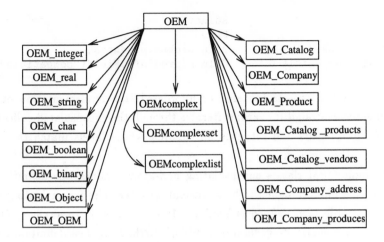

Fig. 5. Classes added by Ozone to our example schema

6.2 Translation from OQL^S to OQL

OQL^S expressions involving OEM operands are implemented by methods defined in the class OEM. This class defines methods for navigation, user-specified coercion, the Construct function described in Section 5.2, and performing different kinds of unary and binary operations (such as arithmetic, boolean, comparison, and set operations). In the remainder of this section, we first describe the use of methods for implementing path expressions in OQL^S. Then we describe the implementation of user-specified coercion and construction. We conclude with a brief illustration of how methods are used to implement mixed expressions.

Implementation of OQL^S path expressions. Structured data is queried by OQL^S in exactly the same way as by OQL on a standard O$_2$ database, i.e., an OQL^S query over structured (pure ODMG) data does not need to be modified by the Ozone preprocessor. However, navigation of OEM objects is performed by methods such as the Field() method, which takes a label argument and produces the set of children with matching labels. Other navigational methods are discussed briefly at the end of this section. Let us illustrate how the Ozone preprocessor rewrites OQL^S queries on OEM objects using the Field() method. The following OQL^S query (on the left) that selects all compatible products for all products in the broker catalog is translated by the Ozone preprocessor to the OQL query shown on the right:[4]

---

[4] We translate all range variables to the "V In…" style, since O$_2$'s version of OQL supports only this form.

```
Select C                        Select C
From                            From
Broker.products P,              P In Broker.products,
P.prodinfo.compatible C         C In P.prodinfo.Field("compatible")
```

For complex OEM objects (ordered or unordered) the implementation of the Field() method is straightforward: it iterates through the encapsulated collection of (*label*, *value*) pairs and retrieves all children whose labels match the label argument to the method.

For atomic OEM classes encapsulating non-atomic values, the definition of the Field() method is designed to be consistent with the rules for navigating past atomic OEM objects as defined in Section 5.1. For each proxy or auxiliary OEM class, Ozone automatically generates its Field() method (at class definition time) using the O_2 *metaschema*—an API allowing schema lookups and manipulations within an application. The Field() method matches the label argument with each attribute, relationship, and method (without arguments) in the class and returns OEM objects encapsulating any matching property or the return value of any matching method. Atomic properties are returned as instances of corresponding atomic OEM classes (for instance, an attribute of type integer would be returned in an object of type OEM_integer), while non-atomic properties are returned as instances of proxy or auxiliary classes (for instance, the produces relationship of a Company object would be returned in an object of type OEM_Company_produces).

As described in Section 5.1, OQL^S allows method invocations on OEM objects with the following semantics: if the OEM object encapsulates an object in a class with a matching method, the method is invoked and a singleton set containing the OEM proxy object encapsulating the method's return value is generated, otherwise the empty set is returned. Methods without arguments are handled in Ozone in the same way as class attributes as described above. Methods with one or more arguments are handled by the Invoke() method whose signature is:

set(OEM) Invoke(string methodName, list(string) argstext)

Note that any valid OQL^S expression can be used as an argument to a method on an OEM object. The argstext parameter lists the actual query texts for these expressions. In a proxy OEM class, if methodName matches any method in the encapsulated class, Invoke() uses the Ozone preprocessor to translate each OQL^S expression in argstext into its intermediate OQL form. If the argument types match the method's signature, Invoke() uses the O_2 API to invoke the method on the encapsulated ODMG object (the intermediate OQL expressions are used as arguments in this call). For example, an OQL^S query invoking the inventory() method on all subjects of reviews by ConsumersInc is shown below, together with its intermediate OQL form:

```
Select C.inventory("camera1")    Select C.Invoke("inventory",
From                                            list(""camera1""))
Reviews.ConsumersInc R,          From
R.subject C                        R In Reviews.Field("ConsumersInc"),
                                   C In R.Field("subject")
```

For any C binding that is of type OEM(Company), the Invoke() method applies the inventory() method with the argument "camera1" to the encapsulated Company object. Since this argument is an atomic OQL expression, it does not need preprocessing. For such C bindings, Invoke() returns a set containing a single OEM_integer object storing the result of applying the method. For all other C bindings, Invoke() returns the empty set.

Path expressions with wildcards and regular expression operators. Recall that path expressions in OQL^S may contain wildcards and regular expression operators [AQM+97]. Wildcards are supported by the Field() method, whose label argument may contain wildcards. Regular expression operators are implemented through standard set operations and three additional navigational methods in the OEM class:

- Closure(): X.Closure("foo") returns the set of all objects reachable from the object X by following zero or more edges labeled "foo".

- UnionClosure(): X.UnionClosure(set("foo$_1$",..., "foo$_n$")) returns the set of all objects reachable from the object X by following zero or more edges whose labels match any one of "foo$_1$",..., "foo$_n$".

- NestedClosure(): X.NestedClosure(query) returns the set of all objects obtained by zero or more executions of query. Variable self is used in the query to reference the object on which the method is invoked.

As an example, the following translation uses the NestedClosure and Closure methods as well as a Union operation to implement a nested regular expression.[5]

```
Select D              Select D
From    A(.B|(.C)*)* D   From
                      D in A.NestedClosure(
                              "Select X
                              From    X in (self.Field("B")
                              Union
                              self.Closure("C"))")
```

Implementation of user-specified coercion and construction. As described in Section 5.1, OQL^S allows an object X in any class C to be converted into an OEM proxy object of type $OEM(C)$ through the user-specified cast expression $(OEM)\ X$. This coercion is implemented in Ozone simply by creating an appropriate object in the proxy class for C. For instance, if X is of type Company, $(OEM)\ X$ is translated by the preprocessor to OEM_Company(X), which creates a proxy for a Company object.

OQL^S also allows an OEM object X to be coerced explicitly to any class C using the expression Coerce($C,\ X$). This Coerce function of Definition 2 is implemented as a method Coerce in the class OEM. One difficulty is that the result of the Coerce function is of type set(C), where C can be any ODMG class in the schema, i.e., we have introduced polymorphism that is not supported by ODMG. In our implementation, method Coerce therefore has the fixed return type set(Object), which is suitable for returning objects of any type. The preprocessor then inserts an OQL cast to obtain objects of the proper type.

Finally, as described in Section 5.2, OQL^S allows the construction of a structured ODMG value of type T from an OEM object O using the expression Construct($T,\ O$). The present Ozone prototype requires T to be a class type and implements the Construct function as a method Construct in the OEM class. For reasons analogous to the Coerce method, the return type of the method is set(Object). Method Construct uses the O_2 metaschema to create an object in the class C, then attempts to construct the different attributes of the object using the rules described in Section 5.2. If the construction is not successful, the empty set is returned. Once again, the preprocessor must insert an OQL cast to obtain objects in the specified class.

---

[5] In this particular example the regular expression could be simplified to A(.B|.C)*, in which case the translation uses only the UnionClosure method, but we translate the unsimplified expression for illustrative purposes.

Implementation of mixed expressions. Mixed expressions involving OEM operands (Section 5.3) are implemented through methods. We will illustrate the comparison operator "<" as an example. In OQL^S, an OEM object can be compared with values of the following atomic ODMG types: integer, real, boolean, and string. For these types the OEM class defines the comparison methods Less_integer(integer value), Less_real(real value), etc. An OEM object also can be compared with another OEM object (the comparison is interpreted at run-time based on the exact types of the values encapsulated by the two objects), and for this purpose the Less_OEM(OEM value) method is provided. The "<" operator also denotes set containment. The present Ozone prototype defines set comparison methods only for those unordered collections types that have corresponding auxiliary classes. In our example schema, we thus define the method Less_set_Product(set(Product) value) since OEM_Catalog_products is of type set(Product), and Less_set_Company(set(Company) value) since the class OEM_Catalog_vendors is of type set(Company). The return type of all of these comparison methods is OEM, and the return value is always one of the following atomic OEM values: OEM_boolean(true), OEM_boolean(false), or OEMNil.

As examples of the use of comparison methods, let X be an OEM object. Ozone translates the expression $(X < 5)$ to X.Less_integer(5) and the expression $(X < \text{``}abc\text{''})$ to $X$.Less_string($\text{``}abc\text{''}$). If Y is of type set(Company), the expression $(X < Y)$ is translated to X.Less_set_Company(Y). Thus, the decision of which comparison method should be invoked is made statically.

7   Conclusions

We have extended ODMG with the ability to integrate semistructured data with structured data in a single database, and we have extended the semantics of OQL to allow queries over such hybrid data. As far as we know, our work is the first to provide true integration of semistructured and structured data with a unified query language. We feel that this direction of work is particularly important as more and more structured data sources incorporate semistructured XML information, and vice-versa. We have built *Ozone*, a system that implements our ODMG and OQL extensions on top of the O_2 object-oriented database system. Our future work will proceed in the following directions:

- *Ozone performance:* We plan to investigate optimizations that would allow the navigation of OEM proxies for structured data to be as fast as standard OQL. We also plan to study general optimizations for navigating semistructured data [MW99] in the context of Ozone, and explore the use of mechanisms provided by O_2 (such as clustering and indexing) to improve performance. Finally, we would like to detect regularity in semistructured data, and determine whether we can exploit such regularity by using ODMG classes to represent such data [NAM98].

- *Object-Relational Ozone:* We plan to define a similar semistructured extension to the object-relational data model [SM96], and define semantics for the SQL-3 query language in order to query hybrid (object-relational plus semistructured) data.

- *Applications:* We intend to study a suite of applications that can take advantage of our hybrid approach, in order to identify any missing functionality and performance bottlenecks. We also plan to investigate general design issues for hybrid-data applications.

Acknowledgments

We thank the members of the Lore group at Stanford University for their feedback on the design of Ozone. We also acknowledge Ardent Software for providing us with a copy of the O_2 database system. Dallan Quass was influential in evolving Lorel to an OQL-like form, and Sophie Cluet and Jerome Simeon provided help with numerous questions on O_2 and OQL. Tirthankar Lahiri thanks Oracle Corporation for sponsoring his doctoral studies at Stanford University.[6]

References

[Abi97]   S. Abiteboul. Querying semistructured data. In *Proceedings of the International Conference on Database Theory*, Delphi, Greece, January 1997.

[ACC+97]   S. Abiteboul, S. Cluet, V. Christophides, T. Milo, G. Moerkotte, and J. Simeon. Querying documents in object databases. *International Journal on Digital Libraries*, 1(1):5–19, 1997.

[AQM+97]   S. Abiteboul, D. Quass, J. McHugh, J. Widom, and J. Wiener. The Lorel query language for semistructured data. *International Journal on Digital Libraries*, 1(1):68–88, April 1997.

[BDFS97]   P. Buneman, S. Davidson, M. Fernandez, and D. Suciu. Adding structure to unstructured data. In *Proceedings of the International Conference on Database Theory*, pages 335–350, Delphi, Greece, January 1997.

[BDHS96]   P. Buneman, S. Davidson, G. Hillebrand, and D. Suciu. A query language and optimization techniques for unstructured data. In *Proceedings of the ACM SIGMOD International Conference on Management of Data*, pages 505–516, Montreal, Canada, June 1996.

---

[6] Oracle Corporation is not responsible in any way for the content of this paper.

[BDK92]   F. Bancilhon, C. Delobel, and P. Kanellakis, editors. *Building an Object-Oriented Database System: The Story of O₂*. Morgan Kaufmann, San Francisco, California, 1992.

[BDS95]   P. Buneman, S. Davidson, and D. Suciu. Programming constructs for unstructured data. In *Proceedings of the 1995 International Workshop on Database Programming Languages (DBPL)*, 1995.

[Bun97]   P. Buneman. Semistructured data. In *Proceedings of the Sixth ACM SIGACT-SIGMOD-SIGART Symposium on Principles of Database Systems*, Tucson, Arizona, May 1997. Tutorial.

[Cat94]   R.G.G. Cattell, editor. *The Object Database Standard: ODMG-93*. Morgan Kaufmann, San Francisco, California, 1994.

[Cod70]   E.F. Codd. A relational model for large shared data banks. *Communications of the ACM*, 13(6):377–387, June 1970.

[FFLS97] M. Fernandez, D. Florescu, A. Levy, and D. Suciu. A query language for a Web-site management system. *SIGMOD Record*, 26(3):4–11, September 1997.

[GW97]   R. Goldman and J. Widom. DataGuides: Enabling query formulation and optimization in semistructured databases. In *Proceedings of the Twenty-Third International Conference on Very Large Data Bases*, pages 436–445, Athens, Greece, August 1997.

[LB97]   R. Light and T. Bray. *Presenting XML*. Sams, Indianapolis, Indiana, September 1997.

[MAG⁺97] J. McHugh, S. Abiteboul, R. Goldman, D. Quass, and J. Widom. Lore: A database management system for semistructured data. *SIGMOD Record*, 26(3):54–66, September 1997.

[MS93]   J. Melton and A.R. Simon. *Understanding the New SQL: A Complete Guide*. Morgan Kaufmann, San Francisco, California, 1993.

[MW99]   J. McHugh and J. Widom. Query optimization for XML. In *Proceedings of the Twenty-Fifth International Conference on Very Large Databases*, Edinburgh, Scotland, September 1999. To appear.

[NAM98]   S. Nestorov, S. Abiteboul, and R. Motwani. Extracting schema from semistructured data. In *Proceedings of the ACM SIGMOD International Conference on Management of Data*, Seattle, Washington, May 1998.

[PGMW95] Y. Papakonstantinou, H. Garcia-Molina, and J. Widom. Object exchange across heterogeneous information sources. In *Proceedings of the Eleventh International Conference on Data Engineering*, pages 251–260, Taipei, Taiwan, March 1995.

[SM96]   M. Stonebraker and D. Moore. *Object-Relational DBMSs: The Next Great Wave*. Morgan Kaufmann, San Francisco, California, April 1996.

Author Index

Lecture Notes in Computer Science

For information about Vols. 1–1899
please contact your bookseller or Springer-Verlag

Vol. 1766: M. Jazayeri, R.G.K. Loos, D.R. Musser (Eds.), Generic Programming. Proceedings, 1998. X, 269 pages. 2000.

Vol. 1791: D. Fensel, Problem-Solving Methods. XII, 153 pages. 2000. (Subseries LNAI).

Vol. 1799: K. Czarnecki, U.W. Eisenecker, Generative and Component-Based Software Engineering. Proceedings, 1999. VIII, 225 pages. 2000.

Vol. 1812: J. Wyatt, J. Demiris (Eds.), Advances in Robot Learning. Proceedings, 1999. VII, 165 pages. 2000. (Subseries LNAI).

Vol. 1932: Z.W. Raś, S. Ohsuga (Eds.), Foundations of Intelligent Systems. Proceedings, 2000. XII, 646 pages. 2000. (Subseries LNAI).

Vol. 1933: R.W. Brause, E. Hanisch (Eds.), Medical Data Analysis. Proceedings, 2000. XI, 316 pages. 2000.

Vol. 1934: J.S. White (Ed.), Envisioning Machine Translation in the Information Future. Proceedings, 2000. XV, 254 pages. 2000. (Subseries LNAI).

Vol. 1935: S.L. Delp, A.M. DiGioia, B. Jaramaz (Eds.), Medical Image Computing and Computer-Assisted Intervention – MICCAI 2000. Proceedings, 2000. XXV, 1250 pages. 2000.

Vol. 1937: R. Dieng, O. Corby (Eds.), Knowledge Engineering and Knowledge Management. Proceedings, 2000. XIII, 457 pages. 2000. (Subseries LNAI).

Vol. 1938: S. Rao, K.I. Sletta (Eds.), Next Generation Networks. Proceedings, 2000. XI, 392 pages. 2000.

Vol. 1939: A. Evans, S. Kent, B. Selic (Eds.), «UML» – The Unified Modeling Language. Proceedings, 2000. XIV, 572 pages. 2000.

Vol. 1940: M. Valero, K. Joe, M. Kitsuregawa, H. Tanaka (Eds.), High Performance Computing. Proceedings, 2000. XV, 595 pages. 2000.

Vol. 1941: A.K. Chhabra, D. Dori (Eds.), Graphics Recognition. Proceedings, 1999. XI, 346 pages. 2000.

Vol. 1942: H. Yasuda (Ed.), Active Networks. Proceedings, 2000. XI, 424 pages. 2000.

Vol. 1943: F. Koornneef, M. van der Meulen (Eds.), Computer Safety, Reliability and Security. Proceedings, 2000. X, 432 pages. 2000.

Vol. 1945: W. Grieskamp, T. Santen, B. Stoddart (Eds.), Integrated Formal Methods. Proceedings, 2000. X, 441 pages. 2000.

Vol. 1948: T. Tan, Y. Shi, W. Gao (Eds.), Advances in Multimodal Interfaces – ICMI 2000. Proceedings, 2000. XVI, 678 pages. 2000.

Vol. 1949: R. Connor, A. Mendelzon (Eds.), Research Issues in Structured and Semistructured Database Programming. Proceedings, 1999. XII, 325 pages. 2000.

Vol. 1951: F. van der Linden (Ed.), Software Architectures for Product Families. Proceedings, 2000. VIII, 255 pages. 2000.

Vol. 1952: M.C. Monard, J. Simão Sichman (Eds.), Advances in Artificial Intelligence. Proceedings, 2000. XV, 498 pages. 2000. (Subseries LNAI).

Vol. 1953: G. Borgefors, I. Nyström, G. Sanniti di Baja (Eds.), Discrete Geometry for Computer Imagery. Proceedings, 2000. XI, 544 pages. 2000.

Vol. 1954: W.A. Hunt, Jr., S.D. Johnson (Eds.), Formal Methods in Computer-Aided Design. Proceedings, 2000. XI, 539 pages. 2000.

Vol. 1955: M. Parigot, A. Voronkov (Eds.), Logic for Programming and Automated Reasoning. Proceedings, 2000. XIII, 487 pages. 2000. (Subseries LNAI).

Vol. 1960: A. Ambler, S.B. Calo, G. Kar (Eds.), Services Management in Intelligent Networks. Proceedings, 2000. X, 259 pages. 2000.

Vol. 1961: J. He, M. Sato (Eds.), Advances in Computing Science – ASIAN 2000. Proceedings, 2000. X, 299 pages. 2000.

Vol. 1963: V. Hlaváč, K.G. Jeffery, J. Wiedermann (Eds.), SOFSEM 2000: Theory and Practice of Informatics. Proceedings, 2000. XI, 460 pages. 2000.

Vol. 1965: Ç. K. Koç, C. Paar (Eds.), Cryptographic Hardware and Embedded Systems – CHES 2000. Proceedings, 2000. XI, 355 pages. 2000.

Vol. 1966: S. Bhalla (Ed.), Databases in Networked Information Systems. Proceedings, 2000. VIII, 247 pages. 2000.

Vol. 1967: S. Arikawa, S. Morishita (Eds.), Discovery Science. Proceedings, 2000. XII, 332 pages. 2000. (Subseries LNAI).

Vol. 1968: H. Arimura, S. Jain, A. Sharma (Eds.), Algorithmic Learning Theory. Proceedings, 2000. XI, 335 pages. 2000. (Subseries LNAI).

Vol. 1969: D.T. Lee, S.-H. Teng (Eds.), Algorithms and Computation. Proceedings, 2000. XIV, 578 pages. 2000.

Vol. 1970: M. Valero, V.K. Prasanna, S. Vajapeyam (Eds.), High Performance Computing – HiPC 2000. Proceedings, 2000. XVIII, 568 pages. 2000.

Vol. 1971: R. Buyya, M. Baker (Eds.), Grid Computing – GRID 2000. Proceedings, 2000. XIV, 229 pages. 2000.

Vol. 1972: A. Omicini, R. Tolksdorf, F. Zambonelli (Eds.), Engineering Societies in the Agents World. Proceedings, 2000. IX, 143 pages. 2000. (Subseries LNAI).

Vol. 1973: J. Van den Bussche, V. Vianu (Eds.), Database Theory – ICDT 2001. Proceedings, 2001. X, 451 pages. 2001.

Vol. 1974: S. Kapoor, S. Prasad (Eds.), FST TCS 2000: Foundations of Software Technology and Theoretical Computer Science. Proceedings, 2000. XIII, 532 pages. 2000.

Vol. 1975: J. Pieprzyk, E. Okamoto, J. Seberry (Eds.), Information Security. Proceedings, 2000. X, 323 pages. 2000.

Vol. 1976: T. Okamoto (Ed.), Advances in Cryptology – ASIACRYPT 2000. Proceedings, 2000. XII, 630 pages. 2000.

Vol. 1977: B. Roy, E. Okamoto (Eds.), Progress in Cryptology – INDOCRYPT 2000. Proceedings, 2000. X, 295 pages. 2000.

Vol. 1983: K.S. Leung, L.-W. Chan, H. Meng (Eds.), Intelligent Data Engineering and Automated Learning – IDEAL 2000. Proceedings, 2000. XVI, 573 pages. 2000.

Vol. 1987: K.-L. Tan, M.J. Franklin, J. C.-S. Lui (Eds.), Mobile Data Management. Proceedings, 2001. XIII, 289 pages. 2001.